PERGAMON INTERNATIONAL LIBRARY
of Science, Technology, Engineering and Social Studies

*The 1000-volume original paperback library in aid of education,
industrial training and the enjoyment of leisure*

Publisher: Robert Maxwell, M.C.

RESIDENTIAL CARE

A Reader in Current Theory and Practice

THE PERGAMON TEXTBOOK
INSPECTION COPY SERVICE

An inspection copy of any book published in the Pergamon International Library will gladly be sent to academic staff without obligation for their consideration for course adoption or recommendation. Copies may be retained for a period of 60 days from receipt and returned if not suitable. When a particular title is adopted or recommended for adoption for class use and the recommendation results in a sale of 12 or more copies, the inspection copy may be retained with our compliments. The Publishers will be pleased to receive suggestions for revised editions and new titles to be published in this important International Library.

SOCIAL WORK SERIES

Editor: Jean P. Nursten

A Pergamon Journal of Related Interest

JOURNAL OF CHILD PSYCHOLOGY AND
PSYCHIATRY AND ALLIED DISCIPLINES

Official Organ of the Association for Child Psychology and Psychiatry

Joint Editors:

Dr. L. A. Hersov, Consultant Psychiatrist, The Maudsley Hospital, London;
Dr. M. Berger, Department of Child Development and Educational
Psychology, University of London.

This journal is primarily concerned with child psychology and child psychiatry,
including experimental and developmental studies, especially developmental
psycho-pathology. It is recognised that many other disciplines have an
important contribution to make in furthering knowledge of the mental life
and behaviour of children. In the absence of a unified body of generally
accepted fact and theory, an important function of this journal is to bring
together contributions of high quality from different points of view.

RESIDENTIAL CARE

A Reader in Current Theory and Practice

Edited by

RONALD G. WALTON

BA(Admin.), MA(Econ.), PhD
Senior Lecturer in Social Work, University College, Cardiff

and

DOREEN ELLIOTT

BA, Dip Ed Rehab
Lecturer in Social Work, University College, Cardiff

PERGAMON PRESS

OXFORD · NEW YORK · TORONTO · SYDNEY · PARIS · FRANKFURT

U.K.	Pergamon Press Ltd., Headington Hill Hall, Oxford OX3 0BW, England
U.S.A.	Pergamon Press Inc., Maxwell House, Fairview Park, Elmsford, New York 10523, U.S.A.
CANADA	Pergamon of Canada, Suite 104, 150 Consumers Road, Willowdale, Ontario M2 J1P9, Canada
AUSTRALIA	Pergamon Press (Aust.) Pty. Ltd., PO Box 544, Potts Point, NSW 2011, Australia
FRANCE	Pergamon Press SARL, 24 rue des Ecoles, 75240 Paris, Cedex 05, France
FEDERAL REPUBLIC OF GERMANY	Pergamon Press GmbH, 6242 Kronberg-Taunus, Hammerweg 6, Federal Republic of Germany

First edition 1980

British Library Cataloguing in Publication Data

Residential care—(Pergamon international library social work series).
1. Institutional care—Great Britain
I. Walton, Ronald Gordon   II. Elliott, Doreen
361'.05   HV59   79-41182

ISBN 0-08-024690-7 (Hardcover)
ISBN 0-08-024689-3 (Flexicover)

Printed and bound in Great Britain by
William Clowes (Beccles) Limited, Beccles and London

FOREWORD

RESIDENTIAL care at its very best is an unsatisfactory substitute for a caring environment with maximum independence within the warmth of one's own family. However, for some people there is no choice. It is, therefore, important that substitute care of this kind is developed in a way which will enhance all of its advantages and minimise its many disadvantages.

The ability to do this is assisted by an enlightened discussion of the issues involved which helps to concentrate the minds of those concerned upon imaginative ways of overcoming the inherent disadvantages of residential care. The papers which make up this volume are designed to prompt such discussion and to provide a basis for the re-examination of practice which should lead to a new and better understanding of the way in which the quality and effectiveness of residential care can be improved.

A welcome feature of this publication is that it includes papers from a number of writers who are not widely known to have contributed to earlier discussion of this kind. This is both refreshing and stimulating and it opens up a number of new avenues of approach which might have a considerable influence upon future practice.

There is a major element affecting the quality of life within a residential care environment which may receive less attention than other considerations in discussions of this kind. It is the relationship between the size of a facility, in terms of numbers of people, and its effectiveness in meeting its objectives. If the most desirable place for a person to be is with their own family it should follow that any substitute environment should be of such size as to discourage all of the worst features of institutional practice and to encourage all of the best features of family life. This may not be easy to achieve, but it should not be lost sight of in the pursuit of other ideals.

A further element in any attempt to improve the quality and effectiveness of residential care is a willingness to test the validity of new ideas and philosophies. The most fertile ground for harvesting thoughts of this kind is from the residents themselves and the paper on residential participation could give a lead in this direction.

The past two decades have been a period of great social change which has developed from the impetus of the postwar desire to build a better world. This process is still continuing and although the momentum may vary from time to time, the discussion encouraged by this publication will assist those who are concerned with residential services to distil their ideas. There is a need for this to proceed with urgency as there is always a danger that if too long is taken in the distillation of ideas the substance of them may evaporate.

December 1979

RUSSELL FRANK
Director of Social Services
Royal County of Berkshire

PREFACE

Residential care is in an important transitional phase, moving from a period in which the major task has been to overcome the negative effects of institutional life, to a future where the overriding tasks will be to maximise the positive potential of residential living within a continuum of personal social service. In arriving at the present position there has been a rich upsurge of literature and study of residential life over the last two decades. This literature is very diverse and scattered, making it difficult for residential practitioners or students on courses to establish a clear perspective on present theories and developments. It is the need to fill this gap that has generated our Reader, which offers a critical examination of current practice and theory in relation to a variety of client groups and models of working. Its intended audience is primarily residential social workers in statutory and voluntary agencies and students'on Certificate of Qualification in Social Work and Certificate in Social Service courses; but it should also be relevant and of interest to professionals in related disciplines working directly in, or in contact with, residential establishments—field social workers, psychiatrists, psychologists, doctors, teachers and psychiatric nurses.

A new element represented in this volume is an underlying assumption that there is much in common in philosophy and practice across a range of residential establishments, and that it is possible to take an integrated approach to the social work methods which may be applied in establishments for a range of client groups. Much of the present literature on residential care is related to specific client groups, and tends to adopt a negative approach. In addition to papers which outline practice in particular settings, other papers are included which cut across client specialisms, and include topics such as the residential task, integrated methods, research evaluation, ethical problems and training issues. Even papers which are concerned with a particular client group throw up analogies and insights relevant to other kinds of establishment.

Only two of the contributions to the Reader have been previously published. The editors were concerned that if the Reader were to be of maximum value to practitioners, a substantial proportion of contributions should be by those currently in practice, and this is so for two-thirds of the contributors. Throughout, there has been an attempt to maintain a practice orientation, with theoretical concepts illustrated by accounts of practice situations. The non-practitioner contributors to the Reader are all involved closely in residential care, by research, teaching or supervision and we also felt it important to have contributions from a resident and a student.

The presentation of the Reader consists of four main sections, each with an editorial introduction and followed by questions to stimulate further study. In the first section "The Task in Residential Care" recent developments, the present state of residential care, and their implications for the "Social Work Task" in residential care are examined.

This provides the context for the second and largest section which deals with processes in residential care; assessment and admission, continuing care, rehabilitation, evaluation and management. A wide variety of client groups is dealt with, some of them by contrasting methods with a psychotherapeutic or behavioural bias and also using combinations of individual and group approaches. The third main section, "Ethical Issues and Residential Care", looks at the moral dilemmas surrounding key aspects of residential life. A final section, "Education and Training for Residential Work", looks at present and future training patterns and how to teach residential theory and practice skills.

We have not attempted to provide a finished or completely unified theory of residential care. But in providing a broad spectrum of practice and theory in one volume, combined with examination of integrating concepts and trends, there is the possibility for practitioners and students to draw on a far wider body of theory and practice than hitherto. In doing so there is an exciting potential for improvement of practice, quality of care, and for the refining of theory tested out in practice. We hope that practitioners, students and teachers alike will be stimulated to further study and experiment in practice, encouraging a shared effort with residents to establish patterns of residential life which are liberating and satisfying.

ACKNOWLEDGEMENTS

The editors wish to express their thanks to all the contributors who so willingly responded to the task of formulating this collection of readings. It is often difficult for those working in residential care to find the time to write about the work they do and we recognise the substantial work it requires in committing themselves to print and sharing their thinking more broadly. Those contributors who are employed by social work agencies have generally had to obtain permission from their employers, to whom we are grateful for facilitating publication in this way. The views expressed in the Reader, however, are invariably the views of the individual contributor and permission to publish does not necessarily indicate agency support for the views expressed. We are each indebted to many people who have influenced our ideas on residential care over the years: to present and former colleagues, both practitioners and academics; to clients of social work agencies and residents of homes with whom we have had the privilege of working; and to students, who continue to be a valued stimulus in developing many of the ideas incorporated in this Reader. *Social Work Today* kindly allowed us to reprint the article on assessment by Denis O'Brien, and also the article on residents' rights by Ron Walton. Finally we owe thanks to Mary Sansom for help in typing parts of the manuscript, and to Mrs Peggy Ducker of the Pergamon Press Ltd for her help during the process of publication.

CONTRIBUTORS

ADAMS, DOUGLAS: Warden of the Britannia Road Hostel, Kingswood Schools, Bristol.

AINSWORTH, FRANK: Social Work Education Advisor, Central Council for Education and Training in Social Work.

BULL, RODNEY: Lecturer in Social Work, University College, Cardiff.

CORNEY, GILLIAN: Social Worker, Leonard Cheshire Foundation.

DAVIES, GARETH: Officer in Charge, Maes-y-Eglwys Assessment Centre, Church Village, Mid Glamorgan.

DAVIES, YVONNE: Training Officer, Mid Glamorgan Social Services Dept.

DAVIS, LEONARD: Lecturer in Social Work, Brunel University.

ELLIOTT, DOREEN: Lecturer in Social Work, University College, Cardiff.

EVANS, SUE: Senior Social Worker, Dr Barnardo's (Wales and West Division).

GALLOWAY, DAVID: Superintendent, Barnardo's Hostel, Cardiff.

GENTRY, GORDON: Headmaster, Danesbury Community Home School, Herts.

GOBELL, ALEXANDER: Senior Lecturer, Faculty of Education, University College, Cardiff; and Co-Principal, Hengrove Special School, Bucks.

GREGORY, WILLIAM: Headmaster, The Special Unit, Kingswood Schools, Bristol.

HALL, STEPHANIE: Assistant Director, Dr Barnardo's (London Division).

JONES, HARVEY: Consultant in Adolescent Psychiatry, Whitchurch Hospital, Cardiff.

LAMBDEN, SHEILA: Training Officer, Coventry Social Services Dept.

LINE, BRIAN: Resident, Le Court, Cheshire Home, Liss, Hants.

LIPMAN, ALAN: Professor of Architecture, UWIST, Welsh School of Architecture.

MANSELL, JAMES: Research Officer, Health Care Evaluation Research Team, Winchester.

MORRIS, BARBARA: Officer in Charge, Silverbrook Treatment Centre, Church Village, Mid Glamorgan.

O'BRIEN, DENIS: Deputy Head, Lisnevin School, Newtownwards, Co. Down.

PHILLIPS, JOHN: Principal Training Officer, Mid Glamorgan Social Services Dept.

PITHOUSE, MARY: Formerly Social Worker, Cardiff University Social Services.

PRICE, MARTIN: Ex CQSW student now working as a residential social worker in Cardiff.

SLATER, ROBERT: Lecturer in Applied Psychology, UWIST, Cardiff.

WALTON, RONALD: Assistant Director, School of Social Work, University College, Cardiff.

WARD, LIZ: Senior Lecturer in Social Work, Bristol Polytechnic.

WILLIAMS, DWYNWEN: Officer in Charge, Ty Clyd Home for the Elderly, Bargoed, Mid Glamorgan.

CONTENTS

PART I
The Task in Residential Care

PART II
Social Work Process in Residential Care

PART III

Ethical Issues in Residential Care

PART IV

Education and Training for Residential Work

PART I

The Task in Residential Care

INTRODUCTION

The roles of domestic worker, nurse, manager and social worker, amongst others, are ones which find expression in the work we call residential care. The lack of a clearly articulated theoretical framework, the lack of an obvious value-system, and the operation of residential care within the context of a variety of "host" disciplines have all had an adverse effect on the definition of the residential task. It has remained ill defined. One consequence has been that those who work in residential care are not accorded recognition by our society that they operate in a professional, specialised role.

Much work needs to be done to identify and clarify the theoretical base and practical skills and techniques of residential work.

One chapter in this section looks critically at some of the factors which could lead to a negative view of residential work. Another discusses some current changes which show that development is taking place, and a third analyses and extends our concept of the residential task.

CHAPTER 1

CRITICISMS AND POSITIVE ASPECTS OF RESIDENTIAL CARE

RON WALTON AND DOREEN ELLIOTT

Residential care is one of the most costly of personal social service provisions and cost–benefit arguments have been used as a means of questioning the continuing provision at present levels, particularly in times of economic constraint. Nearly half of all expenditure on personal social services is spent on residential care and it is a labour-intensive service. Some 80,000[1] people are employed by social services departments in residential care, of whom approximately 60,000 are ancillary staff; this would be substantially increased if the staff of voluntary homes were to be included, for in 1976 there were 58.8 thousand residents in private and voluntary homes in addition to 152.3 thousand residents of local authority homes (children in care; the elderly; the mentally and physically handicapped under 65).[2] Capital costs have to be added to current expenditure on salaries and running costs. Large sums of money are tied up by agencies' ownership of large properties or in financing purpose-built establishments.

Such factors lead to high costs for each client in residential care: £50 per week to keep an elderly person in a local authority home, £70 per week[3] in a children's home and over £100 per week in specialised children's provision. It is often argued that the cost of maintaining a client in the community would be considerably less by using much less costly home help services, foster care and various types of day care. However, hidden costs are not always included in this calculation of community care. For example, figures[4] for the now well-documented scheme for the professional fostering of adolescents pioneered by Kent Social Services Department show that in 1972–3 the weekly cost of keeping a child in a children's home in Kent was £35; in a CHE was £50; and in specialised accommodation over £100 per week might be spent per child per week. The cost of the community care programme is shown as a flat rate of £32.50 plus clothing allowances, giving a total of £42.65–£45.70 depending on age. The cost of social work support, advertising, administration and research are not calculated as a figure per child to be added to the professional foster parents' salary and allowance. In contrast, the costs per head for residential care include subsidiary expenditure such as maintenance and material degeneration, clerical and administrative staff salaries as well as the items more central to the caring function, e.g. staff salaries and the provision of food and clothing.

An illustration such as this shows the futility of comparing residential and community services on a cost–benefit basis unless all the costs are categorised and allocated consistently. A realistic appreciation of the differential costs of services is important in balancing resources with need, but the ethics of using financial arguments as anything other than secondary factors in determining policy at a general level and in deciding the particular form of social work appropriate for individual clients needs to be rigorously examined.[5] If costly forms of care—whether residential or community—are effective in helping clients, their use is fully justified if no cheaper alternative, at least as effective, exists. Cost factors may at times be far more relevant in examining variations between different establishments with the same clientele and purpose; wide variations in cost in this situation provide surer ground for assuming that an equally effective service could be provided in establishments of different size and staffing pattern.[6]

A further forcible financial argument is summarised by Dinnage and Pringle[7] who suggest that the absence of one parent—for various reasons, including homelessness—accounts for a sizable proportion of the children entering care. Therefore, it is suggested, to offer a care service in their own homes to the children of single parents or to provide a new home in the case of homelessness would cost much less than keeping a child in residential care till adulthood. To pay a family's rent to the council costs less than keeping three or four children of that family in residential care but in cases such as this other factors such as the assessment of the quality of life for the children, the emotional security in the family, the level of physical risk the children run, and the opportunities for normal development must take precedence over financial considerations. There could well be situations when, having taken these into consideration, the local authority subsidises the family in the community rather than taking the children into residential care and obtains a financial benefit also. Equally, there will be other situations where despite the obvious financial advantages of keeping the family together this is not a practical possibility and the children will be admitted to care. The central point is that the welfare of the child and family should be the primary factor in making a decision, not the relative cost of service. A consequent implication is that all should be done to maintain individuals in the community through a variety of social policies (e.g. financial support, housing policy) and personal social service. But there is every indication that even with considerable progress in social policies and community support services there will still be substantial minorities for whom residential care will continue to be the most appropriate service. Ironically, the more successful community support services become, the more expensive residential care is likely to be, as residential services would deal with individuals with the severest difficulties and an aggregation of many different kinds of problem. Also, as community care expands (particularly where the more expensive forms of day care are involved) and is extended to those with more serious personal and social difficulties, its marginal cost may rise very steeply. This reinforces the principle that a variety of service should be available with cost a secondary rather than primary consideration.

Other arguments about the value of residential care have been mounted by psychologists and sociologists. It is not the financial costs which have disturbed them, but personal and social losses to individuals whom they have studied. The work of Bowlby[8,9] has had a profound effect on attitudes to residential child care. His ideas were first presented as a report to the World Health Organisation in 1951. The conclusions reached in this report were based on the interpretation of a number of research studies carried out on maternal deprivation over the previous 15 years by many researchers. Research methods used were the direct observation of children, follow-up studies of some of these children, and retrospective investigation of childhood experiences of adults and adolescents experiencing psychological difficulty. Bowlby concluded that a deprived child's ability to make relationships, other than superficial ones, was impaired; that a child would show "inaccessibility" in allowing others to relate to him; that his social relationships would be characterised by deceit and stealing; and that his intellectual development would be impaired. Sometimes these symptoms would persist through adult life. Although Bowlby related his ideas to a wide range of child-rearing situations in natural and substitute families, the implications were clear for residential institutions for children, especially residential nurseries, and had a discernible effect on child care policy and practice. Comparison of the figures for children in care for 1951 and 1966 in the table below show that, whereas in 1951 there were 34.5 thousand children in local authority and voluntary residential accommodation, in 1966 this was reduced to 27.9 thousands.

Children in residential care 1951–69*

	1951	1959	1966	1967	1968	1969
Residential accommodation—						
local authority and voluntary	34.5	27.3	27.9	27.9	28.4	29.5
Under charge and control of a parent,						
guardian or friend	—	1.9	4.4	4.9	5.1	5.4
Boarded out	24.3	28.2	31.8	31.5	31.0	30.5
Total children in care	62.7	61.6	69.2	69.4	69.4	70.2

* *Personal Social Service Statistics*, HMSO, 1977, Table 714.

The figures show corresponding increases in the number of children placed either in the charge of a relative whilst being in care, or placed in foster homes. The inclusion of figures for subsequent years confirms that this position remained substantially the same until 1969 after which date interpretation becomes more difficult as a result of the 1969 Children and Young Persons Act and the creation of social services departments. In the 1970s the numbers of children in residential care increased, but largely as a result of increasing numbers of children in care rather than a dramatic change in policy.

Bowlby's work rightly had an influence on the number of children placed in institutions, but maybe this influence was only partially effective since many residential workers will still recognise that they are asked to deal with some children who should not have been admitted to residential care. This is in spite of the impact of the 1963 Children and Young Persons Act whose content bore the imprint of Bowlby's attitudes, and was based on the principle of family support with admission to residential care as a last resort. However, Bowlby's ideas were challenged, and work continued on the effects of separation and attachment—not least by Bowlby himself—which gradually modified and refined our understanding of deprivation and its effects. Rutter[10] has collated the evidence from a large number of studies in this field from which he concludes that whilst Bowlby's main thesis—that poor early experiences have serious short- and long-term effects on the human personality—is still valid, the contention that the relationship with the natural mother has the central place in this process, is qualified. Attention was drawn to a series of other significant variables which included: the nature and quality of environmental stimulation; the quality of relationship with the mother-figure before separation occurred—not loss but lack or distortion of care in the first place; and the quality of substitute care. Rutter's conclusions are relevant to residential workers and imply that residential care is not inherently damaging, but that its effects largely depend on the quality of care, including the substitute parenting the child receives whilst he is placed in a home. Similarly, whatever the quality of care, clear recognition must be given to the adverse relationship experiences a child has had before care, if staff are to respond appropriately to a child's need.

The maternal deprivation debate relates obviously to children, but perhaps too little regard has been given in residential care to the importance of rejection for adults who come into residential care. Entry implies failure to maintain a role in the community and a realisation that others—family, neighbours, friends—are unable or unwilling to care adequately: it implies rejection. This theme of loss, rejection, and abandonment is touched on briefly by Michael Meacher[11] in his study of the confused elderly, and by Miller and Gwynne[12] in their study of institutions for physically handicapped adults, but has fruitful implications for the quality of relationships experienced by all adults in residential care. Bowlby's original work, based on strong evidence of deficient residential care for children, has proved a rich vein of insight for residential staff. The later refinement and more discriminating theoretical position has changed our view of residential care from a mainly negative experience to one which has a positive potential, with a relevance far wider than deprived children.

Bowlby's concern with residential care was a by-product of a wide-ranging interest in the origins of disorders of personality and social behaviour. By contrast, Goffman devoted a seminal book[13] to the analysis of institutional life, claiming a sociological objectivity and value neutrality but at the same time presenting a picture which sharpened our view of the potentially negative features of residential life, and which, since the 1960s, has coloured the views of social workers and policy makers towards residential care, giving credence to an aura of darkness, dismay and depression surrounding institutional care. Goffman began by classifying institutions into five types:

(1) Those which care for the "incapable and homeless"; this category covers most of the institutions we would normally subsume under the heading "Residential Social Work", homes for the aged and for children being included.

(2) Those which care for people who, at the same time as being unable to care for themselves, represent some sort of threat to the community, e.g. mental hospitals, isolation hospitals for infectious diseases, leprosy colonies.

(3) Those which protect the community: prisons, POW camps, concentration camps.

(4) Those which facilitate a work task: barracks, ships, boarding schools, servants quarters of large mansions.

(5) Those which are retreats: monasteries and convents.

Goffman then identifies four common factors between these widely varying types of institution.

(1) The various aspects of life—work, leisure and rest—are all carried out "in the same place and under the same single authority".[14]

(2) "Batch treatment" of inmates.[15]

(3) All activities are highly organised leaving no "free" time, and with no opportunity for the inmate to participate in the management.

(4) The activities are brought together in some kind of plan which aims "to fulfil the official aims of the institution".[16]

It is these common features which led Goffman to use the concept of the "total institution" to denote the characteristic ethos and encompassing nature of institutional life. Individuals living in total institutions suffered a number of assaults on their personality categorised in the following way:

(1) A loss of individual identity—symbolised by an admission procedure, by institutional clothing and by the searching of possessions at any time.

(2) Endangering of their physical integrity—surgery, shock therapy and beatings are given as examples.

(3) Lack of privacy.

(4) Humiliation—typified by non-reciprocal forms of intimate address, insistence on deference as well as more extreme examples.

(5) Lack of authority—areas of choice are severely limited.

Subjected to the regime of a total institution, inmates react in various ways including: regression; depersonalisation; opting out; intransigence; "colonisation" i.e. acceptance or conversion, with deliberate attempts not to leave. The human consequences of "total" institutions as presented by Goffman may trigger the reaction of dismissiveness from residential staff on the basis of "our home is not like that" attitude. But it is as well not to reject Goffman's analysis out of hand as it is to avoid being seduced by its rhetoric regarding all institutional care as total. The value of Goffman's work in the concept of the total institution lies in the way attention is drawn to some of the implications of institutional ritual and routine, glimpses of which can still be seen in some of our residential homes today. But Goffman's skill in portraying the processes of institutional life should not cloak those aspects of his analysis which are open to question.

The problems with Goffman's analysis are met right at the outset with his classification which includes institutions whose social purposes are very dissimilar; the differences between the five kinds of institution are as great or greater than their similarities. To compare a family group home (where children go out to school and visit the homes of their family and friends) with a POW camp or rigid monastic order is taking the analogy to absurdity. Further, Goffman's conclusions are not based on empirical investigations but on a collection of subjective observations which are not necessarily representative; thus Goffman would himself accept that, whilst he has described the characteristics of a class of institution, the description is an abstract one. He provides us with an "abstract" or "ideal type" of model which can then be used to understand the processes and structure of particular institutions in the real world. Some criticism is therefore based on a misunderstanding of Goffman's sociological method, but Goffman contributes to this misunderstanding by the conviction and power of his descriptions, which impress the reader, rather than his methodological disclaimers. He gives insufficient weight to the varying functions which institutions fulfil, the diverse ways in which they carry out their functions, and fails to recognise that "asylum" in the original sense of the word could still be a valid function. Can an institution, whose central purpose is rehabilitation or integration in the surrounding community, be understood by applying concepts derived from a total institution model?

Commentators[17] have taken up these and other issues. However, we should remain chastened and warned by his work, alive to the possibilities of applying the analysis selectively and with due caution. There is a need to build on this kind of work and to achieve a greater sophistication in understanding the effects of institutions on those who live in them, and also to clarify the concept of the residential task in social work. An unfortunate repercussion of the application of theory to practice is that it becomes either distorted or over-simplified in the transfer. Bowlby's theory is bowdlerised to become "any family home in the community is better than institutional care" or "all natural mothers are better than substitute parents". Goffman's ideas are simplified and mis-interpreted to become "all total institutions are punitive, humiliating and harsh to experience" whilst conversely, as Gilbert Smith has noted, all therapeutic communities may be assumed to be good. The falsity of these crude all-or-none judgements is clear, and obscures the fact that most institutional care contains negative and positive features —one of the main advocates of the therapeutic community has stated that even the most total of institutions is not incompatible with the concept of the therapeutic community.[18]

Turning from Goffman's sociological critique, a rather different standpoint is pre-sented by Barton,[19] based on observation of patients' behaviour in a psychiatric hospital. Barton's organising concept is "institutional neurosis" and results from identifying a clinical condition of individual personality and behaviour as a response to a social institution like a hospital: "Institutional neurosis was said to occur when the original purposes of an institution are ignored, displaced by, or subordinate to increasing pre-occupation with the rituals or symbols of administration or wealth of that institution".[20] Although developed in the context of a psychiatric hospital, Barton, like Goffman, believed his analysis to be of more general application. Evidence that the kind of treat-ment categorised by Barton exists in other institutions has been corroborated by the series of public enquiries into psychiatric and subnormality hospitals and also occasional revelations about children's homes or old people's homes. Barton's approach was similar to Goffman's in providing a list of functions in treatment which contributed towards institutional neurosis, and which were very like Goffman's "characteristics".

(1) Loss of contact with the outside world.

(2) Enforced idleness and loss of responsibility.

(3) Browbeating, brutality and teasing.

(4) Bossiness of professional staff.

(5) Loss of personal friends, possessions and personal events.

(6) Use of drugs.

(7) Ward atmosphere.

(8) Loss of prospects outside the institution.[21]

Unlike Goffman, Barton is openly prescriptive, and having described a series of factors which could be viewed as causes of institutional neurosis, suggests ways of overcoming the contributory factors. For this reason Barton's work is specially useful for the residen-tial worker, with important implications for practice: the maintenance of links with the community/family; resident participation and involvement at various levels of decision-making; a due regard for the individuality and identity (however eccentric) of every resident; a client-centred approach to management which might mean sacrificing smoothly oiled routines to the interests of the residential group. Barton's significance is in moving away from the simple view that "all institutions are bad" towards the position that "some institutions have negative features and it is possible, once the causes are understood, to take action to improve the quality of institutional life".

The discussion of the work of Bowlby, Goffman and Barton has showed how a negative climate can be produced and hang like a pall over residential care, in spite of the fact that the empirical and theoretical basis for a statement like "all residential care is bad" is invalid. Why is this so? A number of other factors combined over the years to reinforce negative attitudes. Some issues on research in relation to residential care are developed in a later chapter,[22] but in the present context it is relevant to draw attention to Dinnage and Pringle's comment[23] that the central focus of research on residential care had been on the detrimental effects of deprivation and institutionalisation, but very little was being done to evaluate how this might be improved. Prosser,[24] in bringing the survey of research into residential care up to date in 1976, points out that this gap has not been filled. How much notice practitioners take of research is questionable, but nevertheless research studies on residential care have contributed by their negative focus to the general unease about residential provision. The goldfish-bowl nature of the residential setting has made it a good target for researchers who may find it easier to control research projects in this environment. Much of the interaction in the residential setting is public to other workers and to other visitors and residents, and is thus more available to criticism than some other social work situations; anyone who has wall-papered a ceiling knows how easy a task it is when observing with two feet firmly on the floor! Few people observe casework interaction in the office or client's home, which leaves an aura of mystery and ignorance about what goes on—bad as well as good practice. In residential care mistakes are more visible and the observer tends to see what is visible—physical care and daily routine—rather than the relationships and planning behind the pattern of life.

At its worst, residential care has been described by Miller and Gwynne[25] as the interval between social and physical death, and the role dispossession, depersonalisation and lack of stimulating environment described as "social poverty" by Jones.[26] The element of social control apparent in some forms of residential work such as psychiatric hostels and hostels and institutions for offenders, raises for some, doubts about whether this work can be construed as social work at all. Fowler[27] points out that the social control element of social work is questioned by the radical who wants to change the basis of society, and by the therapist who erroneously believes that he can work outside the context of societal values. He argues that a valid role for all forms of social work—casework, groupwork, community work and residential work—is at the point of conflict between the needs of the individual and the needs of society. The issues of control and freedom worked with in residential care crystallise and mirror the tensions and conflicts endemic in society in a more diffuse and shadowy form.

The relationship of residential care to other professions with which it works closely is too large a topic to discuss in detail in this present context, but it is relevant to note here that the growth of a casework orientation in social work in the 1950s, and the consequent mystification of social work, led to an increasing gap between mainstream social work and residential care, with the latter's emphasis on physical caring. Training patterns reflected this difference between the professions—illustrated by the fact that fieldworkers could be trained in universities, whereas there were no such courses for residential workers, whose training was shorter and usually at the level of further education.

The lower value and status of residential care was also reflected in the legal framework. Both the 1963 and 1969 Children and Young Persons Acts reflected the need to keep children in the community *if at all possible* (sometimes wrongly interpreted as *at all costs*) and a similar orientation was apparent in the 1959 Mental Health Act. Such legislation brought about a much-needed change in emphasis in our thinking about residential care, but also fostered an attitude that residential care was a last resort when all else had failed and, as such, became associated in people's minds with a third-class form of care. A recent discussion document shows clearly how the pattern of legislation has encouraged thinking about residential care merely in terms of physical provision. In short, the legislation appears to encourage an equation of old age and handicap with illness—an interpretation of residential care as mere physical care.[28]

Through the influence of Goffman, Bowlby and others, whose writings have become known collectively as the "literature of dysfunction",[29] through training patterns which have consistently discriminated against the residential worker, and still do;[30] through the inappropriate use of cost–benefit arguments; and through inappropriate expectations of what such a form of intervention can achieve whilst working with clients in isolation from their community context, residential care has been seen as the "Cinderella" of the Social Services. These factors have, moreover, strongly influenced the legislative framework and it is perhaps surprising that we have any good institutions, given the force of a whole array of negative attitudes. But good institutions do exist and achieve recognisable and worthwhile results, and the residential setting offers the opportunity for positive intervention in social situations. However, very rarely are the positives of residential living put forward in the literature, and the concluding section of this chapter will focus on the need for residential care and its potential for caring and helping.

There are some clients who require 24-hour care and for whom at present residential care is the only realistic alternative: the non-ambulant elderly; the confused elderly who put their own and others' safety at risk—for example, by leaving on gas-taps; some severely subnormal people requiring constant care and supervision. These people may impose an intolerable strain on a family's limited resources, or may have no available family or close friends to help them. Domiciliary services at a level of 24-hour care over a long period (e.g. three or four workers to maintain a round-the-clock service) are just not available at present, and residential care remains the only practical possibility in the present context. It is important to note that this 24-hour group-care function in no way conflicts with the further extension of domiciliary and day-care service (using volunteers and professional staff) for many people with less chronic problems as a means of improving their quality of life.

Another group of people who may continue to be served by residential care are those clients who pose a serious threat to society. This is a grey area but even the strongest critics of residential care accept the qualification that the "protective" and "control" functions of residential care will be necessary for some individuals. However, the quality of a society ought to be judged in part by the quality of care it provides in institutions whose functions include custody or control. There are obvious dangers involved in the definition of what is seen by society as a threat. Whilst the protection of persons and to some extent of property may be acceptable, protection of questionable norms such as the unacceptable face of severe handicap by the community—ought to be rejected. Nor should residential care prostitute itself in trying to offer individual "cures" to problems largely generated by society, through poverty, a decaying environment, and unemployment; residential workers should resist the off-loading mentality by which some sections of the community are happy to see individuals shunted into residential care as a means of avoiding social problems they could realistically cope with, given moderate effort and goodwill.

The concept of residential care as "asylum" in the sense of "sanctuary" or "place of refuge" (OED) is an important one: the child who had been physically or emotionally battered needs respite whilst a more permanent placement is found or until he is returned to an improved home situation. The elderly person who requires protection from hypothermia and the debilitating effects of poverty may need short-term residential care, but this should not cloak the need to reform longer-term social policies to avoid the situation arising in the first place. The mentally ill may require asylum from the pathological interaction of families which have played a major part in causing their condition. Also the child or adolescent rejected through illegitimacy, handicap or social behaviour will require residential care for a time, at least, until the effects of rejection have passed sufficiently to enable him to be sufficiently trusting to form new relationships and bonds. Some handicapped people may well require sanctuary from the strains and pressures of a demanding and sophisticated society, needing either permanently or from time to time the support of residential care.

As well as the extremes of social control and asylum functions, residential care has much to offer as a positive form of social work intervention. It can be chosen as a positive step to provide a context for intensive learning of specialised skills, e.g. simple daily tasks for the mentally handicapped; new physical skills for an elderly person paralysed on one side by a stroke; remedial education for a young person; making skill adjustments to trauma of various kinds such as blindness, bereavement, or paralysis. As well as this educational function the residential settings provide opportunity for helping with emotional and social difficulties. Therapeutic intervention of this kind needs a setting where tolerance and acceptance, warmth and intimacy, understanding and hope, can be experienced for those who have been deprived of such basic needs in their natural group. Righton[31] quotes an example of an adolescent with whom, to his surprise, he had a conversation about the advantages of residential care. The youngster liked the large variety of adults with whom he could have a variety of relationships; he found his family relationships more limited; he liked sharing with a large peer group whom he was not expected to love as he was his brother and sisters; he liked the activities available, often having experienced boredom at home; he liked the large rambling building offering an unaccustomed privacy; and he liked the increased freedom and lack of restriction he experienced in residential care. If space permitted, similar catalogues could be presented of the potential advantages for other client groups.

The word "potential" is used advisedly here. The models of residential provision operating now, still frequently produce separation and rejection, stigma and social poverty. However adversely the negative influences of residential care described in this chapter have affected the quality of care, we may agree with David Ennals that, "Too much is sometimes made of the negatives of residential care. We must never overlook them. . . ."[32] But the negatives, far from being a reason for banishing residential care, provide a programme for improvement and vitalising the quality of residential life. Other developments—increased flexibility of provision, short-stay care, day care and sheltered housing, unstaffed homes as well as long-term homes—will create a continuum of provision which, along with improvements in training and rewards for residential workers, will go a long way towards decreasing "the distance we have yet to travel before we can truthfully say the "positive" scale outweighs the negative".[33]

References

1. D. ENNALS, The role of residential care, *Social Work Today*, **10** (7), 1978.
2. *Social Trends, No. 9*, H.M.S.O., 1978, Tables 3.7, 3.10, 3.13 and 3.22.
3. *Social Service Estimates 1977–8*, Chartered Institute of Public Accountants, quoted D. ENNALS, *op. cit.*
4. N. HAZEL and R. COX, The special family placement project in Kent, *Social Work Service*, No. 12, D.H.S.S., December 1976.
5. See B. UTTING, Residential care—the end or the beginning, for a good discussion of costs in relation to need and effectiveness, *Social Work Today*, **9** (7), 1977.
6. M. KNAPP and D. DAVIES, The costs of residential care, *Social Work Today*, **9** (33), 1978.
7. R. DINNAGE and M. K. PRINGLE, Conclusion and Recommendation, in *Residential Care—Facts and Fallacies*, Longman, 1967, pp. 167 ff. Reprinted in H. PROSSER, *Perspectives on Residential Care*, N.F.E.R./ National Children's Bureau, 1976, pp. 27ff.
8. J. BOWLBY, *Child Care and the Growth of Love*, Penguin, 1965.
9. J. BOWLBY, *Attachment*, Penguin, 1971; *Separation*, Penguin, 1975.
10. M. RUTTER, *Maternal Deprivation Re-assessed*, Penguin, 1972.
11. M. MEACHER, *Taken for a Ride*, Longman, 1972.
12. E. J. MILLER and G. V. GWYNNE, *A Life Apart*, Tavistock, 1972.
13. E. GOFFMAN, *Asylums*, Anchor, 1961 (Penguin, 1968).
14. *Ibid.*, p. 17.
15. See study of residential establishments by KING, RAYNES and TIZARD, *Patterns of Residential Care*, Routledge & Kegan Paul, 1971. "Block treatment" of residents is identified in some of the homes studied.
16. GOFFMAN, *op. cit.*, p. 17.
17. See G. SMITH, *Social Work and the Sociology of Organisations*, Chapter 5, Routledge & Kegan Paul, 1970; and J. JONES, *The Residential Community*, Routledge & Kegan Paul, 1979, Chapter 2.
18. M. JONES, *Social Psychiatry in Practice. The Idea of the Therapeutic Community*, Penguin, 1968.
19. R. BARTON, *Institutional Neurosis*, John Wright, 1959 (3rd edn. 1976).
20. *Ibid.*, p. 75.
21. *Ibid.*, p. 77.
22. R. WALTON, Chapter 19.
23. DINNAGE and PRINGLE, *op. cit.*
24. PROSSER, *op. cit.*
25. MILLER and GWYNNE, *op. cit.*
26. JONES, *op. cit.*
27. D. FOWLER, Ends and Means, in H. JONES (ed.), *Towards a New Social Work*, Routledge & Kegan Paul, 1975, Chapter 6.
28. *Policy Issues in Residential Care: A Discussion Document*, Personal Social Services Council, 1978, p. 22.
29. The phrase was coined by K. JONES in *The Development of Institutional Care*, Association of Social Workers, 1967, p. 14.
30. D. ELLIOTT and R. WALTON, Attitudes and policies for residential training, *Social Work Today*, **10** (24), 1979.
31. P. RIGHTON, Home life, *Social Work Today*, **10** (30), 1979.
32. ENNALS, *op. cit.*
33. P. RIGHTON, Positive and Negative Aspects of Residential Care, *Social Work Today*, (37), 1977.

CHAPTER 2

SOME CURRENT ISSUES IN RESIDENTIAL WORK: IMPLICATIONS FOR THE SOCIAL WORK TASK

DOREEN ELLIOTT

Changes in the practice of residential care come about as a result of the influence of a number of factors. Increased training opportunities, both in-service and professional, should encourage practitioners to question and test out their existing practices. Developments in knowledge areas from the Social Sciences—e.g. in sociological and organisational theory—help to bring increased understanding of the influences affecting a resident's situation both inside and outside the Home. Changes in society's values and attitudes will be mirrored in the microcosm of the residential establishment. Occasionally a tragedy or a public enquiry in one Home or Institution will reverberate throughout the profession bringing about changes in previously accepted practices. Instances such as these receive much press coverage and public discussion, but less often debated are the changes which develop almost unnoticed, but which together form what has been aptly termed "A Quiet Revolution".[1]

The Keyworker Concept

One of the most frequently mentioned, yet insufficiently debated, developments in ideas about residential practice which have taken place recently, arose out of the report of a joint working party set up in September 1976 by the Residential Care Association and the British Association of Social Workers.[2] This report expressed dissatisfaction with the traditional model of practice characterised by: the minimal involvement of the residential worker prior to a client's admission to a residential establishment; the retention of overall responsibility by the fieldworker for any major decisions which had to be taken; and by the withdrawal of the RSW usually on the discharge of a client from the residential establishment.

An alternative model of practice was suggested which involved the concept of a "keyworker". This was seen as a role to be filled by either a fieldworker, or a residential worker who would be responsible for the planning and implementation of an individual care plan for a resident, and who would carry accountability within the organisation for that case. The keyworker would therefore need to call regular reviews and keep appropriate records. The report outlines the factors which would need to be taken into consideration when deciding, in respect of an individual client, whether the field or residential worker would be the more appropriate worker to fill this role. Clearly, if this concept were to be adopted in a social services department, it would involve considerable redefinition of role boundaries. It might involve a residential worker in working with the family of a resident, or a fieldworker spending more time with the client whilst in the residential establishment sharing the "life-space" of that client. Whilst this idea is congruent with recent developments in training[3] and in social work theory,[4] there are many practical difficulties surrounding its implementation.

Many of the objections raised would be expected to be in the area of how far the training and experience of residential workers equips them to undertake this task. Where they are trained, it has usually been with respect to a particular client group rather than the generic based fieldwork training, and residential courses have not usually offered casework/fieldwork placements, so that training has focussed on the skills of dealing with clients in the residential situation. Criticisms such as these may be answered in various ways.

Firstly, it is unsound to imply that there are fieldwork and residential skills which are totally separate and which have no areas of overlap. The diagram (Fig. 2.1) attempts to illustrate this by showing just one area—contact with individuals—on a continuum. One end represents the interview situation in which exchanges are verbally based, where there is a clearly defined beginning and end of the interview, and which is usually task-oriented—e.g. the exchange of information or problem solving. The other end of the continuum represents the life-space of the client in which the worker shares, alongside the client, his daily living experiences.

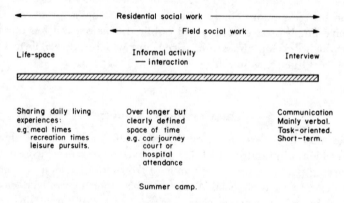

Fig. 2.1. *Intermediate Treatment*

It is apparent that work in the residential setting requires skills covering the whole of this continuum and that some situations in fieldwork practice require the application of what would normally be called "residential" skills, e.g. Summer-camps with children, and Intermediate Treatment. The transfer of skills from one area of practice to another is an area which has been insufficiently explored but for which an integrated methods approach to social work theory offers a framework to define common skill areas needed by both field and residential workers.[5]

Secondly, even accepting that there may well be a considerable area of overlap of skills between fieldwork and residential work, the keyworker concept offers a challenge to in-service training schemes, in which experienced residential workers can be given help and encouragement to extend their skills, and similarly, fieldworkers can take on functions more closely related to the residential task where appropriate.

Thirdly, objections to the possibility of residential workers extending their role boundaries into "fieldwork" situations might be tempered by the fact that approximately 60% of fieldworkers are not professionally qualified. Simon Rodway, in one of few published papers commenting on the keyworker role,[6] suggests that the two crucial areas to be considered in implementing the keyworker idea are accountability and supervision. That supervision is not an established tradition in residential work as it is in fieldwork, and the implications of this, are brought out very clearly in Juliet Berry's study of residential establishments.[7] That the keyworker should have adequate supervision, consultation and support was a requirement incorporated into the BASW/RCA policy statement on the keyworker. Given the differing organisational structures of local authority social services departments, lines of accountability need to be clarified. To whom is the keyworker immediately accountable—to the team leader or Head of Home; to the Area Director, or Homes Adviser?

The complexities of the influence of organisational structure in relation to decision making and accountability about clients entering residential care have been explored and reported by Billis,[8] and although his study was undertaken before the idea of the keyworker was introduced it showed that the decision-making process for a client entering residential care could be improved by a critical analysis of the organisational implications. In a later study carried out in another department by Bromley,[9] two models of interaction between field and residential workers are described. The first is a *prescriptive* model, in which the assessment for residential care, the choice of residential establishment, the kind of treatment and duration of stay would be prescribed by the fieldworker. The second model, and the one adopted by the project, is described as a *collateral* model in which decisions about admission, treatment and rehabilitation are reached by "discussion, compromise and agreement: neither can impose their decisions on the other".[10] The adoption of this collateral model set the scene for the emergence of the role of "Prime Care Agent"—another term for a keyworker. The project groups recognised the difficulties in working with a collateral model in which there was not, as is so often the case in practice, equality of training, status and experience of the people involved. Yet the project went ahead and appeared to have achieved some success in having negotiated a model of practice which allowed for the greater involvement of residential workers in admission and review decisions.

Another attempt to relax rigid role boundaries between field and residential work is based on the work of a single establishment and has been described by Allen.[11] Here the residential staff carry out some fieldwork tasks and there is an attempt to involve the manager of the home into the departmental hierarchy. That other attempts to implement the keyworker idea have occurred up and down the country is apparent in discussion with residential practitioners, but all too few of these have been recorded in the journals. But despite these attempts to implement new ideas such projects are a minority and many departments still work on the prescriptive model of interaction between field and residential workers. Similar studies on the relative roles of field and residential workers in relation to the rehabilitation process, to complement those concentrating mainly on admission, would be valuable. It is significant that, writing $2\frac{1}{2}$ years after the publication of the initial study, there has been such little public debate about this concept of the keyworker, so important for the changing role of the residential worker.

Developments in Social Work Theory

Recent developments in this area have important implications for the residential task. Mounting criticism of the casework method in social work because it tended to treat social problems as the result of individual pathology, and the increased questioning of its effectiveness, along with the application of sociological knowledge and analysis, led to the search for a theoretical framework for social work which would allow for the treatment of social problems as well as individual ones. The recognition that admission to residential care often represents a societal failure, as well as or instead of a failure of the individual client, has far-reaching implications for the role of the residential worker, who can no longer concentrate his efforts solely on the client and expect to solve the problem. His role will of necessity extend to working with the client's family, peer group, and with other agencies at the very least. Lack of space prevents further development of this theme here, but its implications are discussed more fully in the introduction to Part II, Section Two, in this reader.

Resident Participation

Whilst the concept of the keyworker focusses primarily on the role of the worker, another concept—that of resident participation—focusses primarily on the changing nature of the role of resident and by implication, therefore, on the role of residential worker. Perhaps this is a result of the influence of the now well-recognised consumer movement of the 1960s, perhaps also of the slow percolation into the residential setting of social work theory involving the idea of "contract" with the client, and perhaps also from the various ways in which "radical" social work has challenged traditional assumptions and practice in social work. The idea of resident participation assumes various guises, from the increasing involvement of children in their case conferences and reviews, the emergence of unstaffed group houses to units, or simply effecting the choice between tea and coffee at breakfast time or choosing the time at which one goes to bed. The idea of resident participation is discussed here in relation to three levels of decision making.

Participation in daily routines

The same degree of choice exercised by someone in the community with regard to their daily activities is unavailable to the average resident in a home: choice of rising time, meal times and bath times are often determined by routine and the convenience of staff rotas. Choice of food likewise is limited by the need to cater for large numbers on a budget which is often restricting to the most fertile culinary imagination. Residential workers are increasingly recognising the need to introduce staggered meal times, and in the case of the elderly, to move away from the debilitating "hotel" model of care for the elderly, involving them increasingly in making choices relevant to their daily lives. Similar attempts are being made in provision for other client groups, but average practice still lacks a conscious effort to achieve an acceptable degree of resident participation even at this most basic level.

Participation in social work decisions

Even more challenging to the temptation in residential establishments of doing things "to", "at" and "for" people is the notion that they should be "enabled" by involvement in the process to arrive at their own solutions to problems or to determine their own life-style. Perhaps one way to differentiate between "institutional" and "residential" care—terms which are so often confused—is that institutional care consists of doing things "to", "at" and "for" people, with or without their permission, and about which they exercise no choice, whilst "residential" care consists of the worker sharing daily living experiences alongside the resident—which might or might not have a therapeutic goal—and a concept of his role primarily as an "enabler".

The idea of resident participation, however, is not new in institutional care: in writing about the idea of a therapeutic community, Rappoport[12] defines one of the four main characteristics of such a community as "democratisation" whereby each member of the community should share equally in the decision-making process. This might include "therapeutic" decisions traditionally reserved for staff. Pioneers in education, such as A. S. Neil,[13] long ago advocated the value of shared decision making, and in many schools for maladjusted children the daily community meeting has long been one where problems are discussed and rewards and punishments meted out. However in social services departments, the token involvement of a child by bringing him in at the end of a case review meeting, to inform him of decisions already made, has been the only widespread, but not real, concession to participation in "social work" decisions. Any doubt about this judgement can be dispelled on reading in *Who Cares*[14] examples quoted by numbers of children who failed to have understood such, if any, explanations they were given as to the reason for their being in care. The involvement of children and adults in meetings where important decisions are made affecting the future course of their lives is a challenge which residential and other social workers and managers must face squarely. As in most areas of practice there are pockets where these innovations are being made[15] but much more widespread practice of these principles is needed to help to raise standards of care for the client generally.

"Open" record systems, i.e. those to which clients have access,[16] have far-reaching implications for the residential task where, still, in some establishments residential workers have inadequate information provided and where records are often kept in the department and not in the Home. An open record system means: examining more carefully the judgements made about residents and being able to justify them adequately; less use of glib labels e.g. "confused", "aggressive"; including the resident's point of view by inviting the resident to write his reports in the records which would no longer be seen as the "property" of the agency.

A further possible implication of the involvement of clients in social work decisions is the idea of "contract"—a working relationship with mutually agreed objectives and a recognition that both parties have responsibilities in this shared process. The application of this idea, practised in a few agencies, is likely to become more widespread.

A linked concept which is altering the nature of the residential task results from changing ideas about what are acceptable risks to a client in residential care. In a system where the worker is totally responsible for the resident's welfare and is accountable to an agency hierarchy to the exclusion of the resident's responsibility for his own actions, then we have the kind of care described in the case of the elderly by Slater and Lipman in a later chapter.[17] Fear of accusations of negligence on the part of the residential worker if an elderly person slips whilst taking an unsupervised bath becomes more important than the resident's right to privacy. A redefinition of what is an acceptable risk[18] by involving the client in that decision as far as possible is resulting, in some areas of practice, in a better quality of life for the resident.

Participation in the management function, including the selection and training of staff

An obvious but little-practised area of resident participation. The practicality of this would depend to a certain extent on the nature of the client group but has been practised within some agencies and with positive advantages, as Brian Line reports,[19] for both residents and staff in terms of mutual trust, respect and understanding. We should not be deterred from considering this aspect of resident participation because of the existence of some client groups for whom it would not be appropriate to participate—the very young, the confused elderly, severely subnormal residents—for there are a large number of older children and young people, physically handicapped adults, elderly residents, some mentally handicapped and mentally ill residents for whom this level of participation would not be inappropriate, and who should not be denied the opportunity to participate in this way.

Resident Population Changes

The elderly admitted to residential care are older, less ambulant and less continent than they used to be; children in residential care are more "difficult", more aggressive, more "disturbed". Any professional gathering of residential workers can be guaranteed to produce such comments as these. Is it a collective fantasy, or is there a factual basis to these observations? If there is a factual basis, then there are important implications for the residential task to be considered.

Figures show[20] that females over 75 years of age form the greatest proportion of the elderly in residential accommodation in England and Wales, and that during the years 1966–75 the most significant increase in the resident population has been of females aged 85 and over, increasing from slightly over 20,000 in 1966 to over 35,000 in 1975, i.e. a growth roughly the size of the population of an industrial town such as Bridgend in Glamorgan. The second most apparent increase in the resident population is that of females in the 75–84 age group. It would be fair to assume that a large proportion of those residents over 85 may need more physical care and attention than residents needed when the average age of a resident in a home for the elderly was substantially lower. Other figures[21] show that the number of cases aged 65 and over attended by Home Helps increased by 354,000 in the years 1961–76, i.e. by more than 23,000 per year. The one set of figures indicating both a proportionate and numerical increase in residents aged 85 and over, and the other indicating the large increase in the number of cases where Home Helps are used for the elderly in the community, together would imply that the cases entering residential care require more intensive care and support than previously.

Similarly, policies designed to keep children in the community as far as possible by the increased use of fostering schemes or intermediate treatment or other supervision schemes may have resulted in those children who remain in residential care appearing more difficult to manage since the less "difficult" ones tend to remain in the community. A sweeping generalisation, but one which probably contains a large enough element of truth to illustrate the fact that the residential task is a changing one.

Gillian Corney[22] argues in a later chapter that the residential task with the physically handicapped resident is one which is becoming more demanding and skilled, and similarly, as the potential and needs of the mentally handicapped resident are drawn to our attention, both through improved assessment and treatment techniques and through changing attitudes, so the residential task with that client group becomes more skilled and demanding.

It is apparent that if current trends in population continue, then residential social work will need to become one of the most highly skilled and specialised of the personal social services. Important changes in another area, that of salaries and conditions of service, are making this concept of residential work more feasible than in the past.

Conditions of Service

The effect of changed conditions of service on the residential task has been the cause of considerable debate since 1974 when the length of the working week was limited to 44 hours with subsequent reductions to 40 hours.[23]

These changes represent a real attempt to move away from the situation where, for example, the housemother of a family group home was expected to be on duty at all times when the children were around, taking time off during school hours and where relief assistance was provided for perhaps one day a week off duty. Like the mother of a natural family she was expected to be omnipresent. The introduction of a limited working week implies, first of all, increased numbers of staff, when the housemother then becomes the manager of a team, needing to acquire the additional skills necessary for this role. Delegation, co-ordination and communication become all-important, but even where these functions are carried out effectively, the representatives of residential workers have argued[24] that such a system imposes restrictions on the role of the residential worker which are disadvantageous to the relationship with the client. There are some needs which must be met as they arise and the rigid operation of a shift system could easily cut across those needs. One of the main tools used by residential social workers is the relationship between worker and client, and the particular qualities of this relationship cannot always be supplied by the substitution of another worker on another shift. Part of the value of teamwork in the residential setting is that members of that team are involved in unique but complementary relationships with the residents with whom they share their working day. A child care worker may feel it is important to remain with a child after his experiencing problems at school, or on his returning to the Home after running away, or after a painful family visit. A residential worker with the elderly may judge it important that an elderly person is not left alone when death is imminent.

In all aspects of the helping professions, however, it is important to balance the needs of the residents with those of the staff, for whom it is important, if they are to bring a measure of balance and objectivity to their work, that they have sufficient time to devote to family and other interests outside the work. Whilst recognising this principle, residential workers have suggested that to define the boundaries of the task in terms of fulfilling a number of hours rather than meeting the residents' needs[25] does less than justice to the professional role of the residential worker.

Alongside these difficulties in the implementation of a time-limited week are the administrative difficulties in operating such a system: clerical work is increased by the need to keep records of overtime worked, and if staffing establishments are not suitably increased, then the effect of payment for regular overtime may be to discourage the future improvement of client–worker ratios and nullify the original intention which was to reduce the working week in the interests of both client and worker.

A related issue is that of "living-in". The number of posts where staff are automatically expected to live on the job has decreased considerably over the last few years, perhaps more as an expedient solution to the fact that fewer staff are prepared to live on the job than as an expression of a view about the residential worker's task. No doubt the debate will continue as to the advantages and disadvantages to the client of staff living in, but that is a separate question from the provision of 24-hour care, which is often one of the criteria upon which the selection of a client for residential care is based, and which can be provided by non-resident staff operating "sleeping-in duty" rotas and night shifts. Whether the residence of staff on the job creates a better "community" atmosphere and a greater sense of sharing between client and worker, or whether it narrows the worker's perspective and lessens his efficiency by increasing the amount and intensity, if not necessarily the quality, of client–worker contact, will depend on a large number of at present unidentified variables. Future research studies in this area might provide useful evidence. If residential work is to exploit one of its positive features, which is to offer a wide variety of types of care from unstaffed homes to high-ratio staff–client intensive care units, then it may well be important for the profession to lay down no fixed rules about residence. The increasing number of workers living out is likely to result in a better rather than poorer service to the client in most situations, but the option should remain open for staff residence to be determined by the need of a particular post. It is vital that the need is determined by the nature of the post, and not by the personal needs of the staff concerned.

The residence of staff and its related issue of emoluments—i.e. payment for board and lodging—has had important repercussions in the area of salary levels for residential staff. Salary levels have been substantially lower for residential workers than for field-workers, differences even at the lower points of the corresponding scales amounting to around £1000 per annum. It has sometimes been argued that this apparent substantial discrepancy conceals the hidden benefits of board and lodging allowances since residential workers pay subsidised rather than economic rents for staff houses, which can include heating, lighting, repairs, and furnishings and subsidised rates for board. In addition, tax benefits are obvious for such payments in kind. However, as Banner has pointed out,[26] in an economy such as the present one, any savings a residential worker can make are so eroded by inflation as to be valueless, so that when he moves or retires he can find himself homeless and without furniture. The answer is therefore to provide a proper salary in the first place. More recently the rise in property prices has intensified this problem, and it would seem important that if staff are required to live in on the job some account is taken of the fact that they may be running two homes, one on the job, and the other their more permanent home in the community. The issue of a more realistic salary is one which at the time of writing appears to be closer to reality than at any time in the past, and whilst the changes do not include residential workers on the APT and

C salary grades, there is nevertheless a matching of these, and of the SO and PO scales, on which field social workers are employed, with the new grade offered to residential workers. This move marks a major breakthrough in salaries for residential workers and, although there will still be problems of emoluments and property purchase for those who live in, discrepancy in salary rates will no longer be such a great disincentive for people who might otherwise enter residential work.

The possibility of the use of industrial action of various kinds has been an issue in the events leading up to the offer of this award, and as such raises issues about the way the residential task is perceived. Should the ultimate bargaining power of strike action be used by residential workers, when inevitably the most vulnerable groups of clients in residential care will suffer considerably? Views vary, of course, and reactions will depend on a worker's moral and political stance. The Residential Care Association, who lay no claim to being a trade union, but who advise members to join an appropriate trade union, suggest that, whilst the go-slow (e.g. in filling in returns) and the work-to-rule (e.g. overtime ban) are legitimate bargaining strategies, the withdrawal of labour in the form of strike action is not a possibility open to the residential social workers. The advice by the same association that action taken should involve residents and invite them to participate in industrial action reflects a changing concept of the residential task.

Training for Residential Social Work

One factor which should considerably affect the practice of residential social work in the future is the revised pattern of training currently being put into operation, the phasing out of the former pattern of training due to take place by 1980. In 1974 the Central Council for Education and Training in Social Work issued a policy statement[27] which concluded, after examining the nature of the residential task, that it shares with other forms of social work a common knowledge base, common values and goals, clients in a continuum of care, and common attitudes of working, and that there should therefore be a common pattern of training.[28] The Certificate of Qualification in Social Work (CQSW) was suggested as a common qualification for both field and residential workers. Two years later, the proposals about the two levels of training set out in Paper 111 were modified by the introduction of the Certificate in Social Service (CSS)[29] which was to be a less academically demanding level of training.

These changes in the structure of training patterns represented a major change from the complexity of the former training pattern. Residential workers have, however, been rightly suspicious that in this new two-tier pattern of training, that the CSS would become the accepted training for residential workers. A recent study[30] of the secondment patterns of local authority social service departments in England and Wales showed that, apart from a very small number of authorities, few residential workers were being seconded for CQSW training. If standards of residential practice are to be improved, then training both at a professional level and on an in-service basis is vital. Nothing short of emergency measures are needed if the 4% of qualified residential workers is to be substantially increased in the foreseeable future.

The effect of the creation of large social services departments following the Seebohm recommendations have been well discussed and documented in relation to the effects on field social work, but significantly less so in relation to residential work. This area is explored in more detail in a later chapter, but it is worth noting in the present context that residential establishments have remained as isolated as they previously were from the rest of the organisation. The average residential worker has few contacts with other residential establishments and in some working situations his access even to the Home Adviser would usually be via the Head of the Home. Effective consultation is still all too infrequently available and the resources of specialised knowledge about particular client groups possessed by residential workers are not exploited fully, although a recent report suggests that in the case of residential workers with the mentally handicapped, their knowledge and skills could be passed on to workers in non-specialist units and to families caring for the mentally handicapped at home.[31] Perhaps a further development will ultimately be a more clearly defined concept of the residential task by the increasing recognition of the common factors in caring for people outside their own family situations, and a useful transfer, where appropriate, of skills not only between those who care for different client groups in the residential setting but also with those who practice social work in other settings.

This brief discussion of some of the factors which seem to be bringing about changes in the residential task at the present time indicates that much of that change is positive. The mirage of an increasingly skilled and specialised task, which is fully integrated into the continuum of services and glimpsed by residential workers for many years, is becoming more of a reality. Future development depends on many factors, of which the recognition by residential workers themselves of the potential of their profession is perhaps one of the most vital.

Notes and References

1. R. WALTON, A quiet revolution, *Social Work Today*, **10** (33), 1979, p. 20.
2. The relationship between field and residential work. Published simultaneously in *Social Work Today* and *Residential Social Work*, September 1976.
3. CCETSW, Paper 111, *Residential Work is a part of Social Work*, 1974. This document advocates joint training and a common qualification for field and residential workers.
4. See Part II of this reader: Social Work Process in Residential Care.
5. The model put forward by PINCUS and MINAHAM—*Social Work Practice, Model and Method*, Peacock, USA, 1973—suggests the following skill areas: Assessing Problems; Collecting Data; Meeting Initial Contacts; Negotiating Contracts; Forming Action Systems; Maintaining and Co-ordinating Action Systems; Exercising Influence; Terminating the Change Effort.
6. S. RODWAY, "Pie in the sky"?—An employer's viewpoint [on the keyworker concept], *Social Work Service*, No. 19, Mar. 1979.
7. J. BERRY, *Daily Experience in Residential Care*, Routledge & Kegan Paul (Library of Social Work), 1975, Chapter 4.
8. D. BILLIS, Entry into residential care, *British Journal of Social Work*, **3** (4), 1973.
9. G. BROMLEY, Interaction between field and residential social workers, British Journal of Social Work, **7** (3), 1977.
10. *Ibid.*, p. 290.
11. D. ALLEN, The residential task. Is there one? Report on the Highlands Experiment in East Sussex, *Social Work Today*, **9** (7), 1977.
12. R. RAPPOPORT, *Community as Doctor: New Perspectives on a Therapeutic Community*, Tavistock, London, 1960.
13. A. S. NEIL, *That Dreadful School*, Herbert Jenkins, 1937.
14. R. PAIGE and G. A. CLARKE (eds.), *Who Cares*, National Children's Bureau, 1977.
15. See Chapter 15 by D. ADAMS, Hostel Provision for Adolescent Boys. Also G. JENSEN, Reassuring reviews, *Community Care*, 11 Oct. 1978.
16. D. ELLIOTT and R. WALTON, Recording in the residential setting, *Social Work Today*, **9** (32), 1978.

17. R. SLATER and A. LIPMAN, Chapter 18, Towards Caring Through Design.
18. For a fuller discussion on risk-taking in residential care see R. WALTON, Training for risk-taking; applications in residential care, *Social Services Quarterly*, No. 18, Dec. 1978.
19. B. LINE, Chapter 21, Resident Participation, A Consumer View.
20. Social trends No. 8 Chart 3^{14}, p. 67, HMSO, 1977.
21. *Ibid.*, Table 3^{13}, p. 67.
22. G. CORNEY, Chapter 8, Residential Care with the Physically Handicapped.
23. NATIONAL JOINT COUNCIL FOR LOCAL AUTHORITIES' ADMINISTRATIVE, PROFESSIONAL, TECHNICAL AND CLERICAL SERVICES, Circular No. N.O. 271, 4 Oct. 1974.
24. RESIDENTIAL CARE ASSOCIATION, *The Dalmeny Papers, Manpower Problems in Residential Social Work*, 1976.
25. *Ibid.*, p. 6, para. 3:6.
26. G. BANNER, A better deal for residential workers, *Community Care*, No. 31, 30 Oct. 1974, pp. 14–15.
27. CCETSW Paper 111, *Residential Work is a Part of Social Work*, Nov. 1973.
28. *Ibid.*, pp. 9–11, para. 32.
29. CCETSW, *A New Form of Training: the Certificate in Social Service*, 1975.
30. D. ELLIOTT and R. WALTON, Agency attitudes to residential training, *Social Work Today*, **10** (24), 1979.
31. *Report of the Committee of Enquiry into Mental Handicap, Nursing and Care* (The Jay Report), HMSO, London, 1979.

CHAPTER 3

THE SOCIAL WORK TASK IN
RESIDENTIAL CARE

LIZ WARD

Social work in a residential setting is about working with people in a shared day-to-day living experience. Whether the task is providing care for the aged in an old people's home, or containing critically damaged boys and girls inside a locked unit, it is *what is going on* between the people involved that determines the quality of residential care. What the worker says and *how* he says it, what he does and *how* he does it, determines the nature of the worker/resident relationship, which in turn determines the basic mode of intervention. Every incident, however seemingly unimportant, acts as a vehicle of communication: helping or hindering, caring or not caring, demonstrating authority over the resident, or setting the scene for self-responsibility and self-development.

Residential social work is about relationships as they happen and about the way these relationships can be used to enable a person to cope with his life-events, both the ordinary events of living and the particular, problem events surrounding whatever situation brought him into care.

Residential admission represents breakdown, either of a temporary or permanent kind. This breakdown occurs at two interacting levels. First, there is the *personal* experience of breakdown for the individual concerned, the meaning of admission for *him* in terms of his own functioning, behaviour, relationships and life-situation. Then there is breakdown at the interpersonal level, the breakdown *between* the individual and his family, *between* him and important others, *between* him and his social environment, school or work, peer group, neighbourhood and community.

Thus, in responding to the in-care person's needs, residential social work embodies two interacting levels of intervention: (i) intervention relating to the person and his personal states and processes, and (ii) intervention relating to the person and his outside world. For the practitioner, the task has two aspects: (i) working with individuals in the context of the group *inside the residential unit* and (ii) with the residents individually and through the group, *across the unit's boundaries.*

Traditionally, residential workers have been encouraged to concentrate their efforts inside their establishments, leaving almost all outside contacts to outside practitioners. Involvement across the boundaries, however, is a core activity in any form of residential intervention aiming to enable people to cope more effectively with themselves and their environment. Boundary activity increases contact with the community, enabling workers and residents to make connections between life in the institution and life in the outside world. The way a residential unit functions largely depends on how its reasons for existence are perceived by all the people who live in it, and how the workers view the job they are trying to do.

Care, assessment and treatment; custody, control and punishment; whether stated or assumed, are among the most commonly held objectives. Creating a warm, caring environment, building a therapeutic community, or providing secure relationships are familiar explanations of the task. *How* these things happen, however, determines their usefulness. Each of the objectives and explanations mentioned above allow wide interpretation in practice. Assessment can be an invaluable aid for clarifying a problem and reaching decisions on the best available action. It can also be experienced as an intrusion into private affairs. Providing secure accommodation can mean a caring response to a youngster's cry for adult control. It can also mean being locked away and left alone with unmanageable feelings of hate and self-destruction.

Clearly, identical objectives can produce vastly dissimilar results, depending on how they are interpreted by the team of workers, and especially by the officer in charge. Three factors are significant: (i) the team's view of the residential unit, (ii) the team's view of the unit's relationship to the outside world, (iii) the building of these views into a collective value system.

Talcott Parsons[1] has argued that the ". . . value system [of an organisation] must by definition be a subvalue system of a higher-order one, since the organisation is always defined as a subsystem of a more comprehensive social system". Parson's theory of organisations is important in understanding how residential establishments interpret their task. The central theme of Parson's argument is that any organisation, or institution, is a subsystem of a more important or superordinate system (the superordinate system being the society in which the institution operates). The given task of the institution is to fulfil particular functions for the superordinate system. In carrying out this task, the institution reflects its acceptance of the values held by society. That is, the value system incorporated by the institution is a subvalue system of the wider and more generalised values held by the higher-order system, i.e. by society. "The most essential feature of the value system of an organisation is the evaluative *legitimation* of its place or 'role' in the superordinate system."[2] To justify what it does, the institution incorporates into its values a set of attitudes and beliefs that give legitimacy to the ways it performs its tasks, and to its reason for existence as an essential part of society. Thus, whether we examine the most positive or most negative features of residential care, the institution will readily justify its methods of practice. To understand the implications of these methods of practice (that is, to understand what is going on) the organisation must be viewed in context with the values held by its parent society.

For example, the punishing regimes of the Poor Law institutions clearly reflected society's denial of responsibility for the social conditions that contributed to the inmates' failure to cope. While today we have moved towards a more liberal view of the person in care, we are still assigning the institution the task of "doing something with" those people who are failing to cope in the community. Being unable to cope burdens other people with unwanted pressure, so the burden is transferred to the institution. Thus the institution is assigned a double function; to provide care for its inmates, and to provide space for the unwanted feelings of the parent society. Ambivalent values of caring and rejecting are projected into the institution along with the residential clients. If the residential team interpret their role mainly in response to the punitive values thrust upon them, custody, control and storage must become the principal methods of care.

If they perceive their task in terms of protecting the helpless, "looking after" and "doing things for" uncoping people, client dependency on authority becomes the regime. In order to achieve a balance between meeting the needs of individual residents while at the same time legitimising its role within society, a careful definition of objectives is essential.

By defining objectives, agreement can be reached between all those concerned about the operational purpose of the unit's existence, what it hopes to achieve, whom it aims to benefit, and how it intends to function. Objectives should make explicit exactly what the residential unit has to offer. When objectives are shared, understood and accepted, both within the residential centre and across its boundaries, agreement can be reached between the team of workers and the (higher-order) management body regarding policy and practice.

Objectives define basic functions, and must be specific enough to include appropriate limitations. "To provide short-term care for homeless young people" is an open-ended objective. "To provide care and accommodation for a maximum of 15 young people, of either sex, between the ages of 16 and 21, for a maximum of 10 consecutive nights" is more realistic. However, the word "homeless" is vague, requiring explanation. Additionally, the objectives must include reference to the anticipated outcome of intervention; for example, what happens to the youngsters at the end of their 10 night's stay?

A basic objective for any caring establishment is to assess and respond to the needs of its client group. Realistically, the needs of the in-care person are similar to the needs of anyone else. The difference arises in terms of degree. Depending on the pre-admission situation, need for ordinary physical care and comfort may be intense. The youngster on the run may be wretched with hunger, the elderly isolate literally dying from cold, and the angry, frightened teenager, arriving after a night in the cell and a day in court, may be desperate for someone to care for him. Responding to physiological need has sometimes been downgraded as falling outside the social work task. In residential work, however, providing physical care is often the first stage in making the relationship that later becomes the medium for intervention. Using ordinary events, like sharing a meal or helping a person into bed, as opportunities for getting in touch with the "person inside" is an essential skill for the residential worker. The task is to become acutely aware of *how*, as a unique and separate individual, this person functions; *how*, here and now, he is experiencing his admission into care. Awareness of what is going on for him is the important thing of the encounter, enabling the worker to discover the person and his needs without jumping to conclusions about either.

A common pitfall in residential work is for the workers to assume they have more understanding about the needs of the residents than the residents have themselves. Consider, for example, the number of case conferences that occur, specifically for the purpose of decision making, without the views of the subject or his family being seriously represented.

One explanation of the way in which people experience need has been illustrated by Maslow.[3] Maslow describes need satisfaction as occurring in progressive stages, beginning with the lowest. Until basic survival needs are satisfied, for example, need for food, water and air, there will be little investment in higher order needs. When physiological (survival) needs are met, they tend to lose importance, and the person becomes anxious for higher need fulfilment. See Fig. 3.1.

Maslow's theory tends to simplify need requirement. It fails to account for excessive

Some examples

Development and expression of capacities and talents.

Opportunity for new experiences.

Identity, recognition, autonomy, prestige, status, dominance.

Friendship, love, affection. Contact, communications, relationships. Participation, involvement.

Protection from injury. Freedom from pain.

Food, warmth, shelter, fresh air, personal space. Bodily care and maintenance. Fatigue recovery. Sexual needs.

Some responses

Optimal environment for client autonomy.

Scope for interaction across unit's boundaries.

Respect for persons. Client involvement in decision making. Opportunities for self-responsibility and personal achievement.

Minimisation of staff hierarchy. Development of informal atmosphere. Sensitive relations based on mutual trust. Involvement of significant others.

Realistic approach to risk factor. Minimisation of restrictions. (Secure environment—where essential—involving secure relationships.)

Shared responsibility for decisions on house matters. Flexible routine. Respect for privacy.

Fig. 3.1. *Maslow's hierarchy of needs*

need fulfilment at one level as a response to need deprivation at another. Neither does it explain why an individual might crave fulfilment of several need levels at one time. Even so, it is a useful model for understanding need response in residential work. The first two levels, physiological needs and safety needs, can most *easily* be met by doing things to and doing things for the residents. The more assiduously the workers take responsibility for the residents, keeping them warm, fed, clean and comfortable, the safer the residents become. Risk factors are reduced to a minimum. Not uncommonly, children are banned from kitchens because of the risk of burns from fat fryers, and elderly residents are prevented from making tea in case of scalds. Medications taken safely for years are hidden away in case of overdose.

Failure to allow participation in basic need fulfilment acts as a depersonalising factor. Collusive dependency arises, the enforced helplessness of the clients evoking strong parental feelings in the workers, who in turn only function at their best when "looking after" other people. As a spin-off, the residents and the workers grow heavily dependent on the institutional routine, which in severe cases takes over as the principal reason for the unit's existence. When this happens, "getting everything done on time" becomes the real objective, regardless of the objectives that may be formally described.

Belongingness and esteem have their roots in responsibility for self. The person judged unable to make decisions about his own bodily requirements is unlikely to perceive himself as rating much prestige. Self-image is prone to the judgement of other people, and self-esteem dependent on how an individual believes he is perceived by the important others in his life. For the inmate, important others include the workers and the resident group, from whom it is difficult to hide the social insufficiencies that brought about admission. Unless opportunities are available for higher need fulfilment, residents will develop their own fulfilment routes. This is one basis of the residential subculture where status is defined by the number of offences, degree of handicap, or length of stay. When this happens, division between workers and clients is intensified, the institution reflecting those values of the "superordinate" society that demand segregation of the "not coping" from the "coping".

Need fulfilment can most adequately be met when residential experience is based on sharing responsibilities. Client participation does not mean client takeover. Neither does it mean workers will allow severely distressed or damaged clients to take irrational or harmful decisions. Rather, the emphasis is on a *joint effort* towards increasing the individual's ability to manage for himself.

Sharing responsibility begins with admission. If the client is consulted and kept informed, even where little choice exists, he at least has time to make preparations. The more realistic his perception of the kind of institution he is entering, the better he is likely to cope with the demands of group living.

Planning admission includes: (i) clear definition about the reason for admission; (ii) clear definition of expectations, agreement about principal tasks to be accomplished and the anticipated outcome of the residential period; (iii) a time plan; (iv) clear definition about the ongoing involvement of all the workers concerned, and nomination of a responsible or key worker.

Admission criteria form the basis of the intervention plan which, later, will be developed into a contract shared between the client and his worker. Where appropriate, other people will be included: family, friends, a school teacher, residents, members of the care team or other professional workers. The contract involves agreement and decisions about what changes everyone expects will happen, who exactly is expected to change and in what ways, when and how the changes will come about, and what is to happen when change has been achieved. Any contract represents a pact or treaty between two or more parties, each party undertaking to fulfil certain requirements. Thus there must be agreement about which worker, by name, will accept responsibility for the care plan, ensuring that opportunities occur for required activities, and that progress is monitored and goals reassessed in the light of achievements or a changing situation. *The part the worker will play* and the ways he will support the client should be indicated. Additionally, there must be a statement about what the establishment has to offer. The degree of freedom allowed and the amount of group involvement expected must be explained. So, too, the opportunities for developing new skills, or relearning skills which may have been lost.

Goal setting is an integral part of the contract. A first assumption in residential work is that the person in care will gain something rather than lose something from the experience. This means providing an environment that will stimulate personal growth

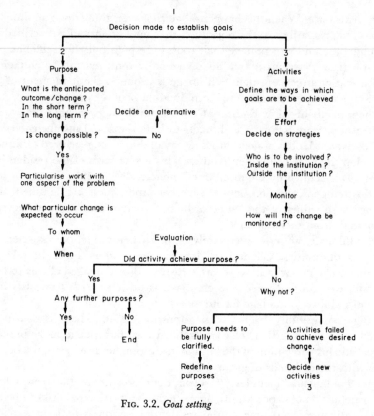

Fig. 3.2. *Goal setting*

and responsibility. But, in practice, admission to care is a public response to the person's failure to manage, or—with the very young, very old and the handicapped—failure to be manageable. The worker's motivation to the job at very least reflects desire to help other people. All too easily, workers and residents are polarised, the workers to care for and control the residents, who in turn are easy targets for a dependency role. Additionally, a group can more readily be managed in a structured, routine-bound environment. Thus, a continual tension exists between creating an environment for client autonomy (which is more demanding on the workers and involves failure risks for the clients), and maintaining a controlled routine (which increases resident dependency but ensures a smooth-running establishment). Overcoming the strain between client autonomy and client dependence lies in combining the giving of care with *goal directed activity*. Then, residential intervention is a period of intensive care, purposefully planned to enable the individual to self-manage his personal states and processes, so enhancing his coping capacities in and with his outside world.

Sheldon Rose[4] has suggested that in working with individuals in a group, three kinds of goals exist: (i) individual treatment goals; (ii) common treatment goals; (iii) goals involving a change in the interactive patterns among group members.

Individual goal setting concerns doing something about activities or behaviours that are problematic for the individual. For a handicapped child, an individual goal might be learning to tie his shoe-laces. For a youngster in trouble, it might be learning to cope with unmanageable flashes of temper. In the latter example, "learning to cope with temper" is too general as a goal statement. How and when the temper happens must be identified, and the goal reduced to manageable stages by division into subgoals. If, commonly, the youngster is cross on waking, exploding into temper at even small irritation, a subgoal might be introduced limiting initial goal achievement to the getting-up period.

Attaching *conditions* to goal achievement helps to clarify how, when and where an activity will be carried out. Conditions keep a goal realistic by imposing limitations. For example: "*When Tara's worker is on duty*, she will help Tara cope with temper at breakfast by sitting next to Tara at the breakfast table." Exactly how the worker intends to help depends on the strategies *agreed* between her and Tara, which in turn depend on the *agreed* policy of the unit. It might be decided to prevent conflict by rapid verbal intervention. A system of fines and incentives might be used, or reality confrontation, feeding back to Tara the way the group experiences her behaviour. Whatever the strategy, it must be shared *in advance*, not in a punitive way, but as a plan for achieving helping results.

Residential social work aims to facilitate interaction between the person in care and his ordinary environment. While Tara's day-to-day tantrums may occur in response to here-and-now causes, they may also represent a response to long-term environmental factors. If Tara is to return home, involving family members in the care plan is essential. Tara is unlikely to be the only person needing to change behaviour, and the *contract* must include the family's contributions, how they intend to behave towards Tara. Aspects of the family environment provoking and sustaining incompatible relationships must be identified and attempts made at modification.

As an interventive method, residential care depends on making connections with the in-care person's pre- and post-residential life. There must be linking with the person's own life-style and personal values. New skills and new experiences acquired in the residential centre will be of greatest benefit when readily transferable into the outside community. It is the client's life, and those who enter into it must guard against imposing their own values into the other's world.

A characteristic of residential social work is the extension of the worker/client relationship into areas of the client's life not ordinarily shared by a social worker. Workers may see residents in bed and asleep, and may help them with the intimate routines of living. Touch is not only inevitable, it is a part of caring. Often the worker and the resident are involved together in the actual situations that contribute to the problem for the resident. The truanting youngster who hates school may find himself firmly escorted to the school entrance by the same worker who plays football with him on Saturdays. The girl who has learned to mistrust adults finds herself in daily confrontation with adults who tell her they care and set about showing it, regardless of her rejections. Sharing in events as they happen, over an unbroken period of time, characterises the relationship between the residential practitioner and his client. What happens today will affect what happens tomorrow, all the group members (whether staff or residents) reaping some of the spin-off of their own interactions.

When a number of group members share a common problem, *common goals* can be established. Giving up smoking or reducing weight are ready examples. Common helping activities can be agreed, the group members acting as a support towards each other. Peer-group pressure is a useful aid to common goal achievement.

A group goal, or as Rose[4] has termed it, an interactive goal, involves the group in achieving something together, and is dependent on each person allowing and enabling others to participate. In an analysis of the phases and components of autonomous group functioning, Polsky and Claster[5] suggest three basic stages for the formation of group goals. First, establishing communication; second, identifying the needs, interests, and problems inherent in the group; and third, converting the need, interest, or problem into a *shared concrete realisable goal*. " 'Needs' refers to individual or group psychological pressures—the internal conditions of the group members. 'Interests' refers to more objective concerns; for example, leisure-time activities that cottage members are attracted to. 'Problems' refers to difficulties and frustrations in the living situation." The authors suggest that when the group identifies its own needs, decides on its own interests, and talks about its difficulties, a kind of "group diagnosis" emerges, forming the base for a shared goal activity.

Consider a beginners' swimming session, arising from a *shared* need to counteract boredom, an *interest* in learning to swim, and the *problem* of a disruptive, bickering group. A simple interactive goal might be that everyone agrees to take one turn helping another person to float, or everyone agrees not to push anyone under the water. While the *common* goal is about learning to swim, the *interactive* goal is about learning to help each other, and having consideration for each other. For goal achievement, a shift in group behaviour is essential, the more boisterous members restraining the temptation to push the less confident into the water, who in turn must learn to trust their peers.

Whether a goal is planned for an individual, for a group, or as an interactive process, a well-formed goal represents a shared statement of intent, clearly describing *who* is involved, what *activity or behaviour* is concerned, and the *conditions* for performing the behaviour or activity. Equally important is a *time* framework, and criteria for *assessing* when the goal has been achieved.

The main areas of work involved in the residential task can be drawn together under five broad headings: (i) individual intervention, (ii) working with groups, (iii) involvement in the community, (iv) care giving, (v) administration. As a way of summarising this chapter, the chart that follows gives greater detail to individual intervention and working with groups. However, all five areas are interdependent. The chart is not exclusive, but aims simply to identify the central activities performed by residential social workers.

The Residential Social Work Task

1. *Individual Intervention*

Client-centred activity	*Environmental activity*
1.1 *Participation at referral*	
(a) Clarifying reason for admission, anticipated outcome, time plan.	Liaison with referring worker(s)/agency.
(b) Nominating responsible or key worker.	Decision *re* ongoing roles of referring worker(s)/agency.
(c) Getting to know potential resident. Identifying and sharing initial intervention plan.	Beginning relationship with family and important others.

Client-centred activity	Environmental activity
(d) Planning admission: Pre-admission visits: worker to client, client to res. centre. Planning date, time, transport, escort. Helping with clearing up unfinished business.	Beginning contract with family and important others.

1.2 *Admission*

(a) Involvement at admission time: Assessing and responding to immediate needs. Providing information, providing support. Linking events in a caring way.	Involving family/important others/ relevant colleagues.
(b) Availability in early admission period.	

1.3 *Planning intervention, making the contract*

(a) Ongoing observation and need assessment. Identifying client's own resources.	
(b) Planning responses, goals, supporting activities, and sharing with client.	Facilitating contributions from family/appropriate others.
(c) Identifying shared and/or interactive goals, and ways of achieving these.	Identifying goals which include family and/or external environment.
(d) Drawing up contract with client.	
(e) Collecting and collating data. Record keeping.	Collecting appropriate reports from outside agencies.

1.4 *Implementing intervention plan (day-to-day caring)*

(a) Activating goal achievement.	Facilitating interactions across boundaries, e.g., involvement with family and/or others.
(b) Promoting client involvement in planned activities: one-to-one counselling, group counselling, task groups, development groups.	Supporting client across boundaries: e.g. family visits, court appearances, hospital appointments.
(c) Using spontaneous event as helping processes, individually and in the group.	
(d) Using routine tasks and domestic chores as helping processes.	
(e) Facilitating client self-responsibility, client participation in decision making.	
(f) Monitoring progress and recognising change. Goal re-evaluation. Ongoing case recording. Preparation of reports.	
(g) Involvement in case conferences. Facilitating client's contribution. Implementing conference decisions.	Facilitating family and/or others' contributions to case conference.

Client-centred activity	*Environmental activity*
(h) Planning and involvement in leisure activities, physical, social, cultural.	Facilitating participation in outside activities: clubs, churches

1.5 *Rehabilitation*

(a) Long-term planning: Monitoring progress towards anticipated outcome of admission, e.g. search for foster parents. Decision making *re*: long-term future.	Provision of long-term resources: e.g. aids for handicap, grants, housing. Educational or occupational progress.
Continuing in care Liaising with ongoing establishment.	*Continuing out of care* Liaison with and supporting family/ foster parents/others. Liaison with external agencies, e.g. medical, domiciliary.
(b) Preparation for discharge: e.g. help with transition to new school, help with accommodation, job finding. Planning discharge programme. Visiting new environment. Supporting at transition stage. Availability at discharge or accompanying client to new environment. Completing/transferring case records.	Activating community support. Liaison with new establishment. Negotiating aftercare support programme.
(c) Availability after discharge: Sometimes providing ongoing friendship, a secure base. Availability in crisis.	

2.   *Working with Groups*

2.1 *Working in the group setting*

(a) Facilitating group interaction. Creating opportunities for group communication, expression, activities. Utilising spontaneous group activity.

(b) Using the group's dynamics: Making positive use of group interaction, pressures, learning, support, resources, subgroups.

(c) Involvement in planning and implementing shared and interactive goals.

2.2 Working in planned group activities and planned subgroups: Planning and implementing group meetings: worker/resident, management, development. Activity groups, leisure groups.

3.   *Involvement in the Community*

3.1 Mobilising outside resources: Family, recreational, educational, cultural, occupational, legal, physical aids and adaptations, medical, psychiatric, housing and accommodation, social security, religious, volunteer services.

3.2 Advocacy and support on behalf of client (as in any of 3.1 above).

4. *Care Giving*

4.1 Caring for the whole person:
   e.g. Sensitivity to need, availability, time, interest, understanding. Developing mutual trust and respect.

4.2 Providing and maintaining accommodation:
   Providing warmth and comfort, personal space and privacy, communal space. Providing and maintaining facilities:
   e.g. laundry, kitchen, bathrooms, hobbies rooms, gardens.

4.3 Providing food:
   Planning, purchasing, preparation, creating meal-time environment.

4.4 Provision and care of clothing:
   Laundry. Ensuring possessions are not lost or damaged.

4.5 Helping with day-to-day living:
   e.g. Getting-up, dressing, bath times, toilet routines, mobility, feeding.

5. *Administration*

5.1 Safety:
   e.g. Fire precautions. Decisions about risk taking. Responsibility for care and maintenance of property.

5.2 Personnel management:
   Selection of staff. Staff supervision, support, training.
   Personnel administration:
   e.g. Staff duty rotas, holiday rotas. Staff meetings. Preparation of job descriptions. Liaison with trade unions.

5.3 Student training:
   Student supervision, assessment, report writing. Preparation of residential group for student's arrival. Links with colleges, tutors, training officers.

5.4 General administration and forward planning:
   Ordering supplies, inventory keeping. Budgeting, banking, petty cash.
   Secretarial work:
   Letter writing, phone calls, record keeping and report writing. Involvement in policy making, internally and with management.

5.5 Interdisciplinary co-operation:
   Facilitating working relationships with colleagues of other disciplines.

5.6 Community involvement:
   Formal contact with outside bodies. Pursuing informal contacts with local community. Facilitating interaction between resident group and community. Promoting residential intervention as a social work resource.

References

1. T. PARSONS, Suggestions for a Sociological Approach to the Theory of Organizations, in Etzioni, *A Sociological Reader on Complex Organizations*, Holt, Rinehart & Winston, 1961.
2. *Ibid.*
3. A. H. MASLOW, A theory of human motivation, *Psychological Review*, **50**, 370–96, 1943.
4. S. D. ROSE, *Group Therapy: A Behavioural Approach*, Prentice-Hall, 1977.
5. POLSKY and CLASTER, *The Dynamics of Residential Treatment*, University of North Carolina Press, 1968.

PART I: QUESTIONS AND EXERCISES

1. Examine the routines in your establishment and match them with the negative features outlined by Goffman and Barton. If you find an aspect of daily living which resembles any of these features, how might it be changed?
2. Identify an aspect of the establishment's structure and pattern of life which you feel to be very positive for the residents. What reasons can you give for this and can you give any evidence that residents do, in fact, benefit?
3. (a) Take an incident from your own practice with a particular resident which you think helped the resident. Describe the incident fully, and explain what the benefits were and what it was in your approach which was positive. (b) With regard to the same incident ask the resident(s) concerned to write a similar account. (If this is not possible, ask them to record their version on a cassette tape.)

   Compare the two accounts of the situation, and note where the views of the incident are the same, and where they differ.
4. What weight is given in your home to physical, emotional and social aspects of residents' lives? Draw up a scale from 1 to 5 for each aspect of living, and give your rating. Explain the reasons behind your ratings, and consider whether in the light of the goals of the Home there should be any change of emphasis.

1	2	3	4	5	Physical
1	2	3	4	5	Emotional
1	2	3	4	5	Social

Little emphasis	Much emphasis

5. Outline your own conception of the social work task in residential care. Does this differ from the task in fieldwork and, if so, what implications are there for co-operation between field and residential social workers?
6. What do you understand the term "resident participation" to mean? What are the implications for the residential social work task if the principle of "resident participation" is accepted?
7. Who is responsible for the following aspects of residents lives?
   (a) Contacts with family and friends.
   (b) Visiting the family of a resident.

37

(c) Reviewing a resident's development, initiating a case conference.

(d) Contacts with school, G.P., Social Security.

(e) Who holds the master file for a resident.

Answer, residential social worker, field social worker or resident for each question. Would a "keyworker" make any difference to the pattern, or are there any other ways of redefining roles to improve service to the client?

PART II

*Social Work Process in
Residential Care*

INTRODUCTION: CRITERIA IN THE
ASSESSMENT FOR RESIDENTIAL CARE

Assessing people for residential care is beset with problems. Many criteria can be used but which to give priority to is less easy to resolve. Criteria in frequent use are: the psychological, physical or social problems of the individual; actual or potential delinquency or mental illness; the individual's rejection of his family or vice versa; the tolerance of the community towards deviant attitudes or behaviour; and the availability or otherwise of community support services. From the professional viewpoint assessment may be viewed as a part of identifying needs and providing appropriate treatment. From the individual client's viewpoint assessment and admission to residential care may be viewed and experienced as a labelling and stigmatising process. Assessment may take place in stages, with different criteria being assigned varying importance according to the stage. The first, and sometimes only, stage is the assessment to remove someone from home. With the elderly, once this assessment has taken place, there may be little opportunity for choice of establishment, and the residential placement made is often the permanent home of the resident. With children there is more often a second stage: after an initial assessment to remove a child, there is a more complex residential assessment to determine whether a child should return home or, if not, which kind of substitute care—residential, fostering, or adoption—is most appropriate.

It is clear that in first-stage assessment family and community attitudes are highly significant criteria, whereas in second-stage assessment physical, psychological or social problems of the individual may be given a greater weighting. The disadvantage of this variation in weighting is that once people are admitted to residential care the initial assessment, often incomplete and a reaction to a crisis situation, may be accepted as permanently valid, and be insufficiently re-examined. If there is a two-stage assessment it is essential that all the criteria are fully examined at both stages. There is an overwhelming case for having as thorough community assessment as possible, as a means of avoiding the risk of admitting people unnecessarily to residential care. If there is second-stage residential assessment the family and community criteria and rehabilitation possibilities should be given full weight, lest there develop a semi-automatic progression to long-term residential care.

Applying criteria in assessment for residential care is a complex task, because the different criteria may be assigned lesser or greater importance by different workers (psychologists, teachers, social workers, psychiatrists, police, doctors) and according to whether the workers are normally located in a residential setting or the community. Thus, the co-ordination of the assessment process, to ensure that all relevant information is assembled in written reports, and that the different perspectives are brought together (as in a case conference), is critical.

The other and perhaps paramount factor is the process of assessment and admission as experienced by potential residents. If they are treated simply as objects of assessment, rather than fully involved participants, the assessment process cannot be other than depersonalising—however benignly—serving the interests of administration and processing the individual in much the same way as an industrial product. Traditional assessment methods tended to locate the problems in the individual. Later much greater emphasis was given to family and social/environmental factors. Recent practice has just begun to look in a more systematic way at involving potential residents and their families more fully in the decision-making process that assessment entails—a process which may have lifelong consequences for the individual. The papers in this section illustrate well these shifts in thinking and practice, and indicate the important efforts which are being made to make judgements with skill and humane concern.

CHAPTER 4

ASSESSMENT, LABELLING OR EXPEDIENCY?

GARETH DAVIES

My involvement in the field of residential assessment has spanned the period of trauma, confusion and anxiety that was the direct consequence of the dynamics of the changes that were brought about by the reclassification of Remand Homes to Assessment Centres, with the implementation in 1969 of the Children and Young Persons Act.

It is my contention that when that specialised assessment facility was suddenly and massively increased, few of the involved people possessed the knowledge base to cope with the new demands. This was to a large extent due to the fact that the role of the former Remand Homes was, as stated by Helen Richardson,[1] mainly the provision of a place of safety, where a delinquent was kept in storage, as it were, pending a court appearance or reappearance, until a decision was reached.

When that decision resulted in the youngster's committal to Approved School, he remained at the Remand Home to await transfer to one of the Classifying Schools (which were introduced in 1942). These establishments defined and classified the type of youngsters who were to be admitted for training to the Approved Schools.

The demands made upon the Remand Home system, therefore, were sufficiently well defined and understood as not to cause them to feel inadequate in meeting them. These goals also minimised the traditional conflicts associated historically with the aims of correctional institutions for young offenders, i.e. the inevitable conflict between goals that are deemed to satisfy the needs of the child, and those that are deemed to satisfy the demands for security from the community. Predictably, as part of the overall correctional provision for youngsters, the Remand Home intake consisted, in the main, of offenders. In my own establishment at that time, of 400 youths admitted during 1967 and 1968, 54% were returned to the community with, of course, recommendations for ongoing professional supervision, change of schools, remedial teaching, psychiatric involvement on an outpatient basis, conditional discharges, etc. The situation, prior to the changes that resulted from the 1969 Children and Young Persons Act, was at least refreshing by its lack of ambiguity, however much it may have been the initial cog in an ineffective machine whose primary concern, after all, was with children and young persons who had been in conflict with the control systems of society. It is, I believe, fair to say that Remand Homes were at the lowest level of the hierarchical provision within the field of residential social work concerned with children and young people.

It is here that I am reminded of the famous seventeenth-century "Nun's Prayer" which included the line "Keep my mind free from the recital of endless details; give me wings to get to the point". That graphic point, in my case, was the elevation, with the implementation of the 1969 Act, in the status of the new Assessment Centres within the regional provisions for youngsters, based on the philosophy that the basis for effective treatment is effective diagnosis, and that assessment is the central element of our child care service. The rapid transition from Remand Home to Assessment Centre, from a basically punitive task to a sophisticated, scientific provision of assessing the problems and needs of children in an endeavour to arrive at a more efficient and appropriate treatment of those problems and needs, predictably led to the initial confusion, anxiety and self-doubt associated with the dynamics of change in institutional settings. Much of that initial anxiety was alleviated by the fact that there were successful models available in the form of the existing Classifying Schools which had been practising the science of assessment since their introduction in 1942, for the former Remand Homes to emulate. With hindsight, I believe our major mistake was in too rapidly implementing changes without basing the change of focus on available resources of skill, knowledge and expertise. It is well to remember that the traditional informal measurement of success had been the effectiveness of the Homes in containing their inmates. At best, the Remand Homes had fulfilled the function of relieving some of the tensions caused by the removal of a youngster from his home and also of providing him with a group-living and a work and play experience that would be a feature of his life-style in an Approved School. For that large percentage of youngsters who were returned to the community following their period of "remand for reports", the experience was perceived as having been salutary and, hopefully, meaningful in terms of the child's future functioning.

The upheaval that was a feature of those Assessment Centres which had formerly been Remand Homes during the first years of change of role and function did not last long. In my own case, I discovered that the demands, expectations and degree of responsibility of the new establishments attracted staff who were excited by the prospect of the new challenge. The majority were trained—although they were inexperienced in comparison with those whom they replaced.

The next stage in our developmental process is remembered as being one of euphoria— brief, misplaced, but nevertheless euphoric. The latter was based upon fantasised assumptions, such as having for the first time the right to refuse to admit certain children (especially re-admitting those whose long-term placements had broken down); formulating unrealistic frameworks of priorities for admitting children, viz. remands to care, interim care orders, place of safety orders, those in care requiring assessment, those in care requiring re-assessment and, lastly, those in care awaiting long-term placement.

We were no longer concerned only with "holding" children and of providing a punitive experience for them in a total institutional setting. The Remand Home regime was indeed a model of the total institution with its depersonalising procedures and dependence upon inmate conformity for survival, despite the hostility and resentment created within that client group by that philosophy.

It is appropriate at this stage to refer to my awareness, at that time of professional transition, of the degree of disillusionment in the sphere of residential care in general. The latter, according to Peter Righton,[2] had suffered from hesitations and confusions for two reasons. Firstly, it was dogged by its Poor Law origins which assigned to it its residual and often custodial function, and thus gave little incentive to staff to think deeply about goals. Secondly, current academic opinion was, with few exceptions, hostile to institutional living, proclaiming that virtually any life-style "in the community" (however poor) was far less damaging to a person than life in a residential unit. This view, according to Righton, had played its part in keeping most current thinking about the goals of residential work at a depressingly low level. This general depression among residential social workers resulted in their being deeply frustrated and alienated from their work. This was very evident in the assessment field where disillusionment replaced the euphoria, due to a lack of direction. This lack of direction was exacerbated by the burden shouldered by Assessment Centres of having to provide a variety of contradictory functions such as reception and shelter, observation, classification and diagnosis, custody, treatment, punishment and substitute care. This demoralising situation was in direct contrast to the promised rejuvenation contained in Section 36 (4b) of the 1969 Children and Young Persons Act, which stated that: "Each regional plan shall contain proposals for the provision of facilities for the observation of the physical and mental condition of children in the care of the relevant authorities and for the assessment of the most suitable accommodation and treatment of these children."

The decade since 1969, however, has been a dynamic period of positive growth with the attainment of many of the ideas and concepts contained within the Act. Nowhere has the success been more graphic than in Regional Assessment Centres, where immense strides have been made towards providing "the best possible diagnosis" as mentioned in Paragraph 33 of the Seebohm Committee Report[3] which led to the Children and Young Persons Act itself. What has added icing to the cake of success is, firstly, the manner in which the assessments have been related primarily to the competence of those who make and use them; secondly, the manner in which the assessment has been co-ordinated with the evaluation of the facilities which are being offered; and, thirdly, the fact that assessment has contributed to a decision-making process which is genuinely geared to the needs of the child. Previously, it is my belief that this had not always been the case: the process of assessment had too often been followed by a placement determined by available vacancies rather than child need. The concept of Regional Planning had much to do with this success and I was fortunate in being appointed to my present senior post at a purpose-built Centre and subsequently involved in the planning process prior to its official opening. This privileged experience afforded me the unique opportunity of being involved in the creation of an effective model which only now is emerging from its infant stage.

Our first task was to define the goals of the establishment and the means of attaining those goals, viz. that the assessment process would attempt to produce a comprehensive picture of the child, his past history and family background, and his physical, educational, social and psychological development; and to formulate a plan for the appropriate treatment of the child. To achieve the assessment goal, the Centre should be a place where a child should be able to feel secure (and therefore, safe). It should be clear that he understood why he was there and that he would be there for a short time only. The setting would not demand conformity, but there should be an underlying sense of control. The need for structure and control would not cut across the maintenance of a moderately permissive climate. A moderate amount of permissiveness, space and a sense of freedom are essential—so that the children have an opportunity to behave in a characteristic way and, within limits, give rein to their anxieties and feelings—to make the observation of their behaviour meaningful. The main purpose of our programme would be to keep the children usefully absorbed and under observant supervision. It would also afford a medium for relationship between staff and children, and although the main function is assessment, staff should, as a secondary goal, feel able to influence, guide and help the children positively when an opportunity occurs. Peter Righton[4] confirmed this latter view when he emphasised that "whatever the instrumental goals any particular home is pursuing—rehabilitation, control, treatment or any other—all homes have an absolute responsibility for providing their residents with satisfying life experiences, and opportunities for the maximum degree of personal growth and self realisation". Righton continued by emphasising the need to develop within the establishment communication networks in which participants are clear about the parts they are to play, the scope and limits of their authority, and where responsibility rests for taking initiatives and decisions. Here the language of roles is an indispensable tool, in order to clarify expectations, set boundaries and regulate interchanges between the role holders.

Before embarking on the task of defining roles, we set out to examine the purpose of residential assessment, which was to look in depth at the child/family functioning so as to work in the most effective manner with the child as a member of his family, even though he may need to be placed away from them. This involved three basic elements, viz. an examination of all available information relating to the child when he was living at home; observation and examination of the child while he was away from his family; and finally, observation of the ways in which the family reacted while the child was away, together with an examination of their feelings regarding the child's possible return home.

It is fairly obvious that, before this stage was embarked upon, we reflected briefly on the take-off stage of any assessment process. When a child is identified as having particular problems that require further investigation, a decision has to be made as to where the process of assessment should be located. Is it possible for the child to be left in the community or should he be taken into a centre where he would be housed while the assessment took place? The importance of this decision was considerable as it had overall implications for the whole assessment process. Indeed, once this decision had been made, it could be said that assessment of the child had begun—it is the first "assessment decision" to be made regarding the child.

The process of assessment has, I believe, three component parts: the period when the child is being assessed, when he is closely examined and observed in all those areas felt to be relevant so that the assessment team may attempt to identify what the child is most in need of; a decision as to where the child should be placed in the hope of meeting those identified needs; and finally, the placement decision, and any appropriate recommendations should be implemented and subjected to an ongoing process of review as the child and family circumstances and needs moderate and change with the passage of time. All assessment should be seen as part of a continuing process, and previous assessments should be used as a guidelines for ongoing work even if they need review or adaptation, and even if recommendations need to be revised. Therefore, there is a need for a routine system of reviews, with all those involved in ongoing work with the child and the family meeting together.

Any treatment plan is effective only to the extent that it is seen as practicable by the residential social workers if the child is placed in a residential establishment, and by the field-based social worker who will work with the family in either event. In reality, therefore, the plan must be workable. The ideal placement should also be clearly defined for planning purposes even in circumstances where such a placement is unlikely to be available.

A comprehensive assessment necessitates, in my situation, the child being resident for a period of 8 weeks. During this period there is observation and interpretation of his reactions to separation from the family; general behaviour patterns, with particular reference to neurotic symptoms or antisocial responses; ability to form relationships with adults and peers; and observation also of the family's reactions as seen at the Assessment Centre, in terms of informal and formal contact.

Our educational assessment is conducted on the premises and is important not only in assessing educational potential, but in looking at the child's ability to mix in a group larger than living groups, and in a more "normal" and familiar child setting.

Psychiatric assessment of the child and the family takes place through interviews at the Assessment Centre. A psychologist examines the child's personality by the use of tests where appropriate, and examines the nature of family interaction patterns, suggesting hypotheses to account for behaviour patterns and possible courses of treatment. Also, the child undergoes a full medical examination, and onward referral is made for necessary check-ups and opinions from specialists.

Comprehensive residential assessment enables the field-based social worker to make a thorough investigation of the family functioning and to assess the effect on family dynamics of the child's removal from home, compared, where possible, with the situation prior to removal. Similarly, he investigates the child's functioning in the community and within the school setting. He also examines the strength of the extended family and the possibility of community support, or pinpoints weaknesses and areas of concern.

It is important that the child's family be present at the Centre at some time during the assessment process for the team members to observe the child's functioning in relation to his family, and the nature of the family unit.

The end product is a concise and focussed assessment of the child which provides: a summary of the child's personal history and current family situation; a summary and interpretation of specialists' reports and of the information thrown up in the case conferences; the ideal recommendation for meeting the child's needs, together with realistic alternative placements. Recommendations are broken down for placement, giving special indications for treatment, together with suggestions for work with the family.

Within the context of the timing of the assessment process, the following guidelines in my setting were implemented. Upon his arrival at the Assessment Centre, the child must be accompanied by such necessary documentation as court orders, court reports, medical cards, admission forms and, where possible, detailed social histories.

By the end of the first week at the Centre, the reports from field-based social workers must have arrived at the Centre and these should lay special emphasis upon a detailed social history of the child, beginning at birth and closely examining events in the child's life up to that time.

The appointed co-ordinator of the assessment process is responsible for collating relevant information regarding the child and circulates it to all concerned. In cases where little is known with reference to the family previous to the referral, it may be necessary to have an information-gathering conference to identify specialist areas of work, and this is held as soon as possible after the child's admission. At this conference, the essential personnel are the field-based social worker and residential workers on the observational staff. Following this early conference, the co-ordinator informs all the specialists concerned in the process, highlighting areas of concern and requesting appropriate and detailed reports to be made.

Other conferences are held as appropriate, and by the sixth week of the child's stay at the Centre, he will have been seen by all the appropriate team members. Some time towards the end of this week, a decision-making conference is held, all reports having been circulated to the assessment team prior to the meeting. The function of this final conference is to examine the reports from all the team members. Following on from this decision-making conference at which a decision regarding the ideal placement has been made, the required placement is secured as soon as possible. It is necessary for this conference to identify the most suitable placement, and also the next most suitable and so on in the event that the ideal placement cannot be realised in practice for some reason. It is imperative, however, that the final recommendation for placement is based solely on the child's needs and not limited by reference to the available resources. This is important not only because it provides a comprehensive recommendation, but also because in this way gaps in provision can be shown up.

In order to fulfil all of the assessment and placement obligations a period of at least 8 weeks is necessary for the full residential assessment of a child. Over the last 2 years (since its opening), during which time some 230 adolescents have passed through my establishment, our planned model has at least proved workable.

With Righton's concepts referred to earlier concerning the need to define member roles, the following were formulated for those specialist members of the multi-disciplinary team involved in our assessment process. The nature and extent of investigation and involvement had, of necessity, to vary in accordance with the needs of individual children.

The assessment co-ordinator, as indicated earlier, is the central cog in the assessment process, collating information, liaising with specialists, and having the responsibility for the production of the final assessment dossier and its eventual distribution.

My own role as Principal of the Assessment Centre is concerned with planning the environment so that all aspects of the child may be observed, and the needs of the child fulfilled; it is also to establish working relationships between the residential staff and the specialists; to train residential staff to improve their observational techniques and enable them to fulfil their respective roles; to act as co-ordinator of the residential staff's observations, putting them in perspective, taking into consideration the composition of the child's group, the personality of the staff, and the degree of stress present within the living unit; to control parental contact in co-operation with the field-based social worker, and interpret the parent/child relationships; to ensure that all the necessary legal documents accompany the child; and to liaise with treatment centres and build up a knowledge of the service provided by them.

The psychiatrist is expected, on the basis of the information provided, to interview the child and, when appropriate, the child and his family; he attends the conferences to evaluate the information made available by other team members as well as the information collated from other psychiatrists who may have been involved with the child at an earlier date; suggests hypotheses to account for the child's problem; plays a part in formulating the treatment plan; is involved in a consultative role with residential and fieldwork staff and in an ongoing way with such things as reviews of placement, and so on.

The Educational Psychologist is expected to assess the educational needs of the children at the Centre, and ensures that consideration is given to such needs in the placement of children when they leave the Centre. This involves the collection of information from the child's previous schools, from the School Psychological Service in the child's home area, and from others who may have information relevant to the child's educational history. He conducts an educational and psychological assessment of the child in the Centre; presents the information obtained to other members of the assessment team, preferably at a case conference; and liaises with the School Psychological Service in the area in which the child is placed.

It is appropriate to emphasise here that adequate educational and psychological assessment can only be carried out if there are sufficient teaching facilities in the Centre. An important element of this is continuous observation of the child in the school situation, which only teachers can provide.

The Medical Officer (preferably a local GP) is expected to conduct a routine medical examination of the child to detect any physical disability, in particular those likely to interfere with the child's normal adapting to his environment or to retard his educational progress, or to influence his choice of vocation; he collects and collates medical documents, including those records in the hands of Health Visitors; interprets medical reports to social workers; provides guidance on educational and vocational placement when medical conditions are involved; prepares medical reports and arranges for the transfer of all medical documents and any medical recommendations to appropriate authorities after the child has been placed.

Our Clinical Psychologist investigates the personality of the child and suggests hypotheses to account for the child's problems; recommends how these problems can best be treated; investigates family interaction patterns, i.e. how the parents' personalities impinge on the child and how the child perceives his parents; suggests how the family can best be supported and encouraged to contribute to the assessment and treatment process.

Our expectation of the field-based social worker is that he provides comprehensive information on the child and his family; provides ongoing observation and support work with the family, focussing on effects of separation, pin-pointing alterations in family dynamics etc.; provides a link between the child and the family so as to mitigate the child's feelings of isolation; visits the child's school to discuss the child's performance and behaviour in and out of the formal classroom situation; ensures that the family and the child are aware of the placement decision and its future implications.

Under my own direction and support, the residential social workers' roles involve creating a living situation where a child should be able to feel secure, and therefore safe, and ensuring that the child understands why he is at the Centre.

My residential social workers deliberately set out to encourage a child to trust them and to confide in them, in order that they can understand the child's problems, his suitability for residential care, his feelings about his family, etc. Success is achieved when the staff members have developed relationships to a point where the children are able to reveal their inner feelings. Our roles within the establishment are concerned with all the basic themes of human life: love and hate, joy and sorrow, birth and death, sexuality and power. The caring process is directly related to the development of human relationships and based on the belief that the individual human being is of value. To know that another person accepts one unconditionally is to be able to accept oneself and, therefore, to be able to be oneself. It is within small group-living situations that personal relationships based on mutuality between staff and children can develop. Human beings want the approval of their fellows, both staff and children; human warmth and praise are, therefore, an essential method of control and can be given through personal relationships in groups sharing common experiences.

The residential social worker must be aware that residential experience separates a child from his family, his peers, his community, and from real life experiences; that the child is, therefore, stripped and cut down to size before his arrival at the Centre, bringing with him a complex of past unhappy experiences and the pain of rejection. It is essential that the staff, in an attempt to make the child's group-living experience at the Centre meaningful, create a real learning situation, substituting personalising for depersonalising procedures from the moment of admission.

The worker minimises the child's separation experiences by encouraging his parents or a family member or friend to accompany him with his own clothes and possessions when he arrives.

The worker ensures that the child's Christian name, his individually chosen clothes, his place for possessions and his bedroom are his preserve, and belong to him rather than to the establishment.

The staff at our Centre ensure that for the first few days the child receives intense concentration from a single member of staff until he is familiar with his new environment and understands what he is expected to contribute, and what the establishment is going to offer him and why; it is ensured that during these first few days he knows when he can again expect to see his parents or any significant outside-world figure.

Finally, in the admission context, the establishment staff can ensure that the child receives some protection over his private difficulties, such as bed-wetting or backwardness, so that he is not exposed to shame and ridicule.

The Assessment Centre's intense small group-living settings enable a child more safely to take risks in expressing his real feelings of anger, frustration and hatred and again begin to communicate them in words as well as actions. The child is helped to appreciate how his reactions affect others; when the whole group is upset, it remains small enough to allow for a "moaning session" which relieves tension and gives time for the adults to listen as well as talk.

Groups do not eliminate hostile behaviour but they tolerate it better than the total establishment: the absconder is welcomed back to warmth, comfort and a meal; the diagnosis of his behaviour is then our first concern. Group-living situations are for problem solving and for the hard work of learning painfully about human behaviour and interaction. Whereas adult groups are usually formed on the basis of sharing common interests and activities, the group in adolescence is essentially a friendship group for solving real-life problems, for exploring relationships and achieving independence. The residential social worker is the adviser who devolves onto the groups as much responsibility as they can carry for planning their lives and activities in as many areas as possible, so that faced with real problem solving, the group recognises the need for social limitations and responsibilities.

Group behaviour is modified by the kind of leadership supplied. Experiments have indicated that the most effective form of leadership—especially in a setting like the Assessment Centre—is the democratic model. This demands that the residential worker is really in touch with the children, sharing his own personality and experiences with them and bearing the pain of total involvement.

As well as providing the resident with what Righton[5] referred to as a satisfying quality of life, the residential social worker in the Assessment Centre setting, he went on to emphasise, needs the knowledge and expertise to fulfil the demands of the following three tasks. Observation, which entails knowledge of what to look for, how to distinguish the important from the trivial, anticipation of future behaviour that needs to be watched and recorded, and a sixth sense for events and feelings in the "underlife" of the group.

Interpretation, to understand the meaning of what is observed and how to relate it to the needs and problems of individual children. To do this accurately demands a sound knowledge base, the ability to learn from continuing experiences and from others more gifted in the art, and a recognition of one's own fallibility.

Recording, entails a reasonable command of written and spoken English, a sense of priorities in problem identification and solving, a capacity to express these systematically and clearly, and a respect for the fact that communication is difficult and the risk of misperception always high.

It is important at this point to emphasise that the observation tasks can only be effective if the quality of the caring is high. Therefore the Assessment Centre should be a place which offers the children a warm and accepting milieu. Many of the children will have had severely damaging experiences, they will be disturbed and resentful and will have failed to respond to the normal social controls. Acceptance alone is not enough; if it is passive, it may do little more than foster dependence. It is necessary that the child should feel that he is being accepted as he is, that he has worth in the eyes of adults. It is this planned acceptance that provides the sort of reassurance from which independence can grow.

The other crucial factor which affects the success, or otherwise, of a Residential Assessment Centre is the quality of pre-admission screening of referrals. This, when effective, can determine accurately whether the necessary assessment can be community based or in an "open" type of local authority Reception/Assessment Centre, or indeed whether the events match the criteria for admission to a Regional Residential Assessment Centre, of the type dealt with in this paper.

From a sample of 500 adolescent boys and girls admitted to my establishments during the period from 1975–8 the criteria for admission confirmed the findings of the Mind Report,[6] i.e. that the youngster's behaviour constitutes a potential danger to himself or to others; that the youngster needs relief from acute stress associated with some emergency or crisis in his family or substitute home; that the child's behaviour within the family exhibits such unusual features that assessment of the child may be severely biased unless his behaviour is witnessed in a variety of controlled situations; that while the youngster's behaviour in his family may be relatively normal, adverse outside influences such as a delinquent peer group or grossly deviant relationships with adults appear to be a more powerful determinant of his mode of life; that the child is persistently refusing school or truanting, especially when little is known about how he is spending his time during the absences from school.

Whilst there are suggested reasons for the referral of children for a period of need assessment in a residential setting, none of them constitutes by itself an absolute criterion, but on the other hand each is relevant to such a decision. It can be said of the children who made up the sample that the majority appeared to be disturbed in many aspects of their functioning, finding themselves unable to relate to a wide range of people—parents, teachers, peers and siblings. Their disturbance was manifested in many ways and the following categories could be isolated, all of which involved extreme forms of acting-out behaviour: youngsters showing a consistent pattern of self-inflicted violence, aggression to siblings, or persistent absconding from home or residential institutions, those who while missing from home commit serious property offences, those whose promiscuous behaviour puts them at risk, who are addicted to drugs, or who are known fire raisers, etc. The criteria do not focus much attention on the actual offences committed, in conjunction with the spirit of the 1969 Children and Young Persons Act which set out to eliminate the distinction in assessment and treatment between the deprived and depraved. Of course, it can be argued that offences are symptomatic of pathological behaviour and that one is really taking as much account of this as of the offence itself.

In almost every case, however, the following criteria relating to assessment away from home arise from a consideration of two factors. At one level, can the child manage and sustain himself effectively in his home environment given the facts of the precipitating occurrence? If he, or his family cannot, then removal would seem desirable. If the youngster is malfunctioning in many aspects of his life, can the home environment manage and sustain his malfunction? If not, removal from home is deemed desirable.

I am conscious of having neglected the question posed in the title of this paper, and this was deliberate. Assessment, and in particular residential assessment, has attained a high level of effectiveness that has not—as yet—been matched by other residential resources for children. Formulated residential treatment provision is not adequately available to profit from the accurate diagnostic reports and recommended treatment plans produced by the Assessment Centre and it is this situation that results in decisions being based on expediency.

Applications to hospital settings for children deemed to be depraved are unsuccessful due to the degree of violence exhibited by them; Community Home schools are too fearful of the arsonist to accept him for treatment; children's homes are too affected by a girl's former promiscuous behaviour to offer her a refuge; children cannot be returned to their families when it is considered desirable because the social casework provision and support cannot be guaranteed; maladjusted and educationally subnormal children are turned down by boarding schools because of their "delinquent" tendencies. The list of examples is inexhaustible.

There is already evidence of a marked improvement in facilities in residential settings due primarily to the policies with (some) regions of encouraging establishments to focus their development on specialisation. The starting point, it seems to me, is for long-term residential resources to examine where their strengths lie and then to offer them appropriately.

Expediency is also to be avoided by even the most sophisticated Assessment Centres, which frequently, because of the degree of sophistication they have attained, are not sufficiently flexible in their approach. This is sometimes reflected in the manner in which every child is processed routinely as opposed to moulding the provision to meet the needs of the individual. This form of expediency is both expensive and wasteful, and often counter-productive to the child's development.

Labelling, or categorising, is a prominent and inevitable feature of social work in general, as it begins as soon as a family or individual with a "problem" seeks the formal intervention of a social work agency, and thereby becomes labelled as being inadequate, or of being a failure, etc., with the consequent stigma of shame and guilt. This is borne out, in my experience, by the three factors common in a significantly high percentage of children in care situations: they were the products of families that were in some way inadequate or disrupted; had low self-images, exhibiting continual evidence of being of little personal worth; and, irrespective of intellectual potential, were educationally retarded.

I would like, in conclusion, to reiterate my belief that, during the last decade, residential assessment of children and young persons has attained a sufficiently high measurable degree of effectiveness and efficiency—measurable, that is, by the success it achieves in realising its goals and by the amount of resources used to achieve those goals—to form the foundation upon which to build an equally effective range of treatment provision for those young "stretcher-cases" of society who make up our client population.

References

1. H. J. RICHARDSON, *Adolescent Girls in Approved Schools*, Routledge & Kegan Paul, 1969.
2. P. RIGHTON, *Heads and Hearts*, R.C.A., 1978.
3. Seebohm Committee Report, HMSO, 1968.
4. RIGHTON, *op. cit.*
5. P. RIGHTON, *Objectives and Methods of Residential Social Work*, 1971.
6. MIND Report, *Assessment of Children and their Families*, 1975.

CHAPTER 5

FROM RESIDENTIAL TO DAY ASSESSMENT IN BELFAST*

DENIS O'BRIEN

For approximately 4 years I had been working as deputy headmaster of a residential unit, in Lisnevin School, Newtownards, Co. Down, assessing delinquents when, after consultations with the Northern Ireland Office, our management board decided that we should close down, transfer to premises at Whitefield House in Belfast and practice day assessment. Some of my colleagues were not altogether enamoured of this decision but I felt that we should accept the challenge, take stock of our past experience, learn from it and then start afresh. The concept deserved a different approach and the remainder of this paper describes how we made the transition and the first weeks of the operation.

A team approach

The idea of an assessment team is not unique but in practice I have found that the term describes a group of people who meet at a case conference to make decisions which may alter the life of another human being. In the weeks preceding the conference the client was observed and tested while living away from his natural environment. In the residential context this meant that he was separated from his home and family. Both the young person and his parents were excluded from the case conference or at best they performed a minor role while the main part was played out ritually by the professionals.

Dockar-Drysdale writes that "those people who make assessments are in an omnipotent position".[1] In my experience not only are the workers attending the case conference omnipotent, but the pecking order amongst the disciplines makes some opinions more powerful than others. Paradoxically, it was often the report of the professional who had been least involved with the client which carried the most weight. My hypothesis is reinforced by a conclusion in the MIND report that "the perspectives on a problem of, say, a residential or day care worker who has frequent and regular contact with a child may well be much more significant than that of a consultant psychiatrist who has based his conclusions on one interview only".[2]

Yet in support of team work Dockar-Drysdale writes, "all need assessments must be made by a group, *never* by an individual collecting information or depending on interview procedure". I felt that somehow this principle had to be embodied in a day assessment system. With a large staff group it was numerically possible to divide into

---

* This chapter appeared as an article in *Social Work Today*, **10** (27), 1979.

teams and, while retaining the same *primary task*, the philosophy of each team could be different. The MIND report also suggests that, "it is impossible completely to divorce the observation and assessment process from the therapeutic and educative one. Assessment is always both a pre-requisite and an accompaniment to help." This statement confirmed our own experience in residential assessment and accordingly we decided to divide the staff group between four teams. Three of the teams would work directly with the children at the day centre. Each team was to develop its own ethos independently, thus conforming to different treatment approaches. The fourth team was to be concerned with "intake" and would be interrelated with the other three.

The members of two teams, the Intake Team and the Family Group Team, were released to commence day assessment in October 1977. I was given the responsibility of leading the Family Group Team and we were allowed a few weeks for preparation and reorientation.

The Intake Team

We decided that the Intake Team would be comprised of four persons, two social workers, a teacher and a psychologist. It had been our experience in the past that on occasions barriers were placed between assessment workers and knowledge held by other agencies on the grounds of confidentiality. However, we believed that quite often the real reason for withholding information was interprofessional rivalry. By having an interdisciplinary Intake Team we sought to eliminate this difficulty and bring about an increase in communication.

Referrals

Referrals are made directly to the Intake Team by the courts. Once a referral is made they initiate enquiries aimed at establishing which other organisations have previously been involved with the client and his family. There is an advantage in getting "first-hand" information. Often a school report is forwarded by a busy headmaster who has completed three or four such documents on the same afternoon. Direct contact with a form teacher or year master by the Intake Team teacher is more valuable. He may also use the occasion to begin negotiations for the client's return to school. Similarly, contact with professional colleagues in Child Guidance or the Schools Psychological Service are made by our psychologist. When necessary he may also undertake intellectual and educational attainment testing.

The social workers on the Intake Team liaise with fieldworkers from Social Services and Probation etc. Usually they receive a copy of the home background or court report on the client. However, since these reports were not intended for our use in the first place and also since they are generally a resumé of the client's circumstances, and say little about the person himself, they are not specific enough for assessment purposes. Nevertheless, they are a useful starting point and through the process of consultation with the author and by follow-up visits to the client's home the gaps are filled in.

Allocation

After collecting and collating the information they have received from all their resources the Intake Team meet and on the basis of their findings they will allocate the case to one of the other teams. This process should only take a few days, after which they pass on the file and indicate goals for assessment, e.g. "to get John back to school" or "to investigate the relationship between Sue and her mother".

Family Group Team

The practitioners in this team are six in number and between us we have 37 years of experience in residential work. Three of the team, Thompson, Mabel and Martin have trained in residential child care, while Arty, Mary and myself (Denis) have a teaching background. I completed the SCRCCYP course at Bristol University in 1975/6 and during the same year Mary had postgraduate training in the Education of Maladjusted Children at London University. Her training included practical experience as a play therapist in a Child Guidance Clinic, one aspect of her work at the day centre.

Philosophy

The team is committed to the concept of assessing and treating children within the context of their family. Our basic premise is that when a young person is referred by the court for assessment this very procedure creates a crisis situation for the whole family system. Hansell writes that "arranging the treatment system to achieve close timing between precipitating events and the entry of help, takes maximum advantage of the unusual flexibility of cognition and affectional attachments during the crisis state".[3] It is while this state of crisis exists for the family, and their cognitive processes are enhanced by it, that the team will intervene. Since the young person is still living at home then the crucial decision of whether he will remain there or not has still to be made.

Contract

I am sure that one area of social work practice which is often overlooked in assessment centres, remand homes and other residential establishments, is contracting. I am not speaking here of micro-contracts made between residents and workers from day to day but of a contract which runs throughout the period of intervention. I expect that one reason for the absence of contracting with children in residential work is because often the client has been imposed in the situation, e.g. sent there by the court. I felt that the practice of day assessment of children and their families would depend upon a workable contract. Middleman and Goldberg write that "a service contract may be said to exist when both worker and client explicitly understand and agree upon the task to be accomplished and what the worker will do to help accomplish it".[4]

Before a juvenile is referred to us for assessment a magistrate asks both him and his parents while in court if they will agree to this procedure. When the young person, his family and the fieldworker visit the day assessment centre a few days later they are met by one of the team who will make a contract with this group. While any contract is subject to negotiation the following is a draft of how we proceed.

(1) You have been asked to visit Whitefield House because of your agreement in court to allow your son/daughter to be assessed.

(2) We have an obligation to submit a report to the court at the end of the adjournment period.

(3) Whilst the immediate problem seems to be the behaviour which led to your son/daughter appearing in court, this problem must in some way affect the whole family and therefore we will want to take an in-depth look at the situation.

(4) To make a complete assessment it will be necessary (a) for your son/daughter to attend the centre every day, (b) for your family to meet regularly with the Whitefield staff during this period.

(5) If you agree to these conditions then you will have the opportunity to contribute to the assessment report and to attend the Case Conference.

At this point if an agreement is secured the assessment worker makes a firm arrangement for the first in a series of family meetings and settles a date, pick-up time etc. for the boy or girl to commence attending the Centre.

While this contract is explicitly made between ourselves and the family there is an implicit assumption that the fieldworker will want to be involved. We began by expecting him to participate as a co-therapist at the family meetings but after experiencing some difficulty we recently decided to consult the fieldworker between meetings instead.

Family Meetings

We have meetings with a family throughout the period of assessment. Two members of the assessment team participate as co-therapists at all family gatherings and, while the frequency of the meetings will vary, six to eight meetings are the norm. Initially, all members of the child's immediate family are invited to attend and the family circle may be widened to include significant others whenever this seems appropriate and if all participants agree. Eventually it may be necessary to work with dyads, triads etc. of family members or indeed with the parental or sibling subsystem. In our work with families we are concerned with understanding and changing the transactions between people rather than trying to effect change in any individual. In the beginning we held the meetings in the family home but experience has shown that the therapists are more influential when the family meet at the Centre. The family meetings are held in the afternoons or evenings.

It is our practice to begin each meeting by restating the purpose for which the group has gathered. We stress to the family that there can be no secrets between members of our assessment team and that the events of the meeting will be discussed with our colleagues at the Day Centre. We resist any attempt by a family member to take a worker into his confidence, since we believe that "private practice" may lead to collusive relationships and negate the therapeutic process. We find it best to avoid beginning the first meeting by working on a hypothesis and prefer to canvass the opinions of individual family members on how they see "the problem". The team meets together between family meetings to agree on the hypothesis which can be tested at the second and subsequent meetings with the family.

The purpose of the family group meetings is twofold. On the one hand we hope to discover how the family system really works and to expose underlying feelings of perhaps guilt or conflict within the group. At the same time a therapeutic intervention is made when a shift in the balance of pathogenic relationships within the family system is facilitated. Frequently we find that real communication between family members begins as a result of being drawn into a meeting by us and often "family secrets" are shared or acknowledged for the first time. When disagreements between family members occur we manage the situation rather than avoid it for, as Zuk writes, "family therapy is the only therapy in which patients come with an established history of conflict and with a well-developed means for expressing or disguising it".[5]

Travelling to the Centre

The day begins for the children when we collect them from their homes and ends when they are "set down" again the late afternoon. The driver is always accompanied by one of the assessment team who will actually call at the homes of our clients in the mornings. In this way we take the temperature of the home situation on a daily basis. Moreover, I feel that we have also picked up valuable clues and made positive gains for our assessment on the doorstep as the following illustrations show.

Mabel called for Jane each day at 8.45 a.m. She was always ready and waiting by the garden gate. One morning Mabel was about 10 minutes earlier than usual and Jane wasn't in her usual place. On calling at the house Mabel was greeted by the girl's step-mother who said that Jane was at a friend's house nearby. Just then Jane appeared, brushed past her step-mother and entered the house to collect her coat. There was no exchange of greeting between them. Subsequently Mabel discovered that Jane left the house each day at 8.00 a.m., when her father was going to work, and walked around for a while returning only when time for her collection by the bus was near. This gave us our first insight into inter-familial relations in this house.

When we met David's parents for the first time his mother was untidy and withdrawn while his father was suave and seemed to have some insight into the boy's behaviour. After Arty had been collecting David from home for about 1 week the boy's mother beckoned him into the house one morning and showed him bruises on her body and on the arms of David's sister which she alleged had been caused by her husband. At the next family meeting the husband agreed that he beat his wife and children regularly.

On other occasions we received positive indications that our work was becoming effective and the following account is just one example.

William's adoptive parents were separated and he lived with his mother. He was seldom out of bed when Mary called in the mornings. Our bus waited regularly while William dressed and made ready. But following our third family meeting when his mother had painfully disclosed that her marriage had broken up because of her psycho-sexual problems, William was always ready and waiting when Mary arrived.

Programme Activities

Between 9.30 a.m. and 1.00 p.m. we provide programme activities at the Centre. There is a timetable and the young people are divided into groups for periods of about three-quarters of an hour during the morning. I believe that maladjusted children need the security that this structure gives and "acting out" behaviour is reduced accordingly. However, the Beedell principle of "only child treatment"[6] is embodied in the programme with one or two of the team always employed with individual children. Each child has one period of formal education daily while the other activities provided by the team, i.e. craft, play therapy, guitar lessons, art, PE, are educational in the broad sense of the word. I consider that it is essential to remember that our primary task is assessment and not education. Otherwise it would be so easy to become so thoroughly involved in teaching that the client's problems remain "buried between the cracks in the floorboards" while we cling tenaciously to our traditional roles.

Group Work

The first hour each day is spent in group therapy and all staff and children attend. As the facilitator I begin by setting a time boundary and explaining the purpose of the meeting. The children are reminded that the common element in their presence at the Centre is that they have been referred for assessment by the court. I explain that their task in the group is to "work on their own problems" and suggest that they should help each other. They are reminded that the staff attend the meeting to see how the children are "shaping up" since our task is to prepare a report for the court on each one of them.

Our experience has been that confusion and silence prevails for a time but eventually some of the children will advance defensive ploys which we reject. The effect on the children, when the normal paternalistic responses of the staff group are replaced by unfamiliar and demanding ones, is that they release feelings which had hitherto been suppressed. We encourage the examination of these feelings but our assistance is non-directive. While some children cannot verbalise within the group they often express themselves non-verbally and it has been our experience that in individual sessions with staff afterwards they are often quite forthcoming.

We have three other groupwork periods each week which are devoted to exercises in communication through touch, play and movement. Again all the staff and children are involved in holding, balancing, tests of strength and stability etc., i.e. a range of activities aimed at building up confidence and increasing trust. As we are running a day centre without the normal institutional controls, we have found this work to be invaluable as a means of establishing rapport and building relationships based on sensitivity and trust.

Recording

My experience in the residential assessment situation was that any behaviour of an individual which conflicted with the standards laid down by the regime was noted most frequently. I believe that if we are to gain insight into children's behaviour then first of all we must become more aware of ourselves. For if adults are not conscious of their own feelings they are likely to unconsciously act them out through the children. Therefore I asked the team members to record those feelings which they might have about individual children.

There is also a question about what the children are feeling during interactions with us. In other words what is the subconscious meaning behind their words and actions? We are trying to develop the habit of therapeutic listening and of picking up non-verbal happenings and then recording the total experience including the verbatim conversation.

We have a "needs assessment" meeting on each child after he has attended the centre for about 2 weeks. Then the recordings are examined and discussed openly and we attempt to assess the state of the individual child. State here refers to the level of his ego development and in some cases the exact syndrome of deprivation. A treatment programme is outlined and we initiate the work reviewing progress weekly. The format of the need assessment is described by Mrs B. D. Drysdale in her paper in *Consultation in Child Care* and we consider evidence of "panic" or disruption when making our diagnosis.

Consolidation

I think that I can best illustrate how the various strands of day assessment combine, by giving a resumé of Sean's case. He was referred with a presenting problem of stealing and truancy. At 12 years of age he had completed a period of probation, attended Child Guidance and the Schools Psychological Service and was under supervision of the Social Services.

At our first "needs assessment" meeting the team decided that we hardly knew Sean as he was all "locked up" and did not really communicate. He seemed anxious and needed a great deal of ego support.

The first family meeting revealed that Sean's parents were rejecting him to such an extent that they agreed their home would be a better place if Sean was removed from it. However, Mary and Arty also discovered that Sean had been the constant companion of his maternal grandmother who died when he was just 5 years old. Coincidentally, Sean's stealing began around that time and his truancy began when he was 7.

When we reviewed the need assessment the team felt that Sean's emotional growth was arrested around his fifth year. During play therapy Sean had related to Mary some "good experiences" he had with his grandmother. These were centred around eating and drinking together. So we decided that Mary should have an adaptation, a localised regression, with Sean by replicating the experience he enjoyed with his grandmother.

Actually Sean was quite moved on the occasion and took off his coat for the first time and talked expansively about his grandmother. From that time onwards he progressed rapidly. His very expression changed and he verbalised more in group sessions and family meetings. Not only did he commence "working on his problems" but began to help everyone else talk through theirs.

Meanwhile at the fourth family meeting Sean's father disclosed that there was friction between himself and his wife. He confessed that because he was some years older than her that he regarded Sean as a rival. By the time the sixth meeting was held the boy's parents had clearly been drawn closer together again for the first time in years.

We also arranged a meeting in Sean's school with the headmaster and some other teachers. Sean, his parents and social worker attended, together with Mary and Arty. The school was prepared to be flexible in Sean's timetabling and we gradually re-integrated him into the educational system.

Case Conference and Report

Sean's Case Conference was typically informal, attended by himself and his family throughout, together with his social worker and all six members of the "family group assessment team". A recommendation to the court that he should remain living at home under supervision of his social worker was agreed. The assessment report was not a concentrated diagnosis but was simply empirical, i.e. an account based on experience, observation and experiment.

Postscript

It is early days yet to say whether or not our assessment/treatment of young persons has been effective. But the results so far are encouraging and between October and July we have worked with over 50 children and their families. We have also phased out completely our residential assessment system, and the remaining staff are working as two more day assessment teams.

Indeed, I feel that we are only now experiencing all the painful reality of children's lives, a reality from which we were so well cocooned in the residential world.

Although we have only just begun day assessment and thus realise that we will still encounter many problems and difficulties, I feel that this is a really worthwhile venture, and view the future with enthusiasm and optimism.

References

1. B. Dockar-Drysdale, *Consultation in Child Care*, Longman, 1970.
2. MIND, *Assessment of Children and their Families*, 1975.
3. N. Hansell et al., *Decision Counselling Method*, Department of Psychiatry, Northwestern University Medical School, Chicago, 1969.
4. R. R. Middleman and G. Goldberg, *Social Service Delivery: A Structural Approach to Social Work Practice*, Columbia University Press, 1974.
5. Gerald H. Zuk, *Family Therapy: Formulation of a Technique and its Theory*, Eastern Pennsylvania Psychiatric Institute, Philadelphia.
6. C. J. Beedell, *Provision for Play-Groups in a Reception Centre*, R.C.C.A. Review 1971.

CHAPTER 6

COLLECTING AND USING DATA FOR ASSESSMENT

E. STEPHANIE HALL

"Perchance my too much questioning offends."

(Rev. Henry Francis Cory 1772–1844, Dante Translation 1812 Canto 18 line 6)

Some Social Service Departments are attempting to look at assessment at the point of referral and have set up Intake Teams. I have yet to come across one team which has a member skilled in residential practice. Capitalising on the specialist knowledge of a qualified residential practitioner would bring another dimension to assessment at the point of referral. It is erroneous to think that this kind of specialist knowledge applied to assessment can only be used in a high cost residential establishment and in isolation to the total assessment picture.

The input of a residential practitioner's expertise at this stage could also have a spin-off to

(a) rationalisation of resources

(b) future planning

(c) workload management.

Maybe residential workers are left out because admission to residential care is still seen as a failure, and not seen as Chris Payne says it should be, as complementary to other Social Services.[1] I believe once this happened and residential services were seen as complementary rather than as residual, and were considered at the point of referral, much more could be done by way of prevention work.

This kind of thinking could also have far-reaching effects on the type of future residential service which is developed to meet the need of early intervention. Instead of waiting as at present for the collapsed state before residential intervention is considered.

This is already happening in relation to the drive towards fostering and adoption. Jackie Langley and Tess Sinnot, Child Placement Co-ordinators in East Sussex[2] have said that by increasing foster home placements they are beginning to affect the type of residential placement being made, and are having some influence on decisions concerning the future use of residential establishments, e.g. change in their method of working. They say this kind of influence does not always make them popular.

Nevertheless, I believe this type of influence is bound to happen. Certainly in my own agency we are taking steps to change our methods of residential work to complement the work of our Fostering and Adoption Section.

If we believe in integration as being an effective way of giving the best service to our clients we must be courageous in our approach to change. How can these changes be made? One way this can be done is to take a long hard look at the way we collect data and make assessment for admission to residential care and to see if we can cross boundaries without too much difficulty within the existing system.

In general terms there are negative and positive aspects as to why data is collected in any Social Service agency. The negative side is the fact that we have limited resources and therefore we have to be selective. This applies to social work intervention *per se*. Whether it is carried out by the Social Service Departments or by the voluntary sector.

The positive side is that data collecting and assessment makes for the rationalisation of the use of these limited resources whether it is for macro planning or for highly specialised service delivery. There is also the spin-off of specific research based on data collection. This particularly applies in an agency such as Barnardo's where we have to be selective. Therefore, our residential units have clear criteria for admission which are based on Strategic Agency Objectives (see note (3)). Tactical Objectives to meet these Strategic Objectives are then set for each residential unit. Those residential units from which the ensuing model for collecting and using data for assessment for admission is taken are those units set up for emotionally and socially handicapped children. Age range 5–16.

The Tactical Objectives for these are:

1. The creation and maintenance of a powerful healthy open environment based on a synthesis of thinking in an attempt to create living/learning space or life-space.[4]
2. To adhere to Structured Admission procedure.
   (a) Completion of application form.
   (b) Visiting of child and significant adults to unit prior to admission.
   (c) To make provision for Intake Conference.
   (d) To make case plans at time of admission.
3. To make provision for 6-monthly review.

There are other objectives related to staff training and development and also research, but although they have a significant part to play in the dynamics of each unit they are not part of the purpose of this chapter, therefore they have not been elaborated.

Readers of this chapter might want to give up at this point, particularly, in the light of what I have said previously about the need to broaden referral and intake procedure, and the generalisations I have made, but one thing I have learnt through the years is that often the biggest changes come from the smallest beginnings.

Once after a sub-office meeting in which we had been clearly told there was no new money for growth some wit wrote on the notice board "We have no money so we must think". Often in these days of mad pressure we have lost the art of thinking. Making the best out of what we have whilst still looking towards the big changes that are needed.

Another spin-off from making the best of what we have is coming to the realisation that by doing so we stop throwing the baby out with the bath water and truly value what we have. Much of what we have had comes from the hard graft of other generations of committed social workers.

The Model

Data for assessment is collected, viz.:

1. Application forms;

2. Observations;
3. Intake Conference which takes the form of direct questions and answers.

It should be noted that data collection and assessment are synonymous in that, during the whole process from the point of referral to admission, the two go hand in hand and constitute one process of checking and rechecking facts which are gathered, comparing each against the other. The technique for doing this, if it can be called a technique, is that described by Specht and Vickery. "The substance of our practice to support the client is often a combination of knowledge, skill, expertise, insight, intuition which often criss-crosses to and from into systems other than our own, and use a mix of lower level theory to achieve results."[5]

1. *Application forms* (written communication)

These are usually sent after a telephone enquiry for a placement. The application form asks questions which are used multipurposefully both by managers for statistics and research into trends, future development and planning, and by practitioners for case planning. Questions are asked about the direct nature of the problem, e.g. why is residential care being sought? Questions are asked about what section of what Act the child is being brought into care. Again these are used multipurposefully to clarify the extent of the delegated authority and responsibility the agency and residential worker will be asked to carry.

Preliminary casework plan questions are asked such as short- and long-term goals. These questions are related to the time a child is expected to remain in care and what will happen to him when he leaves. In this concept I heartily agree with Nancy Hazel that children placed in residential establishments are in transit. "It is never their final destination",[6] although much of today's practice by both residential and field workers acts as if it were. This kind of practice must have, through the years, influenced planning policy and be one of the root causes of the problem which faces many of us, that of the destination of a child coming out of long-term care at 16-plus.

This is not to gainsay that some children will benefit from and will prefer long-term residential care.[7] If this is the situation plans must be made to ensure the quality of life and the maximising of potential which will ensure a total independence in the community at adulthood. This is not something which will happen on a hit-or-miss basis. Hence our questioning how long is the child likely to be in care, a question which can often offend, particularly if seen as a challenge. These completed application forms are then studied by the Head of Unit and his staff. If they feel at this stage that they can help in the situation presented to them, they invite the social worker and client to make a visit to the unit with plans for the child to remain for a period. The social worker is encouraged to bring with them parents or other significant adults in the child's life. It is now that the second stage of information gathering takes place.

2. *Observation*

This is a delicate time, as in all initial contacts, because it is here that true engagement takes place. Although the need for the skill of initial engagement is recognised from the first point of referral to the agency, a non-empathetic telephone response at referral can often take a long time to overcome.[8]

The observation skill and development of residential staff is essential, for they are reaching out into another system—perhaps several systems, the family system, other social work agency systems. They will also want to begin questioning the realities of other of the client systems of which they have some written knowledge, such as school or work systems.

They will wish to explore the quality of the relationship they will have with the social worker, the parent or other significant adults in the child's life.

During the period the client will remain in the unit, the limitations and expectations of the adults of the unit will be explained in detail, e.g. if it is a hostel, then the expectations are that the young person will work and pay his way. If the child is a school refusal the unit's expectations will be explained, telling the child the resources which are available for his support and help. Every endeavour will be made to show the child/young person the realities of the residential care he can expect. The boundaries will be explained as realistically as possible. The child/young person will be given the opportunity to talk with other residents to get the feel of the place. If groupwork is part of the unit's function, or outside activities are part of the dynamics of the unit, these too will be explained. In fact anything which will help the child or young person to understand—if only in a limited sense, according to age and intellect—what is happening to him.[9] Observation of the child/young person's cognitive ability at this stage can help tremendously at the case planning stage, particularly if a contract of working with the child is being contemplated.

This period of time will also be used to make a judgement about which member of the residential staff will become the child's contract adult. The contract adult will be the child's primary care agent whilst in residential care and will also be, if the case plan requires it, the person who will work in tandem with the field social worker.

The concept of contract shown here in this model is actually based on the work of Lydia Rappoport and her work on *Crisis Intervention as a Mode of Treatment*,[10] where she talks of "mutually agreed upon goals", i.e. engagement with the client or other workers in some kind of work agreement. It does not always mean a casework relationship even with a client. It can often be a business arrangement, and always is a business arrangement when field and residential workers decide to work together on one or more elements or targets of the case plan.[11] This idea of breaking down the case plan into small elements or targets will be explained later under the heading Case Planning.

The next stage of collecting and using data for assessment is:

3. *Intake Conference*

It is here that there is a specific group meeting of child and significant adults which will also include the contract adult. The purpose of this meeting is to make a final assessment of all the information, to make a mutually agreed decision to admit the child, and to make a case plan. As the case planning is based on the total information it is important that such information is checked openly by the Chairperson, usually the Head of Unit.

These meetings can be illuminating and stimulating particularly if parents are present.

They can also be threatening, and the Chairperson must be skilled in knowing how to reduce the threat so that the work of case planning can proceed.

Once the case plan is made by mutual agreement, it will not be changed unless all those who met to make the plan meet again and change it. The plan is updated at the review when again all interested parties meet. In this way the child is never in a position where there is no plan or where plans are changed, when there is a change of staff either field or residential. It is also logical to expect that once a child has experienced this type of intervention his expectations will be that he will also be involved in the plans being made for him, whatever the circumstances might be which call for a change of plan.

The illuminating experience of the group meeting can often produce quite startling results as in a case in which the whole focus of the plan changed. I have not had the experience described by Bruggen, Byng-Hall and Pitt Aikens at Hill End Hospital[12] where they have a similar-type admission meeting which always includes the parent or parent figure, of the admission being refused by the parents as they now felt able to cope. This action was attributed to relief of pressure by the offer of a place and the coming together of the parents in mutual understanding at the admission meeting.

I have had the experience when chairing such a meeting at which the long-term plan was to be fostering for three young children after a period in residential care, where the mother and cohabitee, who were present, decided that they would have the children after the period in care.

Finally:

The Case Plan

This particular case plan has been specifically designed for use at the Intake Conference and takes cognisance of the process of the Model of Collecting and Using Data for Assessment for Admission to Residential Units for Emotionally and Socially Handicapped Children. At the time of writing it is fairly hot off the press, and as such it has not been thoroughly tested.

Its purpose is an attempt to conceptualise further the idea of contractually based work and integrated methods of working between field and residential workers.

It is also an attempt to move away from the actual psychopathology of the child being admitted, although this question is not shied away from if it is there to be asked, but even then it does not take up the whole focus of the plan. This is also an endeavour to remove the blame the child often feels and the stigma so graphically spelt out in *Who Cares*.[13]

Another purpose is an attempt to move towards partialised problem solving. Often the problems which face a child and significant adults alike at admission to care are so immense that we are immobilised by the overwhelming effect. By breaking down the problem into small elements or targets which can be worked on by more than one person, the problem becomes more manageable. This way it is also possible for more than one target to be worked on at one time possibly by two or more people. Thus we have the elements of possible integration between field and residential workers and also the engagement of the client in the work agreement.

There is also the element of accountability for all concerned to get the work done within time limits.

This focus on time limits for specific targets has the effect of showing that it is not always necessary for the child to remain in residential care whilst certain work continues, e.g. if part of the problem is shown to be relating to the natural home and this is sorted out in 6 months, whilst another part of the problem was the home environment which had been estimated as taking 12 months to sort out, it might be possible for the child to return home whilst work still continues in the environment.

The plan is in the form of a matrix on a single sheet of paper. On the left-hand side it asks six questions related to the child being admitted to care and forms the vertical axis. The horizontal axis asks: is the problem or reasons for the admission in the personal development of the child, in the family, the environment or the school? The family, the environment and the school have been subdivided as many children come into an establishment either from foster home breakdowns or from other planned substitutes such as another residential home where perhaps the relationship has broken down. The last point, H, on the horizontal axis asks what is the relevance of the unit to the identified problem.

On the second sheet there is room, if necessary, for an elaboration of the case plan.

The most important part of this elaboration is the priority rating given to the concept of partialised problem solving. Going back to the idea of the overwhelming size of a problem it is sometimes easier to clarify those things which need urgent immediate attention and those which can be safely left.

Example of Practice Using Model and Case Plan

Tom is a 16-year-old about to leave school. An attractive, articulate lad of average intelligence.

He has had a chequered career. Several court appearances, a period in Detention Centre. No social services involved up to that time. At a subsequent appearance a Care Order was made. He was admitted to an Assessment Centre, followed by a committal to Community School, from which he absconded. He disappeared from view, finding a flat with two other lads. He and the other lads were finally arrested for burglary.

He was admitted to a children's home, where he began to pay serious attention to his situation. He was under the threat of Borstal which was staved off by the social worker. Tom received a deferment of 6 months and was required to appear in court again after 6 months. From the children's home he attended school and made very good progress.

His parents saw his care and control as the responsibility of the social services. Since his admission to the children's home, their relationship with the social worker had become more productive.

It was felt that although Tom had made very good progress at the children's home, he had outgrown their provision and would continue to do so after he started work. He wanted to work with a construction company.

Application was made for him to be admitted to an Adolescent Unit.

The above information was gathered as described in the model (1) "Application Forms" (written communication).

Tom visited the unit with his social worker, Tom staying overnight. Tom's parents had been invited by the social worker but they refused.

During the stay overnight the second process of the described model (2) "Observation" was used. A residential worker whose interest lay with delinquent boys isolated from parents and whose workload could take on another contract was the adult who took over this observation process.

The next day Tom and the contract adult decided to proceed to the next stage, "Intake Conference". This Intake Conference had been arranged but Tom knew that there was a choice at this stage. If either he or the contract adult had grave reservations about the proposed admission these would be honestly discussed with all concerned in the time set for the Intake Conference and the application withdrawn by mutual agreement. The element of choice highlighted at this stage is one that is built in during the whole of the data collection and assessment. It is based on theories related to criteria for admission to particular units, and mutually agreed-upon goals. To take any action with or on behalf of emotionally/socially handicapped young people, they must be involved in deciding and agreeing goals.

The Intake Conference

Present: Tom
         Social worker
         Head of Unit
         Head of children's home where Tom had been living
         Contract adult
         Senior Residential Officer in the Chair. (This person is Supervisor/Consultant to Head of Unit.)

Here a mutual decision was made to admit Tom to the unit. This decision was made after all written data was openly checked, including the statutory obligations related to Tom's care.

All members of the group including Tom were able to say something of their observations of the unit, its function, its relevance to Tom's needs and what Tom might be able to contribute to the unit.

Case planning

The six questions on the matrix planner (see case plan proforma) were asked. Why is Tom being admitted? From the data the conference had, both written and verbal, it was plain that the significant adults in his life felt that Tom was still in need of care and control and that it was not possible for his mum and dad to give this care and control. Tom was asked to honestly face up to these facts and was encouraged by the head of the children's home Tom was about to leave about the progress made at that unit. Together the group were able to look at the need for children to have significant adults to support them, and bring them up until such times as they are able to stand on their own in society. Tom agreed that he was still vulnerable due to his past convictions.

The head of the children's home was able to say he and his unit could no longer give Tom the care and control which it was felt Tom needed during the next year as he started work and became an adult. This did not mean that they did not want anything more to do with Tom but would be glad to see him and to be kept informed of his progress.

This gave the lead into looking at the role of Tom's parents at this point in time, and the group were able to discuss the significance of Tom's parents to him. The social worker was able to say the kind of support he was offering to Tom's parents. Tom appeared to draw comfort and gain in confidence when he could see that there was more than one reason why he was being admitted to the unit. This kind of honesty between adults and children at this stage is the beginning of a mutual support system which does not get bogged down and overwhelmed by any one problem. It helps the child not to carry with him the total burden of blame and guilt at having to be in residential care, but to face up honestly to his share of responsibility. What is to be gained by Tom's admission? It was agreed that being admitted gave everyone time to build on progress already made and time to build on other support systems in the community in readiness for Tom to leave care.

What change is hoped for? This brought a reality to what is possible. No high flying but down-to-earth possibilities and facing the reality of Tom having to find a home of his own in the community. How will this be made? It is here that the conference realises that effort has to be put into reaching what is seen to be possible.

Who will do the work? Action with and on behalf of Tom—the contract adult, the social worker, Tom and the head of the unit begin to make links. This idea of helping each other, honestly discussed, strengthens the mutual support system. The social worker admits he does not find it easy to communicate with Tom's parents. The contract adult says he will need help in this direction. Tom says he knows his parents best.

How long will it take? Time limits are agreed, including the date Tom will be admitted to the unit. Space does not allow for full analysis of the dynamics of what is happening at the case-planning stage, and of course it is not as simple as it sounds. What appears to happen is that adults and child face up to their responsibilities in the here-and-now situation and plan to take action on specific targets. In Tom's case plan there were four targets.

(i) *Tom's personal development*—it was hoped that the unit's environment would help in this direction, this would be achieved by working to the case plan with the unit head building in the following: Tom's case to be discussed at staff meeting before admission.
Points for discussion at staff meeting:

> All staff to be aware of targets.
> Tom's progress since he began to pay attention to his situation.
> Why he cannot be restored home and the need to be ready to welcome his parents into the unit if they decide to visit.
> The possibility that Tom's case will need to be discussed with the psychiatrist on one of his visits to the unit, particularly if Tom begins to act out some of his unresolved rejection by his parents.
> Being aware that this is not a target at the moment. Support contract adult and receiving feedback from him at staff meetings.

(ii) *Family*—do not see themselves as being able to offer care/control. It is unlikely that Tom will return home to live but his family are important to him. They are also important to the unit's environment if they are to help Tom to a stable independence. Time starting immediately, fading off after 6 months, to be reviewed.

(iii) *Peer group in the community*—Tom has a girlfriend. Social worker says it appears a good relationship, and could be the start of more appropriate peer group relationships. Tom is a keen footballer. Unit has a five-a-side football team which visits and plays other teams in the area. Community links need to be established now for flat lodging later on. Time starting immediately, reviewed in 6 months. Maximum 2 years.

(iv) *Employers*—Tom wishes to work with a construction company who have a training scheme. He is willing to take a labourer's job to start. He is willing to travel. Tom will need help to negotiate what he wants from the work situation.

All four targets will be worked on by Tom, the contract adult and the social worker, in the following way:

Contract adult's work—actions

Being part of environment work.
Communicating and receiving feedback from social worker on his work.
Using his relationship with Tom:

To help Tom keep his links with the family.
To help Tom with his efforts to find suitable employment.
To help Tom with business arrangements, board lodgings payments, social
    security, etc.
To help Tom with personal matters—sex education, etc.
To help Tom bring his friends to the unit.
To help Tom become aware of his responsibilities to the environment.
To help Tom form links in the community.

Clearly stating what his role is to Tom.
Receiving supervision on his work on targets from senior staff of unit.
Contacting Tom's parents as representative of unit. Working the timing and nature of introduction through his supervisor and links with social worker. Using this contact as means of starting a relationship with the parents, by explaining what his role with Tom is.

Later he might be able to interpret to Tom their behaviour and Tom's behaviour to them, on a basic level. Being aware he is into family dynamics, and that there is at present a limited family target of keeping lines open. If there is any marked change in the parents' attitude, which should be picked up via supervision and feedback from social worker, a case conference should be called so that all are involved in change or plans.

Tom's work—action

To be involved in the environment. Making his contribution to this by, as he suggested at intake, talking to other young people who are trying to take serious consideration of the situation.

Attendance at unit community meetings.

(1)

TABLE 6.1. *Case plan for child to be admitted to residential care*

Name Tom   Age 16   Referring Agency —

	Personal development of child (A)	Family Natural (B)	Family Planned substitute (C)	Environment Home (D)	Environment Planned substitute (E)	Referring Agency School — Home environment (F)	Referring Agency School — Planned substitute (G)	Relevance of unit (H)
Proposed admission date: — Name of unit: — Name of social worker: — Name of contract adult: —								
Why is the child being admitted to residential care? (1)	In need of care and control (see over)	Mum and Dad unable to give care and control	Tom has outgrown small family group home	N/A	N/A	N/A	N/A	Can offer a care and control structure
What is to be gained by his/her admission? (2)	Time for Tom to build on progress already	Time for separation with understanding and harmony	N/A as Tom has outgrown grown unit but Tom will visit	Time to suss out possible future contacts (see over)	N/A	N/A Tom left school this week	N/A	Have time to give to plans
What is hoped for? (3)	1. More stability 2. Start work (see over)	Communication between Tom/parents	N/A	Stable links	N/A	N/A	N/A	Have staff who can work as a team with Tom/social worker

How will this be made?	(4)	Tom giving serious thought to his life (with help from contract adult/social worker)	By trying to interpret to each what is happening to Tom	N/A	By Tom/social worker + contract adult looking for links	N/A/	N/A	Ability to accept adolescents growing up
Who will do the work?	(5)	Tom supported by Unit/social worker/contract adult	Tom by still visiting contract adult/social worker	N/A	Tom by taking up opportunities which are open to him	N/A	N/A	Unit has the ethos for working in the here and now
How long will it take?	(6)	Not certain. It is hoped 1–2 years	6 months		6 months			Unit can be committed for 1–2 years

Date plan was made: As at Intake Conference

Who was Present? Tom,
Unit Head,
Social worker,
Contract adult,
Head of children's home.

Who will have copies? All those present at Intake Conference

(2)

TABLE 6.2. *If necessary—elaboration of case plan*

Number and letter of elaboration	Description of problem	Effects of problem	Further action	Priority rating
1A	Tom has had a chequered career of delinquency.	Tom in trouble with police. Is likely to go to Borstal if present plan breaks down.	Tom to continue progress already made. Contract adult to discuss Tom's progress in taking responsibility for his own care and control.	Top priority on going support from contract adult, social worker and Unit.
2D	Although Tom cannot live at home with his parents he likes the area and wishes to have bedsitter accommodation there eventually.	In the past Tom has mixed with the disruptive delinquent element in the area.	If Tom wishes to live in his original home area more positive and supportive links must be made.	Top priority will be given to finding positive link. Low priority to finding a bedsitter possibly 6 months' time
3A	Work is difficult to find but Tom is willing to start as a labourer on a building site.	It will not be helpful for Tom to be out of work. If he cannot find work he will start a course at a College of Further Education.	Tom and contract adult must actively seek employment.	Top priority.

Cleaning his room and cooking his own breakfast.

Visiting his family.

Getting to know his community is another way than at present, e.g., as he is keen on football, trying to gain a place in the hostel five-a-side team who play local youth clubs. Inviting his girlfriend to the unit.

Actively seeking the kind of employment he wants. Being aware that he has positive links through unit, contract adult and social worker to help him achieve those things he agreed he wanted at intake conference.

Social worker's work—action

Visiting unit, being aware of what goes on, having a meal, attending case conferences, reviews, etc.

His continuing relationship with Tom, keeping this on a level to match agreed targets.

His statutory obligation with Tom's parent. Being aware of how the family are feeling if target is being met. Feeding this back through contract adult.

Together with contract adult working on keeping lines open, each being aware that it is not the present target to restore Tom to his parents. If the focus changes, then a new plan must be made with new or slightly different targets involving all who made the original plan.

All targets will be reviewed at the 6-monthly unit review.

Notes and References

1. H. SPECHT and A. VICKERY, *Integrating Social Work Methods*, Chapter 12, Attitudes to Residential Care, p. 201.
2. *Adoption and Fostering*, **92** (2), 1978, p. 25.
3. The words "strategic" and "tactical" have been used by me as a shorthand explanation. For fuller details see *Social Values, Objectives and Action*, by JIMMIE ALGIE.
4. A. TREISCHMANNS, J. K. WHITTAKER and K. BRENTANO, *The Other 23 Hours*, Aldine, 1969.
5. SPECHT and VICKERY, *op. cit.*, Part 2, p. 107.
6. N. HAZEL, Children in care should be in transit, *Community Care*, 5 July 1978.
7. D. CLOUGH, Residential care: positive alternative, *Adoption and Fostering*, **92** (2), 1978.
8. See chapter on Making Initial Contacts in A. PINCUS and A. MINAHAN, A Model for Social Work Practice, in SPECHT and VICKERY, *op. cit.*, p. 97.
9. ALGIE, *op. cit.*, Chapter 4, Positive Pole, p. 83.
10. *Crisis Intervention as a Mode of Treatment, Creativity in Social Work*, selected writings of LYDIA RAPPOPORT, edited by S. N. KATZ, Chapter 5, p. 103.
11. PINCUS and MINAHAN, *loc. cit.*
12. P. BRUGGEN, J. BYNG-HALL and T. PITT-AIKENS, The reason for admission as a focus of work for an Adolescent Unit, *British Journal of Psychiatry*, **122** (568), Mar. 1973.
13. R. PAIGE and G. A. CLARK (eds.), *Who Cares*, National Children's Bureau, 1977, p. 16.
14. F. HOLLIS, Contemporary issues for caseworkers, *Smith College Studies in Social Work*, **XXX** (2), 1960.

CHAPTER 7

AN ASSESSMENT CHALLENGED

DWYNWEN WILLIAMS

In an attempt to determine to what degree admission into residential care may add to, or may often cause, confusion in the elderly it was decided that a concentrated observational exercise should be carried out with a lady resident, who had been assessed as being "confused and mentally disorientated".

Mrs J. was admitted in the first instance to Home A a few days after the death of her husband, whom she had nursed at home for some considerable time, having lived in this house for 40 years. She was taken out of Home A to attend the funeral of her husband and was returned that same evening. Her behaviour in the following 9 weeks appeared to confirm the original assessment of confusion and disorientation; she was continually attempting to leave Home A to return to her own home, and at times became aggressive. As a result of great pressures on the staff at Home A, since they had three "very confused" residents there who were all making attempts to leave, arrangements were made for Mrs J. to be transferred to Home B. It was thought that by separating these three residents, pressure would be relieved and the danger of someone being injured by traffic immediately outside Home A would be avoided.

Admission

Mrs J. arrived at Home B at 3.00 p.m. with a social worker and her son-in-law. She appeared quite rational and was in fact quite aware of her new surroundings and commented that she liked the front carpet very much. I welcomed her to Home B and introduced her to a care assistant who was with me at the time. Our first discussion, which took place before she removed her coat, and while sitting in her bedroom, was about her chapel, her room, and the fact that she hated sewing but enjoyed crocheting. Mrs J. showed a little reluctance to remove her coat and hat, but eventually this was done and general discussion about her room helped this awkward moment to pass. Mrs J. was then left in the capable hands of two care assistants who helped her to place her clothes in the wardrobe and drawers.

While this was taking place I had a discussion with Mrs J.'s son-in-law who told me quite frankly that he had in fact travelled some distance overnight to stop this transfer taking place. When I asked him his reasons for this, he stated that his wife, (Mrs J.'s daughter) was very distressed, and that they felt that to move Mrs J. out of her natural environment (meaning that Home A was nearer to her original family home) was completely wrong. He straight away added that after having spent a few hours in the company of his mother-in-law and the two other "confused" ladies in question, he could quite understand the reason for the transfer. Apparently, while he was there the three residents has been planning a method of leaving the building together; this conversation surprised and shocked him. He stated that even though his mother-in-law had shown signs of "confusion" for some time, she had not been aggressive, but in the company of the other women she had shown considerable aggression and her language was not the kind she normally used. He then left and Mrs J. was shown around the home and introduced to other residents and staff. During tea and up to 5.30 p.m. Mrs J. was quiet and took part in discussion directed at her.

The First Evening

Mrs J. was sitting in a lounge when one of the residents rang the bell to inform us that Mrs J. was preparing to "go home". When I approached her she was aggressive, and stated that she was Mrs J. and that no one could force her to stay. She then said that if I did not show her how to get out she would smash the doors and windows. I told her that I had no intention of forcing her to stay but that her doctor had said that she was extremely tired and needed a rest, so I thought it best if she stayed a while until she had recovered her strength enough to take care of herself. After my walking up and down the corridor with her a number of times her aggression gradually ceased and she admitted that she was in fact "so very tired". She was persuaded to sit down in her bedroom. In the conversation which followed Mrs J. still insisted that she should go home because of the danger her brothers and sisters were in during her absence. She was encouraged to talk about her brothers and sisters and it emerged that she had brought up the family of nine children when her mother died. Mrs J. was only 16 years old at this time. Mrs J. was a trained soprano, and was apparently heading for a promising career in singing when her mother died and it became impossible to continue with the career she had hoped to pursue. Mrs J. then looked after her family, the youngest being 4 years of age. She eventually married and moved to her own house, but her father used to insist on her cooking, cleaning and washing for him. During the Depression her sister, then 15 years old, had to go to London to take a job "in service". Mrs J. gave her sister half her clothing "to be tidy going to London", she took her to the local station and put her on the London train, and said she had not seen or heard from her since that day. Another sister died, but Mrs J. could not remember how old she was, though she remembered that the sister had a surviving daughter who did not bother with Mrs J. at all.

She remembered the names of four brothers, but she was not sure about the other two. She remembered that one had married a girl from her village, and that he had been killed in the Second World War. She believed that two brothers still lived in the London area. Mrs J. then had a baby girl, the daughter who now lived some distance away and who Mrs J. said did not want her. It was this daughter's husband who had accompanied Mrs J. on her admission to Home B. She also had had a baby boy who died tragically at the age of 15 months. He had apparently fallen down a small step at home but no one thought there was any bad injury. She says that for 6 weeks he cried quite a lot and one day she noticed a patch on his knee turning black. He was admitted to hospital where they amputated a gangrenous leg, and he died 2 days later.

Throughout the past hour references had been made to her husband's death, but she had quickly gone on to change the subject. However, she did finally say, "Yes I've had a hard life, I've lost my brother and my husband in the last few weeks. My husband went into hospital and had his two legs amputated." Mrs J. then went on to say that she had been in hospital for an operation to remove her gall bladder, and that she and her husband had ceased to have sexual intercourse. By this time Mrs J. was extremely tired and changed and went to bed without any trouble at all. No sleeping tablets were given. Her words before she went to sleep were "I don't think the Queen would be treated better than this". Mrs J. was observed frequently throughout the night, but she slept all night with no disturbances.

Day Two

Mrs J. woke in a happy frame of mind, washed and dressed herself, chatting to Mrs S. —her room-mate—quite sensibly. Mrs J. took note of all around her during the day. She read the daily papers, watched television and tidied up the top of her locker and dressing table. The day was a pleasant and uneventful one for Mrs J. until 5.45 p.m. when she started to show signs of agitation and stated that she was contacting the police to inform them that she was being held prisoner. I offered to contact the police for her and she immediately said that she had done nothing wrong, and there was no need to see the police. Her aggression was easily coped with by staff involving her in other subjects of discussion. She was calmed down in about three-quarters of an hour, and returned to the lounge of her choice where she talked and watched television until she went to bed at her desired time (10.15 p.m.). Again, Mrs J. was observed frequently during the night but she slept all night.

Day Three

Mrs J. was very pleasant when she woke and said she was looking forward to her cup of tea in bed. She rose from bed, washed and dressed herself, and put on clean under-clothes. She was obviously much more at ease with her surroundings today.

During the course of the day, Mrs J. discovered that Mrs B., one of the other residents, was known to her and they chatted about days gone by in their village. Mrs J. also started forming a relationship with Mrs M., one of our day care ladies. This relationship advanced so that when Mrs M. went into the kitchen to help with the dishes, Mrs J. joined her, and they spent half an hour seeing that the dishes and cutlery were all put away in their right places. Mrs J. took great interest in the other ladies who were knitting items ready for our summer fair in June. She decided she would crochet something but after a few attempts she gave up and said she had not done this for so long her hands were hurting. She did, however, say that she would try again tomorrow. We decided not to attempt to encourage her to keep trying. Mrs J. did maintain her interest in what she saw going on, but purely as an observer.

Early in the evening, Mrs J.'s daughter telephoned to speak to me. When the call was put through to me I asked the staff to try and get Mrs J. to my office so that if she wished she could speak to her daughter when I had finished. Her daughter stated that since her husband had returned home after transferring her mother to us, she now felt a lot easier about the situation. She felt helpless being so far away and asked my opinion of her mother's being transferred at some time in the future to a home in the area in which the daughter lived so that she could carry out what she thought were her duties to her mother, thereby maintaining their natural relationship. I stated that at this present time we would be feeling our way very quietly and patiently with her mother and hopefully, in time, some of the confusion might clear, thereby enabling her mother to live as full a life as possible. We would not mention transferring her mother at present. She agreed to this, and was surprised when I said that her mother was waiting to speak to her. Not having seen Mrs J. for the past hour, I warned her daughter that it was possible her mother could at this time of the day be a little aggressive, but that this was not the general pattern throughout the day. As it turned out, my fears were groundless. Mrs J. was delighted to speak to her daughter, and she was quite rational during the conversation. Mrs J.'s daughter left a message with one of the staff saying that this was the first positive response she felt she had had from her mother for quite some time. Mrs J. returned to the lounge and watched the television until she went to bed at 10.30 p.m. when she was obviously in a good frame of mind. She slept all night again without disturbance.

Day Four—Mrs J.'s Birthday

Mrs J. woke in a good mood, washed and dressed herself and spent a happy morning opening birthday cards and receiving good wishes from the staff and residents. She received a lovely bowl of flowers from her daughter.

Mrs J. decided to sit in the quiet room, which is adjacent to the front door. The front door had been wide open most of the morning but Mrs J. had not shown any obvious interest in it, even though she had walked past it to go to the toilet.

We watched closely but not obviously. Mrs J. did not attempt to leave or state any desire to do so.

The morning passed, Mrs J. having had discussions with residents who usually spend their day in the quiet room, and after lunch Mrs J. helped to wipe the dishes and put away the cutlery. She returned to the lounge where the ladies were knitting and she tried to do some knitting herself. She became very frustrated and angry when she could not do the knitting. At this point she was taken for a walk around the home to meet some other residents. Mrs J. obviously enjoys the company of others, and was quite happy with the personal introductions. She appeared to adopt a very benevolent attitude with some of the residents, and she did not appear to be aware, I believed, that she was in a residential setting herself. We both returned to the office where she told me how sorry she felt for the people she had just met, and how awful it was that they had no home to go to.

In the evening she ate a good supper and stated that the food in "this place" was very good, but about an hour later, around 7.30 p.m., Mrs J. became agitated, though not aggressive. She stated her concern for her brothers and sisters. When reminded that these brothers and sisters were all either married or dead, she appeared to realise her confusion and stated how silly she was to have forgotten. Mrs J. then spent some time going over events that had eventually led up to the death of her husband. No mention was made of her admission or residence at Home A. Finally about an hour later she became very tired, went to bed and slept all night.

Day Five

Mrs J. washed and dressed herself and appeared to be in a happy frame of mind.

At 8.30 a.m. she had a good breakfast and helped to clear and wash the dishes, after which she sat in a lounge with some other ladies, and generally discussed the weather, television and papers. At coffee time, she collected the cups and stacked them neatly for staff to take away. During lunch she started worrying about her father and who was going to put his food right for him, after lunch becoming very agitated and wanting to go home to look after her father. She insisted that we were forcing her to stay by keeping her locked in. A member of staff put to Mrs J. the facts regarding distance from Home B to her own house and the problems of transport. Mrs J. then decided that it was too cold to leave just then and said "When I'm a bit stronger, I'll get someone to take me home in the car". After a walk around inside the home she returned to the lounge and appeared to be more settled in.

Around 3.30 p.m. Mrs J. had a good tea but refused to help with dishes. She slept from 5.00 to 5.15 p.m. in the lounge, after which she watched television for short periods but appeared very unsettled, getting up and walking around corridors and dining rooms looking for "Dilys".

At 6.35 after having had a very good supper, she did not feel like clearing the dishes: she said, "I've worked hard all my life, I don't see why I should wash dishes for you."

Later that evening there was an incident when Mrs J. was discovered trying to break the other ladies Easter bonnets in the lounge. She was restrained from causing any more destruction, by gentle force and persuasion. Mrs J. then asked to go to bed because she was very tired. At 8.00 p.m. she needed help to undress for bed, and went to sleep almost immediately.

Day Six

Mrs J. slept until 5 a.m. when she woke in a very distressed state. She had had a nightmare about her husband but could not remember the details, only that she felt sure he was alive. She was given a cup of tea by the night staff who stayed with her until she had gone through the stage of returning to a realisation of the "here-and-now" situation—about half an hour. Mrs J. then went back to sleep until 7.00 a.m. She appeared to be extremely quiet on waking, and did everything mechanically throughout the day. When attempts were made to include her in what was going on, she closed her eyes and appeared to shut herself off from personal contact. She ate less than usual and went to bed when asked if she was tired at 9.30 p.m.

At 11.00 p.m. Mrs J. got out of bed and went into the lounge. She was given a cup of tea and biscuits by the night staff because she said she was hungry. She returned to bed 11.45 p.m. and slept all night.

For the next 12 days Mrs J. had no distressing episodes, but appeared to be settling in and gaining knowledge of the group she had spent most time with. Most of the time she was a passive member of the group but now and again she would contribute conversation with them and therefore add stimulation to the group. At times she would entertain them with a song and all of them agreed that she had a good singing voice. She slept uneventfully every night.

Day Eighteen

Mrs J. attended the Day Centre for tea along with 22 other residents; she seemed to enjoy this and also entertained the people at the centre.

Day Twenty-Two

Mrs J. complained of feeling tired and weak. She was seen by the doctor who prescribed a course of iron tablets. During the following week Mrs J. seemed much better, eating well and each day seemed to bring more confidence.

Mrs J. complained of sore mouth and headache; Solphadeine was given for the headache, and Bonjela applied to her mouth.

Day Twenty-Eight

Mrs J. appeared to be feeling well. Her daughter telephoned and arranged with Mrs J. to collect her and take her for a holiday to her home by the sea at the weekend— in 5 days time. During those few days, Mrs J. was busy, having been involved in the preparation of her clothes and personal items to take on holiday. She was very happy and looking forward to her holiday. The evening before she was due to go away Mrs J. had a bath and one of the staff washed and set her hair. She wanted to go to bed at 6.30 p.m. but was encouraged to stay up until after night drinks at 8.30 p.m. This was done because it was thought she would wake very early and the time would seem never ending to her until she was picked up at 1.00 p.m. the following day.

Day Thirty-Three

Mrs J. woke at 6.45 a.m. She dressed immediately after her cup of tea. She did not want a cooked breakfast in case it upset her on the journey.

At 12.30 p.m. after lunch one of the staff gave her undivided attention to Mrs J., helping her with her clothing, her hair, and to contain her agitation about what she thought was the lateness of the arrival of her daughter. Mrs J.'s son-in-law arrived at 1.10 p.m. and they all left at 1.20 p.m. Some of the residents and staff were outside to see Mrs J. off.

Day Forty-One

Mrs J. returned to the home at 4.30 p.m. She was very happy but very tired. When she came into the home she was welcomed by staff and residents who were interested to find out if she had enjoyed her holiday. I asked her son-in-law how the week had been, and he replied: "Surprisingly it went very well; I think she enjoyed herself." After having a cup of tea with Mrs J. he left to return home. After supper, Mrs J. sat and told the residents who were interested about her week with her daughter. She went to bed at 7.30 p.m. and slept all night.

Day Forty-Two

When Mrs J. awoke she thought at first that she was still at her daughter's home; it did not appear to distress her when she realised that she was in fact back at Home B. After breakfast, Mrs J. asked if she could help with the dishes. This she did, and for the rest of that day she had great delight in telling in detail the experiences of the past week, and during the following days she settled quite well and enjoyed her new-found popularity within her group, as she now had so much more than some of them to talk about.

Day Forty-Eight

At 2.30 a.m. Mrs J. was discovered out of her bed, agitated, and wanting to go out of the building. The night staff persuaded her to sit in the lounge and gave her a cup of tea. They talked to her for almost an hour. Her main concern, it appeared, was that all her belongings were still in her own house and she was afraid someone would break in and steal them. She was assured that her daughter had in fact cleared out most of her furniture, but that someone would be contacted in the morning to verify this. Mrs J. then settled down and went to sleep about 3.30 a.m.

The following morning I had a long chat with Mrs J. about her position, her house, her daughter and any other subjects Mrs J. brought up. She was still naturally upset over the death of her husband. Mrs J. also said that she could not manage to live on her own, but that her daughter would like her to go to a home like Home B though in her daughter's area, so that Mrs J. could be near her. Mrs J. felt that in some ways this would be very nice, because then she would see her daughter more often and have the opportunity of visiting her daughter's home when it was convenient. But she would not like to spend too much time with her son-in-law as they did not get on very well. Mrs J. said that she was quite happy in Home B and was concerned that if she moved then she would not like it so much, but she obviously was giving this move some very serious, intelligent thought.

During the course of this conversation Mrs J. was informed that there was still £54.00 outstanding on her husband's funeral bill, and that she would be receiving insurance money and the death grant due to her in the near future. These amounts totalled £50.00 so there would be £4.00 to add to it to clear the bill. She became upset and said that she wanted to pay this as soon as possible, because she had never owed anyone a penny, and until she had paid it she would not have done her duty to her husband. I promised to take her to pay this bill as soon as the money came through. We then discussed her house, and she said that she would like to check to see if there was anything in the house that she would like to keep. This could be arranged for the same day we were to go to pay the funeral bill.

Once again it appeared that the pressures of facing up to and accepting reality brought resulting disorientation. By 11.00 p.m. Mrs J. had been into a gentleman's bedroom situated next door to her own and left her shoes there, also used his drinking glass and had lain down on his bed. She had also entered a lady resident's bedroom two doors away from her own, taken her nightdress out of her drawer, put it on, and then got into the lady's bed. Both residents were extremely upset but after their beds had been changed, as they had demanded, they went to bed. The following morning I explained to both residents some of the reasons for this distressing confusion, and assured them that a close eye would be kept on the situation. These explanations were accepted. Mrs J. was put to bed and slept all night apparently unaware of the upset she had caused.

As a result of this incident the two residents involved asked for keys to their bedroom doors. These I gave them on the understanding that they did not lock the doors when they were inside. This they agreed to, and have not gone against this agreement up to the present time. Neither of them smokes, and the master key is available to staff in charge.

About a month later a case conference regarding Mrs J. was held at Home B. This included the Social Worker, the Senior Residential Officer, the Senior Social Worker and Officer-in-Charge of Home B. The current situation regarding Mrs J. was reviewed but there had been no obviously uncharacteristic episodes since the episode in the previous month.

The intended visit to the funeral director and the planned visit to Mrs J.'s home were the topics of conversation in the next few days.

Day One Hundred and Three

Mrs J. and the Officer-in-Charge left Home B at 9.30 a.m. after an uneventful morning, the funeral director was expecting us at 10.00 a.m. When we arrived Mrs J. apologised for the delay in clearing the bill, but assured him that if she had not been ill it would have been paid before. Mrs J. had accepted this duty as her responsibility and carried it out perfectly, without any sign of confusion. We then went to her home which was in a street that was obviously part of a very close community. The next door neighbour had the key to Mrs J.'s house and when she came to the door she was very pleased to see Mrs J. as were a dozen other neighbours whom we saw in the following hour, including old and young alike. Mrs J. was very anxious to go inside the house and yet at the same time was anxious to greet her neighbours in the proper manner. We did, however, eventually go inside the house, and after a quick look around as she walked through, Mrs J. immediately picked up the dishcloth and proceeded to clean the hand-basin which was in a dirty condition.

During the next hour, Mrs J. went from extremes of delight to those of distress when small items and photographs were found. She put together things that had personal meanings to her to bring back to Home B for her room. We talked all the while about her husband, their experiences together, good and bad, about her neighbours and about her family and her village. At one stage Mrs J. said she thought she could manage if she came back home, but she eventually worked out for herself that she could not live and manage alone after all. After collecting all her chosen possessions and putting them into the car, we were invited into next door for tea and biscuits. At no time at all during these two visits were there any indications of confusion, there was just pure down-to-earth grief, and loss of a life that had been led in a very close community. Mrs J. wished everyone goodbye, and invited them all to call to see her. As we drove out of the street, Mrs J. said, "That was a great street, we all had some smashing times there, we were poor, but we enjoyed ourselves."

Since that day there have been no episodes of confusion, depression or other distressing incidents. Mrs J. now talks freely about her family and husband, and her life in days gone by, and they are all in the proper context. She is now looking forward to a holiday with her daughter again, when it is hoped a visit to a residential home in that area can be arranged, so that in the event of Mrs J. having a transfer there she will be able to say she knows where she is going.

Discussion

Mrs J. had been living under great strain prior to admission; nevertheless, she was able to carry out the task of caring for her husband and herself in her own familiar surroundings that gave her comfort, confidence and security. Her husband's need of her made her own life purposeful. When Mrs J.'s husband died, she was removed from her familiar, secure home and placed in a completely strange, alien situation while suffering the trauma of the loss of her husband.

She was taken from Home A to attend her husband's funeral and then returned that same evening to suffer her grief with strangers. I believe she found this situation intolerable, and therefore she began the process of denying her husband's death. From her point of view her continual striving to return to her own safe and comfortable surroundings was being obstructed and this resulted in her showing a natural aggression. Her move to a second home, even though this was done to protect Mrs J. from physical harm. must have added greatly to her mental anxiety and therefore added pressure to what was already an extremely traumatic experience.

Due to a concentrated effort by all staff, it was possible to help Mrs J. return to the "here-and-now" situation by living through and accepting her grief. Sadly, I have to admit that due to levels of staffing in homes today, plus the increasing disabilities of residents, it is impossible to guarantee every resident a similar opportunity to the one happily given to Mrs J.

The opportunity to take responsibility for her financial commitments arising out of her husband's funeral expenses helped to restore her confidence, and the visit to her own home was important. Through this visit she was able to recognise the reality that she was at this time unable to look after herself, she was able to retrieve cherished possessions, and say goodbye to her neighbours in a way which had not been possible when she first left her home. Invitations to the home offered at least some prospect of continuity with her former life.

The case of Mrs J. illustrates how we tend to use the word "confused" too often and too lightly. In this instance a bereaved person was reacting to a situation which she did not fully understand: the admission in quick succession into two strange living situations where the routines and life-style were totally different from the way in which she had lived her life for many years previously, combined with her fear that her daughter would reject her. Her difficult behaviour was a natural reaction to her unhappy situation.

As residential staff, we need to be aware of these issues and, as far as possible, prepare residents carefully beforehand for admission with a number of visits. If in the case of emergency admissions this is not possible, then residential staff need to be able to respond appropriately to the feelings of a resident when they present themselves in actions.

Further Reading

BREARLEY, P. C., *Residential Work With The Elderly*, Routledge & Kegan Paul, 1977.
HANSON, J., *Residential Care Observed*, Age Concern, 1971.
MEACHER, M., *Taken for a Ride: Special Residential Homes for Confused Old People*, Longman, 1972.

PERSONAL SOCIAL SERVICES COUNCIL, *Residential Care Reviewed*, 1977.
ROBB, B., *Sans Everything*, Nelson, 1967.

All the above titles deal directly with the elderly in residential care: TOWNSEND, P., *The Last Refuge*, Routledge & Kegan Paul, 1962, though outdated now in some respects, is still useful particularly to show the developments and changes which have taken place.

Related topics of interest might be:
GOLDBERG, E. M., *Helping The Aged*, Allen & Unwin, NISW Series, 1970, a study of the effects of the work of field social workers with elderly clients.

More general studies of the elderly are:
BREARLEY, P. C., *Social Work, Ageing and Society*, Routledge & Kegan Paul, 1975.
BROMLEY, D., *The Psychology of Human Ageing*, Penguin, 1974.

Issues raised in relation to this chapter might be followed up in:
FELSTEIN, I., *Sex in Later Life*, Penguin, 1973.
HINTON, J., *Dying*, Penguin, 1967.
KÜBLER-ROSS, E., *On Death and Dying*, Tavistock, 1970.
TUNSTALL, J., *Old And Alone*, Routledge & Kegan Paul, 1966.

INTRODUCTION: AN INTEGRATED
APPROACH TO CARE AND TREATMENT

What is residential social work? The term is used to describe a wide variety of roles occupied by those who are employed to look after others living in groups outside their natural families. Thus, it is used to describe work with a range of client groups, within at least four professional disciplines, and the operation of a wide variety of modes of care. The table shows the range of provision and different models of care, and one way to begin to define the role of a residential establishment might be to identify the point or points in each column appropriate to that establishment. It will be apparent that a large number of combinations are possible for any one client group.

One way of looking at the concept of integration is in bringing together the disparate client groups, knowledge and practice areas illustrated in the table and to look at the common elements in the way practice takes place. The integrating factors would appear to be in the area of values, processes and skills common to work with each of these differing client groups, and common knowledge areas from the social services and other disciplines.

Values

Social work in any setting operates within a value-context. A recent discussion document[1] describes a value as that which determines what a person thinks he ought to do, which may or may not coincide with his wishes, his interests or his actions. A value therefore becomes a socially accepted standard guiding an individual in the making of choices. The document considers concepts which would find broad agreement among social workers in most settings: respect for persons, reflected, for example, in the use of the idea of contract expressing mutual rights and obligations in the client–worker relationship; respect for life, a value which sometimes holds conflict for a social worker trying to uphold the autonomy of a client, for example in cases of NAI, in abortion-counselling, and in working with suicidal clients. Other values identified in the discussion document are: acceptance—the attitude which recognises the inherent worth of an individual irrespective of his actions: confidentiality, and individualisation. Social work literature abounds with discussion on values and identifies them in various ways, but the present purpose is merely to illustrate that it is possible to recognise a common value-system across what would appear to be a great diversity of practice in residential and other settings in which social work is practised.

Processes' Skills and Techniques

Common processes are apparent not only in the differing models of practice in which residential care operates, but also in other social work settings. The assessment of social situations, engagement or the beginning processes in the formation of relationships; sustaining those relationships in order to bring about change of some kind; disengaging from and terminating those relationships; these are all stages which are apparent in all social work settings. Similarly, the skills and techniques used in these situations to achieve agreed goals are common in many areas of social work practice, and some of these are listed in column 4 of the table.

Knowledge Areas

The knowledge needed by all social workers again indicates common ground. Knowledge drawn from a variety of academic disciplines is needed if a social worker is to attempt to understand the functioning of individuals and groups within their social context. Thus, knowledge drawn from psychology, sociology, philosophy, medicine and law should inform the way in which a social worker in any setting intervenes in a social situation.

Another way of looking at the concept of integration is in the context of integrated methods in social work theory. This represents an attempt to provide a conceptual framework for the activities involved in casework, groupwork and community work approaches as well as residential social work. It is sometimes also called a "unitary" approach. The major contributors to this approach are Bartlett,[3] Pincus and Minahan,[4] Goldstein[5] and Specht and Vickery.[6] This approach emphasises the importance of choice of method of intervention in relation to the needs of the problem as opposed to the training of the social worker. Much social work practice in Britain continues to be casework oriented because this has been how workers were trained until recently, irrespective of whether other methods of social work intervention might be more appropriate. This kind of approach has important implications for residential work.

In any form of social work, the way in which a problem is defined determines the nature of the intervention to deal with that problem. One important factor in determining the residential task has been the way residential provision has been used as a response to a particular form of problem definition. People who are admitted to residential establishments are usually seen to be no longer capable of maintaining themselves in the community or have behaved in ways which offend society's mores or break its laws. They are seen to have experienced a breakdown in their social functioning and so the problem is defined in terms of individual deficiency or pathology. Any intervention either to "cure" the problem, or where this is not possible to alleviate the symptoms of it, is therefore seen to be that which focusses on individual change. It leads to a system of residential care where the worker deals only with the resident within the boundaries of the institution, where the fieldworker's role is mainly prior to admission and where other people and agencies are contacted usually only to collect the information required to assess the client's situation (Diagram 1). An alternative way of describing the problem being experienced by a person resulting in admission to residential care would be to see it as a breakdown in the informal and formal helping network around that individual in

1	2	3	4	5
Client group	Model of provision	Function of establishment	Methods of intervention	Professional group
Physically handicapped—(children and adults)	Unstaffed group home	Substitute home	Casework/relationship work	Social services
	Sheltered accommodation		Counselling	
Mentally handicapped—(children and adults)	Hostel	Asylum (refuge)	Groupwork	
	Residential home		Family therapy	
Sensory handicap—(children: deafness, blindness)	Community home	Therapy/treatment	Individual and group therapy	Education
			Therapeutic community	
	Family group home		Milieu therapy	
Disturbed/maladjusted (children)	Hospital	Education	Psycho-drama	
			Transactional analysis	
Deprived/rejected (children)	School	Assessment	Behaviour modification	Medical
Elderly	Hotel		Social skills training	
	Detention centre		Token economy	
Mentally ill	Borstal institution	Social control	Teaching	
Homeless	Secure accommodation		Community work methods	
Offenders	Prison	Punishment	Advocacy	Penal

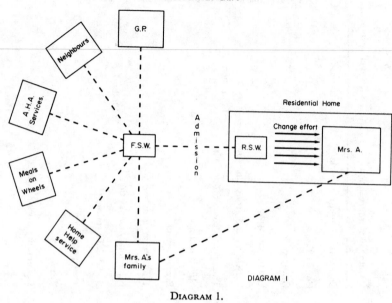

DIAGRAM 1.

the community. The following case sample illustrates how these two ways of defining the problem might result in differing strategies of intervention:

> Mrs A. was a widow in her early eighties, who after a fall and hospitalisation for a broken thigh found herself back at home, partially recovered, but less mobile than previously, partly due to the accident and partly due to the worsening of an arthritic condition. She became depressed and was worried about having another fall and lying injured for many hours as she had few callers. She began to neglect her food, the house and her person, and was referred to social services by the community nurse on a routine visit after she appeared to be very confused during their conversation. The subsequent occasional and short visits of the Meals on Wheels service twice a week and the Home Help did not improve the situation sufficiently and at her own request she was admitted to Part III accommodation.

This situation might be seen as an individual problem experienced by one elderly person, in which case improvement was brought into the situation by the provision of a substitute home with help on hand whenever required (Diagram 1). On the other hand it might also be seen as a failure of resources and policy to provide the amount of help she needed and similarly of family and neighbourhood networks, who were unable or who chose not to provide assistance. Admission to a residential home might be seen as a positive step to help her over a crisis, but in this case it would be important to work with the client's family and neighbourhood, perhaps locating and co-ordinating volunteer help, and to work at policy level to improve domicilary services with a view to the client's return to her own home if she so wishes (Diagram 2). This type of intervention, where there are other targets for change than the individual client, and where the method of intervention is one or more methods which are chosen as being the most appropriate to the problem, can be seen as an integrated approach to social work intervention.

In the situation illustrated by the second diagram, the client is deliberately moved

DIAGRAM 2

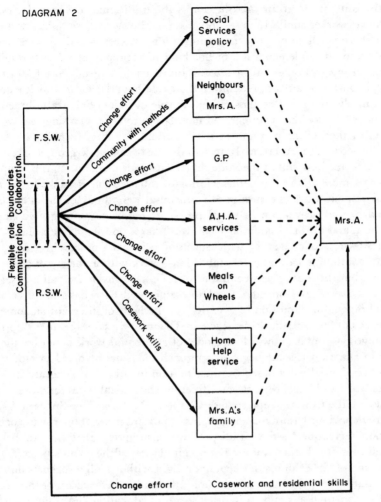

DIAGRAM 2.

from the central focus of the change effort, though this approach does not preclude worker–client interactions of the accepted kind. Other "targets" for change are brought within the compass of the social worker dealing with the case. Thus the Meals on Wheels and Home Help services are challenged and pressured to increase their services in the interests of a whole group of clients in similar circumstances to Mrs A. Social services policy becomes a legitimate target for change as the need for a peripatetic residential service (i.e. where the residential workers move into the client's home for a short time) to cover crisis situations is recognised. Community work skills are brought to bear in the motivating and co-ordinating of volunteers, and the setting up of a street warden scheme, again recognising that Mrs A. represents a whole group of clients in the area with similar problems.

The situation represented by the second diagram raises the question as to how the change effort is divided between field and residential workers. Liz Ward has examined some of the issues involved in working across the traditional role boundaries,[7] and the idea of the keyworker similarly raises these issues. However these tasks are divided, it is clear that there needs to be good communication between social workers operating in these roles, and an implementation of this kind of approach could well result in a different kind of integration—that of a team approach where residential and field social workers collaborate as a team, redefining their role boundaries, in which case there are important implications for the possible future role of residential establishments.[8]

Thus one way of looking at integrated methods in relation to residential work implies a choice of method of intervention or combination of methods which are most appropriate to the needs of the situation. It implies the use of casework, groupwork, community and residential method, but at the same time transcends these divisions by implying that in most cases more than one of these forms of intervention is likely to be necessary. Unilateral responses are the product of unicausal definitions of social problems, the recognition of multi-causation in social problems requires an integrated approach to their solution, and in this residential social work has a positive part to play.

In the following section dealing with aspects of social work process in residential care— assessment, continuing care and rehabilitation—work with a variety of client groups is represented, but there are areas common to those in terms of the value-base, the skills which the worker draws on, and the knowledge used as a basis for that work. The chapters also contain discussion of a variety of methods of intervention some of which clearly represent the situation identified in Diagram 1, some begin to approach the issues involved in moving towards a model of residential work based on the situation identified in Diagram 1, some begin to approach the issues involved in moving towards a model of residential work based on the situation identified in Diagram 2.

Readers will also be aware that very different theoretical bases for work with people in the residential setting are represented. Chapter 12, "Susan, the Successful Resolution of a 'Severe Behaviour Disorder' ", highlights important issues about the use of behaviour modification techniques*—the validity of the assumption that human behaviour is determined by reward; the ethics of the manipulation of the client's behaviour and the administration of, for example, a sleeping draught without full awareness on the part of the client that this is part of the programme; the undoubted success of the programme; the use of this method as opposed to other forms of education and training to alert staff to such important issues as to how to reinforce behaviour appropriately. These and other issues are discussed in Chapter 12, and in Chapter 10—"Social Learning and Residential Care", and also in Chapter 11—The C.U.S.S. Group Home. They are issues which like many others in the helping professions have no easy, clear-cut answers, but they are ones about which residential workers should formulate their own opinions as individuals and about which the profession as a whole should begin to work towards an accepted code of practice.

Chapters 13, 14 and 15, on the other hand, show clearly some of the issues raised by the practice of residential social work within a psycho-dynamic framework: the complexities involved in the term "relationship work"; the emphasis on intra-psychic, and inter-personnel processes at the expense of wider considerations, involving the structure

---

* A more general discussion of some of the ethical issues is to be found in I. Epstein, The Politics of Behaviour Therapy: the New Cool Out Casework, Chapter 9 in H. Jones (ed.), *Towards a New Social Work*, Routledge & Kegan Paul, 1975, and in D. Jehu (*et al.*), *Behaviour Modification in Social Work*, Wiley Interscience, 1972.

of society and the cultural roles and expectations placed on certain groups within that society—e.g. adolescents or the elderly—and the resulting problems experienced by those groups of people as well as individuals within the groups.

Readers are not being asked to take sides in the war between behavioural and psychodynamic psychology, or to become militants in the cause of radical social change as opposed to therapeutic strategies of intervention—implying that these stances are always mutually exclusive—but to consider carefully the issues involved, to be aware of the positives and negatives within each approach, and to recognise where there is basic agreement or incompatability in the underlying assumptions of each approach, as part of the process of improving service to the client.

The evolving concept of rehabilitating residents who may have been institutionalised for long periods, and the trend towards shorter stays in residential care, has led to an increasing focus on rehabilitation as part of the residential process.

In the early development of the philosophy and practice of rehabilitation there were many disappointments and failures. This was because of an inadequate appreciation of the long-term effects of institutionalisation and of the intensive preparation and support that residents would need before returning to the community and when they re-entered the community. More recently, rehabilitative programmes have analysed far more precisely the practical and social skills which are needed for leading a normal life in the community. Residential life has itself become less institutionalised and many establishments now include, in addition to skill training, intermediate settings which are very similar to those which a resident will encounter in the community, ranging from bed-sit accommodation on the premises to separate units in the grounds. These intermediate or halfway schemes enable residents to take a greater responsibility for all aspects of daily living and to use skill they have been developing at an early stage of their residential experience.

Previous chapters show that all establishments now carry a rehabilitation function to some degree. The contributions in this section demonstrate that with clearly formulated objectives and strong individual support and attention it is possible for residents who might have been thought unlikely to adapt to ordinary community life to make good progress, and attain a relatively satisfying and independent style of life. Success is dependent on strong commitment to rehabilitative goals, a carefully designed programme, and imaginative use of human resources, professional and voluntary, both in the residential setting and in the community.

The chapters in this section, then, reflect the present state of practice, which is itself in a stage of development, but which also contains much potential for an improved service to the client.

Notes and References

1. *Values in Social Work*, CCETSW, Paper 13, 1976, Chapter 2, para. 2.05, p. 14.
2. *Ibid.*, Chapter 2, para. 2.08, p. 15.
3. H. M. BARTLETT, *The Common Base of Social Work Practice*, New York, 1970.
4. A. PINCUS and A. MINAHAN, *Social Work Practice; Model and Method*, Peacock, USA, 1973.
5. H. GOLDSTEIN, *Social Work Practice: A Unitary Approach*, Columbia, USA, 1973.
6. H. SPECHT and A. VICKERY (eds), *Integrating Social Work Methods*, Allen & Unwin, National Institute of Social Work Series, No. 31, 1977.
7. L. WARD, Chapter 3, The Social Work Task in Residential Care.
8. See D. ELLIOTT, Integrated methods and residential work, *Social Work Today*, **9** (24), 1978.

CHAPTER 8

RESIDENTIAL CARE WITH THE PHYSICALLY HANDICAPPED – A VIEW FROM A VOLUNTARY ORGANISATION

GILLIAN CORNEY

Miller and Gwynne, in their pilot study of residential institutions for the physically handicapped and young chronic sick, *A Life Apart*, which was first published in 1972,[1] describe two models of institutional care, one of which, the "warehousing" model, represents all that disabled people fear most when they face the prospect of entering a residential home. In depicting the "warehouse", Miller and Gwynne describe a state in which the disabled person, rejected by society because he can no longer play any useful part in it, irrevocably enters an institution with impenetrably strong boundaries between itself and the outside world, so that he in effect suffers social death. Once inside the institution, he then surrenders all individuality and becomes more and more apathetic and lifeless, until he eventually succumbs to physical death.

This picture of residential homes thus having the primary task of "warehousing" or "storing" disabled people during their transition from social to physical death, is indeed a terrifying one, though it undoubtedly represented an accurate description of many institutions when Miller and Gwynne first published their study. Sadly, some such establishments still exist and as many people, disabled or not, still believe that this is the only kind of existence possible for the handicapped person in care, it would perhaps be useful to begin this consideration of residential care for the physically handicapped in 1978 by looking at the way in which many homes have moved very surely away from the warehouse model.

Physical Accommodation

It has been increasingly recognised by many organisations, not least the Cheshire Foundation, that the opportunity for the disabled resident to maintain his identity and remain very much alive must begin from the point of his admission, when he should have a room of his own, if he wishes, which he can furnish in his own way and in which he can enjoy complete privacy. In order to make this possible, then, many homes have engaged in large-scale building extensions in order to provide single-room accommodation in previously unsuitable big old buildings, while the newer homes are purpose built with single rooms. However, most homes also recognise that some people, particularly those who have been in institutional care all their lives, may prefer to share a room, and they are now including in most building schemes some double rooms, which can also be used by married couples.

Many residents, therefore, bring with them into the home furniture from their home in the community, while many of those who have been in care for some time are increasingly choosing to spend some of their Mobility Allowance in refurnishing newly acquired rooms. Thus, in many places, the visitor is aware of being invited not into an institution but into 15 or 20 different and often beautifully furnished homes within a home.

This is the beginning of enabling the resident to maintain individuality within the general life of the institution.

Activities and Work

Most residents coming into care will have had to give up work because of their disability long before admission, and many, too, perhaps having become increasingly helpless, will have given up even their leisure activities. In such a situation most are utterly depressed, feeling that they have no useful role to play in their family or in society at large, and many thus come feeling that they might as well resign themselves to tackling the inevitable basket-work which many people still regard as being the main activity of the physically handicapped.

Some homes, sadly, still do provide only this kind of activity for their residents but, happily, there are many others where, while residents do engage in craftwork, they produce really impressive products as part of a much wider undertaking. These are groups of residents who are entirely responsible for a business venture in which they order supplies for their work, and are responsible for the marketing of their products and for the financial considerations involved in such an enterprise. They share the profits that they make amongst themselves at an agreed rate.

One obvious difficulty that could arise in this situation is that of the different degrees of disability suffered by the workers in such a unit, disabilities which mean that one resident, though working to his utmost, might only be able to produce half the work done by a more able-bodied companion. This problem some units have overcome, with a decision made by the participating residents that people will be paid according to the hours they spend working, regardless of how much they actually produce in that time, provided that they are working to the best of their ability.

Apart from sharing profits amongst their workers, many groups also use part of it to buy something for the home which all the residents can enjoy, including those who cannot work. In doing this, the working members feel that they are making some useful contribution to the society of the home in which they live, and most enjoy the opportunity to give rather than always to receive.

There are, however, residents who, prior to illness or accident, have led very varied and active lives and, having no interest in craftwork, nevertheless want and need to be useful members in the society of the home. Increasingly, then, many such residents are being encouraged to accept responsibility for much of the day-to-day running of the home, from being involved in policy-making decisions as full members of management and admissions committees, to running the bar or the shop (including all the ordering of supplies and managing of accounts), planning and co-ordinating work done by volunteers in the home and entertaining professional and lay visitors. One home within the Cheshire Foundation has recently published a report[2] listing no fewer than 42 varied jobs which are the sole responsibility of some 38 of its 54 residents.

Given such activity, which involves considerable responsibility in many instances, residents are not merely being "kept active", but are clearly aware of making an important contribution to the community in which they live. In learning to accept such responsibility, residents also have an opportunity to grow and develop personally, their individual ability recognised and nurtured—the surest antidote to the threat of social death.

However active the community in which they find themselves, many residents, nevertheless, would like most of all to undertake paid employment outside, or to follow a career of their own, working from the home. This is because society still clearly values most those adults who can distinguish themselves by achieving independence and success in a career; while, for the disabled person, the ability to follow paid employment is one of the surest signs to the world at large that he has triumphed over disability and can still compete with his able-bodied peers. An as yet small number of residents with secretarial and book-keeping skills are, then, employed doing office work within particular homes, while some residents with these same skills are able to use them in employment in the community at large. A number of residents follow full-time work as clock and watch repairers, music teachers and academic tutors from particular homes, doing jobs in which they are much valued by the village and town communities in which the home is situated. A still smaller group of residents are highly successful artists, earning a considerable annual income.

The difficulty for any resident seeking to follow any sort of employment within a residential setting is, of course, the vexed problem of finance. The majority are sponsored by their local authority, and understandably that authority demands that a resident should make a contribution to his fees if he begins to earn. While some local authorities are prepared to allow residents to earn up to £10 per week without expecting a contribution to fees, others are less generous. Meanwhile, for the highly successful artist, life can be even more difficult, as he finds that all of his earnings may be taken up by his fees, unless the home itself is prepared to waive some of its charges.

Thus, as things stand at present, people in residential homes who are self-employed have little financial incentive to work, while those who accept jobs in the community at a rate which is not going to affect their fees not only lose their own status as valued workers but also arouse the wrath of fellow workers who fear "cheap labour". This very difficult area of existing policy has now been taken up at government level by the Legal and Parliamentary Committee of the Royal Association for Disability and Rehabilitation and the matter is still under discussion.

Activities Involving Risk

While many residents enjoy being involved in activity in terms of craftwork, or their own particular career, or in the general running of the home, with all the connotations in such activity of making a worthwhile contribution to the life of the home, there are many others who prefer to follow activities which bring pleasure only to themselves. Such residents sometimes meet opposition from staff and management committee members who voice a view still held by many of the public at large that disabled people should somehow be ever-grateful for all that has been provided and should, in return, devote any energy they may have to contributing to the life of the home.

Gradually, however, there is a growing awareness in many homes that to pay lip-service to the idea of offering residents as full and active a life as possible and then to complain if they choose to engage in activities that are purely pleasurable to themselves is somehow hypocritical. There is also an awareness that, far from being always saintlike and self-sacrificing, the disabled, like any other group of people, have amongst their number people who choose to live life simply to please themselves. Thus many homes are now far more prepared to rearrange meal times and to release staff for escort duties for residents who want to follow some activity of their own such as frequent visits to public houses, theatres, concert halls, or sports such as fishing, gliding and sailing.

Some of these activities clearly involve some degree of risk, and this again is a thorny problem which is being very firmly dealt with by staff and management committees. For many of the public still feel that people with physical handicap are somehow mentally handicapped too, so that the residential home must have a custodial responsi-bility. Understandably, mentally able and alert residents who want to pursue some activity which could involve risk find it totally frustrating that they should be banned from doing so simply because the staff and management committee of a home fear adverse public reaction should any accident occur. While management committees in charitable organisations are only too aware of the effect that adverse public opinion could have on the contribution of much-needed funds, nevertheless the more forward looking of them are now firmly of the opinion that, if a resident is fully aware of the risks he is taking, then he must without question be allowed to take those risks in the pursuit of any activity of his choice.

As an extension of this, some homes are encouraging decision-making by residents regarding activities within the building, which could put everyone at risk, e.g., smoking in bed. Some resident groups, then, not only make their own rules as to what is permis-sible in this respect, but also impose their own sanctions for the breaking of those rules.

Thus in yet another area of life, residents in taking responsibility individually and collectively for their own activities and for the risks involved in pursuing them, are able to experience further opportunity for personal growth and maturity.

Relationships within the Home

One cannot look at ways in which residential homes for the physically handicapped are seeking to avoid the social death of their residents by offering both the opportunity and the encouragement necessary for residents to maintain their individuality and to continue to develop as people, without looking at the opportunity afforded residents to make and develop relationships within the home. It is above all through meaningful relationship with other individuals that human beings develop best, through feeling valued and loved, and it is so often the lack of opportunity for such relationship that has prevented people long in institutional care from maturing. Meanwhile, for the newly disabled person, the lack of opportunity for such relationships in the future is, without doubt, one of the things he fears most about moving into care.

Miller and Gwynne[3] make the observation that staff in institutional "warehouses", who see their task as having total responsibility for the socially dead beings within their charge, inevitably regard resident relationships as extremely threatening, because residents in relationship with others, deriving support and developing individually as a result of friendship, are less easily controllable and far more likely to question the regime in the institution.

While few staff in residential homes today would admit to regarding resident relationships in this light, there are many who, while they will encourage resident freedom and participation fully in terms of work or leisure activity, are nevertheless very anxious at the prospect of residents making individual relationships other than general ones within the home.

Most would explain this anxiety in terms of not wanting to see residents hurt in personal relationships which go wrong. They quite rightly point out, too, that it is doubly difficult for people to recover from an unhappy relationship in residential care when, unlike the situation in the community at large, they cannot avoid seeing their former friend daily, at every meal time, with little chance of avoiding contact.

While staff express these fears about resident friendships which do not have a sexual element, they are undoubtedly even more anxious about male/female relationships and particularly about homosexual relationships. With some staff, this concern is undoubtedly because they have not come to terms with their own sexuality, particularly with regard to their feelings about disabled people themselves having sexual needs. Again, some staff concern is centred round the question of public opinion and what would be said if it were known that residents in a local home were enjoying sexual experience. Whatever the real reason for staff anxiety about such involvement, however, it is most often voiced in terms of a belief that residents are emotionally immature, factually ignorant about sex, inexperienced and therefore certain to get into difficulty. While this may be true of some residents, it is equally true of many able-bodied people whose right to such relationships few people would deny.

The activities of the Committee on the Sexual Problems of the Disabled, during the last 5 years, have done much to publicise the sexual and emotional difficulties of people with disability. As a result, many staff and management committees are now accepting that physically handicapped residents have a right to enjoy relationships of all kinds, accepting the risks of being hurt, in the same way as any other individual. The privacy of single-room accommodation has made the experience of sexual relationship far more possible, and more and more homes are prepared to offer married accommodation, as well as active aid in terms of advice and physical help with the sexual relationship, if this is asked for. As yet, however, no Cheshire Home is able to offer accommodation to couples who want to have children.

There are some residents who, while enjoying a physical relationship with another resident or someone from the general community, do not want to marry. Many homes are now defending the resident's right to such relationship, provided that it is carried on discreetly; while homosexual relationships between consenting partners are also being increasingly viewed in this light.

While staff and management committees who adopt such views are well aware that they run the risk of adverse public opinion, they are nevertheless prepared to take a stand on the grounds that resident relationships, sexual or otherwise, are yet another aspect of the risk-taking that is part and parcel of life for any human being—a part of life which no disabled person should be denied experience of simply because of his disability.

The Boundaries of the Institution

(a) *Contact with the outside world*

It is impossible to actively encourage residents within a residential home to engage as far as possible in leisure and work activities such as those enjoyed by members of the community outside, without making the boundaries of the institution itself far more flexible.

In the more obvious way, this has been achieved by fewer and fewer homes insisting that "All visitors should report to Matron", so that anyone visiting a particular resident is able to go straight to that person's room to be entertained there in privacy. To this end, in many homes, residents have their own facilities for making snacks, while other homes have provided informal kitchen areas where residents and their guests can cook for themselves. While more and more effort is made to ensure that a resident is admitted to care in a home as near as possible to his own area, in cases where relatives or friends have to come from a distance, many homes can offer accommodation for a minimal charge, while close relations can, if they wish, sometimes be accommodated in the resident's own room.

Most homes also welcome frequent visits from people who take an interest in the home and help residents in various ways—e.g., letter writing, sewing or simply in providing friendship, if this develops. Fewer and fewer homes encourage the invasion of their premises by groups on "sight-seeing tours", however, as residents understandably object to having people simply coming to stare at them, though many residents are quite prepared to meet freely in discussion with either lay or professional visitors.

Much more, however, residents are leaving the residential home to meet people in the community at large, rather than waiting for people to come to them. This has been made far more possible first of all by the introduction of much better aids, especially improved electric chairs which have made the disabled far more mobile. Again, more and more homes are recognising that residents do not want to go into the community only for "outings" in a vehicle clearly proclaiming that they are disabled; therefore, in addition to a mini-bus, many homes have an ordinary car which residents can book for their own excursions, excursions which they can now more easily pay for out of their Mobility Allowance. The siting of the newer purpose-built homes right in the centre of towns, rather than in the depths of the country has also made ready contact with the general community far easier—so too has the legislation that has meant that all new public buildings must be accessible to the disabled, while more towns and cities are publishing their own guides outlining accessible facilities.

As a result, residents are able to spend far more time in the community pursuing activities enjoyed by the able bodied. In this way the boundaries of the institution have become far more flexible for the resident, while hopefully the fear and prejudice of able-bodied people, which seeks to keep residents locked away, will be broken down in time, as the groups mix more freely.

(b) *Return to the outside world—rehabilitation*

While such opportunities to maintain easier contact with the community at large have made life in a residential home far more acceptable to many residents and broadened the horizons of many who had experienced only the old style of institutional care, nevertheless, for many residents, there still remains the knowledge that basically the home is the place in which they must stay until they die, given that there is no cure for their condition and that they have no family to care for them.

To some extent, there is an element of choice for residents in voluntary homes such as Cheshire Homes, for they can seek a transfer to another home within the Foundation, whose atmosphere may be better suited to their needs. An increasing number of such transfers occur each year, no final decision being made until the resident has spent some 3 months as a trial period in the home of his choice, to see whether it really is the place where he will be happiest.

While it is reality, therefore, that some disabled people will always have to remain in residential care until they die, there are many other residents for whom there is now a clear opportunity to return to the community. These are people who, in the past, had to be admitted to care simply because there was no alternative if they could not cope completely independently. Now, with better community services and better allowances to enable disabled people to pay for help, together with the requirement under the 1970 Chronically Sick and Disabled Persons Act, that local authorities should suitably adapt accommodation and provide all the necessary aids for people with handicap, more and more residents are finding that they can return to the community. It is to be hoped that still more will be able to do this, with the increase in the "Crossroads" type of domiciliary care scheme, which provides help in their own home for people who need rather more assistance than can be provided by the Home Help, Meals on Wheels and Community Nursing Services. Many more local authorities, too, are providing sheltered housing schemes with warden-controlled accommodation for the disabled as well as the elderly. While other groups, such as Habinteg and the Cheshire Foundation Housing Association, are also seeking to provide such accommodation which will make life in the community far easier for disabled people as well as providing integrated living with the able bodied.

Apart from the practical facilities required to enable residents to return to the community, there are very real psychological considerations. The variation in the time it takes for people to come to terms with disability and to learn to function with a degree of independence again is tremendous. Hitherto, medical rehabilitation centres have provided excellent assessment of the disabled person's potential recovery, but, because of pressure on beds, have been unable to allow people to stay for more than 8 to 12 weeks normally. Many people need far longer to be both physically and psychologically rehabilitated; one of the most encouraging tasks of the residential home, therefore, can be to provide the right kind of atmosphere and opportunities for residents to learn to cope with their disability to the point of maximum independence once more. A number of quite severely disabled residents who have recently left Cheshire Homes to return to the community have made the point that without the 2, 5 or even 10 years spent in the residential setting regaining confidence they would never have been able to contemplate such a move, however many practical services had been available outside.

Thus, the idea that some residents can be rehabilitated to the point where they can return to the community is not a myth created to keep residents optimistic and to save staff from despair, but, given careful and expert assessment of the resident's potential and the right kind of atmosphere for positive rehabilitation, can become a reality. This need for expert assessment is now being recognised far more in homes, though some have for many years used medical rehabilitation centres in their area. In many areas, however, no such centres exist; for this reason, the Cheshire Foundation is now considering the possibility of providing some form of assessment centre of its own.

Emotional Needs—The Acceptance of Deterioration and Death in the Institution

While life in many residential homes is undoubtedly richer and more hopeful than ever before for many residents, there is still the underlying reality that many do suffer from degenerative illnesses which are going to gradually deprive them of every vestige of physical independence before death eventually comes. Clearly, it is much easier and happier for both staff and residents to live and work in an atmosphere where each resident is able to participate fully and to move from achievement to achievement in terms of greater independence; yet any home which ignores the very real needs of residents who psychologically or physically are too ill to achieve, simply creates for them a setting which is as soul destroying as that of the "warehouse" model to the active resident. Miller and Gwynne[4] describe these establishments in which the lack of ability or desire to achieve is classed as failure, as providing the "horticultural" model of care. This is seemingly far more desirable than the warehouse model at first sight, but fails just as dismally to meet certain areas of resident need.

It would appear that this horticultural model of care is perhaps the next step forward for some homes from the warehouse ideal. Recognising the need to move away from rigid institutionalisation, there is a violent swing to the opposite extreme, in which every resident is all at once inundated with opportunities for freedom and individual expression, and is almost overnight expected to achieve independence whatever his physical or mental state. Whether this attitude is a swing away from paternalistic institutionalisation, or a way of making life tolerable for staff, it is not an acceptable form of care for many residents, and it is, therefore, heartening now to find homes that have moved a step further towards more appropriate care.

These are homes in which it is recognised that, while the atmosphere must be one of encouragement to growth and achievement, nevertheless a real look at individual need is certain to reveal residents who, for whatever reason, will never achieve much psychological or physical independence, and who will need to be dependent to a considerable degree on staff and other residents. Yet, if such residents are not to be treated according to the warehouse model, even in their utmost mental and physical dependence, they must be treated with dignity, care and individuality to the end of their days, without being made to feel that they have failed and that they are an intolerable burden on the life of the home.

Many homes are recognising, too, that even their most able and articulate residents, who usually enjoy a rich and active life, may have periods when depression and despair overtake them. This perhaps occurs when they are aware of a further progression of their disease, or when they recognise, because of another birthday or the death of a friend, that life is slipping by and that there is little time left for experiencing the many things that they have never been able to do.

Such despair, unless recognised and dealt with, either becomes chronic and is all too often labelled "apathy", or it is manifested in an anger and bitterness that turns itself towards more able residents, towards staff or towards the very fabric of the institution.

So often this kind of anger is labelled as "manipulation" to be dealt with firmly and angrily, and conflicts in the home thus mount, as the resident's real need to have his depression dealt with is not properly met.

Every resident, therefore, needs staff caring for him who are sensitive to the changes in his need and who are equipped to deal, now with his desire for greater independence, now with his need to depend, without at any time making the resident feel that he has failed by wanting to express either part of these two basic facets of the adult personality.

Staff in Residential Homes for the Physically Handicapped

The task of staff in any kind of residential home is surely the most demanding one in the whole field of work in the caring professions, for there is so much more involvement demanded in actually living with people in need, as opposed simply to visiting or treating them periodically. The worker with the physically handicapped is under particular pressure, because he works with so many residents who have considerable intelligence and ability but who will often be unable to achieve their fullest potential, however good the home, because of the severity of their physical disability. Many will also be deteriorating physically, though they may survive in this state for many years, thus placing a considerable strain on the physical and emotional resources of staff.

In the days when resident need was seen as the need for bodies to be cared for adequately and no more, many staff in homes for the physically handicapped were trained nurses who brought to the task all their nursing expertise, but also many of the defences of the nurse, as described in Isabel Menzies's classic paper.[5]

Now that a different ideal of residential care is the goal for many homes, the task for staff has become so much more complex. They must certainly have the expertise to deal skilfully with physical need, for no resident can feel happy with an untreated pressure-sore, however happy the atmosphere of the home. In addition, staff must be prepared to relinquish old ideas of the "control" of residents and be prepared to share with them in the running of the home on a far more equal basis. Staff must have the willingness and vision to encourage residents to the greatest degree of physical and emotional dependence, and yet also have the sensitivity and strength to bear with the resident who needs to grieve about the tragedy of his life or the fear of his impending death. On top of all this, staff have to face the criticism of management committees and the public at large, for allowing residents the freedom to engage in risk-taking activities or relationships, where such ventures go wrong and cause emotional hurt or physical injury or death.

A formidable task indeed, especially as only a small percentage of residential staff have any training. It is heartening to discover, however, how many are now seeking far more assistance and training for the job they do—heartening to find staff, for instance, asking help as to how best to offer comfort to dying residents, or seeking aid in dealing with a resident whom they have failed to help effectively themselves.

In order to meet this staff need, which must be provided for if resident need is to be effectively met, the Cheshire Foundation is about to appoint regional training officers, in addition to three counsellors already in post, who will not only help senior staff with particular problems of staff training, but will also encourage all staff wherever possible to follow nationally recognised courses. In the meantime, many Heads of Home are finding that their staff and their residents are being considerably helped as a result of the holding of regular staff meetings in which staff can openly express their difficulties and receive advice and support.

Conclusion—Looking to the Future

Residential care for people with physical handicap is presently in a state of transition, with some homes barely a step away from the regimes of the old institutional model, while other homes now truly seek to provide "maximum opportunities for independence, activity participation, mobility, fulfilment of intellectual, sexual and emotional needs, education and training, therapy and counselling".[6]

Looking to the future, there are clearly going to be changes in the kind of disabled person seeking residential care, for with a shift in government policy towards the priority provision of community services, rather than institutional buildings, far more disabled people may be expected to remain in the community for a much longer time. Already, the indications are that applicants for residential care are generally much older than previously. The differing needs of such residents will obviously alter the task of the residential homes they enter.

Again, advances in medical knowledge, with the development of techniques such as amniocentesis, so that pregnancies likely to result in the birth of a deformed child can be terminated, should mean a reduction in the number of handicapped children being born in the future. In another area, should the increasing amount of research into multiple sclerosis result in the discovery of a cure, then most homes would at once lose half their residents.

While there will then be less demand for residential care for the physically handicapped in future, with applicants coming, on the whole, from an older more disabled group, there will always be a demand for such care for some people. Hopefully, the provision made will become even more appropriate to resident need, if disabled people themselves continue to make their feelings known about the kind of provision they most require, in the way they have begun to do in the past decade.

References

1. E. J. MILLER and G. V. GWYNNE, *A Life Apart*, Tavistock, 1972.
2. Le Court Admissions Policy, Discussion Paper, Appendix 3, September, 1978.
3. MILLER and GWYNNE, *op. cit.*
4. *Ibid.*
5. I. E. P. MENZIES, *A Case Study in the Functioning of Social Systems, as a Defence against Anxiety*, Tavistock Institute of Human Relations Pamphlet, 1970.
6. *Residential Care Reviewed*, pp. 10–11, Para. 2:14, Report of Personal Social Services Council, 1977.

CHAPTER 9

POSITIVE CARE FOR THE ELDERLY

DWYNWEN WILLIAMS

Providing good, positive care for a number of elderly people with individual needs and various disabilities "under one roof" is a difficult but not impossible task. If residential workers have discovered for themselves why they have made the decision to "care" and have determined what their objectives are in attempting to create a "caring" situation for many in one building, then a large part of the problem is solved. Before caring for others, we must recognise our own day-to-day life and be aware that our desires, needs and life-style are those of an individual person. When we are aware of these facts, then this should help us to recognise the individual needs of every elderly person needing care and make every attempt to cater for these varying needs. It should not be too difficult to make it possible for residents to fulfil their lives in a way that maintains their dignity and individuality and also helps them to retain a feeling of usefulness to themselves and other members of society.

Some people may say this is fine when residents are physically and mentally able, but every human being, regardless of disabilities, has a strong desire to achieve, and given the encouragement and opportunity, everyone can turn these desires into successful action. I remember working with a gentleman who was paralysed from the neck down; the achievements that were experienced with just a little encouragement and support were phenomenal. There were days of anger, distress and disappointment, but all these feelings faded when a seemingly impossible task was completed successfully.

Provided that the residential worker does not impose his own standards on residents, and expect them to accept without question a life-style that is completely alien to their own desires, then some level of understanding can be reached, and providing good positive care for individual residents becomes an interesting, challenging and satisfying task.

It is important, when caring for elderly people who may be feeling that they have outlived their usefulness, to provide daily new challenges that will produce positive thinking and actions and thereby positive results. This is possible only if the residential staff team has a positive attitude to life and the task in hand. Negative means "nothing"; therefore if staff attitudes, actions and thoughts are negative, then they can expect to add "nothing" to the lives of the people in their care. By providing food, warmth and cleanliness, care is being given, but by merely providing support for these physical needs, the residential worker is only adding weight to and perpetuating the mistaken idea that elderly people require little else but these comforts and a few kind words when there is time or when an elderly person has the ability to express the desire for attention.

A well-planned admission into residential care is important if the trauma of change is to be minimised. In the cases of emergency admissions this is not always possible, but I believe it is possible to reduce the number of "emergency admissions", for we find that many have in fact had social work involvement for some considerable time. It is possible now for prospective residents to visit the home either on a day basis or for a short-term stay. These arrangements enable an elderly person to make a decision while being in possession of all the facts that may affect their life if they accept residential care. If desired, the residential social worker could visit the home of an elderly person; this would help in determining individual needs and desired life-style. The elderly person would feel more confident in his own surroundings and be more likely to ask personal and pertinent questions. These procedures would all help to produce positive results and increase the feeling of freedom of choice for the elderly person.

After admission to a residential home, it is necessary for the field social worker to continue to give support until such time as the resident indicates satisfaction and trust in the residential social worker. This continuation of fieldwork support also helps to prevent a resident from suffering the feeling that he has been totally disconnected from his previous life. If a person is to experience a good positive life in residential care, then his previous relationships and former life are a necessity to him and must not be disregarded; in fact, they are the stones on which to build his new life.

To ease the immediate post-admission distress which occurs, it is necessary to provide specific support from two members of staff; two additional staff are necessary to cover off-duty periods. Giving two staff this responsibility can eliminate many distressing incidents such as a person not knowing which way to turn and whom to turn to when trying to find toilets, bedrooms and dining rooms, etc. To place a new resident in the position of having to cope with at least 40 new, unknown faces and personalities, not knowing which one can answer your questions and help you, is an unsatisfactory situation and one that can easily be avoided. A new resident needs a specific person to relate to in the immediate admission period. When he has gained in confidence and is familiar with the building and daily routine then he will embark on the challenge of making new friends, and his ability to widen the circle of relationships will increase, taking in members of both staff and resident groups.

All members of the staff team—and this includes external staff—should be aware of the objectives of the home and it is necessary for regular discussions to take place between all members of the team. This would ensure that all are working to one end, and if there are strong feelings regarding procedures, then these can be discussed; good communication helps eliminate negative actions and also prevents confusion and mistrust amongst residents which arises when different answers are given by different staff members regarding policies and routine in the home.

All staff should recognise the importance of listening to individual points of view being expressed, they must be aware that feelings are expressed for a specific reason and that they need to respond to these statements in specific ways. Training of staff is necessary if they are to have the ability to recognise such things as distress presenting itself through aggression, or other troubled behaviour. Training makes staff more aware of the subtle ways in which residents can be hurt and also gives them the confidence to deal with presenting situations.

Maintaining links with the community is necessary if attempts are to be made to lessen and eventually remove completely the stigma of "them" and "us".

Joint social activities can be arranged where residents either visit clubs and theatres, or members of clubs in the community are welcomed to the home. Many people in the "outer community" are very keen to involve the homes in any activity, and providing there is genuine interest shown by members of staff and resident groups, then this is an avenue of great positive stimulation. Relationships that are created in this way have to be nurtured very carefully, for the least indication that visitors are causing more work and problems within the home can destroy weeks of hard work in an hour.

It is necessary to persevere with presenting various activities as some residents may not appear to appreciate what is being done. It may be that the activity is not what they desire, so if you change and challenge continuously, soon you will find a selection of activities that involve the maximum number of residents. If they have the choice they will choose, if there is nothing to choose from, then why should they bother? Talking to residents usually presents quite a selection of ideas, and if staff really work at it, residents themselves will be responsible for supervising many activities, e.g. bingo sessions and coffee evenings. Arranging a summer fair does not only provide one day of interest, for if preparations are made months before, then small items that residents have been given the opportunity to make can amount to a great deal of task hours that can then be seen to be of use when they are sold to swell the home fund. It is necessary that residents see the benefits of any effort they make. Whist-drives, draughts tournaments, and cheese and wine parties are just a few of the social evenings that can be arranged with little effort, yet the interest and motivation they create amongst staff, residents and visitors provides an opportunity for positive support and action.

To be successful in providing these activities, a great deal of listening and discussion is necessary. It is wrong to assume that we, as staff, know how much and what type of activity suits the residents. A home must be run for the benefit of residents and not to suit the convenience of the staff. Many staff defend quite strongly the fact that residents have "freedom of choice". If we really sit down and discuss just what areas residents have complete freedom of choice in, I believe we would find it would be nearer the truth to say that we only pay lip-service to this statement.

As our homes are built and staffed today, it seems impossible to enable residents to actually decide such things as time of rising from bed, time and type of meals, whom they would like to sit by in the dining room and lounges, and many more decisions that we, as staff, make for ourselves each day. As staff who are aware of the needs of the elderly it is our responsibility to let the people who plan the homes know just what areas need to be improved in the buildings so that we have a better chance of improving the quality of the lives of residents, e.g. the provision of residents' kitchens and more space available for social activities, very often activities have to take place between meal times because the only room available is the dining room.

Great interest and enjoyment is experienced when 37 residents are given the opportunity to choose their own wallpaper and paint for their rooms. It takes about 6 weeks for books and colour charts to go around, but what a great 6 weeks! Then comes the excitement as each room is completed, every one different! Even the blind people can have patterns and colours described to them, so you see there is no excuse for denying this right to anyone; even residents who are "confused" have great delight in expressing their opinions in these matters. Staff need to be very positive if this venture is to be successful, for administrators and decorators have to be convinced of the benefits of such choice, since it is obvious that it is much quicker, easier and cheaper to have every room decorated in an identical manner. There has to be personal commitment on the part of all staff for they will be asked their opinions of choices made, and should see this as a privilege given to them by residents. When residents realise that their requests for staff time are not considered burdensome, then life takes on a different meaning for them and eventually for staff too.

For too long admission to residential care has been seen as "a last resort", "the end of the road", and unfortunately the greatest offenders in this case have been social workers themselves. How many times has it been said, "when you go in you won't have to do a thing". Statements such as, "you won't have to worry about your bills" or "you can sit back and let someone else do the work and the worrying for you" are very frequently used to encourage a person to accept residential care. What in actual truth is being said is "you can no longer make decisions and care for yourself" or "admit to yourself that your body and mind are old and tired and society is afraid to let you continue to take risks because they would feel uncomfortable for a while if anything happened to you at home".

To attempt to rehabilitate a suitable resident when he has been convinced that he no longer has reason to try is a very difficult task. If rehabilitation is to become possible, even if it is only with a small percentage of residents, then all members of the care team need to be aware of the possibilities that exist within residential care, to bring about success in this area. There must be a coming together of positive thoughts and ideas between field and residential social workers. If this does not happen, then we are never going to move forward and improve the quality of life of the residents in our care.

When staff make it obvious that they have a great desire to improve standards and a real need to support residents in their efforts to remain individual persons with a reason to live their lives to their fullest extent, then, and only then, will residents feel confident that residential life is not a play taking place on a stage where everyone has to pretend and take on a role to avoid being considered a nuisance or a troublemaker and a burden to the more youthful members of our society.

A Case Study

Mrs A. was admitted as an emergency case under great duress. She had for some time been living in extremely dirty conditions and had neglected herself physically; she had not washed for some months and had failed to secure for herself adequate nourishment.

Many requests had been received for social work involvement from neighbours and eventually from Meals on Wheels and Home Helps who had failed to obtain access into Mrs A.'s house. Mrs A. was eventually persuaded to come into residential care having been given the assurance that this was a temporary measure until her home could be redecorated and she was well enough to return.

When admitted, she was quite ambulant and protested loudly over being removed from her home. She was, however, obviously in need of physical care and nourishment and was given a cup of tea and a meal on admission. Recognising that no matter how sensitively the task of bathing Mrs A. was carried out there was obviously going to be intrusion on her person and added distress to an already destructive situation, this task was eventually successfully achieved. Being aware that Mrs A. would have been more humiliated if other residents had met her in her extremely dirty and odorous condition helped the staff to complete their task without feeling they had "committed a crime" against another human being. Mrs A. told us later that she was glad that we had supported her in her attempt and desire to achieve a standard that made her feel socially acceptable; it was, she said, because of her dirty condition that she had refused to have the Home Help and Meals on Wheels ladies in.

Mrs A. gradually settled down to a daily life which included preparation for her eventual return to her own home. She was supported in her efforts to launder personal clothing, lay table, and secure for herself meals with good nutritional value, and she went shopping for personal items. She also saved some of her weekly money at the Post Office. Mrs A. would ask daily when she would be returning home; eventually she was considered to be as physically fit as possible, so this together with her desperate desire to return home seemed to be the indication that she was now ready to resume caring for herself at home supported by Home Help, Meals on Wheels, and 2 days per week attendance at a day centre.

Enquiries were made regarding the position of her house and it was found that there was some question regarding its demolition, due to the fact that it was in an extremely bad condition. While discussions were taking place regarding her house Mrs A. began to show signs of frustration and aggression; the time passing was quite unacceptable to Mrs A. and she became fearful of never going home.

These incidents were contained extremely well due to the fact that all residential staff were aware of the situation and when questioned by Mrs A. everyone could reassure her with similar answers. Mrs A. was encouraged to maintain her desire to return home.

During the waiting period a number of meetings took place in the home involving Mrs A. Officers and staff in the home, the Senior Residential Officer, Mrs A.'s field social workers, both past and present, the Senior Social Worker, Housing Officer, Meals on Wheels and Home Help Organisers, Mrs A.'s general practitioner and a Centre Organiser.

These meetings involved discussions as to the ability of Mrs A. to support herself adequately with the maximum support available from various agencies. Comparisons were made by both field social workers as to her condition on admission compared with that at the present time, and the question of placing Mrs A. back into a possible situation of risk was discussed and measured against the fact that she had during the waiting time become used to a great deal of continuous company which had appeared to give her much pleasure. Mrs A. soon made it quite clear that even though she had been comfortable and had enjoyed her stay she would still prefer to be in her own home, and in fact she added that she hoped the other residents would soon return home too.

In one meeting which did not include Mrs A. many widely varying opinions regarding advantages and disadvantages were expressed and the possible eventual outcome of discharging Mrs A. from residential care. By looking objectively and positively at all statements made, it became possible to see that some of the fears expressed stemmed from a resistance to place oneself "at the mercy of" public outcry in the event of a possible tragedy. Lack of support from society and upper management in the event of a seemingly preventable incident gave weight to some of the fears being expressed.

Eventually it was accepted that Mrs A.'s personal desires and needs could only be fulfilled if she could be returned home, and this move was put into action. Mrs A. was presented with the key to accommodation in a sheltered housing complex as it had been decided her own house was beyond repair. Mrs A. would have preferred to return to her own home but accepted the offered accommodation quite happily.

Residential social workers need not feel that they are alone in their efforts to achieve what is best or what is desired by the residents in their care, for there are many people in the care team who have the desire to be involved, the desire to use their expertise together with others in an attempt to achieve for elderly people their desired life-style. When there is integrated experience and expertise then elderly people can feel reassured that all is being done and that many people "really do care" what happens to them.

Comment

Mrs A.'s situation raises several important issues. What weight should be given to the elderly person's own wishes? It is clear that residential staff in this situation were taking on an advocacy role for the resident and initiating action with a variety of external workers. How possible is it for such a role to be a normal and accepted part of a residential worker's function? One interpretation is that a residential worker was acting as a *de facto* keyworker although this was not formally recognised by the agency. Another feature of this situation was the pattern of communication within the home, which enabled all staff to work in the same way with Mrs A. How might this style of communication be aided by formal structures for communication in a home? Initially, gentle force and persuasion were used to secure Mrs A.'s conformity with certain standards, even though her longer-term desire for self-determination was respected. Social control and self-determination co-existed with a different balance between them during the period between admission and discharge. A fruitful way to explore some of these issues could be to role-play a conference about Mrs A. about half-way through her stay.

Further Reading

The further reading list at the end of Chapter 7 contains some references to the subject of this chapter, as does the Bibliography at the end of the book (p. 337).

CHAPTER 10

SOCIAL LEARNING IN RESIDENTIAL CARE

ALEXANDER GOBELL

Residential care is an expensive form of provision, and in several areas the evidence of success in terms of readjustment and rehabilitation is not impressive. In this paper I wish to look at some of the ideas from social learning theory that have been shown to be successful in different caring situations.

The cost of keeping a child in a community home or residential school is usually about the equivalent of the cost of the salary of a full-time social worker, or even two in some cases. If one social worker is thought able to help the number of clients that make up a normal case load, the cost of residential placement seems high, and we should be justified in having equally high expectations of good results. Yet there is little good evidence that residential care produces any better results than the very much cheaper interventions that retain the child within the community, such as foster care or community projects.[1]

Of course there are other reasons for residential care, such as the care of the elderly, the infirm or the handicapped, or custody of offenders, where the primary purpose is not readjustment. Although the criteria for success are even more difficult to disentangle, there is still the need to justify the relatively high allocation of resources, and find the best methods of caring that we can.

Having spent many years working in residential settings with children, I feel that I have seen and experienced the benefits that those children have enjoyed. I have seen them blossom and surmount their problems in ways that it would be difficult to imagine in other settings; and colleagues feel the same about other client groups. Therefore I care intensely that good practice should be followed, and successes recorded where possible.

There are many admirable residential establishments, doing excellent work with different client groups using a great variety of approaches.[2] I have a high regard for the work of several self-styled "therapeutic communities", where the caring, the support and even the love shines through. But so far they have presented no firm evidence to indicate that their successes are any better than those recorded for spontaneous recovery—and we need better evidence than that for such a high commitment of resources.

Some of the best evidence for changes in client groups comes from the application of procedures derived from social learning theory,[3,4] which are systematically employed to modify behaviour. I can understand why people who have worked a life-time to bring about personality changes in clients, or to ameliorate the effects of inadequate early experiences, seeking to understand the deep workings of people they are trying to help, will be very reluctant to use techniques that focus, at least initially, on the surface

111

behaviour. But only the obtuse can now deny the evidence for the success of behaviour modification within its own terms of reference: to help people change behaviour that is a problem to them. (I am aware that the last statement begs some important questions about who decides which behaviour is a problem. That question will be taken up again when I come to discuss some of the ethical considerations.)

I have come to believe that behaviour modification (which is the term used here for the practical application of the principles of social learning theory) has a place in the re-adjustment and social development of many people. I also believe that there are lessons to be learned from social learning theory that are useful even for those of us who do not want to adopt the approach wholesale, and it is my primary purpose here to pick out some of the aspects of social learning theory that it seems important for all practitioners to be aware of, whatever their approach. I also want to introduce some of the procedures that I am at present finding useful with several client groups, and which I think hold great promise in residential care.

The Importance of Giving Attention

Most people want some attention from other people, and will go to considerable lengths to get the attention that they feel they need. One of the major functions of the helping professions can be seen as the giving of attention to those in need of it, in the form of comfort, support and even advice, and in this form it is seen as an important part of helping. But it is not altogether simple or straightforward, and some of the complications need to be recognised and understood if the effects of giving attention are not to have unfortunate effects which can be the reverse of what is intended.

In the first place many of us feel that deviant behaviour is often attention-seeking and a cry for help. Warm, caring adults then swallow their frustration at being disturbed or hurt, and give the child or other client loving attention. It seems to be an admirable thing to do—sometimes in response to appallingly disruptive behaviour. We tell ourselves that there must be a good reason for the behaviour and for the child needing the attention that he succeeds in getting in this way. But could we be reinforcing that deviant behaviour by allowing him to get attention as a result of it?

There are many well-documented reports showing that attention is reinforcing of behaviour in various client groups, so that behaviour attended to does increase. One that is often quoted is by Harris and her colleagues[5] who observed that a 5-year-old child tended to withdraw from the peer group and play alone, whereupon the adults came and gave the child their attention. In this case the child's solitary behaviour was regarded as undesirable by the adults and they wished to help her to become more sociable. But the action they took, paying her attention when she was solitary, had the reverse effect to that intended. Their attention was reinforcing the solitary behaviour, while the social play with other children was ignored by the adults. When the adults ignored the child when playing alone, but gave attention instead when the child was playing with other children, the pattern of behaviour changed.

The need for attention may well be genuine enough, but if the behaviour that succeeds in attracting attention is the behaviour that will be reinforced, then care obviously needs to be taken. It is not uncommon for children to find that the only way they can be sure to get attention is by misbehaving. It does not matter if the attention is that which accompanies a telling-off or punishment. That may be preferable to the child to no attention. The adult is then engineered into a situation of reinforcing that behaviour by giving it attention—although the intention is to stop the behaviour. It is in this sort of circumstance that many investigators have found that there are benefits in ignoring deviant behaviour, which will then decrease. But this has to be accompanied by giving plentiful attention meanwhile to desirable behaviour.[6]

It must be emphasised that there is no suggestion that clients should be deprived of the human attention that we all seem to need. Rather the reverse: that more attention should be given to clients in many situations. What is suggested is that we need to be careful about which behaviour is being reinforced by the attention we give to it.

Praise and Encouragement

Giving a client praise and encouragement for what he or she has done is a potent way of strengthening or increasing that behaviour. There are many impressive studies that bear witness to the effectiveness of praise. Becker[6] carefully observed and recorded the considerable beneficial effects of teacher praise on really quite disruptive children in classrooms, simply by getting the teacher to praise the children much more; and to praise them for their appropriate behaviour, instead of reinforcing their bad behaviour by giving it all their attention. Staff in residential and day settings are often very surprised at the dramatic results that systematic use of praise can have on behaviour.

In view of its demonstrated effectiveness it is surprising that teachers use praise relatively so sparingly. Investigations have found that they use negative "telling-off" statements several times more often than positive, praising statements in the classroom, and Fish and Loehfelm[7] write about "Verbal approval: a neglected resource". I do not know of similar investigations in residential situations, but my informal impression is that there still tends to be a preponderance of negative, critical, telling-off comments.

"Catch them being good", is a splendid catch-phrase when dealing with children in any setting,[8] and, although the wording may not be so appropriate with other client groups, the sentiment remains a desirable and effective one.

Effective though praise has been shown to be in helping to change behaviour, it is not without its hazards. For example, if someone is flooded with over-effusive praise, the praise will tend to lose both its reinforcing effectiveness, and its discriminative message that some behaviours or productions are approved of, and others not. In addition, if the praise is felt to be too easily earned for something that is not seen as praiseworthy by some standard, then it may actually reduce motivation to do better. "If that is considered to be so good, then why should I bother to try to do better?" Easily earned praise tends to set limits to performance in this way.[9]

It may be awareness of hazards like these that lies behind the reluctance to use praise more, especially with children. We don't want to risk children becoming "big-headed", or "above themselves". But there is the danger of going too far the other way, and underusing a very useful tool. It may seem inappropriate to praise the excellence of something if it has clearly not reached the standard expected, but it may be possible to praise the effort that went into it, or some part of it, or this production compared with a previous one.

Many of us seem to find direct praise difficult to accept. We tend to respond by saying something like: "Oh, it was nothing", or "It really wasn't my doing." This may be a result of our own experience of meagre praise, but we should be keen not to pass this on, in view of the demonstrated effectiveness of praise in shaping behaviour.

Modelling Effects

By modelling is meant the way that people learn new behaviours from the example given by others, and copy that behaviour. The idea has, of course been around for a long time, perhaps particularly strongly in work with children in the concept of identification. Bandura[3] has given the idea a central place in social learning theory, claiming that most of what we learn is a result of imitating the models we see. Although this is particularly important in children, where behaviour patterns are being established, it plays a part in influencing behaviour at all stages of life.

Bandura and colleagues,[10] in now classic experiments, showed that children who watched an adult attacking a life-size blow-up doll, subsequently also attacked the doll in a similar way, whereas children who had not watched the adult did not attack the doll themselves. Many subsequent studies have demonstrated that children copy a wide variety of behaviours, both aggressive and passive, from a variety of models, including filmed people and even cartoon characters.[11] Modelling has been used to help various adult client groups to overcome fears by showing them models coping with those fears,[12,13] or appropriate social behaviour by watching models;[14] and even very difficult adolescent delinquents have learned pro-social skills through procedures that included modelling.[15,16]

Clients in residential settings are exposed to a great variety of models: there are the other clients who may be setting all sorts of undesirable examples, as in the highly successful criminal training establishments where delinquents are placed in custody. There are also the visitors and casual contacts among staff, and the models that appear on television and films. But especially potent models are provided by those people who have immediate care, and will be seen as having power over clients. This influence will be especially great if the care-giver manages to form a supportive and warm relationship with the client.[3]

This puts a great responsibility on those care-givers, who need to be aware of the effects of their behaviour; of the cheerful and optimistic, or the grumpy and negative model they are providing. The old adage of "Do what I say and not what I do" gets right to the heart of the matter. To tell a client angrily not to be angry is to give a double message, with the likelihood that the action will speak louder, and more effectively, than the words.

It would be tedious, and inhuman, for staff to skip smilingly about all the time. Indeed, the most potent models in some of the studies have been those who seemed to share the clients' problems and modelled their successful handling of them.[17] But life in a constant gloom or irritation cannot seem worth living for, and if we can set a realistic example of behaviour that makes life seem good overall, then we will be modelling a world that looks worth having.

Inducements (Material and Activity Reinforcers)

Smarties have a lot to answer for. They have given behaviour modification a bad name by caricaturing it as a process of popping sweets into the mouths of compliant children. The trouble is that many young children are very partial—and susceptible—to sweets, which can only too easily be used as bribes. But responsible use of material reinforcers, including food, is a more complex matter.

In the first place, material reinforcers will tend to be used only when more usual methods have failed to get results. Secondly, they will be used for a short time, with the aim of moving on to more widely available reinforcers, such as praise, attention, good marks, self-approval and a sense of achievement, as soon as possible.

Even so, they do often cause a sense of unease. Children, or adult clients, it is felt, should conform without the need for such inducements; if something is worth doing, then it should be done for its own sake and not for some different, extrinsic reinforcer. I find this view very understandable, at least on the surface, and I tend not to want to use material reinforcers until I have failed to help with other methods. Perhaps I delay longer than I should in some cases. For at a deeper level I believe that far from being unethical to use material reinforcers with children who do not respond in other ways, I regard it as unethical *not* to use procedures that I and others have found to be successful. Therefore with a child or adult who finds praise aversive, or who has learned to suspect the motives of someone who tries to give attention, the giving of sweets or something else may be a way to overcome these blockages to normal human interaction. If the child finds the material reinforcer pleasurable, then that pleasure will tend to spread to the person dispensing it, and to the attention and praise of the donor, which will in turn become reinforcing enough. Or better still, the pleasure provided by the material reinforcer will spread to the activity that one is wanting to encourage, and the activity can itself become pleasurable.

A good example is reading, for children who have found learning to read a problem. There is often a long history of failure, and the learning activities may have become aversive. Yet, in order to learn to read, the basic skills have to be practised and mastered, and this will appear to be at least boring, and probably distasteful. If a child can be induced, by material reinforcers, to practise the skills found to be necessary to learn to read, then he has a chance of achieving the happy state where reading itself becomes a pleasure, and external reinforcers are no longer necessary. Many studies have shown that this can be a highly successful procedure. Staats and Butterfield[18] demonstrated its success with an adolescent delinquent school failure, who made good reading progress.

I continue to be surprised at the difference that some material reinforcers can make with certain children. Even when a child appears to be well motivated, not excessively anxious, and putting all his attention on the learning task (in other words apparently doing as well as he is capable of), the use of an appropriate reinforcer can make a dramatic difference. This may affect not only his application, but his learning skills such as retention and decoding. It is probably only personal experience that will persuade sceptics that people can be induced to perform above expectation if the reinforcers are right. In an area of such importance as reading I would argue that it was justified to use material reinforcers if other methods have been tried and found inadequate.

Of course not every activity will become self-reinforcing. If something is in itself boring or aversive, then it should be no surprise that once the external reinforcers have been faded out the activity soon ceases. In fact this seems to me to be one of the safety mechanisms that protects us from being too manipulatable.

Successful use of all sorts of material reinforcers has been reported with many different client groups, of all ages. The list of items used is very long, including all varieties of food and drink, small toys and games for children, make-up, clothing, books, cigarettes, etc. The obvious, but important, factor is that the client should value and want the item badly enough to be motivated to produce the aimed-for behaviour. It does not matter how attractive something may appear to a staff member—it is the client's perception that counts in effectiveness terms. Insensitivity to this factor sometimes leads to frustration, when clients do not react to rewards chosen by staff members and can be seen as unresponsive or even ungrateful.

On the other hand, the material reinforcer must also be acceptable to the staff: I have an objection to sweets for the damage they do to teeth, and to cigarettes because of the health hazards, and both can become addictive. Yet both sweets and cigarettes are used extensively in residential care, both by behaviour modifiers and by those who find that they can be a successful bridge in early relationship building—and can then be difficult to withdraw. This brings into sharp focus the ethical issue of whether the means justifies the end, and each situation has to be weighed up on its own merits; are the dangers worth risking for the benefits to be gained? However, if sweets and cigarettes are being given out, at least care can be taken that they are not given following disruptive behaviour in such a way to reinforce that behaviour: as when a cigarette is given to someone in a temper, apparently to placate him or her—for the way to gain a cigarette will soon be learned.

I have found that using material reinforcers in the context of a contract is a most successful practice, and this will be explored below, after looking at the use of activities as reinforcers and the use of tokens.

Activities as Reinforcers

The same principles apply in using activities as with other types of reinforcer, but their use often seems to raise fewer objections, they can be cheaper and they also seem to have particular advantages in the residential setting. One of the most frequent complaints one hears from people in schools and hospitals is that they are bored, that there is so little to do. "The empty hours" has been an emotive catch phrase used to express concern about this. Yet, as some schools and other residential institutions have shown, there are countless opportunities for interesting and rewarding activities available if the staff have the energy and initiative. In fact, the extra time available in residential settings can be seen as having especial advantages, such as that of giving time to develop new interests.

One of the problems can be that when staff have completed what are seen as the essential chores, there is too little energy left to initiate entertaining activities with unenthusiastic clients. There can be a powerful pull to rely on the "telly" or allow the apathy of people with problems to be an excuse for inactivity.

It is here that building activities into a reinforcement programme can help: activities are offered as reinforcers to clients for achievement of desirable behaviour or performance. In the first place, if the reinforcers do their job in inducing the desired client behaviour, then less staff energy and time will need to go into achieving these results. I certainly found in classroom teaching of disturbed children that I felt less emotionally drained and exhausted when I used a system of reinforcers, and I had more energy for therapeutic interaction with the children and for joining in beneficial activities with them.[19]

Secondly, staff need to find activities that are motivating to clients, and are thus encouraged to explore new ideas, and look at the individual needs and interests of the clients.

In the third place, there seems little doubt that, for most clients, when activities are earned they are more valued than if they are gained as of right and without personal effort. I have found that some craft or game which was freely available but which no one seemed to want to use suddenly became very popular and sought after when children had to earn the right to do or play it.

Finally, staff come to see that leisure activities are an essential part of the treatment programme rather than as an extra, bolted on to help fill time. When they form part of a programme as reinforcers of the behaviour that is seen as marking progress, then they take on that extra value.

Tokens

The use of tokens makes a system based on reinforcers more flexible: as stars, marks or counters can be given out immediately following some behaviour, and back-up reinforcers can be exchanged for the tokens at some convenient time. Although the tokens tend to become valued for themselves (like money), it is possible to build a tolerance of having to wait for the main reward, which is one of the aims with several client groups. It is possible to base the entire treatment programme of a school, home or hospital on the use of tokens, and many successful examples have been reported.[20,4] Such a token economy requires extensive and continuing organisation. The ones I know seem to be in a continual, and healthy, state of development. They vary greatly, some being rather impersonal and timetabled; others buzzing with achievement and breathless industry. But there always seems to be someone at the hub who really enjoys generating the ideas, the graphs, charts and general paper work which their continuing operation seems to demand.

A Cautionary Note

I must not leave even this brief consideration of extrinsic reinforcers without recording my concern that there are some basic things that should not be used as reinforcers, because this always implies the possibility that clients may be deprived of them. In my view, the basic physical needs of food and comfort should not be put at risk, and therefore not made dependent on behaviour. I am also very uneasy about imposing more than the briefest periods of isolation from the company of others. Nor do I think that one should use activities that could bring important benefits to a client. For example, I have found swimming to be of great benefit to disturbed children, and I would therefore not want to make all swimming a reinforcer which a child could fail to earn. A basic, nourishing diet, and sufficient warmth and comfort also seem to me to come into this category.

There are, however, clients who will only respond initially to a very narrow range of reinforcers. With these I would think it permissible to use "extra" swimming, extra or special foods, or extra comfort as reinforcers, as a temporary measure. Of course, this begs the important question as to what should be regarded as basic and what as extra. This is the sort of difficult and sensitive question that is sharply posed by behaviour modification procedures, and which has to be carefully and responsibly faced in consultation with all those concerned with the client's welfare, including the clients themselves where possible. This point will again be touched on in the section on the ethics, but leads on now to looking at ideas for involving the clients in their own programme.

Contracts and Self-Modification

Contracts have been shown to be most useful procedures in all sorts of situations. They consist of an agreement between two people in which each agrees to do or give something on stated conditions. They are often written agreements where a client undertakes to behave in a specified manner, or produce some work and in return is promised a reward. Most material or activity reinforcers can be used, and the client's part can be flexibly tailored to suit many problems and levels of ability, as long as verbal communication is possible. I have used contracts with children from about 7 years upwards, to help change behaviour or produce work. McAuley and McAuley[21] report several successful examples, including highly oppositional teenage problems. They show how contracts between parents, between parents and children, and between therapist and parents and children can be used, and provide a very clear set of guidelines which include the careful definition of behaviours, the negotiating process and the form of contract. Gambrill[17] describes the use of contracts with all ages and several categories of client groups, including alcoholics, depressed, mentally handicapped and emotionally disturbed people.

De Risi[22] has suggested the following form of contract, a copy of which can be kept by the client or displayed.

CONTRACT

Effective Dates: From_____ to_____

We, the undersigned parties, agree to perform the following behaviours:

If_____ then_____

_____   _____

_____   _____

Bonus:_____

_____

Penalty:_____

_____

Signed_____

Signed_____

This formalising and recording of both the target behaviour and the reinforcer can be especially valuable in the residential setting where a client tends to interact with several staff members and it can be a problem to keep everyone informed about the current treatment procedures, and contracts can be an aid in providing consistency for the client.

One of the most satisfactory aspects of using contracts is the way they can be used to involve clients in setting their own targets and choosing their own reinforcers. When they are first introduced, most client groups will need to have the targets set for them. But once they get the idea, clients bring forward behaviours that are a problem to themselves, and ask for a contract to help change that behaviour in a direction they want. For example, I have had children asking for help in controlling their aggressive behaviour, or in organising themselves to do their work, or to control their own swearing. It provides the client with an opportunity to bring matters forward that are worrying to her or him, which may not otherwise have been recognised as important enough.

The contract needs to be seen as an agreement between equal partners, both of whom take on certain obligations. Some people are fearful of the possibility of wrangling about the terms of the contract, with a kind of "shop-steward" mentality developing, demanding a higher price for less. This seems particularly worrying for those professionals who have tended to see a client in a dependent role, especially if the client is a child. But another way of looking at the process of negotiating the terms of a contract is as the development of the skills needed for coping with disagreements and quarrels. These are skills lacking in many client groups, and McAuley and McAuley[21] suggest that the practice provided by negotiating contracts can be a help in learning to avoid aggressive confrontations, for they involve the ability to give as well as to take, and finally to accept a compromise.

The selection of reinforcers can often be left to the clients to choose from the start, with the obvious constraints of expense, safety and feasibility. It is frequently a surprise to the professional what sensible reinforcers are chosen by clients who would be expected to make excessive and impossible suggestions: children with a record of school failure and resistance, choosing extra reading or number work, art work, day-dreaming time, as well as TV and radio programmes, games and hobbies.

This has taken us into the use of self-modification and self-control. Not only can the targets and reinforcers be chosen by the clients, but the recording of behaviour and achievement, and then the dispensing, to themselves, of the chosen reinforcers. There are many studies that demonstrate the successful use of self-modification techniques and their potential in helping people.[23]

These approaches commonly involve self-observation and keeping a careful check on the target behaviour, often entailing the making of records of such things as number of people spoken to, number of angry or praising words used or amount of food eaten. Sometimes clients are taught to give themselves verbal instructions, which helps to bring behaviour under closer control. For example, Novaco[24] got clients at risk of losing their tempers under provocation to say to themselves: "Stay calm. Just continue to relax", "Time to take a deep breath." This sounds close to the age-old method of counting to 10, or reciting the books of the Old Testament, but Novaco showed it worked with people who had records of violent tempers, previously resulting in dangerous assaults; and this has been a group that has proved very difficult to help by other means.

Reinforcers can be anything that takes the individual's fancy. For some it will be a drink or cup of tea, for others a delayed purchase or a treat. Both Novaco[24] and Meichenbaum[13] have found that self-praise and encouragement is also successful, so that clients are taught to say to themselves (probably under their breath): "That was well done. I'm improving."

If this patting of ourselves on the back seems strange, even distasteful, we should perhaps remember how many people criticise themselves, to themselves: "You silly fool, you should know better than to do that." "You're just no good. You always do the wrong thing." We should at least be aware that what we say to ourselves may be affecting our view of ourselves and thus the ways we react.

The importance of giving this self-control to our clients lies not only in respecting their own choice of their behaviour and performance, and working with what Carl Rogers[25] has called the "Quiet Revolution" of power to the individual person, instead of vesting all the decisions in the hands of the so-called helping professions. These procedures also seem to hold the best hope that the improvements attained within a residential setting will be maintained outside, when there are no staff present to be immediate dispenser of extrinsic rewards.

To expand this point, it is necessary to realise that although it is relatively simple to modify most behaviour within a controlled setting, such as a residential school, when clients return to their previous environment, improvements do have a tendency to vanish. For example, in the case of delinquents, within a residential setting their reinforcers can be controlled, and their behaviour modified to conform to the demands of that setting. But on their return home the situation changes, and they are again exposed to reinforcers of their delinquent behaviour, so it cannot be any great surprise that they will return to the previous delinquent behaviour. However, if clients can be helped to dispense their own reinforcers to themselves, especially if it is for behaviour they have themselves chosen, then there is a better chance of that behaviour surviving, even after they have left the residential haven. It may look like a pious hope in the case of delinquents, but there are hopeful signs—for example, in the work at Pioneer House.[4] With other client groups there are stronger signs of success,[17] and self-modification seems to me to exhibit the humanistic face of behaviour modification: providing people with a tool to modify their own behaviour.

Punishment

A full discussion of punishment and its effects goes far beyond the scope of this paper. It is a huge and complex subject with views ranging from David Wills's[26] plea for complete abolition of punishment, to the use of electric shocks with autistic children to stop them head-banging themselves to destruction.[27]

There seems little doubt that punishment, or often the threat of punishment, will stop behaviour, and attempts to tell us that it does not work seem to be mistaken. There does seem to be an equation of effectiveness with the severity and likelihood of the punishment being administered on the one side and the expectations of the rewards of the behaviour on the other. This points to the necessity not only of being consistent in using punishment, but also of being sensitive to an individual's perception of the value of behaviour to him- or herself. It makes nonsense of the practice of administering standard punishments to fit stated misdemeanours. For if punishments are made severe enough to deter everybody, then they will be far more severe than is *necessary* for the majority.

And it is in this question of severity that one of the principal hazards of using punishment lies. For by its nature punishment has to be unpleasant and even somewhat feared. It is well established that fearful feelings tend to be contagious, not only from person to person, but fear of what someone does or may do spreads to the person himself, to his surroundings and to things associated with him. Therefore, fear of the threat of punishment becomes fear of the punisher, fear of the place, and even fear of the other people there. This may be part of the explanation for the very widespread anxiety about going to school felt by so many children from time to time.[28]

This harmful effect may be at least partly counteracted by ensuring that any fear of punishment is more than balanced by warm, caring and rewarding aspects or the people and environment. This must be especially important where the population is as captive as it is in a residential setting. It also seems that punishment administered by otherwise warm and caring adults is more effective, possibly because it also involves the temporary withdrawal of the rewarding aspects of that relationship; and punishment can therefore be lighter and yet still be effective.[29]

Another aspect of punishment that needs careful consideration is the modelling effect. The punisher is providing an example of behaviour which involves being stern and often angry, or, in the case of physical punishment, violent. Therefore the effect can be quite the reverse of what is intended. The child who is smacked for aggressive behaviour is getting two contradictory messages, of which the action message seems to speak louder than the verbal one. The angry telling-off for rudeness seems to fall into the same category. Bandura and Walters[30] found that the children of parents who used physical punishment tended to be more physically aggressive themselves. Although I know of no study that has investigated children who have been angrily scolded, I have often heard children berating their peers or younger children in a scolding voice, using the words their parents or teachers have used.

Overall, punishment appears to be a much more complex procedure than is often thought. It is not easy to ensure its effectiveness, and the repercussions are difficult to predict. However, it is woven into human relationships, especially those of children with adults, where there are disappointed expectations and failed goals, as well as actions taken for the ultimate protection of clients. The use of positive measures in the form of reinforcement seems to be less complicated and hazardous, but where punishment is deliberately used it would seem to be important to monitor its effects, both the intended and the side-effects.

Time Out

One punishing procedure that has been successful in modifying even extreme behaviour with a variety of client groups is "time out". Essentially, this means removing someone from the situation where his behaviour is regarded as deviant, and keeping him for a time somewhere that is less reinforcing. There are reports of rather extreme uses of time out, where clients have been put in rooms on their own, and if the clients have been very violent, this has sometimes entailed specially reinforced rooms to contain them.[31] This extreme use has naturally caused concern and anxiety, even distaste, for the procedure. But basically there is no need to go to such extremes, and time out is really nothing more than a way of using the age-old method of excluding a child or other client from a room or activity because of deviant behaviour which, for instance, is disturbing other clients. Investigations of time out have identified some factors which help to make it a successful procedure to use, and which are important to know about if any form of exclusion is to be used, and I will look at some of these briefly now.

Above all, the situation from which the client is to be removed must itself be providing reinforcement. For example, if a child is to be removed from a classroom for misbehaviour, and the classroom is aversive for him, then the action of exclusion may in itself be reinforcing to the deviant behaviour, and in future when the child wishes to get out of the classroom situation he knows he merely needs to repeat the deviant behaviour that worked before. If time out is to be used, then it must be "time out from positive reinforcement" which is its full name.

It is not at all an essential part of the procedure that the client has to be removed from the room; one can have a time-out area in a room, or simply separate someone from the group or activity which he is disrupting. Nor does the exclusion need to be for long. I have used time out for a matter of 2 to 3 minutes with children[19] and there are reports of fairly brief periods used with different client groups.

The second thing to ensure is that a client is not removed to somewhere more reinforcing, where he finds he prefers to be. If a child is taken from a classroom and put, say, in the corridor, where he greets passers-by, waves to friends in the opposite classroom, and generally enjoys himself, then the time out will again be reinforcing to the deviant behaviour that got him excluded. The same might apply to removal to the room of another member of staff, or the procedure often used in residential settings, removal to bed or bedroom. There is no necessity that time out should be spent in isolation, but if there are other people present one has to ensure that they do not provide so much reinforcement that the client prefers to be with them rather than in the place from where he was excluded. The rule for this seems to lie in a balance, where the reinforcement to be obtained in the original setting sufficiently outweighs any reinforcement in the time-out setting.

A final point concerns the process of getting the client into the time-out place. If it is accompanied by a lot of anger and physical violence, then the same hazards apply as with the other forms of punishment. But if time out can be used calmly and caringly, with the minimum of physical intervention, before the angry reactions break through, then a good rather than a bad model of handling behaviour can be given.

At present I feel that time out is a useful practice, which has a place where other more positive attempts to deal with difficult problems have failed.

Recording and Assessment

A very important requirement in any helping process is to know whether we are succeeding in what we set out to do; are we helping the client? But measuring human progress is an extremely difficult endeavour. Progress tends to be uneven, with spurts and regressions, and therefore the moment of assessment may be crucial. Measurable changes may be very small, but just those small changes may be the important ones. However, in spite of all the difficulties, it is an endeavour that we ought to undertake: in the first place we need to provide ourselves with evidence of results, and in the second place it is important to be able to communicate the success or failure of particular practices, both to colleagues and to the clients themselves and their families.

Behaviour modifiers have put rather more effort into recording and evaluating their procedures than most of the rest of us. It is sometimes objected that this has been possible because behaviour modification focusses on superficial and often rather trivial behaviours, simply because they are observable. It is true that there are many reports of the modification of apparently minor behaviours, such as paying attention in class, swearing less or eating less, etc., and that the results show small changes. However, these changes may be very important to the client concerned. There are also plenty of published reports of attempts to deal with the most severe problems, such as autism, psychosis, toilet training of extremely mentally handicapped patients, delinquency, where other attempts to help have shown little success.[4,17,27]

It is interesting that quite often when behaviour is defined and then observed it seems to moderate and cease to become a problem. This happens frequently enough to have earned the name of "base-line therapy". It does not happen predictably enough to be relied on, but when it does happen it can be regarded as a happy bonus. This is particularly noticeable in self-observation for self-modification procedures.

Once intervention is started, then further observations of target behaviours enable one to monitor the effects of the intervention—bearing in mind the effects of maturation and changed circumstances outside one's control. Procedures can then be decided on according to the observed results, changing when they are not working and persisting where there are positive enough improvements. It is such an obvious factor of intervention that one can only wonder at the frequent absence of such monitoring, where procedures are used with blind faith in their effectiveness, apparently based on authority, or some past successful experience, with little current evaluation.

Records of progress, or lack of progress, are important whatever intervention is to be used. Behaviour modifiers have developed techniques of observation and recording that would be worth investigating by anyone interested in assessing their results, whatever intervention procedures they are using. Details can be found in most of the books on behaviour modification.[17,21,23]

Ethical Considerations

Of course behaviour modification raises ethical issues. Any endeavour by people to alter the behaviour of others must raise issues of right and wrong, perhaps especially within the confines of a residential establishment where the opportunities for avoidance are reduced. Who decides what is desirable behaviour? Who decides whether it is acceptable to use food, money, cigarettes, as reinforcers—and by withholding them as instruments of punishment? Who decides how quickly progress can or should be made, or how uncomfortable or deprived clients should be allowed to feel?

There is no doubt that measures have been used in the name of behaviour modification that have not been acceptable.[32] These techniques can be used by the unwise and unscrupulous, as can other techniques with equally undesirable results. But we also have to ask ourselves questions about who has the right to deny clients techniques with demonstrated results and benefits.

To me the ethical issues highlighted by the practice of behaviour modification are relevant to all "helping" procedures. The choice element sometimes put forward as differentiating behaviour modification from other psychotherapies seems to be something of a red herring: clients can be involved in setting goals, negotiating contracts and choosing reinforcers, and choice is central to the self-modification procedures; whereas an authoritarian practitioner of another persuasion can deny any element of choice or consultation,[33] and of course neglect and cruelty can diminish the dignity of clients whatever the persuasion of the professionals.

The ethical issues that are particularly sharply focussed by the residential setting need to be guided by a code of practice, which will safeguard the basic human rights and standards of clients according to the mores of the society within which they apply. Such a code must apply to client groups whatever procedures are being used.

Concluding Comments

In this paper I have tried to indicate some of the ways in which the principles of social learning theory operate in a helping situation such as residential care. In the space available the treatment has had to be superficial, and it would be wrong to suggest that results are quick or easy—for using behaviour modification demands planning, consistent application and considerable effort in monitoring results.

But, whether one decides to use behaviour modification as a deliberate approach to the problems of residential care or not, the principles still apply, and will be operating to encourage and reinforce behaviour, or discourage it, whether deliberately or incidentally. Therefore it would seem important to try to understand those principles, at least to ensure that they are not working against our endeavours, and hindering our efforts to help.

References

1. H. Prosser, *Perspectives on Residential Child Care*, NFER, Slough, 1976.
2. M. Wolins (ed.), *Successful Group Care: Explorations in the Powerful Environment*, Aldine, Chicago, 1974.
3. A. Bandura, *Social Learning Theory*, Prentice-Hall, Englewood Cliffs, 1977.
4. E. L. Phillips, E. A. Phillips, D. L. Fixsen and M. M. Wolf, Achievement place: modification of the behaviors of pre-delinquent boys within a token economy, *Journal of Applied Behavior Analysis*, **4**, 45–59, 1971.
5. F. R. Harris, M. M. Wolf and D. M. Baer, Effects of adult social reinforcement on child behavior, *Young Children*, **20**, 8–17, 1964.
6. W. C. Becker, C. H. Madsen, C. R. Arnold and D. R. Thomas, The contingent use of teacher praise and attention in reducing classroom behavior problems, *Journal of Special Education*, **1**, 287–307, 1967.
7. M. C. Fish and E. E. Loehfelm, Verbal approval: a neglected resource, *Teachers College Record*, **76**, 493–8, 1975.
8. R. W. McIntire, *For the Love of Children*, Behaviardelia, Kalamazoo, 1970.
9. M. V. Covington and R. G. Beery, *Self Worth and School Learning*, Holt, Rinehart & Winston, New York, 1976.
10. A. Bandura, D. Ross and A. Ross, Transmission of aggression through imitation of aggressive models, *Journal of Abnormal and Social Psychology*, **63**, 575–82, 1961.
11. A. Bandura, E. B. Blanchard and B. Ritter, Relative efficacy of desensitization and modelling approaches for inducing behavioral, affective and attitudinal changes, *Journal of Desensitization and Modeling*, **13**, 173–99, 1969.
12. D. Meichenbaum, Examination of model characteristics in reducing avoidance behavior, *Journal of Personality and Social Psychology*, **17**, 298–307, 1971.
13. D. Meichenbaum, *Cognitive-Behavior Modification*, Plenum Press, New York, 1977.
14. R. M. McFall and D. B. Lillesand, Behavior rehearsal with modeling and coaching in assertive training, *Journal of Abnormal Psychology*, **77**, 313–23, 1971.
15. I. G. Sarason and V. J. Ganzer, Modeling and group discussion in the rehabilitation of juvenile delinquents, *Journal of Counseling Psychology*, **20**, 442–9, 1973.

16. M. H. THELAN, R. A. FRY, S. J. DOLLINGER and S. C. PAUL, Use of videotaped models to improve the interpersonal adjustment of delinquents, *Journal of Consulting and Clinical Psychology*, **44**, 492, 1976.

17. E. D. GAMBRILL, *Behavior Modification: Handbook of Assessment, Intervention and Evaluation*, Jossey-Bass, San Francisco, 1977.

18. A. W. STAATS and W. H. BUTTERFIELD, Treatment of non-reading in a culturally deprived juvenile delinquent: an application of reinforcement principles, *Child Development*, **36**, 925–42, 1965.

19. A. F. GOBELL, Experience with some behaviour modification techniques, *Therapeutic Education*, **3**, 32–7, 1975.

20. T. AYLLON and N. H. AZRIN, *The Token Economy: a Motivational System for Therapy and Rehabilitation*, Appleton–Century–Crofts, New York, 1968.

21. P. McAULEY and R. McAULEY, *Child Behaviour Problems: an Empirical Approach to Management*, Macmillan, London, 1977.

22. W. DE RISI and G. BUTZ, *Writing Behavioral Contracts*, Research Press, Champaign, Ill., 1975.

23. M. J. MAHONEY and C. E. THORESEN (eds.), *Self-Control: Power to the Person*, Brooks/Cole, Monterey, 1974.

24. R. W. NOVACO, *Anger Control*, Lexington, Heath, 1975.

25. C. R. ROGERS, *Carl Rogers on Personal Power. Inner Strength and its Revolutionary Impact*, Constable, London, 1978.

26. D. WILLS, Legislation is not enough, *Times Educational Supplement*, p. 19, 17 Nov. 1978.

27. O. I. LOVAAS and R. L. KOEGAL, Behavior therapy with autistic children, in C. E. THORESEN (ed.), *Behavior Modification in Education*, (NSSE), University of Chicago Press, Chicago, 1973.

28. T. Moore, Difficulties of the ordinary child in adjusting to primary school, *Journal of Child Psychology and Psychiatry*, **7**, 17–38, 1966.

29. R. H. WALTERS and R. D. PARKE, The influence of punishment and related disciplinary techniques on the social behavior of children, in B. MAHER (ed.), *Progress in Experimental Personality Research*, *Volume 3*, Academic Press, New York, 1968.

30. A. BANDURA and R. H. WALTERS, *Adolescent Aggression*, Ronald Press, New York, 1959.

31. R. B. BENOIT and G. R. MAYER, Time out: guidelines for its selection and use, *Personnel and Guidance Journal*, **53**, 501–6, 1975.

32. T. HEADS, Ethical and legal considerations in behavior therapy, in D. MARHOLIN (ed.), *Child Behavior Therapy*, Gardner Press, New York, 1978.

33. S. SUTHERLAND, *Breakdown*, Weidenfeld & Nicholson, London, 1976.

CHAPTER 11

THE C.U.S.S. GROUP HOME: A REVIEW OF PRINCIPLES AND PRACTICES IN THE CARE AND TRAINING OF MENTALLY HANDICAPPED PEOPLE

MARY PITHOUSE

Over recent years there has been growing optimism about the ability of mentally handicapped people to learn new skills and achieve greater personal independence, thereby enjoying fuller participation in the life of the community. A group home, set up by Cardiff Universities Social Services (C.U.S.S.), has been a means of exploring these possibilities. The project shows how the abilities of mentally handicapped people are often grossly underestimated, and that with the right environment and the right teaching, levels of competence in daily living skills can be significantly increased. In terms of day-to-day living this increase in "levels of competence" has exciting prospects and very satisfying results for the individuals concerned.

Levels of skill development have a direct bearing on the kind of life a person can lead, on the amount of control he can exert in his immediate environment, on the range and complexity of his relationships with other people, on his job prospects, and on many other things that affect what is loosely but meaningfully described as the "quality of life". An example is the difference between sitting for an afternoon facing a TV screen (which requires very few skills) and taking a bus into town to go shopping (which involves a fairly complex sequence of specific skills). If a mentally handicapped person is helped to increase his repertoire of skills, he will have more independence, more choice, and a greater chance of leading the kind of full, active and interesting life that most of us would want for ourselves.

In this paper I would like to draw on the experiences of the C.U.S.S. Group Home to show how certain principles and approaches have been used with great effect in helping mentally handicapped people develop their abilities. I shall be looking at day-to-day management practices, training and the quality of the environment. But first a brief review of how the Group Home started.

C.U.S.S. originated in the late 1960s as a loosely organised group of undergraduate students, engaged in a variety of traditional voluntary activities. One of the projects running at this time involved a group of mentally handicapped children and young people living in Ely Hospital, Cardiff. The students took the children out each Saturday morning to the cinema. In doing so, they became aware of the kind of conditions the children were living in (conditions which had little in common with developing child care practices). They saw the children growing up in bleak, comfortless wards, with no personal clothing or possessions, no privacy, few lasting relationships, and little contact with the outside world. Taking children to the cinema seemed a useless exercise in view of these other gross deprivations. The students believed that there had to be a better way of providing care, and the idea of a Group Home took hold.

What, then, was wrong with the hospital system? While professing rehabilitative aims like any other hospital, there were few opportunities for learning everyday skills. This was due to the scale and organisation of the hospital itself. If residents were ever to have a chance of living in the community, how were they to learn to serve—let alone cook—meals, when the plated meal service provided for everyone? How could they learn to cross roads in a large hospital complex where everyone walked in the middle of the road? How could they learn to take care of clothes when the central laundry catered for all irrespective of their abilities? The hospital system fostered the dependence of its residents and worked against the acquisition of skills. The students noted more subtle effects than this; one of the attributes testifying to "severe handicap" in the eyes of the staff and poor prospects for rehabilitation, was inappropriate or disruptive behaviour—for example, screaming, rocking, head banging. But this kind of behaviour occurred in wards where there were few or no materials for constructive activities and few adults to interact with outside of physical care routines. Often, badly needed attention could only be obtained by disruptive behaviour. In short, the ward was an abnormal environment that produced abnormal behaviour, which in turn was taken in all good faith by staff as evidence that the patients needed hospital care.

Other major criticisms of the hospital model have been specified[1]

(1) It has inhibited the maintenance of family links of handicapped people. The problem of availability and cost of public transport obviously limit the extent to which families will visit a hospital. The stigma that attaches to mental hospitals may also be expected to contribute to a low visiting rate. Yet mutual contact is of paramount importance for the handicapped person and his family.

(2) It has concentrated research and development in the hospital, neglecting the potential for community care of the handicapped person.

(3) It has concentrated resources in the hospital, preventing the development of independence in the individual and causing the admission of those needing only partial support and the continued care of those needing little help to live outside.

(4) It has disguised the individuality of handicapped people by emphasising their common problems.

(5) It has disguised those aspects of the total nature of handicapped people which are the same as for non-handicapped people.

By segregating handicapped people in large numbers in abnormal surroundings the hospital model stigmatises them as different, helpless and hopeless. The very existence of the long-stay hospital maintains the stereotype: it "shapes our concepts of mental handicap itself, our values, our fears and even our willingness to assume that the problem is one primarily for medicine and nursing".[2]

In 1971, C.U.S.S. re-organised itself to specialise exclusively in mental handicap and became a registered charity. The setting up of a Group Home was now a firm objective. A long period of planning, negotiating and fund raising followed. Opposition from some people in the traditional hospital disciplines had to be overcome, and it was the support of the then Welsh Hospital Board that tipped the balance in favour of C.U.S.S. A grant was secured from the Kings Fund Centre to employ two trainers to work at Ely Hospital and in 1974 a 4-month rehabilitation programme was set up to prepare five residents from a potential group of eight for Group Home living.

The results of the rehabilitation programme were adequate but disappointing. This was due to the limitations of the hospital environment as a training ground for Group Home living. The lack of domestic-scale equipment meant that domestic skills appropriate to living in an ordinary home could not be learnt. There was also a conflict of values and goals: the rehabilitation programme aimed at increasing personal choice, responsibility and independence. The institution required uniformity and a strict routine. The institution's norms tended to prevail. In short, it was found that training for group home living could not be carried out with much success in an environment devoid of domestic scale and detail, and within a daily regime that is geared to the institution's needs rather than those of the individual.

By this time the search for suitable accommodation for the Group Home was becoming more urgent. The City Housing Department had been approached, but nothing suitable was offered. The basic criterion in the search for accommodation was that the home should be of normal domestic scale and design with no special features that would distinguish it from the surrounding neighbourhood. Not more than two should share a bedroom; cooking and bathroom facilities should be typical of a family household, and there should be a communal living room. No separate living areas for "staff" were to be provided since this would encourage "social distance" between handicapped and non-handicapped residents, characteristic of institutional patterns of care. The search came to an end in March 1974 when University College offered to house the project in one of its own properties close to the Students' Union.

The size and design of a building that serves as a residential establishment has important implications for the relationship between its residents and the people living in the neighbourhood. A large purpose-built unit immediately signifies that its residents are in some way different from the surrounding population. It sets them apart as a separate group and suggests that they are not like the rest of us. An ordinary house in an ordinary street does not evoke this impression; one expects to have something in common with people who live in normal, familiar surroundings. This simple measure of allowing handicapped people to live in ordinary homes can go a long way in helping their integration and acceptance by the local community.

The Group Home opened in July 1974. Four students live with five mentally handicapped young people, all of whom were classified by the hospital as "severely subnormal". These five were amongst the group of young people with whom the students had been working since the early days of cinema outings. Apart from severe mental handicap, two of the residents have serious speech difficulties, one is diabetic, and one is epileptic with a minor physical handicap.

The home is financially self-supporting in that the residents receive either student grants or supplementary benefit, they share bills and all pay the same economic rent to the university. Residents attend adult training centre or their college classes during the day, while at evenings or weekends they share household tasks or participate in leisure pursuits that make as much use of the neighbourhood facilities as possible. Student holidays are covered by other students or social work students on placement in the Group Home. Support comes from the full-time social workers, employed to develop community links and monitor progress in the home. Other volunteers also lend support by visiting the home and sharing some time with the residents. When the home opened there was an immediate increase in ability all round; more was learnt in the first 3 months than in the previous 3 years. This showed the enormous scope for developing the potential of these five handicapped people, given an environment rich in opportunities for informal learning and daily decision making, together with a structured approach to training. The progress made by the residents since leaving hospital has been documented using standard assessment procedures.[3]

The role of the student resident is part teacher, part friend. In the early months emphasis lay in the training aspect of the role, because of the need for developing basic skills like crossing roads, preparing simple meals and doing household jobs. At this time activities in the home were closely organised, much more so than they are now. A simple checklist was used, with which each resident's activities were reviewed at the end of the day. A rota system was set up to allocate tasks in the house such as cooking, washing up etc. and to arrange times for individuals to do their laundry and ironing. With increasing mastery over such skills and training aspects of the student's role have since become less marked. Greater attention can now be paid to the development of individual interests and hobbies, and the widening of friendships outside the home. In the past the students living in the Group Home have mostly been in their second year at university. More recently there has been a trend towards older volunteers, including graduates and working people. After their year of living-in the volunteers, almost without exception, continue their friendships with the residents, and often offer their experience and ideas to the new volunteers. The turnover of resident support injects new enthusiasm and energy into the project and provokes a constant re-appraisal of developments. Problems of recruiting volunteers for the home have occurred, and at present there is discussion on how much support should be provided in the future, but these questions are particular to the Group Home and not immediately relevant to this paper.

In the second year of the Group Home's operation a debate arose over how much time the social worker should spend in the home and how she should fulfil her role in monitoring care in the home. A clarification of roles, relationships and practices was called for. The task was to make these as specific and objective as possible.

The students and social worker set about drawing up these guidelines in the form of an operational policy, now called the "Guide to Good Practice". The work of King, Raynes and Tizard[4] helped initially by drawing attention to particular institutional practices which we wished to avoid. These include:

(1) Rigidity of routine.
(2) Block treatment. This means the general regimentation of residents in groups for certain activities such as bathing and toiletting.
(3) Depersonalisation. This refers to the lack of personal possessions and privacy or the lack of opportunities to make decisions and choices.
(4) Social distance. This refers to the extent to which staff and residents mix together; whether, for example, they eat together or separately.

The Guide to Good Practice sets standards that are incompatible with institutional patterns of care and guards against these features developing in the home. Paragraph 45, for example, is aimed at avoiding rigid routines: "Mealtimes shall be flexible enough to allow for (i) individual choice and (ii) participation in other activities." Paragraph 40 is to do with social distance: "No areas in the home shall be restricted exclusively **to** non-handicapped or handicapped residents." Paragraphs 38 and 39 are concerned with depersonalising effects: "The privacy of individual rooms shall be respected at all times", and "Residents shall have access to their rooms at all times."

The full aims of the Guide to Good Practice are as follows:

> To specify procedures for the assessment and training of each handicapped individual resident in the Group Home, to maximise social, emotional, intellectual and physical development.

> To specify management practices and content of interaction between handicapped and non-handicapped residents in order that appropriate behaviour of each group is reinforced and to specify the least restrictive environment for individual growth and development to take place.

> To specify practices governing relationships between the residents of the home and the officers, members and staff of C.U.S.S., and visitors to the home.

While such a detailed set of procedures and practices may seem overly formalised and impersonal, it is actually essential that practices formulated and promoted in the home are objective, consistent and specific. Only in this way will personal rights and relationships be protected. Choice, flexibility and decision making have to be "built in" by specifying certain practices, like those quoted above.

Related to this is the point that objective guidelines for practices in a residential setting remove the element of personal authority from relationships between staff and residents. By defining in detail the pattern of care, the rights of the residents and the role of staff, an operational policy can help reduce the risk of personal authority becoming vested in individual staff members. For most of us, authority is felt through the existence of public rules and laws; we are also subject to the influence and demands of individuals and groups in our private lives. But within this private sphere most of us have the means to avoid unwelcome control. If someone tries to exercise such control, we could probably find the words to retaliate or negotiate or find a way to manoeuvre ourselves out of the situation. Mentally handicapped people tend to have fewer means than most of us for exerting counter-control. This is one reason amongst many for developing specific guidelines for management practices in a residential setting.

In the operational policy we tried to specify practices that add up to "high-quality care". There were two features we wanted to preserve and encourage: firstly contact with the community, through the use of local facilities, shops, pub, launderette etc.; and secondly a high level of engagement within the home. Much is learnt through interaction and participation and so it is important that a living environment provides scope for this. Basically this means that residents should have easy access to appropriate materials and interested staff. One way to measure the quality of care in a residential setting is to look at how many residents are engaged with people or materials, in their environment. Compared with an institutional setting the Group Home is, by its nature, conducive to high levels of engagement: there are tasks to do around the home, there are people to talk to and activities to share. Even so, we thought it important to set down formal guidelines to help ensure high levels of engagement. For this reason the operational policy states that "residents should always be offered a choice of at least two engaging activities in their leisure time", and it further specifies how much time should be offered by the student residents for activities shared with the handicapped residents

on an individual basis. Standards like these can help to establish a daily living environment that maximises opportunities for learning.

Within C.U.S.S. the operational policy is a valuable instrument for the social worker
to use in monitoring standards in the Group Home. Because it is an impersonal document it enables disagreement to be handled in an objective way through reference to its
contents. The operational policy is a developing document, it allows for changing concerns and developing practices. Anyone can propose alterations to the document; these
are taken to a meeting of the Group Home residents and the social worker for discussion.

Over the past few years the thinking that has guided training procedures in the Group
Home has developed with the input of new ideas from various sources. In the early
stages of the project, the contribution of the Senior Clinical Psychologist at Ely Hospital
was important in directing the students towards the principles of learning theory. This
formed our basis for understanding how behaviours are learnt, and offered approaches
that were useful in helping the residents acquire new skills. Learning theory provides a
technology that works in producing direct change in individuals. One of its chief merits
is that it demands a high degree of specificity. It requires that we state clearly what it is
that we are trying to achieve and how we intend to achieve it. This explicitness is often
lacking in other therapies. However, its effectiveness in shaping individual behaviour
raises ethical issues and I should like to discuss some of these, as they relate to training
in the Group Home. But first it may be helpful to look briefly at the principles of learning
theory and some of the techniques that derive from it.

One of the basic tenets of learning theory is the concept of reinforcement. This
emphasises the relationship between behaviour and its consequent events. Some events
will increase the frequency of behaviours and these are commonly called rewards, or in
the more precise language of learning theory, positive reinforcers. As the infant develops,
the range of positive reinforcers extends from basic physical comforts to social reinforcers
such as the attention and interest of other people. It is important to recognise that not
all positive reinforcers come in the form of formal rewards or praise. There are many
events that may have this function for any one individual. They may derive from the
behaviour of other people or events in the non-social world such as a beautiful view
rewarding the climber. The important thing about learning theory is that it directs us
towards the context in which behaviour takes place. It shows that where a behaviour is
followed by a reinforcing event it is more likely to be repeated and when a behaviour
goes unrewarded it is less likely to recur. In teaching an individual new skills we can
arrange for a reinforcing event to follow a desired behaviour and so increase its frequency. In the early stages of teaching a new skill, where a "breakthrough" is needed
we may wish to use an "arbitrary" reward to strengthen the required behaviour. This
is a reward that does not derive naturally from performing the behaviour but is under
the control of the teacher. For a child this may be a sweet or a favourite toy. In the long
term however, it is important that the consequences for performing the behaviour in the
teaching situation match those operating elsewhere. Otherwise the behaviour will not
generalise to settings outside the teaching situation. Training programmes should therefore eventually incorporate the use of "natural" reinforcers, if the person is to use the
skill in other situations. However, it is not always the case that a person's living environment will contain natural reinforcers for performing certain skills. A hospital, for
instance, may be particularly sparse in these. The natural reinforcer for speech, for
example, is the influence it has on the listener; if a child on the hospital ward has no-one

to speak to, developing speech is not worthwhile. The important thing about the Group Home is that it provides normal opportunities and natural reinforcers for developing skills.

The concept of reinforcement also helps in understanding how events may support inappropriate behaviour. The other day I was in a room with a group of young people some of whom were mentally handicapped. Two were volunteers in the role of care givers. Some of us were watching TV, others were playing table games or leafing through magazines. The atmosphere was quiet and relaxed. It then happened that one handicapped young man got up and started turning the switch on an electric point on and off. The volunteers responded with alacrity; he received a lot of attention and was invited with plenty of good humour and persuasiveness to sit down. Once he was seated the volunteers went back to their previous activities. A few minutes later he got up again and began playing once more with the switch. The volunteers repeated their efforts. And so it went on. It was a situation where inappropriate behaviour was being reinforced by the response of others, while the individual's appropriate behaviour was going unnoticed. Having identified attention as a powerful reinforcer for this individual a different strategy could be adopted. This would involve rewarding only appropriate behaviours with attention and praise, thus strengthening them, and withholding attention for the inappropriate behaviour. In this way we would be dispensing the same reinforcer but linking it to the desired behaviour rather than inappropriate behaviour.

The principle of scheduling rewards is an important part of learning theory. This has to do with how frequently rewards are given. There are two phases, continuous scheduling and partial scheduling. In the early stages of learning a new behaviour it is important for a person to be rewarded every time he performs the behaviour. This enables him to see clearly what is expected of him and is known as continuous scheduling. Once the behaviour is well established, it is possible to change to a partial schedule. This means that the reward is not given on every occasion that the behaviour occurs but intermittently. Providing the behaviour is well established, intermittent rewards will be sufficient to maintain it. The principle of partial scheduling also operates to maintain undesired or inappropriate behaviours. This occurs when people in an individual's immediate environment are, without realising it, intermittently rewarding a particular behaviour. The behaviour pays off part of the time and for this reason it is repeated.

Shaping is another useful principle of learning theory. It involves breaking down a complex skill to small steps and teaching these steps in sequence. Rewards are delivered at each stage. Breaking a skill into small manageable steps is important because it means there is far less chance of failure; and the success achieved in learning each small step is encouraging and rewarding for both the client and the teacher. If a programme does not succeed it may be that the teacher has not identified appropriate reinforcers for the client or that the task has not been broken down into small enough steps. Either way it is a problem of programme design rather than a reflection of the client's abilities.

Because these techniques are effective in changing a person's behaviour and may involve manipulation of his physical or interpersonal environment, their application must be critically examined from an ethical point of view. For this reason C.U.S.S. has an ethical review body, composed of people who are removed from the day-to-day running of the Group Home. The members meet regularly to review the goals and methods of training in the Group Home. A review body of this kind has to have clearly formulated questions and checks to work from and its first task is to formulate these.

There are two main areas to consider, firstly are the goals of training right for the client? Secondly, are the methods used in attaining these goals consistent with the rights of the individual, most importantly his right to choose not to participate in a programme of training?

The selection of goals is an area that is heavily influenced by our own values. We must be explicit about these values and how they affect the choice of goals. In the Group Home the principles of normalisation and integration are explicit values which influence the choice of goals. We are concerned with enabling the residents to acquire skills and behaviours that will allow them to participate as much as possible in the normal life of the community. The operational policy makes the following basic statement on the choice of goals: "Training shall focus on skills which are frequently used, and which enlarge the resident's independence and control of his environment within the context of personal responsibility and respect for others." Initially we can say that training programmes should aim to extend an individual's independence and control of his environment by enlarging the range of abilities with which he meets the world. Goals must be consistent with the needs of the individual and not primarily with the needs of the institution or residential establishment. It can happen that certain teaching objectives for residents are favoured because their attainment will make the task of care staff easier. Given the pressures on residential staff this may be understandable but it is not always satisfactory for the client. For example, many hospitals emphasise toilet training as a priority for young handicapped children to the neglect of teaching other skills. It could be argued that training in language skills is a more urgent priority because research suggests that there is an optimum period for language development in infancy, while there is no such optimum time for toilet training. Care staff may prefer to concentrate on toilet training because it will make life easier, but in terms of the child's needs language training may be the more urgent priority. The statement from the operational policy points to another check that can be made on the choice of training goals; Is it a skill that is used frequently? Does it fall within the range of skills that most of us use on a regular basis? The skills chosen as goals for training should be ones that will be used and maintained in the course of day-to-day living. We can also ask of a teaching objective: Is it a skill or behaviour that will open up opportunities for further learning? Is it one that the individual can build on? An example is learning to greet a visitor in an appropriate manner. This is valuable because it opens up possibilities for acquiring skills in conversation, for sharing knowledge and for forming relationships. However, one of the most important principles for the review body to check in any training programme is whether the client was involved in setting the goals—was the programme planned with his participation? This is a fundamental principle of Goal Planning[5] as it is carried out in the Group Home.

These are some of the questions that need to be asked concerning the selection of goals, but how do we ensure that the methods used for achieving these goals are also ethically sound? Learning theory shows that by arranging for a reinforcing event to follow a desired behaviour we can increase its frequency. By withholding reinforcement it is possible to reduce the frequency of a behaviour. It has been noted that in the early stages of establishing a new skill an arbitrary reward may be necessary to strengthen the required behaviour. From an ethical viewpoint the use of such rewards must be treated with extreme caution. The Group Home's operational policy rules out certain things which may not be supplied or withheld as rewards:

Activities and experiences which significantly contribute to the learning and development of the client shall not be withdrawn as a withdrawal of reinforcement. These activities shall always include the following:

(1) anything which contributes to the physical welfare of the client, such as food, appropriate clothing and medical care;

(2) attendance at adult training centre or other place of work;

(3) access to training programmes;

(4) access to the social worker or relatives.

Initially then, we can say that these activities and experiences must always be available to the client as of right. But if we use other activities, goods or experiences as rewards an ethical problem may still arise in terms of their availability to the client: where a client's access to a particular object or experience is made entirely contingent on his performance of a desired behaviour, coercion is present. Whether these rewards are defined as "luxuries" or "privileges" is beside the point. If we deprive a person of something that is normally available in order to use it as a reinforcer, the person has no room to dissent. If, for example, a trip to the cinema is identified as a reward for a particular client and this reward is made contingent on his participation in a particular training programme, coercion is implicit. If we use this particular activity to encourage and reward participation in a training programme, we have to be sure that the client has access to this activity through other means. From an ethical point of view, it is preferable to make use of rewards that derive directly from the programme of training, these are the natural reinforcers. A simple example is using the phone: if a resident participates in a programme to learn how to use the phone the natural reinforcer is that he will be able to ring his friends and relatives when he so desires. He will be able to do this without having to ask for help or waiting until it is convenient for someone to assist him. The reward is intrinsic to the programme. By highlighting these natural rewards for the client, rather than using arbitrary rewards, ethical problems are greatly reduced. Certainly there are times when a person, by reason of his age or degree of handicap, cannot appreciate the natural rewards of learning a particular skill. It may then be necessary to consider the use of arbitrary rewards in programmes that seek to establish important skills. Where arbitrary rewards are incorporated into training programmes, ethical review procedures are particularly important as a means of safeguarding the rights of the client.

Concern for the ethical problems involved in behaviour change techniques highlights the need for a model that will guide the planning of individual programmes. Goldiamond[6] has made an important contribution. He is concerned with the ethics of behaviour-change programmes and the need to develop a programme model that preserves the rights and dignity of the individual whilst making use of the investigative and analytic techniques of applied behaviour analysis. Goldiamond's model of programme instruction derives from what he calls a "constructional approach" to problems. This approach contrasts with the "pathological orientation" that presently dominates the helping professions. Characteristically, we reflect and focus on what is wrong, on the deficit or disturbance in a person's day-to-day living pattern. We concentrate on the stress involved and the possible means for eliminating it. Diagnoses and classifications are based mainly on these undesirable patterns which require elimination. Apart from the negative features of labelling which may derive from this approach, there is an additional problem in knowing when successful elimination has taken place. This is particularly so in mental illness where disturbed behaviour is attributed to a vague underlying pathological state. Eliminating the pathology is made the therapeutic aim but how can we know when this has been achieved and how can we predict that future disturbance will not recur? In contrast to this eliminative approach, the constructional approach focusses on positive goals that will strengthen and enlarge the client's repertoire of skills. The aim is to directly increase the available options or extend social repertoires. As a by-product of this change the undesirable pattern is likely to diminish. The model requires that goals are set in terms of clearly observable behaviour. This means that we can be sure when the desired outcome is achieved. Essential to the constructional model is contracting with the client on the outcomes and procedures that are considered worthwhile. The contract requires an explicit statement of our areas of concern and requires our being limited to them. All others are reserved for the client.

Goldiamond argues that examining disturbed behaviour can be useful if we analyse what is going on in behavioural terms. He suggests that the distressing symptom or problem behaviour may provide what he calls the individual's "critical consequences", these being the responses that the individual feels he must have from those around him. If a symptom successfully produces this response it will be maintained, even at high personal cost to the individual himself. Goldiamond suggests that what the individual wants is usually legitimate but he has had to resort to unusual tactics to get what most of us obtain through conventional means. The repertoires may be disturbing to others, and he may be jeopardising his own interests through using them, but they are the only means he has for obtaining the response he needs. The task, then, is to increase the individual's repertoire of behaviours which will produce the desired consequences, so that extreme tactics become unnecessary. This analytical approach is particularly useful in working with mentally handicapped people whose skills for obtaining desired responses from others may be limited. The approach is a positive one, it suggests that we use the problem behaviour in a constructive way, to help understand the individual's pressing needs, and then concentrate on building repertoires that will enable the individual to use other, more conventional means for obtaining what he wants.

Goldiamond's model of programme instruction corresponds with the principles and techniques of Goal Planning. There are four basic elements, firstly the "target or outcome". This involves defining the outcome of the programme in terms of observable behaviour. Global aims such as "developing the client's potential" or "enhancing his relationships with other residents" have to be redefined in terms of specific behaviour. Goals that seek to eliminate undesirable behaviour have to be redefined in positive terms that state what the client will be doing when the goal is achieved. Secondly, there is the "entry behaviour or current relevant repertoire". This involves identifying the client's current strengths and the skills he already has which can be used in building new repertoires. In using Goal Planning procedures in the Group Home, we make a list of each resident's strengths and needs. The resident is present when this happens and helps to make the list. The needs indicate possible training goals and the strengths are those things that the resident can already do or enjoys doing. As far as possible the resident's strengths are incorporated in the methods used to achieve the goal. This makes the programme more enjoyable and satisfying. If, for example, a client has skills in the use of money and likes new clothes, a programme to teach him to go into town to shop for clothes on his own will build on strengths he already has. The third element of Goldiamond's model is the "sequence of change steps". Again these are expressed in terms of observable behaviour. Each one consists of a requirement that either differs in requiring more from the client than the previous step, or is the same but involves less help or prompting from the instructor. The fourth element of the model concerns "progression-maintaining consequences". This involves looking at ways that progression through the successive steps of a programme may be maintained. Goldiamond suggests that progression through the programme will itself be reinforcing, providing that the client sees the final outcome as worthwhile. In the Group Home we have found it helpful at times to highlight the progress being made in a training programme by using a simple chart that the client understands. He can then chart his own progress towards the final goal. This helps to maintain his interest and participation in the programme.

Goal Planning was introduced to the Group Home in 1976 with the advice and support of the Applied Research Unit in Mental Handicap in Wales. It made an important contribution to the quality of training in the Group Home by stressing the need for written plans, clear language and the involvement of the client in planning programmes. Training is now based on written individual programme plans in which the goal, the sequence of steps for reaching the goal, and the methods used in each step are all stated in clear language. Each plan contains information as to who will do what in each step of the training process. In the Group Home two standard forms are used: one is for the full details of the goal plan, showing steps, methods and the target date for at least the first step. The other is a goal-plan summary; this lists all the goal plans that a client is currently working on. The use of written goal plans means that information can easily be passed on to the ethical review body. It also means that information can be passed on to the Adult Training Centre. Certain programmes are treated as confidential to those living with or closely involved with the client and, as a general principle, the permission of the client is sought before information is passed on to other agencies.

So far I have neglected to say much about day-to-day living in the Group Home. Information of this kind can be obtained in a recent report.[7] Instead I have tried to focus on general principles and practices which may be applied to other residential settings for mentally handicapped people. Living in the Group Home has produced tangible benefits for the residents. These can be measured reasonably objectively through assessing the level of their skills and their contact with the community. In summary, three important features stand out: firstly, care is provided in an ordinary house which encourages integration in and acceptance by the local community; secondly, management practices within the home allow for individual decision making and the application of a wide range of everyday skills; thirdly, training is based on written plans with specific goals and methods, the client is involved in planning his programmes and they are regularly reviewed by an ethical committee. If to this we add the commitment of caring and interested people, we may be approaching a service that really does give mentally handicapped people the chance to develop their skills and live as full members of the community.

References

1. Cardiff Community Health Council and Vale of Glamorgan Health Council, *Future Services for Mentally Handicapped People in South Glamorgan*, 1977, para. 5.

2. P. TOWNSEND, The Political Sociology of Mental Handicap: a Case-Study of Policy Failure, in D. BOSWELL and J. WINGROVE (eds.), *The Handicapped Person in the Community*, Tavistock, p. 435.
3. *C.U.S.S. Group Home Special Report: an Evaluation of Assessments Carried out to Measure the Social Competence of the Residents Before and After Discharge from Ely Hospital, Cardiff*, 1976, available from Cardiff Universities Social Services, Joint Students Union, Park Place, Cardiff.
4. R. D. KING, N. V. RAYNES and J. TIZARD, *Patterns of Residential Care*, Routledge & Kegan Paul, 1971.
5. P. S. HOUTS and R. A. SCOTT, *Goal Planning with Developmentally Disabled Persons*, Department of Behavioural Science, Pennsylvania State University College of Medicine, 1975.
6. I. GOLDIAMOND, Toward a constructional approach to social problems: ethical issues raised by applied behaviour analysis, in *Behaviourism: a Forum for Critical Discussion*, **2** (1), 1974, pp. 1–84.
7. *Report '79*, CUSS, see 3 above.

CHAPTER 12

SUSAN: THE SUCCESSFUL RESOLUTION OF A "SEVERE BEHAVIOUR DISORDER" WITH A MENTALLY HANDICAPPED YOUNG WOMAN IN A COMMUNITY SETTING*

JIM MANSELL

Effective interventions exist for many of the behavioural deficits of severely mentally handicapped people.[1] But there is little evidence that these interventions are much used in existing services.[2] This is particularly true for mentally handicapped people with dangerous or severely disruptive behaviour. Although precision teaching methods have been used successfully to teach alternatives to troublesome behaviour, in practice the major response to what is called "severe behaviour disorder" is the provision of residential care in a long-stay mental handicap hospital. Of the nine in every hundred mentally handicapped people who bear this label, seven are in hospital.[3]

The proponents of the traditional long-stay hospital claim that only in this setting can those with such "severe behaviour disorders" be satisfactorily dealt with.[4,5] However, the transfer of severely mentally handicapped people with disruptive or dangerous behaviour to such long-stay hospitals has not been shown to result in the learning of alternative "adaptive" responses.[6] Conditions in these hospitals vary widely, but they provide nothing like a normal family and community life for their inmates. What the hospital setting actually provides is a basic custodial environment in which troublesome behaviours can be contained and tolerated.

Many people still argue that the prospect for moving away from the traditional pattern of mental handicap services is much limited by the presence of a significant proportion of mentally handicapped people in these hospitals whose behaviour is so disruptive that it cannot be successfully managed in smaller, more home-like surroundings, among ordinary houses and shops in the community. This is, for example, the view of the Government's Development Team for the Mentally Handicapped.[7] And so planners continue to upgrade or replace wards in existing large hospitals, transforming old institutions into new institutions and accounting for much the greater proportion of capital expenditure available for mental handicap services.[8] Proposals continue to be made for the building of specially contructed "secure" and "semi-secure" units for the segregation of people categorised as having varying degrees of severe behaviour disorder.

Thus, at a time when the future of mental handicap services in Britain, as in the United States and Scandinavia, is held to involve the gradual abandonment of the

---

* The author would like to thank John Clements and Judith Jenkins for their comments on a draft of this paper.

traditional long-stay hospital in favour of better domiciliary services and residential care in small, locally based homes, the problem of severe behaviour disorder is still a focus of the debate. For it is on the belief that the mentally handicapped have among their number a significant proportion of people who can only be contained in a traditional hospital setting that the defenders of the *status quo* base their claim.

This discussion concerns the development, and successful resolution of, a "severe behaviour disorder" in a young woman with severe mental handicap, shortly after moving from a long-stay hospital to live in an unusual kind of group home in the community.

Subject and Setting

Susan had lived in a long-stay hospital for the mentally handicapped from the age of 6; on 13 July 1974, just before her nineteenth birthday, she moved out to live with eight other young people in an ordinary house in the inner city.* Four others (three men and one woman) had come with her from the hospital at the same time and had lived with her on one ward for children at the hospital for 6 months before the move. The other four residents were all students at the nearby University or Technical College.[9]

The handicapped residents were all categorised as severely mentally handicapped but nevertheless all had many skills. All could walk (one with difficulty), no-one had seriously disruptive or troublesome behaviour, all were able to wash, dress, use the toilet and feed themselves—although in the latter areas each needed constant checking and prompting to reach a standard acceptable at close quarters in an ordinary household. Three of the handicapped residents could talk and follow clear and simple instructions; the other two talked very little, and other people needed practice to understand what they said; one also had difficulty with comprehension.

Susan had been one of the oldest and most able residents on a ward for children at the hospital, and had held a trusted position in helping nursing and domestic staff. Susan wanted to be a nurse "when she grew up", and she sought and was allowed to carry out routine ward tasks such as making beds, running errands and sorting laundry. She spent as much time as possible in the company of staff, interrupting conversations and interfering in other activities.

After the move out from hospital, Susan still adopted a "staff role" in relation to the other handicapped residents; she was easily distracted and her level of ability in many areas was very low. She was unable to use most household equipment (in the first 3 months Susan accidentally broke the iron once, the ironing board three times, and needed very close supervision using the vacuum cleaner, gas cooker and gas water heater) or the recreational materials the others used, and would sit and mimic an activity while watching the others, joining in their conversation. Her low level of ability was a constant source of concern to her and she often asked to be taught things, but her very poor comprehension of verbal instruction and lack of manual dexterity made this a slow process, and Susan appeared most comfortable when she was the centre of attention but not required to do anything other than talk or mimic the activity of others.

---

* This is the same unit described in the previous chapter by M. Pithouse. The specific methods described should not be taken as fully indicative of present work at the group home, where change and development have occurred with the passage of time, as in any residential unit.

The most easily distinguished feature of life in this household in the first few months in the summer of 1974 was the need for the student residents to teach and monitor the carrying out of the simple household tasks by the handicapped residents.

This emphasis on household skills lent itself to the use of standardised procedures for teaching each task as a sequence of very small, easily mastered steps. Sometimes written teaching programmes were used, but most often the students developed the procedures on an *ad hoc* basis. The student residents were familiar with the use of the simplest behaviour-modification techniques, having worked closely with the clinical psychologist at the hospital in developing procedures to teach student volunteers to teach skills to handicapped children and young people (including the five former residents). Verbal praise was given as the reinforcement for correct performance of each step of the task. In the small group setting of the household the problem of ensuring consistency of approach was easily overcome and the students felt that this was a good enough reason for written programmes to be dispensed with. Neither did the students keep routine data on the frequency of the behaviours being taught; they reasoned that data collection would be too time-consuming, as teaching was being carried out in virtually every aspect of daily life.

Specific Problems

Six weeks after the move out from the hospital, Susan began to disrupt activities in the home. Susan would often be the last to go to bed. At first this was no problem, but in early September she began to refuse to stay up on her own, in the first few days turning the radio on to full volume, later pulling others out of bed, banging on doors and singing and shouting. Also, she began to refuse to do household tasks or carry out requests, making it more difficult for others to see to their own needs. On these occasions the others—both student and handicapped residents—tended either to argue with Susan or to avoid her, ignoring her behaviour. Using the same approach as in teaching skills, the students tried to provide praise and attention contingent upon appropriate behaviour; thus, during periods of disruptive behaviour, students attempted to withdraw attention. For example, attempts by Susan to wake people up at night were dealt with by a student taking her back to the living room without speaking to her, and then returning to bed himself.

Susan became more and more disruptive during the next 14 days. Every daily task became the scene for confrontation; a new urgency was introduced when Susan began to scratch, hit and bite the people she lived with. These attacks were accompanied by temper tantrums with periods of screaming, of up to 15 minutes at a time. Thus, only a few weeks after moving out of hospital, Susan's behaviour had become a serious problem, threatening her own future in her new setting and the whole project itself. The other handicapped residents had most of their own activities disrupted and were quick to complain to Susan, suggesting that she would be sent "back on the ward". She herself was very upset by the whole idea of returning to the hospital and would promise in response to "be good". The students were concerned that if Susan's attacks increased then it would be difficult to resist her transfer back to hospital if the statutory agencies made this a condition for their continued support for the project.

The students asked the clinical psychologist advising on the project for help in working with Susan to overcome the problem without transfer back to hospital. The next day, the people living next door to the house complained about Susan and argued that she should be sent back to hospital. This was the first solution proposed by the representatives of the health and social services agencies monitoring the project, but after negotiation with the students and psychologist they and the neighbours agreed that in the first instance a teaching programme would be tried.

Objectives of the Teaching Programme

In preparing the teaching programme, two areas of problem behaviour were identified. These were: firstly, Susan's attacks on other people, destruction of furniture and personal effects and disruption of activities; and, secondly, generally poor levels of performance across the whole range of self-help, household and leisure activities. Susan's poor performance was included as a problem area partly because Susan herself made unfavourable comparisons between her own performance and that of the other residents, and also because it was felt that the disruptive behaviour might have been learned, at least in part, as a response to getting low levels of praise and attention in the course of carrying out everyday tasks. In hospital, Susan had also behaved disruptively on the rare occasions when corrected or reprimanded by staff.

The immediate objectives set were, therefore, that Susan should carry out everyday tasks, including going to bed, without disturbing others and without screaming or attacking other people; and that the students should reinforce Susan for smaller steps in her performance of everyday activities and pay more attention to raising her level of competence compared with the other handicapped residents.

The Teaching Programme

The teaching programme involved two components. The major component was a token system combined with verbal praise. Students placed counters into a glass jar in full view in the room where Susan was working; at first each counter was given for periods of about 1 minute during which Susan behaved non-disruptively, by talking quietly, co-operating in recreational activities or carrying out housework or self-help tasks. Counters were not placed in the jar if Susan was interrupting others or if she refused to carry out a task such as laying the table or washing up after a meal (in the case of housework tasks, another resident undertook Susan's share and consequently received everyone's thanks). If she actively disrupted activities, counters were removed one by one from the jar at intervals.

Counters were redeemed for two kinds of tangible reward. Five of every ten counters in the jar could be immediately exchanged on receipt of the tenth counter for a very small piece of chocolate; the other five were saved and used at the end of the evening to exchange for clothing and accessories to be used the following day. The evening exchange was introduced in an attempt to make the decision to go to bed more attractive for Susan who was very concerned about her appearance and for whom the opportunity to choose clothes each night was an important consequence. From the start of the teaching programme Susan's choice was restricted and the students laid out a set of clothes for her; Susan used her tokens to vary and add to the choice of clothes and accessories.

Similarly, Susan's going into her bedroom was the occasion for choosing a coloured nightdress; actually getting into bed and saying "Good-night" was the occasion for giving four counters and, for the first few nights, a small piece of chocolate.

Because of the requirement of deciding to issue or withhold a counter every minute or so, each student paid much more attention to Susan's performance, and the students became more careful in their teaching of skills to break down tasks and instruct for smaller steps.

The purpose and content of the teaching programme were explained to Susan who was an eager participant. The scheme was introduced on 16 September, and used until the end of October 1974. During October, an addition to the basic programme was introduced in response to a request to be involved from Susan's parents. Susan kept an additional "savings account" where saving ten counters a day for each of 7 days earned her the privilege of speaking to her parents on the telephone. If ten counters had not been saved each day then a student would give a progress report over the telephone to her parents, but Susan would not speak to them. In practice this turned out to be a very important incentive for Susan.

In addition to the token system, the programme included the prescription by a medically qualified psychiatrist of a sleeping draught (chloral hydrate) to be given on occasions of prolonged screaming. Susan was not told of this component of the programme.

As with other teaching programmes, the students collected no systematic data on the frequency of appropriate or inappropriate responses when the teaching programme was first used. From 23 September onwards, each instance of Susan refusing to carry out a task was recorded by the students at the request of the psychologist. The only other data collected were routine assessments completed in August 1974 and January 1975 using the Progress Assessment Chart 2^{10} (PAC 2). The assessments were completed by a student resident on each occasion, according to the manual for completion of the chart; there was no procedure for introducing a second observer to check reliability of the observations made.

Results

The introduction of the token system was soon followed by markedly improved levels of co-operative behaviour for much of the time. From a daily occurrence, instances of tantrumming, attacks on other people and disruption of activities recorded in the diary declined to three in September and one in October. On 16 September, the first day of the token system, Susan finished the day with no counters, refused to go to bed and attacked her room-mate; on 22 September, the seventh day, Susan refused to carry out any of her share of household tasks and this was the occasion for argument and a temper tantrum; on 25 September similar refusals were recorded but there was no other disruption; on 17 October Susan refused to go to bed or to stay up alone quietly, pulling her room-mate out of bed. On 22 September and 17 October, the sleeping draught prescribed by the psychiatrist was used—the only instances where this happened; on the other occasions any disruption was tolerated until it ceased without intervention.

The most dramatic change observed was the recorded frequency of Susan's refusal to carry out household tasks. Typically, Susan would, in answer to a request from another resident, say "No", before going on to overturn materials or to attack someone. On the morning of 23 September, the first day on which these instances were recorded, Susan is recorded as saying, on being wakened by a student after sleeping through the sound of her alarm clock, "No, I'm not going to get up! No! No! No! No! No!" She then got up. The next instance was on 26 September; when asked if she wanted to use the hot water for a bath, Susan replied "No—no bath". This took place in the bathroom; 10 days previously it would have been met with a reasoned explanation of the consequences for Susan and everyone else of not using the hot water at the right time; on this occasion, as on 23 September, the student left the room immediately to record the exchange in the diary kept in the living room. On returning, Susan was observed to be in the bath. The only other time Susan refused to do something in this way was on 17 October when the sleeping draught was eventually used.

The routine assessments made in August 1974 and in January 1975 also showed improvement in Susan's behaviour. The scores of the two PAC 2 assessments are shown below. In each subsection of the chart, the individual can score up to six points depending on his or her level of competence.

		August 1974	January 1975
Self-help:	table habits	3/6	5/6
	cleanliness	3/6	5/6
	care of clothes	3/6	6/6
	mobility	1/6	2/6
	health	1/6	2/6
Communication:	language	0/6	3/6
	money	0/6	0/6
	time and measures	0/6	0/6
	writing	0/6	1/6
	reading	0/6	0/6
Socialisation:	shopping	0/6	2/6
	social graces	1/6	5/6
	home assistance	1/6	3/6
	financial dealings	0/6	0/6
	social initiative	0/6	2/6
Occupation:	manual activities	1/6	4/6
	leisure occupations	2/6	5/6
	application	2/6	4/6
	speed and reliability	1/6	5/6
	timekeeping	2/6	4/6

Discussion

Susan's disruptive behaviour was just the kind of problem that proponents of the long-stay hospital for the mentally handicapped claim cannot be dealt with anywhere else. The claim is not that such problems can be resolved through systematic treatment which is possible only within the confines of the traditional hospital, but that only there can disruptive behaviour be tolerated and controlled. Support for this view is claimed because of the widespread practice among residential homes and hostels for the mentally handicapped of refusing to admit, or transferring out to hospital, any resident who exhibits behaviour which is troublesome or dangerous.

This view of the nature of "severe behaviour disorder" involves a profound pessimism about the prospects for change. If this were the only approach to the problem, all that would be left to parents or staff faced with the practical problem of dangerous or disruptive behaviour of a person in their care would either be some kind of saintly tolerance (with the restructuring of daily life to contain the problem, completely disrupting the ordinary programme of social and recreational activities in the family home or the residential unit) or, alternatively, the crude restraint of locking people up in back wards or secure hospitals, tying them down or damping down their general level of activity with drugs.

The development of an alternative, problem-solving approach, which can occur in the statutory services, instead of the pursuit of ever more secure facilities in which to lock people up, is a major priority if the movement to community care is to succeed. The assumption that the problem is, in the day-to-day practical situation, inherently intractable is less and less acceptable as more examples of this approach are provided. Neither should the problem be seen as a failure on the part of individual handicapped people; as the conditions and consequences of the problem behaviour are, at least to some extent, found to be under the control of those caring for the individual, so the problem is in part the product of their activities.

In Susan's case, some of the origins of her disruptive and dangerous behaviour may be seen in a hospital environment relatively impoverished of simple human contacts and providing extremely unusual living arrangements for its inmates. Similar episodes of disruptive behaviour, though of shorter duration, had occurred in hospital, and Susan was held to be unsuitable for life outside the hospital setting. But it is more important to look at Susan's behaviour in the setting in which it was defined as a problem by the people living and working with her—at the conditions under which it occurred and the consequences for Susan in the household of which she became a member.

The successful resolution of Susan's problem behaviour confirmed the students in their belief that their mistakes had actually caused the problem. From the first they had used praise and attention to reinforce the performance of each step in every task being learned by the handicapped residents, but the individualised nature of the task was hard to maintain. The handicapped residents themselves compared progress and criticised poor performance (and Susan was as critical as anyone else), and the students went along with this. Susan made slower progress than the others and in consequence received less praise and attention. The students had made praise and attention difficult to get by un- intentionally requiring a level of performance from Susan dictated by what the *other* handicapped residents had achieved.

Given this situation, the students found the contingent provision of praise and atten- tion difficult and under some circumstances impossible, so that on some occasions they found themselves unavoidably involved in attending to Susan when the criteria for performance were not being met. In retrospect, it seems very likely that over a period of 15 to 20 days in which Susan developed disruptive and dangerous behaviours, the students actually arranged her environment in ways which systematically shaped more and more disruptive behaviour. For example, when Susan began to stay up later than the others, turning the radio to full volume, one of the other residents (usually a student) would return after a while to ask that the volume should be reduced; when the student reasoned that this was maintaining Susan's behaviour the practice was stopped. When Susan began to bang on people's bedroom doors, singing and shouting, this too was ignored; only when she began to come into rooms and pull people out of bed did students respond—by taking her back to the living-room in silence and then returning to their own rooms (in fact the intervening step of locking bedroom doors was tried by all the other residents, but Susan's room-mate then became the only target).

A similar procedure may have occurred when Susan began to disrupt other activities by, for example, removing or destroying the materials being used. If this was ignored, by for example picking the materials up and starting again, Susan attacked one of the other residents and everyone responded by pulling her off the victim. Once matters had reached the stage where this was happening several times each night the end of the evening was the occasion for a prolonged temper tantrum in which Susan's screaming would continue even when no-one else was present.

In effect, a step-by-step programme was unwittingly provided in which Susan could most easily obtain attention from her fellow residents if she adopted a more disruptive pattern of behaviour. So important was this to her that even complaints, reprimands and eventually actual restraint by other residents was enough to maintain the progression. Thus, attention from other residents was for Susan a critical consequence;[11] making this consequence contingent upon performances which were very difficult for Susan made the alternative performances of disruptive behaviour that much more effective—although at a massive cost to Susan and those around her. The very rapid change in the overall level of disruptive behaviour with the introduction of the token system may be seen as, at least in part, due to making the critical consequence more freely available.

Another major point about the approach used by the students to deal with Susan's disruptive behaviour is that it was what Goldiamond calls "pathological" in orientation[12]—it was largely concerned with eliminating particular responses from Susan's repertoire in order to solve the problem. Thus, from the very first, the problem was seen as the need to eliminate disruptive behaviour, to eliminate attacks, to eliminate temper tantrums. Goldiamond contrasts the pathological approach with what he calls a "constructional" orientation to social problems, in which the objective is to build on the existing behaviour: "the focus here is on the production of desirables through means which *directly* increase available options or extend social repertoires, rather than *indirectly* doing so as a by-product of an eliminative procedure. Such procedures are *constructionally* oriented; they build repertoires." This distinction has important practical consequences; in Susan's case it would have meant the difference between ever more extensive efforts to withdraw praise and attention for the increasingly large periods of the day when she was not achieving the desired standards of performance and systematic teaching programmes to build on the existing skills she had. As it was, only the crisis brought on by Susan's disruptive behaviour provided the occasion for a shift in emphasis towards a constructional approach.

In this respect the use of a token system was particularly appropriate—not because tokens form a tangible reward, easily made contingent upon performance (which they do), but because the presence of a pocketful of counters and a procedure for using them cues even the most insensitive teacher into looking for successes, no matter how small. As more everyday skills were acquired Susan obtained attention and praise at much less cost to herself and others; disruptive behaviour was no longer necessary. The PAC scores provide an indication of the increase in Susan's social competence; from a score of 21 items in August to 58 in January, out of a possible total of 120 items.

A further point concerning the procedures used by the students to deal with Susan's behaviour is the importance of the collection of routine data on problems and successes in achieving particular targets. The students living with Susan and the other handicapped residents were involved because they had wanted to demonstrate the possibilities for caring for severely handicapped people outside the traditional mental handicap hospital, in community settings where there were more opportunities for achieving the stated aims of services for mentally handicapped people. Among their criticisms of the hospital, the presence of bizarre and heavily structured patterns of daily life were among the most important. Consequently, in the house they rented there was much emphasis on creating a "homely environment", a "substitute family home" in the same very general terms used in stating the targets of most residential facilities. The students' view of what made for a good place to live in included only the minimum apparatus of precision teaching; the routine collection of basic data and the introduction of tokens were, at first, both avoided.

The consequences of this attempt at being "natural" were that nobody had hour-by-hour information showing which things were going well and which were going badly, and that no direct feedback on the students' teaching methods was available with any precision. The importance of tokens as a "hard" form of data has already been referred to; in addition, the careful attention paid to the frequency of problem behaviours at the suggestion of the psychologist placed the problem in perspective against the strengths of the individual concerned.

Susan still lives in the same house with the same group of handicapped people (the students have moved on and been replaced with others). At no time has there ever been any question of Susan being re-admitted to hospital. The people who live with her report that she has as many strengths to give as any other resident; she can now for example, walk to a launderette several streets away and do her own laundry; use local shops and amenities; answer the telephone, give appropriate replies, relate simple events, deliver messages reliably, as well as carrying out the basic tasks in her home, including cooking one evening meal for nine people each week. In 1978, Susan went abroad on holiday for the first time with her parents.

For the future planning and development of services, the successful resolution of the problem presented by Susan's disruptive behaviour provides one more example to illustrate the weakness of much current practice in providing for the care of severely mentally handicapped people. Susan's case points to a more helpful approach. It emphasises that behaviour develops within a social context, and that a major influence in this social context is the behaviour of the people who spend their daily lives with the individual. It suggests that more attention is due to the performance of these people, and to the resolution of behaviour problems, than to the containment of disruptive people in poor-quality institutional environments.

Susan's case suggests also that successful staff performance, which manages disruptive behaviour in a humane and sensitive way, is not possible only in the setting of the traditional mentally handicapped hospital. This, together with the evidence that a traditional hospital will not solve behaviour problems more successfully than community settings, indicates that the rationale of disruptive behaviour being "inevitable", "unchangeable", and merely "containable" is not sufficient to justify a person's transfer to, or continued placement in, hospital.

The defence of the long-stay hospital as the *only* form of residential care which can successfully deal with people whose behaviour is disruptive or dangerous is, therefore, premature, and certainly no basis on which to commit large amounts of scarce resources, the effects of which will have to be lived with for years to come. The move away from the large traditional mental handicap hospital has drawn its strength from many sources, not least from the inadequacies of the hospitals themselves. It will be appropriate to continue to develop services in smaller, more homelike facilities, nearer to the families of the handicapped people served, in line with the principles which are supposed to form the basis of current policy.[13]

But in doing so, it will be important also to develop the practices and procedures which front-line staff can carry out with people like Susan that will result in disruptive behaviour being prevented by good patterns of care, and being successfully managed and resolved where it does occur. As such procedures are developed, it may be that the small residential unit, staffed by people who work with the same clients on the same unit every day, working to a set of expectations generated in part by ordinary people living in the surrounding community, turns out to have rather more advantages than the proponents of the traditional mental handicap hospital currently suggest.

References

1. G. BERKSON and S. LANDESMAN-DWYNER, Behavioural research on severe and profound mental retardation (1955–1974), *American Journal of Mental Deficiency*, **81** (5), 428–54, 1977.
2. DEVELOPMENT TEAM FOR THE MENTALLY HANDICAPPED, *First report: 1976–1977*, HMSO, London, 1978.
3. A. KUSHLICK and G. COX, The epidemiology of mental handicap, *Developmental Medicine and Child Neurology*, **15**, 748–59, 1973.
4. (a) A. SHAPIRO, The clinical practice of mental deficiency, The Blake Marsh Lecture, 1968, *British Journal of Psychiatry*, **116**, 353–68, 1970.
   (b) A. SHAPIRO, Fact and fiction in the care of the mentally handicapped, *British Journal of Psychiatry*, **125**, 286–92, 1974.
5. ROYAL MEDICO-PSYCHOLOGICAL ASSOCIATION, Memorandum on future patterns of care for the mentally subnormal, *British Journal of Psychiatry*, **119**, 95–6, 1971.
6. J. W. PALMER, A. KUSHLICK and B. J. DAWES, *Evaluation of Locally-Based Hospital Units for the Mentally Handicapped in Wessex: Report on Professionals' Following of Rules, Some Consequences for Clients, and Changes in Demand for Residential Care*, Winchester: Health Care Evaluation Research Team, Research Report No. 123, 1977.
7. *Ibid.*
8. CAMPAIGN FOR THE MENTALLY HANDICAPPED, *Plans and Provisions for Mentally Handicapped People*, Enquiry Paper No. 4, London, 1976.
9. CARDIFF UNIVERSITIES SOCIAL SERVICES: *Group Home Rehabilitation Programme: First Report*, 1974. *Group Home Project: Second Report*, 1975. *Group Home: Special Report*, 1976.
10. H. C. GUNZBURG, *The PAC Manual*, National Association for Mental Health, London, 1969.
11. I. GOLDIAMOND, Coping and adaptive behaviours of the disabled, in G. L. ALBRECHT (ed.), *Socialisation in the Disability Process*, University of Pittsburgh Press, Pittsburgh, 1976.
12. I. GOLDIAMOND, Toward a constructional approach to social problems, *Behaviourism*, **2** (1), 1–84, 1974.
13. DHSS, *Better Services for the Mentally Handicapped*, Cmnd. 4683, HMSO, London, 1971.

CHAPTER 13

METHODS OF TREATMENT IN A PSYCHIATRIC UNIT FOR ADOLESCENTS

HARVEY V. R. JONES

Introduction

As the 1970–9 decade has gone by, the National Health Service's contribution to the residential and day care of troubled adolescents has increased. There are now 50 or more so-called Adolescent Units.[1]

They vary in their treatment approaches, range of children taken, and in their philosophies. Some common themes can be identified. A description of one such unit will follow, with emphasis on the treatment methods employed and on some possible implications for other settings.

Description of the Young People's Unit, Whitchurch Hospital, Cardiff

No two Units are alike and no Unit necessarily stays the same for very long. Five years after its opening, the Young People's Unit at Cardiff is currently the base for various aspects of an NHS adolescent service. The outpatient work, home visiting, consultations at other agencies etc. will not be described here, although serviced from and staffed by some same members of the team that operates within the Young People's Unit.

Here the focus is upon the day and inpatients treated at this Unit. Up to 16 or 17 will be attached at any one time. Of these perhaps two or three will be day patients. The age range taken is 12 to 19 years with the main emphasis usually on the 14- to 16-year range.

The scheme runs on a weekly boarder basis (Sunday evenings to Friday evenings) in a modern four-wing one-storey building. The residential section occupies two wings, the Unit school a third, and the interviewing outpatient suite a fourth.

The building is in a corner of a psychiatric hospital campus, the hospital being some 300 yards away at its nearest point.

A generous amount of field adjoins the building. The inside does not have many spaces suitable for energetic young people in spite of being purpose-built. A flat roof, easy to climb onto, provides too easy a play-space alternative for some.

Whilst the style is in places "over-clinical", bright colours predominate. Adhesive cellulose tape is allowed for posters etc. A sense of continuity and "history" is helped by framed photographs of events and excusions taken of various patient and staff activities over the years.

The staff is comprised of a heterogeneous group—14 nurses (on a three-shift system) and three teachers work exclusively with this client group. Other full-time and part-time professional staff from the Adolescent Service (hereafter called "clinic staff") give varying amounts of their time to the in/day patient service. They include five psychiatrists (three of which are in training), a senior social worker, and clinical psychologist and/or child psychotherapist.

Undergraduate trainees of various disciplines undergo placements, usually not more than one or two at a time. Secretarial, receptionist and domestic assistant staff (all with duties over and beyond the inpatient service) complete the staff group.

The timetable

This is partly structured, with moderate free time. Sunday evening sees people returning from weekends at home. Monday to Friday mornings start with a 15-minute "payover" of news from the nurses to the school and clinic staff. A 45-minute "community meeting" follows. (These and other events will be described later.)

Whilst the adolescents (*qua* pupils) attend the school, the clinic and nursing staff spend 1 to 1½ hours in daily staff meetings. These either transact general administrative business of the therapeutic community, or review cases, or have a staff-training focus.

The lunch-hour is followed by another school session. The school day ends with a half-hour meeting between adolescents, teachers and nurses. The weekly day routine is interrupted by visits to the hospital gymnasium and the municipal swimming baths, a shopping expedition, and a psychodrama group, all at fixed points. Each adolescent will also have an individual psychotherapy session of about 45 minutes duration once or twice a week, or possibly (perhaps once in 3 weeks) a family psychotherapy session. On Monday evenings each patient and his/her family attends one of two 1-hour multifamily groups, taken by selected members of the nursing staff. Other evenings are free for activities in or out of the agency. The adolescents and the nursing group struggle to keep the balance between legitimised and non-legitimised activities. Apart from informally prepared snacks, food is not prepared in the Unit kitchen, but provided by the hospital centralised kitchen.

The patients

Instead of presenting a statistical picture of the 130 inpatients and day patients treated in the first 5 years, a clearer idea may come from briefly listing the patient group as sampled at a given point in time and couched in terms of their "presenting problems".

Inpatients

(1) A 19-year-old young man readily retreating into his own private world. He was admitted after two or three violent assaults upon his parents.
(2) A 17-year-old middle-class girl with anorexia nervosa.
(3) A 16-year-old only daughter of totally deaf parents, having presented with acute school phobia.

(4) A 15-year-old boy with an alcoholic father. He is extremely agoraphobic and withdrawn.

(5) A girl of 15 admitted having shown severe truancy and mildly promiscuous behaviour.

(6) A 14-year-old boy whose presenting problem was of a mixed emotional conduct disorder with emphasis on delinquency.

(7) A 15-year-old girl who had shown partial school refusal, social withdrawal, somatic symptoms and a history of three intentional overdoses of drugs.

(8) A 13-year-old girl with conduct disorder, consequent to supposed sexual mis-behaviour in the family, admitted from a Social Services Assessment Centre.

(9) A 14-year-old boy from a one-parent family, having a very neurotic mother. He presented with intractable school refusal.

(10) An 11-year-old boy exhibiting considerable depression and social withdrawal.

Day Patients

(1) A 15-year-old boy who had had episodes of hysterical blindness, frightened of his own and other people's aggression.

(2) A 15-year-old girl detaching from an inpatient stay. She had been exhibiting disordered behaviour in school, aggressive behaviour and promiscuity.

(3) A 15-year-old boy from a very broken home with considerable psychosexual confusion. He was transferred from a community school.

(4) A 14-year-old boy who is very socially frightened subsequent to a spell of extreme alopecia areata (patchy baldness) and the recent death of his father.

(5) A 14-year-old girl with school refusal as part of a grief reaction to the death of her mother some months before.

Referrals are made from various sources: general medical practitioners, Social Service departments, educational psychologists, etc. Nearly all inpatients and day patients will have had several weeks of outpatient individual and/or family treatment first. Emergency admissions are rare (the crisis preferably being dealt with by focussed outpatient and domiciliary work).

The usual length of stay is 6 to 9 months, with some staying shorter and a few longer (up to, say, 18 months). Most are treated as inpatients (weekly boarders), a few as day patients (exclusively, or as a prelude or as a detaching phase to a residential stay). Most have further but limited outpatient follow-up.

The Philosophy of the Agency

Most organisations thrive if they have a declared sense of purpose and rationale for functioning. For an agency working with disturbed adolescents, this is particularly essential. The theoretical base is comprised of three themes:

(1) Construing adolescent breakdown in terms of *maturational* breakdown. The jargon for this draws on psychoanalytic theory, attachment theory and family interaction ideas.

(2) The notion of the agency being a *therapeutic community* (as modified for the special situation at hand).

(3) Viewing the focus of the work as being *triangular*: Unit/patient/family.

(1) *Maturational breakdown*

It is felt important to relieve the patient and his family of certain of the ordinary expectations of being a patient. If one is viewed as sick (especially near a psychiatric hospital), one might be mad, not responsible for one's actions, needing to become passive and "good", and then perhaps one can be cured (or not, as the case may be) by experts.

Furthermore, "treating" people (in both senses of the word) in the style implied above, when they are at a sensitive point in their identity formulation, builds in risks of permanent incorporation of such patterns. It may well be better to develop ways of looking (by staff, patient, peers and families) at themes to do with trouble on the journey between childhood and adulthood.

The adolescent has to re-negotiate his position in relation to his own body, to his family, and to the world around him. Aggressive drives take on new meanings; sexual drives become differentiated as novel and strong experiences. These are complicated processes and one or other can go wrong—sometimes as new matters, as if in a clear sky; sometimes as a follow on from troubles in childhood. One's identity has to be crystallised in both its sexual and vocational aspect. These difficulties may present fairly directly, e.g. the youngster who complains, "I do not know what is to become of me." More often the starting point in the trouble-shooting is a symptom—depression, fear of school etc.

Even then the symptom may not be owned by the patient—but complained of by the family or the school, or by society (e.g. via the courts). The agency's task is to redefine problems in maturational terms.

(2) *The therapeutic community*

Having considered symptoms as meaning various types of breakdown in the process of growing up, the next step is to help the client realise he is being invited into a sort of human laboratory, but not as a guinea pig. He is being invited to enter a community where new things can be learnt. "Come in, and do some of your growing up here. We shall take a look at it with you and see if we can help you work at it." That is *not* written over the door but one hopes the implicit message becomes explicit. The notion at large of the therapeutic community is often distorted or too specialised. Adolescents need amongst other things structure, not a *laissez-faire* or over-permissive environment. Discipline, control and structure are compatible with the title, notwithstanding some of the (often incorrect) impressions formed about some therapeutic communities.

Social analysis and a readiness to use many of the experiences that come to hand are the corner-stones of such treatment. Emphasis on clear inter-staff communication, attention to individuality and blunting of hierarchical pyramids plays an important part too. If the essence of the treatment is the facilitating of maturation within the adolescents, then one thing that is essential is a structure which allows the staff to "grow" too. This aim is complex (see Krohn *et al.*[2] for a fuller consideration of it). Staff working with disturbed adolescents are particularly prone to crises of morale, with or without intra-group staff tensions. If the carers are not given a feeling of being cared for, much is lost. Adolescents are very reactive to group tensions (be they family groups or staff groups) and act out accordingly (Evans[3]).

(3) *The family*

The above will have already indicated points relevant to the family: especially the separation process active throughout adolescence, and the passivity of relatives if an expert is treating their kin (Jones[4]). Two themes must be added. The first draws on notions about family interaction, particularly the manoeuvres by which one member of a family becomes a patient—with symptoms reflecting dysfunction in the group as a whole. The second theme is to do with the issues of guilt, rivalry and competition for ownership, endemic when the care of one's child is in part, or wholly, vested in the hands of others for longer or shorter periods.

Because of these factors, huge stores of emotion can build up, vested in either family, or client, or agency. The family may wish to dissipate supposed guilt—or block positive changes in the child (especially if those are dramatic or go beyond a certain threshold). The child may enjoy a certain power and prestige by manipulating news between his home and the Unit. The staff in the Unit may get filled with self-righteous anger about "those terrible parents", etc.

It has been implied above that this agency is in the business of producing change. How? Does one create a nurturing environment where biology can simply take its course? Does one operate a "reformatory" (behaviourally orientated, or otherwise)? Does one create an environment sufficiently secure and patronising so that regression occurs, and then the child relives (in healthier ways) some of the traumatic points in his past? Does one take an opposite view—state that the past is passed and corrections have to be made from present resources, keeping an eye on the present and future (and not the past)? All these styles are theoretically possible.

A compromise is aimed at here. The adolescent is given a fair amount of social feed-back about the system he is in (the therapeutic community); he and his family can also do likewise—but to a lesser extent—about them as a family group.

The staff will strive to understand the messages and conflicts represented by the adolescent's behaviour. Much decoding may be required, a task requiring skill, patience and training. Then the difficult job of implementing the feedback, in comprehensible terms to one and all in the system, goes on.

Regressing is sometimes focussed upon (going back to earlier events, memories and ways of coping), but is only allowed against a struggle. This is perhaps a subtle point. The adolescent may need to "go back" to get something inside the self healed. The pro-cess, however, is not made too easy, lest it be adopted as a flight from stress and a substi-tute to finding new and more adult ways of coping. A paraphrase might be: "Go back there (or stay back there) if you must—but come back to us now. Here and now is safe; and maybe the future has got some fun in it."

Specific Aspects of the Therapeutic Programme

These will be enumerated separately, although each part of a network, and each showing characteristics special to them in this context. They would show different features in other settings, and be operated differently.

Individuals of most ages find themselves in groups of different sizes. In growing up, the adolescent needs to be able to cope with such differences, as well as with differing proportions of peers and adults. Thus can the changes be rung by structuring the programme with such issues in mind.

Privacy

We are, after all, inside ourselves all the time. The Young People's Unit acknowledges a right to privacy—either in the physical sense of going for a walk by oneself, or to one's room—or in the sense of not being over-intruded upon.

One to one

(a) *Patient to Patient:* as in families in which siblings can be a powerful influence, patients need each other in personal and intimate ways. Free time in the programme makes due allowance for this, with the minimal rules necessary to ensure acceptable levels or social propriety, etc. Pairing of an excluding and/or over-intense nature is critically examined in other parts of the therapeutic matrix. Visits by friends from the outside world are also facilitated.

(b) *Patient/staff:* these are either informal—on a random, casual basis with staff of *all* sorts (including e.g. the YPU secretarial staff)—or formal, i.e. designated psychotherapy.

(c) *Individual psychotherapy:* all clients are assigned to one of the clinic staff for once or twice weekly psychotherapy sessions. The orientations of the different therapists are varied. The sessions provides a disciplined point in the week, in which the patient can take stock of his programme and progress, and share what he wishes. For some adolescents the value of such a session is that of an opportunity (used intensely) for a private one-to-one compared with the "goldfish bowl" of much of the rest of the week. For others their defensiveness and mistrust of intimacy is greater, and can perhaps be more readily upheld in such a context; there are lots of other people with whom to talk, lots of other activities in which to let off steam.

The confidentiality boundary is a tricky one in this programme slot. Talk with one's psychotherapist is the place in which privacy can most be guaranteed (from the rest of the week's events with people), but patient and therapist have to decide jointly whether some hidden things should be shared with the rest of the community.

Medication with psychoactive drugs is only used very rarely. It would be the therapist's responsibility to supervise this—but not physical/medical problems. If an adolescent requires treatment or examination for "medical" matters, one of the other medical staff would deal with this, not to complicate the therapeutic alliance unduly. (See Miller[5] for some further views on this.)

Small groups

Given that each patient has an "individual" therapist, it would not be appropriate to have a small therapeutic group with functions overlapping those or the former.

Two special-task groups occur weekly however.

(a) *The "split" group*—i.e. two sex-split concurrent 45-minute groups, one for the boys, one for the girls, each conducted by a male and female staff pair; the focus is allowed to be broad, but in an atmosphere temporarily freed from heterosexual strain. This is a chance for another sort of privacy because most other formal activities are of both sexes.

(b) *Psychodrama.* This event expresses the constant struggle for adults with adolescents. How is one to understand, harness, translate, handle and control adolescent behaviour? Whilst adolescents are more self-conscious and oppositional to action techniques than many adults, the scope for personality growth and change is freer. Conflicts are more accessible, defences more transparent.

All the patients are expected to attend, supported and led by a staff group of four or five people. Weekly sessions last 60 to 90 minutes, with a "de-briefing" session for the staff group after.

The group canvasses ideas, problems, recent events etc. that can be worked on through either formal psychodrama, or a role-play, a family sculpt or other technique.[6,7,8] Discussion is then encouraged in an attempt to integrate the experience. The intensity of this truly kaleidoscopic experience varies widely from session to session.

Large groups—community meetings and staff groups

As in most aspiring therapeutic communities, the Community Meeting is an essential constituent. The meeting with which the daily programme starts lasts 30 to 45 minutes and consists of all available patients and staff; the smaller meeting at the end of the school day lasts 20 to 30 minutes, with all the patients, but only the nursing and teaching staff.

The purpose of the latter group is fairly simple—an exchange of news about the day at school (or wherever else people have been), and a chance to plan the evening.

The main Community Meeting is a more complex affair. It is the chief forum for looking at all sorts of issues, both at the individual and group level. The staff have to resist making it too "patient focussed". It would be as unbalanced to do this as to hold a family therapy session centred only on the children's behaviour.

The form of leadership and structure varies. At one time the most senior nurse present was chairman. A more recent experiment has been to choose a staff subgroup of three people to lead it, not all necessarily being available each day. People sit around the floor of the largest room in the Unit in a circle. There is scope for retreat, e.g. under the table-tennis table. Sometimes the group allows this; at other times the retreater is dealt with more confrontingly.

Staff and/or young people will sometimes change places, e.g. to support someone in distress, or to "break up" a distracting subgroup. Headings for discussion are sometimes used, e.g. worries, complaints, news, announcements.

The focus varies but is more upon general issues, and issues of general relevance stemming from behaviour (and/or trouble) in one or two people in the group. The staff has to be reminded sometimes that it is not a group therapy session in the accepted sense, though it can have elements of that. The dynamics of large groups are complex, and have to be seen as different from small ones.[9]

Staff meetings

These are held daily—but the function varies from day to day. The Monday and Wednesday meetings last 40 minutes, and at these general administrative matters are discussed. The Tuesday meeting is very brief (because it is followed by a psychotherapy seminar for the clinic staff), but is held to support the principle that there is a need for daily and frequent communication in such a staff system. The Thursday morning meeting lasts $1\frac{1}{2}$ hours—the "case review" meeting being a self-explanatory title. The Friday morning meeting lasts $1\frac{1}{2}$ to 2 hours. It has either an educational focus, led by a team member or outside speaker, or is more given to a look at relationships within the staff groups. The nursing team meets for a weekly staff-support group regarding the multi-family meetings (see below). Once a month an 8.00 p.m. "night meeting" is held with the night nurses. Matters relevant to the latter, and to the day/night regime culture clash are considered.

The multifamily groups

Two concurrent groups are held, an hour long, and each conducted by a cotherapy pair of selected nurses, each Monday evening. Parents are expected to attend with their children who are inpatients or day patients, and siblings are encouraged to come too. Such sessions are crucial in attempting to manage the tension in the patient/family/hospital triangle mentioned earlier. They also help exchange information and work through guilt and sharing issues, such as the conflicts about who "parents" the child—the staff or the parents?

The Young People's Unit School

School is part of any youngster's life and is an essential part of the regime. Emphasis is thus put on the "going to school" process.

The three teachers each take part in general staff meetings, with one also as a member of a cotherapy pair in the split-sex small groups, and another in the psychodrama group. The teaching staff are the primary responsibility-takers for the patients during school hours; the nurses the rest of the time.

The school adheres to normal school term and holidays, but the Unit is open for nearly all the year. Youngsters need to learn how to cope with leisure and boredom as well as with school work.

Some Process Issues

Control

This is put first because it is the issue over which so many like facilities can founder. By definition, any agency importing disturbed adolescents is importing a large fund of disturbed behaviour and feeling.

The Unit is physically not very lockable, nor designed for over-zealous ongoing surveillance. People can run away. This feature is abated by one of the more extreme sanctions being that of being suspended from the Unit to home for a few days—to think things over. This turning upside down the pattern of locking people up or losing home-leave privileges for absconding inverts quite a lot of home-seeking behaviour.

The agency does not consciously admit an adolescent who will be too very great a tester-out/or acter-out in the system. Such people fare more happily in a more physically secure and structured regime.

Emphasis is put upon trust and group agreements in the attempt to contain disturbed behaviour. Acknowledgement of a degree of shared responsibility is repeatedly made. The youngsters are sent bills for the damage they do—not "let off" on the pretext of being too crazy or too deprived. However, on grounds both of expediency and mercy, the bill is often relatively nominal.

Staff support

This topic follows on naturally from the above one. It is important. Staff can readily get "burnt out" and/or disillusioned when attempting to produce change with disturbed young people in a vigorous way, if their own needs are not met. If not supported accurately, staff will either leave, fall sick, project extra tensions into the client or revise the ethos of the agency in such a way as to make it more rigid and defensive. The price of peace achieved the latter way is a more institutional regime in which the client contains his distress more—and in so doing makes it less available to the processes of change.

All staff doing psychotherapy get personal one-to-one supervision of that work as an additional buttress.

Intimacy and distance

A proposition must first be put forward. In residential work a professional can only tolerate a finite quantity of contact with the client. There are alternate ways of doing this. Either one can spend a lot of time being with the clients but holding oneself back—or being with them for a lesser time, but in greater contact. It is the latter model that is used in the Young People's Unit. The NHS nurses' 8-hourly shift system tilted the initially-formed choice in this direction.

The weekly boarder system too gives everyone a break from intensive work. It also brings the adolescents and their families into regular reality-testing opportunities, a reciprocal chance for *them* to do some work.

Staff, by having differing roles depending upon their jobs, can take up different professional stances that are comfortable for them. Not everyone has to be the same "distance" from the client. Taking up a comfortable psycho-social distance for oneself (knowing others will be at other points) leaves one comfortable—and means the adolescent is more likely to be relating to a group of professional people who are feeling comfortable—with consequent increased security and peace for him. Staff are not asked to be all-rounders, omni-versatile. They also need permission not to have to handle issues that are too difficult for them, given their respective temperaments, skills and training.

Self-esteem

This can be a key theme for adolescents in trouble. Some have had deprived pasts and therefore feel they are no good. Others are currently in big troubles, and so also judge themselves poorly—perhaps as all bad, or even very mad. The consequences of poor self-esteem are varied, but always undesirable. Some adolescents carry round with them a feeling of poor inner worth and consequent depression (see Baker[10]). Others put on a puffed-up but fragile claim to "bigness" with a lot of bravado. All with low self-esteem have a poor tolerance to frustration.

The large-group handling of this depends vitally on morale in the staff, i.e. staff-group self-esteem. This is only sustained by constant attention to staff support (as above). This support must minimise its emphasis on hierarchies. If the people at the bottom of the professional ladder are left feeling poorly valued, not important, and without scope for growing professionally, what hope has the client of escaping the same trap, these being the staff with whom he is most readily and commonly in contact?

Symptoms

Health Service derived disciplines and agencies naturally think much in terms of symptoms, and have clients referred via symptoms.

Whilst initially a symptom is a ticket for the journey of professional attention and treatment, it can be used differently once the individual is in the system. In adolescents, symptoms are usually expressed and described by others, e.g.: "He won't go to school", "She won't eat and is only 5 stones in weight", rather than "I am anxious and depressed", or "I can't stop all this hand washing and checking whether the gas taps are off".

The aim in this therapeutic community in this context is to redefine the symptoms in relationship terms, e.g.: "He has difficulty in controlling the way he rebels against authority", "She is having difficulty in separating from her mother"; and secondly then to "forget" the symptom. This does not mean cure—just a translation into issues to do with living and growing up. Thus medication usually becomes an unimportant and irrelevant weapon in the fight towards maturity.

Leadership

A leader's task is (a) to help a group with its task, (b) to see the group does not fall apart, and (c) to see that the individuals of whom the group is comprised do not fall apart. In the Young People's Unit, being an NHS agency, the overall leadership is vested largely in two consultant psychiatrists, one of whom is the author of this chapter. The NHS organisational format, however, gives them a larger measure of responsibility than of power. From the bureaucratic point of view the only staff for whom they are administratively responsible are the medical staff, but they have overall and final clinical responsibility for their patients. The nurses are responsible to the NHS nursing management structure. The teachers are employed by the Local Authority Education Department, the social worker by the Social Services Department.

Paradoxically this division puts more responsibility upon people to work together in a more democratic, weakly hierarchical, system, and one consonant with a therapeutic community. People have to find ways of trusting each other, and working at personal and professional differences. In so doing, something exciting and satisfying is achieved. It is a constantly changing dynamic process. One hopes it is one with which the adolescent patients can identify, and thus be in contact with yet another developmental process which will assist their maturation.

Conclusion

One National Health Service Adolescent Unit has been reviewed from both the descriptive point of view, and in terms of the ideologies from which it draws.

The argument has been developed that a psychiatric base has a role to play in the handling of disturbed adolescents. This can be done without recourse to institutionalising and other mechanisms often associated with psychiatry at large.

Adolescent psychiatry makes use of a wide variety of relevant theories, techniques and personnel, and this is a useful treatment resource for a variety of (but not all) young people in severe difficulties.

References

1. ASSOCIATION FOR THE PSYCHIATRIC STUDY OF ADOLESCENTS, *Register of Adolescent Psychiatric Units*, 1976.
2. A. KROHN, D. H. MILLER and J. LOONEY, Flight from autonomy: problem of social change in an adolescent inpatient unit, *Psychiatry*, **37**, 360–71, 1974.
3. J. EVANS, Conflicts, Crises and Tension within a Residential Unit, *Proceedings of the Vth Conference*, ASSOCIATION FOR THE PSYCHIATRIC STUDY OF ADOLESCENTS, 1970, pp. 61–72.
4. H. V. R. JONES, Families and Hospitals, *Proceedings of the Xth Conference*, ASSOCIATION FOR THE PSYCHIATRIC STUDY OF ADOLESCENTS, 1975, pp. 20–24.
5. D. H. MILLER, The Development of Psychiatric Treatment Services for Adolescents, in J. C. SCHOOLAR (ed.), *Current Issues in Adolescent Psychiatry*, Brunner/Mazel, New York, 1973.
6. H. V. R. JONES and J. ALONSO, Psychodrama in an adolescent unit, *Therapeutic Education*, **3** (1), 31–37, 1975.
7. H. V. R. JONES, Psychodrama with adolescents, *Nursing Times*, 1978, pp. 2052–4.
8. R. SHUTTLEWORTH, Psychodrama with Disturbed Adolescents, in S. JENNINGS (ed.), *Creative Therapy*, Pitman, London, 1975.
9. L. KREEGER (ed.), *The Large Group*, Constable, London, 1975.
10. R. BAKER, Adolescent depression: an illness or developmental task?, *Journal of Adolescence*, **I** (4), 297–307, 1978.

CHAPTER 14

RESIDENTIAL WORK WITH ADOLESCENT GIRLS

BARBARA MORRIS

Introduction

It is perhaps significant that little seems to have been written about this particular "client group", i.e. these young people who have long been the subject of immense social work concern. Maybe the concern and anxiety has disabled the helping activity, and indeed the sparsity of literature related to sound experience and practice may reflect the scarcity of provision.

It would be wrong to undervalue the writing that does exist, although much seems to be related to particular areas of pathology, and equally wrong to devalue considerable and consistent efforts that have existed in small pockets throughout the country for many years, to which many girls and helpers are profoundly indebted. It would also be an omission not to acknowledge the richness of the pioneer work which has been done with groups of youngsters of both sexes where the emphasis on the girl group has not been highlighted. Many good things done "through a glass darkly" have not been highlighted because of the humility surrounding what actually is "effective"; what helps young people to "grow up" and grow on and what helps youngsters to become both stronger and braver?

Having all but said that nothing in this chapter can be new, it will also be obvious that almost everything shared is highly subjective, viewed from the horizons of life experience and what to many will seem very limited work experience. It is also hidebound by the perspectives of working with and for youngsters of my own sex. These are fundamental influences to be acknowledged when individuals, whether alone or in groups, attempt to help, change and influence the lives of others.

The thoughts put together relate to years of teaching adolescents, years spent in the Probation Service, but mainly experiences shared over the last 3 years working with about 200 teenaged girls in a regional assessment unit, and now a CHE which has just, somewhat miraculously, achieved its second birthday. Trying to provide good "child care" is exacting and difficult. In addition to this, girls, if in need of residential care, should also need the kind of "treatment" which is part of a "problem-solving process". This is both difficult to provide in a one-sexed environment which in itself has a negative institutional aspect and is, of course, a very skewed environment. It is also difficult to provide for this most disturbed and deprived group of youngsters within the existing systems and patterns of Child Care Practice, which recently seem to have become somewhat dominated by Conditions of Service.

The Residential Environment as a Response to the Girls'
Situations and Problems

This is at present the only Community Home with Education on the Premises the region provides for adolescent girls. Forty girls live in six small group units. Many are far from home and 50% are currently homeless. All will know the heart searching and accompanying sentiments that go into the removal of girls and women from home. They are subject to far more sympathy than boys and viewed traditionally and culturally in quite a different way. This probably contributes to ideas about different needs which may be quite unfounded. It can be concluded, however, that the girls with whom we live, work and share, represent and have experienced extremes of despair, deprivation and often emotional damage. This in itself makes the viability of institutional care highly questionable because, too often, we feel ourselves faced with a mountain of despair.

Few generalisations can be made with any confidence, but all "our girls" have been rejected by some other part of the caring system—an experience shared by all other Community Homes with Education. True, there have been constructive "moves on", but many girls need not be in this particular form of residential care had there been "more room" in an emotional sense in other forms of children's home. It is significant that these other smaller group homes are almost entirely dominated by female staff.

Frequently in the most "normal" and stable family situation we see in all its subtlety this "no room" or "not enough room" syndrome. It seems an unfortunate physiological coincidence that middle-age uncertainties in parents, especially in mothers, often coincide and conflict with the uncertainties of their adolescent daughters. The bonds with the parent of the opposite sex can become intensified, perhaps excluding, and situations and feelings can become so distorted that someone takes flight into illness, running away, or is pushed out further and rejected. We experience the victim of this not unusual phenomenon as the teenaged girl who becomes "beyond control", runs away and whom "no-one understands". There has not been enough space for two or more females. Frequently, however, when more room is made, mothers who have failed at this stage to parent, are often able to befriend, albeit in a somewhat complex, sibling-like way which can often be used well.

Can it be that this same pattern exists in many of our small group homes where often the help and managment of the teenaged girl breaks down time and time again and the youngster is moved on? This is seen many times in youngsters whom we feel need never have been moved on had other residential settings been more aware, stronger and braver, and grown-ups had more room and compassion for the younger woman. Many of these youngsters present few behavioural problems after they have arrived with us. It is not because there is more staff or more structure (though they are better paid!), or that there are Secure Units etc. Although there are a multitude of factors, including the child's ability to put into practice in a new setting what she has learned from the old, there are real questions to be asked about attitudes, expectations, understanding, support and space.

Although these questions must be asked about girls who have been moved on, "chucked out" or inappropriately placed, for many reasons they add some balance to the girl group here which would otherwise be made up of the most grossly deprived, damaged and delinquent, and therefore further questions would need to be asked and more problems posed about the viability of such an environment, where the population is so skewed and the personalities so vulnerable.

Other or additional problems bring the girl (many actually present themselves) into residential care. Very many have had destructive sexual experiences which have not only been premature but even deviant. Grossly disrupted family patterns have heightened incestuous feelings at an emotional and often a physical level. The normal girl/father attachments have been cruelly distorted or destroyed at critical periods. The beginnings of trust and dependency have been abused and violated by grown-ups, many of whom themselves are still in infancy. Many girls are homeless, including those who have been bereaved. Some girls are away from home as the result of crisis arising in adolescence, which has already been discussed; others have agonising problems at school. All have had problems of school attendance and under-achievement. Many are the victims of neglectful subcultures and have run wild and free with no external or internal controls, and personality structures then become fragmented. Some are compensatorally delinquent related to their earlier deprivations and may need primary care, substitute programmes and/or the breaking down of potential addiction to delinquent patterns which may fall into abeyance when other more basic needs are satisfied. A few girls are entrenched in delinquent subcultures learned from infancy but are not essentially emotionally deprived or disturbed. These girls have a strong sense of stigma and often feel that justice has discriminated unkindly against them especially as they are only too aware of the contribution the neglected subcultures in which they have been reared have made to their problems. These are a cross-section of the predominating problems all contributing in the growing girl to enormous lack of personal worth, lack of self-esteem and feelings of failure and despair.

The cost of residential care is enormous, not only in financial terms, but much more in the emotional price paid by those who are "in care". Girls "in care" can suffer separation, cultural shock, loss of the familiar, group living with people who are not of of their choice and with whom they may be incompatible, frequent over-exposure and the likelihood of reduced opportunities for personal responsibility. Because of this, residential social work must be more than caring and containing and must make a real contribution to growth and to alleviating at least some of the problems which have necessitated coming into care or "being sent away".

Integration as a Guiding Concept

The concept of "integration" can be very helpful as a major objective in working with adolescent girls. "Integration" in relation to personality growth has a special analytical meaning which is very important, but the word can also be used more simply and usefully. If the adolescent girl is admitted to care or still "in care", so little of her total life spectrum is functioning. Everything has broken down. The family, if in existence, is unintegrated, dysfunctional and has been split. School attendance and achievement is abysmal. Girls are often socially and culturally impoverished, often financially poor and occasionally in indifferent health. Morale and self-esteem are depleted, confusion about personal identity is haunting, as is uncertainty and fear about the future. Years of destructive experience have diminished motivation and often the very real strengths of the youngsters have been eroded by anxiety and guilt. Our aim as a team of family, friends, field and residential social workers, teachers and other helpers, should be to try to establish confidence and courage in trying to rebuild in all areas of functioning so that the girl can become more whole, more integrated and more certain in some, if not all, areas of her being. We illustrate this with girls by a sputnik-like drawing with spiky arrows flying off outwards in all directions representing the bits of themselves that they know about. What we try to achieve are the arrows steadying up in straight and balanced directions pointing inwards and nourishing the centre of the sputnik which we call the self. It may sound a bit messy but it is basically simple to illustrate and girls understand and help us to understand further.

This has, obviously, to be a team approach involving all the key people mentioned before. There needs to be great flexibility based on knowledge, skills and the child's own attachments. It is a great challenge to both communication, co-operation and co-ordination, and calls for not only sound therapeutic methods but clear therapeutic and administrative management. There is little room for woolly-minded charisma or the dominance of leadership's whims. Every worker involved, whether field, community, home or school based, needs a clear understanding of the task and of his or her particular flexible role in it.

How do we do it? At the risk of piety it needs to be restated that what we do is a reflection of what we are and, irrespective of essential methods and systems, the ability to help and heal is related to one's awareness, concern and preoccupation with children. The echoes of "nobody cares" hit home because seldom can the quantity or quality be good enough, and the cost to the helper in terms of debilitation and impoverishment can be too high. This is not a counsel of despair but a need to be aware of oneself and one's own fluctuating resources if one is to survive and work with the demands, insights and incisiveness of teenaged girls.

Great emphasis needs to be placed on the living environment/atmosphere or milieu, whatever it may be called. This is the only factor that can remain relatively consistent when we are working a 40-hour week, have reasonable leave, time is spent in training and there are some staff changes. The prevailing ethos in itself can help to create a sense of security, predictability and consistency.

Treatment Principles and Practice

Some fundamental principles in the treatment of girls become part of this working environment. The interaction and daily task is based on what we call the "person principle". Girls are confronted with their problems and helped to change destructive flight/fight patterns, but the emphasis is on the common human needs of sensitive human beings, not on systems that are geared only to the prevention of problems (though there is a place for helpful safety systems to be incorporated). Relationships are primarily on a person-to-person basis, grown-ups are not dominant or necessarily right, there is no subordination, and "respect" does not "sit on anyone's chair" by virtue of that person's position. Much emphasis is placed on treatment of the individual rather than a uniform response to particular kinds of behaviour, and there is a very limited and (hopefully) constructive use of "punishments". It is emphasised that girls must be seen in the light of their total life context and that on the whole their perceptions of their problems are probably the most accurate. Not all youngsters have the ability to determine much of their own future because of the distortions of damaging experiences. The issues of staff responsibility in determining boundaries, controls and some decisions are inescapable, but having said this the goals, values and objectives girls set for themselves are often realistic, valid and based on much self-awareness and insight. These must not be ignored.

Although much of this may seem somewhat radical, to some it is quite familiar. Girls have responded to this kind of environment with a readiness and alacrity which was quite unexpected, and comparisons of "unfairness' and areas of conflict have been rare. It may also have been easier to introduce girls to this pattern of living because they have not been subject to the traditional and cultural patterns of care which have prevailed in institutions for boys.

Much emphasis is placed on attainment and success in a domestic sense, in the small school-room groups and in such areas as community service. This, however, seems implicit in all child care. Nearly all of this is achieved within small group involvement or on an individual basis. Nothing takes place in the large total group, except a morning pre-school "community meeting". It is felt that girls do not take kindly to larger group activities, but this is more a whim of a female Officer-in-Charge, rather than the result of any evidence.

Small group living, i.e. up to eight girls, is fundamental to our treatment concept. Girls and a small staff team (of up to five or six) live and work together in six House Units. The domestic maintenance is the responsibility of this group and they are entirely self-catering. Interaction and proximity is intense, as is the potential for sound relationships. It is often an uncomfortable, demanding experience where expectations of toleration, sharing and understanding of each other is high. Much is learned about "living together" and many social and emotional techniques and skills, which may be new to many girls, are tried and practised, and it is hoped these will help the youngsters function better when they are eventually in domestic situations of their own choosing.

So much of "institutional" living can be the result of particular quirks and whims of the leaders involved and there needs to be continuous and sensitive awareness of this. The culture tends to be tender and strong rather than assertive and tough, and much emphasis is placed on the development of femininity and the more positive aspects of the female role. This, in effect, means that girls are helped to become domestically able. Sexuality, both in terms of marriage and motherhood, is discussed with some real teaching and girls are encouraged to look pretty in whichever way they feel most themselves. Much of this may sound banal and "old fashioned", but these areas, together with some job achievement and creative leisure opportunities, are felt to be where most girls will find their major opportunities for any sort of fulfilment in future.

A simple treatment plan covering all areas of functioning is made by each house team involving the youngster concerned. It is related to all areas of functioning, involving family, friends, social workers etc., plus additional resources, such as club leaders, psychiatrists and friendly neighbours. It is reviewed every month. Counselling is a major feature of each girl's programme where her progress in all areas is collated and co-ordinated, and emphasis is placed on how she has responded to the confrontations which take place on both a planned and a spontaneous basis within the daily living pattern.

As yet there is no particular counselling style—it is questionable whether there should be. Each member of staff is a counsellor and what they know and feel, as well as who and what they are, is focussed on the needs of the child. It is usually task- or goal-orientated, directed to the girl's self-discovery, rather than a grown-up imposition of advice, and must help girls not only to discover themselves and face problems which can be made more manageable but also to share facts and feelings helpfully. Over-interpretation, which can be way off the mark, is avoided, as is more awareness than the youngster has resources with which to cope. There is much praise and encouragement for every small area of growth. The more planned counselling must have focus and time boundaries because girls will talk for hours and "go on and on and on". Without these boundaries they may be left with helpful feelings and relationships, but other vital aspects may be lost by sheer duration. The various balances are fine and this sounds easier than it is, but in working with girls much apprehension has been lost and people have felt safer because the talking over of problems soon becomes part of the culture.

Group work with girls can take various forms. There is the small group living setting which gives rise to enormous informal opportunity for girls to learn more about themselves, make changes in behaviour and generally grow. The numerous conflict situations arising within relatively unselected groups gives exacting, exhausting and stimulating experiences beyond measure. Girls and grown-ups learn much about themselves and each other and participation and sharing is never more real. Opportunities can arise from menu planning, sponsored walks or "somebody's nicked my jeans" or "boyfriend". It is, however, vital to emphasise that many opportunities will be and must be missed. We cannot forever be looking self-consciously for useful moments etc. Life is also about having fun, having rows, getting on and getting out, managing one's depression and boredom and living within a restricted budget. These are group living and learning aspects the girls are stuck with. They do not need to be somewhat artificially laboured.

More formal group work for which staff have some training or "go on courses" takes place in house meetings, various committee meetings and special groups for discussing areas such as bereavement, contraception, work etc., or often in relation to particular girls' problems. These groups take place in the houses, in school, or can be specially set up for selected groups of girls. They need special planning, support and guidance, but there is much in the way of helpful literature and experience to help develop this area of the work.

Girls are always seen within the context of their families and that which is good in the most tragic of situations is capitalised upon. "Ongoing" work is done with families by fieldworkers and by residential workers in conjunction with each other. Families come to visit and to stay and, where possible, some families come regularly for "family therapy". A basic principle is that "all people can change" (even though the degree of change is questionable) and many grown-ups who may not be able to parent can possibly befriend. For over half our girls their family is no longer there. Parents are unknown, scattered, totally rejecting or dead. This high proportion is an indictment on existing child care practice. Even in these circumstances it is vital for the child to remember, recall or imagine what she needs to know about herself. Much that is rememberable is suppressed by pain, so personal identity is further confused. Much talking goes on, places of the past are revisited, old friends etc. contacted and some scrapbooks are made to help put together the pieces and thus aid "integration". Girls learn to express and survive the bad bits and become stronger to go on.

Much gaming, sociodrama, squiggles and charades is incorporated into the daily life and provides not only fun (every child's prerogative), but useful material for treatment. There are now a number of available and useful books on simulations and exercises which guide and help workers develop confidence to make up their own experiences which will enable girls to communicate and become freer and more confident. Most girls will join in if grown-ups initiate, participate in, and "mess around" in these simple, useful and often provocative activities.

Leisure and creative activities often present quite a short fall. Apart from the therapeutic potential, life is more than work and problem solving (or should be). Residential care should not seek to over-organise kids out of their individuality or to avoid boredom and depression at all costs. But putting things together, having interesting and enjoyable experiences, doing something new and planning does something enriching or gives "kicks" which makes everyone bigger and more interesting, and widens thinking and feeling experiences. These things can be so simple and lead to all kinds of social skills and practice in being and doing together. There is often a reluctance from grown-ups to develop these activities. Either their own childhood culture may have been somewhat limited and they have perhaps not been parents themselves or residential life in itself may be somewhat culturally flattening.

There is no particular exclusive method or style that is effective with adolescent girls. Methods arise out of sound basic principles which are applied individually with as much sensitivity and flexibility as possible. In discussing these methods, it is essential to emphasise that no aspect is the prerogative of one particular area of the unit or of any particular staff group. Much work discussed goes on at school, in house units and in the night. Our work with adolescent girls owes much to the small group of night staff who help individual girls and often a group when "the dark is light enough", and many are troubled and fearful, or even when many need to talk about a provocative late-night film. Bed times, as are meal times and getting-up times, are periods of much sensitivity. We are much indebted to those rather solitary group of workers who really use these night hours so well.

Dealing with Girls' Emotional and Sexual Development in a Single-Sex Regime

Having seldom worked with adolescent boys, it is difficult to be specific about particularly sensitive areas peculiar to working with adolescent girls. A one-sexed environment does little to help the adolescents developing perspectives or experience. It is artificial, poses unnecessary problems for therapeutic management in trying to create a balanced life-experience, and can put extra pressures on male staff, who can often be viewed by female staff and girls with distorted perspectives. These statements are open to the most hilarious as well as serious misinterpretations and in themselves would take yet another chapter of discussion. Where girls have had deprived, damaging or distorted experiences with the opposite sex, the role for male staff carries special responsibilities. It is as prey to the worker's own personal response as is working with one's own sex. We, both men and women, are especially vulnerable to the young woman in acute distress, especially with the awareness of her potential motherhood. Many need to be gathered up and held both emotionally, symbolically and physically. Staff must have the confidence, training and knowledge of when and how to hold and "hold on" if many youngsters are to develop trust and relationships which will help them to grow, for it is of this very experience that the child has been deprived.

Male staff particularly, though not exclusively, need help in managing transference and potential counter-transference situations. They need to understand how aggression, violence and sexuality in many people, especially the most deprived and damaged, are inextricably linked, and how the insensitive or thoughtless management (of which we are all guilty) may trigger off a chain response of which no-one is consciously aware.

Much can be said about the use of the power of the grown-up. The residential social worker is in such a powerful position in relation to those who are not only "not yet grown up", but for whom all else has failed. The things we say, do and are have immeasurable and unknown impact. Grown-ups have in the past violated our girls because the child has been so vulnerable. Our responses can so often reactivate the fears which belong to events of the past and the child's response is out of all proportion to the current incident. An awareness of the power of the grown-up and humility in using it is essential to becoming "child centred". It is only this awareness that can help us manage our more primitive needs for dominance and meaningless "respect" and "prestige" and that can counteract the effect that some of our early cultural experience has implanted regarding the expectation of masculine and feminine sex roles. Too often it is ghosts of the past and of cultural expectations that cause staff to say "We could do with more men around here". This may well be true but for other than the obvious reasons being expressed.

Culturally it is expected that girls can be more overtly emotionally expressive. Fortunately they usually are, or can be helped to be articulate; they cry, can extend themselves to touch, hold and embrace. There may be less barriers to feelings that need to be reached when working with girls, and staff may need to learn to be unafraid of this. It is when these feelings manifest themselves in violence towards herself or others that the situation becomes more shocking and workers can find themselves disabled, disturbed or even provoking the situation further. The management of this kind of violence, when the child is in panic or inflicting ugly self-injury, needs much knowledge, support and discussion. It must not be dismissed as "manipulative" or "attention seeking", which are words quite unhelpful to sensitive understanding of children's needs.

Much needs to be understood of the girl's low self-esteem, the need for excitement, the crisis-reared child, the release of accumulated tension and unbearable fear and destructive guilt. Much violence is provoked by grown-ups who carry these expectations of some girls and are in themselves "tension bearers". Others do not know enough about the particular youngsters with whom they work and the grown-up may be working under personal duress. Violence is often managed by further aggression or more emotional injury. Too often little is understood of the youngster's sexual experience or perceptions and there is the unhelpful expectation that the male staff will "sort it out" (although just occasionally their assistance may be essential). These outbursts can often be avoided. They can be worked with constructively and sensitively by grown-ups who of course are afraid, but who know that the child is much more afraid. Our understanding and good practice develop as we become more experienced and honest with ourselves and each other. Let's not pretend that these things do not happen as we share and learn together. Neither is there any place for pushing around "blame". Guilt is to be shared. Blame is diminishing. If one person makes a conscious or unconscious error, it could be any one of "us" in this shared environment.

Conclusion

These, then, are some practices and experiences learned whilst working with adolescent girls within a residential setting. Nothing can be said to be exclusive to girls or even a particular age group. There can be no particular model but only an eclectic approach gained from experience, awareness and sound theory. This account in itself is full of generalisations and points that often lead or may lead nowhere.

Like any other "pattern of care" the efforts and attempts described call for a particular pattern of management. The residential unit must be seen as an integrated part of a wider complementary system of care if the objectives of integration in a personal and social sense are to be achieved. Resources must be available in terms of psychiatric, administrative, educational, financial and domestic consultancy, which can widen perspectives, and add to skills whilst keeping reality in mind. There is a need not only for clear understanding of the task which is somewhat different for each individual girl but for clear systems of organisation, communication and recording to see that each other's work and actions are co-ordinated into a helping continuum. Team organisation and leadership is vital with clear understanding of roles and functions within the larger and smaller team.

Training and opportunities for further learning and sharing is essential for all staff, not only for fuller understanding, but for the development of skills and practices which help youngsters and grown-ups to grow in strength together. Some of this training will lead to college-based professional qualifications, together with the experiences which equip workers for leadership and policy- and decision-making roles. Other training may be differently based and take place with individuals and/or groups and will have a specific task or focus. There are key people to be involved in training programmes who are part of the wider organisation, but vital to training is the person who works alongside and the child to whom we need to listen. Nothing need be said about "support". It should be able to be taken for granted.

In working with any child in care, especially adolescents who are still "here", much could be said about leadership. For the pattern described here it needs to be central and involved rather than hierarchical and autocratic. Leadership at all levels needs to be specially aware of all resources available and to be able to identify the need where there are omissions. Sound management training is as essential as therapeutic ability. There is a great need to be able to recognise and work with the feelings of other workers, i.e. the feelings of anger, despair, helplessness and uncertainty, as well as to be able to combat one's own intrinsic professional loneliness. A discussion of leadership issues is in itself a subject of length and depth.

It is a profound if not shocking fact that by mid-teens the girl "in care" may have been in residential settings for most of her life. Although there are a few girls who may need sheltered care for the greater part of their lives, it is tragic if during mid and late adolescence, girls have to move to yet another institutional setting. The greatest need and omission in existing provision is not only for greater understanding and acceptance of the adolescent girl and her needs, but for some real domestic base. This may not and for many will not be their original home but must be some intimate domestic situation which many have never experienced, even though they are expected and expecting to be mothers and home-makers in the future. This is where the key learning for the girl's future life can really take place. What we can helpfully and hopefully do in residential care can only be by way of preparation for this next step which for so many still does not exist.

Further Reading

As noted at the beginning of this chapter, the literature on work with adolescent girls is sparse, but the following references may be helpful to readers wishing to follow up this area:

J. COWIE, V. COWIE and E. SLATER, *Delinquency in Girls*, Heinemann, 1968 begins with a survey of the literature from 1920, and contains a substantial bibliography.

G. KONOPKA, *The Adolescent Girl in Conflict*, Prentice-Hall, 1966 contains accounts of the use of groups in working with girls in the residential setting.

H. RICHARDSON, *Adolescent Girls in Approved Schools*, Routledge & Kegan Paul, 1969 is a research study outlining the social background and other characteristics of girls in an assessment centre at that time.

More recent accounts of work in this field have been mainly in the form of articles. A useful list of articles on *The Care and Management of Adolescent Girls* has been compiled by *S. Rugg* for the DHSS bibliography series—No. B83, July, 1977—and is obtainable from the DHSS Library, Alexander Fleming House, London.

The psycho-dynamic approach to treatment outlined in this chapter might be followed up with:

B. DOCKAR-DRYSDALE, *Therapy in Child Care*, Longman, 1968.

I. SALZBERGER-WITTENBERG, *Psycho-Analytic Insight and Relationship*, Routledge & Kegan Paul (Library of Social Work), 1970.

J. MOFFAT, *Concepts in Casework Treatment*, Routledge & Kegan Paul (Library of Social Work), 1968 contains a brief discussion of the concept of transference and counter-transference.

CHAPTER 15

HOSTEL PROVISION FOR
ADOLESCENT BOYS

DOUGLAS ADAMS

Number 43 Britannia Road was initially conceived as a third stage of a continuum of care within Kingswood Schools, the constituent parts being secure, semi-secure and fully open, these representing the stages of progression before a child goes into the community. There was, however, a conceptual change even before the semi-secure provision was built; it was realised that there could be no such thing as semi-secure: it had to be either secure or open. This resulted in the building of the open wing of the secure unit, which in many ways acts as a hostel for the secure wing.

The staff of Kingswood Training School use, for the majority of their boys, outside resources. They also have provision for boys to work out while still resident at the Training School. They also provide, like the open wing, the opportunity for the boys to be involved in community-based activities such as Youth Clubs etc., which reduces the need for them to use the facility of "43".

The development of Community Homes Schools has brought about the situation where there is almost no provision equivalent to that of the former Senior Approved Schools. This can also be linked with the fact that there is a considerable number of adolescents who find themselves in care especially under Section 1 of the 1948 Act, who do not require the full resources that would be available in Community Homes Schools but who need a living base to be able to practise life skills and are in need of a supportive caring environment.

Number 43 has no "typical" resident; the boys have come from all over the southwest of England and the range of behaviour they have manifested in the past is very wide, from those boys who have committed grave physical assaults to the multitude of property offences and those boys whose only "offence" has been not to be wanted. When deciding upon a boy's possible admission it is very important, in my view, to try and balance the peer group as far as is reasonably practicable; in operating this principle it is possible to accommodate a wide variety of boys and behaviour so that the boys can achieve their independence to a meaningful level.

Number 43 is a single-storey building of functional design which provides living accommodation for 11 young men whose ages range from 15-plus to 18-plus. At one end of the building there is staff accommodation in the form of a three-bedroomed house. Number 43 itself consists of a "quiet" room, large lounge/dining area and kitchen. There is an office for the Warden, a General Office, toilets, bathrooms, utility room, 10 bedrooms, nine for boys and one room is used as a staff sleeping room for those who work overnight. Then, at the other end of the building, there is a two-boy living unit which is independent of "43", with its own entrance, kitchen and bathroom and two bed-sitting rooms. The purpose and ethos of this part of the unit will be described later.

The methodology of the unit is not limited by any one model. We, in fact, are prepared to use any method that will achieve our desired aim, that is to help each boy in the unit to face up to the realities of his own situation. It could be said that we are, to some extent, behaviouralist orientated, but not without being aware of the pitfalls of operating this type of system. It is a realistic approach, we feel, to confront each boy with the type of behaviour that he manifests, pointing out how this might cause difficulties to him as it will prove unacceptable to the vast majority of the community in which he lives and works, yet showing him alternative forms of behaviour that will be acceptable and help him to survive in a harsh and unsympathetic world. This necessarily means that each boy will be responsible for his own behaviour and that he must accept adult responsibilities. If this breaks down and the boy commits further offences, we feel that it is best he be treated in a realistic manner by us and the courts and the agencies of social control. However, the present system of administration of justice, which allows many children to collect numerous convictions before they are treated in a realistic way, often does more harm than good in that the children have contempt for the courts and all that they represent as being ineffective.

The use of team meetings is of the utmost importance to maintain the amount of collective observation that is necessary, so that any changes in behaviour in the boys can be met by a concerted staff group. Team meetings are used for discussion of all staff issues from the very trivia of residential life to extreme problems that staff may find in the handling of children. They can also be used for staff to talk over new ideas and new concepts and for other members of staff to introduce ideas that they may have read about. This general "educational" role can be very rewarding. As a time used for reflection on our own behaviour and handling of situations they are very valuable learning exercises. The discussion of new admissions and the collection of reports and data on possible new admissions are carried out at team meetings.

In general, when a boy is referred to "43" it is expected that a recent assessment be available. This is read by all the staff of "43" and notes are made by each member of staff. These are brought into discussion at the next team meeting. If possible, and it usually is, one member of "43" staff will be present at the last review of the boy if he is at Special Unit or Training School or the Assessment Conference at Kingswood Assessment Centre. This necessarily means that good links have to be forged with the referral agencies and good methods of communication have to be established. It is also important that each boy is introduced to the idea of "43" while he is at Kingswood Assessment Centre or any other agency, and to its aims and expectations of him, so that he is able to cope with the pressure and demands that will be made of him.

On admission, the boy signs a contract for his room laying down the basic conditions of residence at "43". This is an attempt to make the rules similar to those used in lodgings and bedsits such as the boys will find on leaving "43".

When permission has been given for a boy to go out in the evening he must return by 9.30 p.m. unless, due to special circumstances, he has been granted an extension.

All boys must be in bed by 10.00 p.m. and quiet with lights out by 10.15 p.m.

Radios, record players etc., may be played at reasonable times at a moderate volume but must be switched off by 10.00 p.m. If such appliances continually cause a nuisance they may be confiscated.

"CONTRACT"

43 BRITANNIA ROAD.

I understand and agree that the conditions of my being allowed to live at 43 Britannia Road are:

Accommodation is leased to boys on the understanding that they are liable for any loss or damage to the furniture, furnishings and decorations therein.

Rooms are inspected weekly by staff.

A deposit of 50 pence is required in respect of room keys. This deposit will be refunded when the keys are returned but will be forfeited should the key be lost.

The Warden and staff have duplicate keys and are entitled to enter any room should the need arise.

Guests are not allowed in the building except with permission of staff and then only in communal rooms.

Boys are expected to help with the running of the establishment and domestic chores will be shared.

Laundry facilities are available on the premises but may only be used under supervision of staff.

No alcohol is allowed on the premises.

In the majority of cases the boys who are resident at "43" are of working age and therefore engaged in full-time employment.

Each boy is given his own room and he is responsible for its upkeep and he has to attend to his own laundry. In the utility room there is an automatic washing machine and a tumble drier. When a boy first arrives at "43", if he is of working age, he has to be prepared to work and in fact initially take any job that is offered to him. This may appear to be forceful; it is, to an extent, but in our experience it is easier to find the "right" job which each boy would like if he is already employed.

This idea means that the staff of "43" need to build up a close relationship with local employers and the staff in Job Centres and Careers Offices. It is a good sign of this relationship that for the majority of the time all the 11 boys are either at school or in full-time employment. A member of staff of "43", besides being part of the care team, also has to foster the necessary links. It is hardly surprising that after a few years we can boast of a group of sympathetic employers who know that they will receive support if they are prepared to take on what at first might appear to be a "difficult" boy. It is not uncommon for an employer, after having taken on one of our boys, to be prepared to take on another. This would only happen if he were confident of the support that he would be given. There are, however, invariably a number of boys who will still be receiving full-time education either within Kingswood Schools, in local comprehensive or education units for school phobia such as the Bayswater Centre.

Dealing with boys of working age means that there needs to be staff cover from 6 o'clock in the morning or even earlier, to make sure that they leave for work on time, that they have had sufficient breakfast, that any packed lunch has been prepared by the boys who need it, and to be around to encourage the boys as to the virtues of a working life. The level of support each boy will need varies, the greatest support will be necessary for those boys who have never worked or who find holding down a job difficult. Those boys who have set up a steady work pattern will be encouraged to get themselves up and to start organising their own lives. Later on in the morning those boys who go to school, usually no more than three out of a total group of 11, will be called and got ready for school etc., so that by 9 o'clock each morning all the boys will be out of the building. This is the time in the day when the staff on duty can start to look towards the administration sides to the job, the record keeping, contact with social workers, employers, schools etc. If a boy is out of work it is expected of him to work around "43" during the day. However, the search for a new job is of paramount importance. The work he is expected to do is cleaning, cooking, preparation for meals. No boy is allowed to do nothing. It is common for the boys who are in work to ask what the out of work boy has done during the day. There is a great deal of pressure to find work both from the staff and the peer group.

When the boys start to arrive home from work they will go to their rooms to wash and change before coming back down into the communal areas. In the majority of cases a meal will have been prepared by one of the Housemothers or if there is a boy out of work he will have had to cook it with help from the Housemother. The meal is usually held around 6.00 p.m. to make sure that as many of the boys as possible are able to get together around the meal table and talk together amongst themselves and staff. The boys then are responsible for the clearing away and washing up of the dishes.

After the meal it is time for those boys who want to go out and who are allowed out to negotiate the time of arrival back with the staff on duty. If it is important in the boy's eyes to do something, it is best that he is encouraged to do it but to act in a responsible manner, so that if he has to be up for work at 6.00 a.m. he cannot expect to stay out until midnight every night of the week and hope to hold down a job. The privilege of late nights is afforded to those who are in work on a regular basis and it means that adult responsibilities are met with adult privileges and given each boy's behaviour the degree of privilege will vary accordingly.

Relationship Work

However, there are often boys who have not yet been able to make the transition from what can only be called the "total care" of other establishments and the realities of adulthood and they will need to be helped in many areas of social interaction. We feel that it is our role to help to broaden each child's outlook while still accepting that there may be overriding cultural bonds that will put some fetters upon this type of work.

By the use of local resources such as Youth Clubs, sport facilities, adult education and Further Education colleges and the particular skills of individual staff members it is possible to give each boy a wide choice of activities. However, it is important that while each boy is encouraged to take part in activities, pressure is never brought to bear on anyone who wishes to opt out of any activity in order to convenience staff. As far as possible the staff team try at first to encourage the boys to take part in any activity but in many cases they will find their own level and the pace at which they wish to travel. It would be worthwhile to point out that this is often the first area of self-determination for many really institutionalised boys; as so often is the case, care means a diminished responsibility for the boys. By attempting to give back that responsibility it is possible for a boy to accept his responsibility very quickly and respond to this "adult-like" treatment by progressing rapidly through the treatment programme.

On the other hand, this approach can backfire on the boy when he progresses for part of the programme but gets frightened when faced with certain realities. By trying to work through problems associated with relationships the boy with the very hard chauvinistic attitude towards women can often be very frightened when, as with one boy, his girlfriend finishes with him. In this case this was such a shock to the boy that his behaviour deteriorated rapidly and his attention-seeking behaviour became of concern to staff because of possible self-inflicted injury. There is a risk that, if you are hoping to work on a realistic basis with adolescents, situations such as this must be faced up to and with good staff support can be worked through, to help the adolescent to achieve independence. It is important that each boy be helped to acknowledge the potential effects of his behaviour by pointing out difficulties he may encounter when living in an unsympathetic world and how to cope with them. Thus, the boy who used female underclothes as a masturbatory aid needed very careful and sensitive counselling by the staff. He also needed protecting from possible ridicule from the other boys.

We feel that there is no need for the setting up of a regular counselling session with individual boys, but with good staff communication particular individuals who require help can be given that help as and when they need it either by their telling staff—which can take many forms, sometimes verbal but more usually in acting-out behaviour—or by staff observation of the peer group dynamics. This will help staff to highlight areas that need particular attention. By the time a boy has reached the end of his treatment programme he will start off any counselling session because he will have built up a trust in staff members and he will want to talk. It is very interesting to be around when one of the "older" boys tries to help a "younger" one and to see if they find this frustrating and ask, "Was I like that?"

The development of good relationships between the individual staff members and the boys is of the utmost importance, for without the mutual trust that we have tried to build up the task we attempt would be hopeless. If the consumer of what you offer understands why you are offering it and how it can help him, then he is more likely to accept what you have to offer. This can often be the most difficult and frustrating task residential workers can undertake and staff must not expect gratitude. I do not say that this will apply in all areas but when dealing with adolescents it is a prime objective to help residents to understand what is happening to them and how they can help to control part of their lives. This brings us back again to the point that care so often diminishes the responsibility of the child. How is this responsibility re-established?

The first area in which we tried to increase the responsibility of the boys was to invite them along to their individual case conferences. This move was welcomed in principle by the first group of boys involved. It is a common feeling amongst adolescents that so much of the care decision making is done behind their backs. There are, however, many drawbacks, but these have not been insurmountable. When (as in any case conference) the boy is faced with several difference viewpoints he feels threatened (what adult would not in such a situation?) but this is alleviated by involving him by letting him hear what members of staff and social workers and parents have to say, and at the same time giving him an opportunity to take part in the decision-making process. It is essential to encourage staff members and social workers to rid themselves of the safety they find in holding reviews in camera; that is to say not to pull any punches with regard to what they say, but to have the confidence to say those things with the lad and parents present. It is encouraging to note that few problems have been encountered in inviting the boys and parents to case conferences. The involvement of all the parties concerned is, in my opinion, of primary importance. It has also become our practice to invite the boy's employer or immediate supervisor to the case conference; we have found that they are keen to attend and take a greater degree of interest in the boy because of this involvement.

It may have crossed your mind to ask, what if boys refuse? They may have been in care so long that this whole concept could frighten them. If after trying to persuade them to attend they still feel unable to do so then you can give them a copy of the last case conference and try to get other boys who have attended their own reviews to reassure them. Even after this it has been known for some lads not to be able to face their first review, yet it is quite common for them to attend subsequent ones. An interesting side-line of this area is to point out that those lads who are admitted direct from Kingswood Assessment Centre without being in care before are, in the main, more ready to attend the first review. It would appear that the longer a lad has been in care the less likely he is to wish to attend.

In this connection, we had a very frustrating experience. A very repressed boy, who was committed to care because of a very grave physical assault, had been brought to the point of virtually facing complete responsibility. He had been in residential care for $5\frac{1}{2}$ years, most of it in a secure environment. The DHSS were interested because of the nature of his offence and wished to attend the review that was called to discuss whether or not the lad could leave care.

The boy had attended the previous review while with us, together with his father and the domiciliary social worker still involved. The DHSS representative expressly requested the exclusion of father and boy from the review. This request was acceded to, but with hindsight it is doubtful whether this should have been done. This incident is illustrative of difficulty that some adults carrying responsibility, either direct or indirect, find in entering into meaningful discussion with clients.

It is also illustrative of the contradictions and complications underlying the practice and the perceived objectives of social work interaction. It was clear from the DHSS representative's viewpoint that the expediency of social control and management were of prime importance. This is an interesting example of what Jeff Hopkins in the *British Journal of Social Work*, **8** (4), 1978, in his article Models of assessment in social work, describes as the management model, this being the argument that represents social behaviour as something to be contained and administered.

The next specific area where we attempt to increase each boy's responsibility is our approach to activities that can give a sense of achievement and hence increase self-esteem, yet not losing sight of the fact that many activities that are offered in residential establishments do nothing to foster independence but are used as a method of containing children and tiring them out. When I first started to work at "43" the range of outdoor activities was quite limited and this must be the case because of the type of staff and their ability. In common with many establishments, it was the practice at holiday periods to group the boys up, provide them with food, equipment and transport, and whisk them away to South Devon for such activities as swimming, fishing and walking. Although this is the only way to conduct outdoor activities in many establishments, given the work we are trying to do in "43" it was totally inappropriate.

To this extent we had to have a re-appraisal of the resources that are within easy reach of Kingswood. These consisted of a very active Youth Service run by the County Council and many other private bodies. Coupled with this there is easy access to the Mendip Hills, the Wye Valley, the Forest of Dean and the Avon Gorge. It was on, or rather under, the Mendip Hills that the first of these activities took place—caving. This was fairly easy to get off the ground with two members of staff being interested. During the first weekend that caving was offered all but one of the nine boys in "43" took part. After the initial enthusiasm had waned there were four boys who were very keen. As the boys became more experienced the trips became more and more adventurous, with the boys able to free dive water-filled passageways known as "sumps" and to tackle 85-foot ladder pitches with a stream falling on them. For them to feel that they had succeeded in something and seen things which were excluded from the vast majority of people was good to see.

The next problem that we came up against was how the boys were going to be able to equip themselves and to meet other young people taking part in similar activities. We were fortunate in that it was possible for "43" to assist in the buying of the basic equipment that was needed. The local Youth Associations were able to provide an answer to the second problem through their outdoor activities club. An example of how this worked was when two boys were entered on their advanced caving course in the Brecon Beacons. They were more than a match for the other people on the course and the course was of a two-fold benefit; it increased the boys' self-confidence and they met ordinary people taking part in outdoor activities, proving that it was not something confined to residential establishments or school.

However, opportunities for activities that can operate under this principle are vast— not only outdoor activities but any activity that will help the lads to mix with the outside world. One thing that does contradict this principle is the idea of helping each lad to have car driving lessons; by meeting half the cost of the first 10 lessons it provides an avenue to an acceptable qualification, i.e. a driving licence. The importance of all the types of activities is to gear them to things which the boys can on the one hand find exciting and which are, on the other hand, legitimate while being reasonably within their financial grasp, so that they can carry them out after they have left care.

Preparation for Leaving

The next stage to which we extended the use of "43" was to convert part of what set out as a laundry room into a small self-catering area. This was specifically set up with the idea that any lad who was, on leaving "43", going to live in a bed-sit/flat type accommodation, would not have an "Ideal Home" type of kitchen but fairly basic facilities. The facilities that we provide are a sink, a "Baby Belling" type cooker, a limited set of pots and pans and enough crockery for two people. All boys should be able to use this facility, but obviously priority is given to boys who have to achieve total independence because of their circumstances. But for those who may be returning home, often a month of self-catering is sufficient to impart some of the skills that they may need to use if they are to survive if the home breaks up after they leave care.

The usual format is that after 3 months of being catered for by "43", and after the first case review, it is recommended that before the next review they have at least started on the self-catering scheme. There is such a demand for the use of this facility, because of the prestige attached to it, that if we were not very careful it is possible that some boys would try to stay longer on the scheme by, say, making a mess of the last week of their month in the hope that we will keep them on it until they "totally" succeed. This is where careful observation by the staff is essential to make sure that we are fully in the picture.

The process starts with the boys on the self-catering scheme paying a fixed rent; it may be necessary to explain that ordinarily the rate of rent is pre-set by Avon CC directive. But the present charge for self-catering boys is a fixed amount at two-thirds the maximum rent. They have to buy their own provisions and plan menus. In the first place they get a lot of help from the staff, and any boys who take part in the scheme are shown how to shop, where to look for bargains and the essentials of cooking on a limited budget of only buying seasonal provisions when at their best and cheapest.

At first there is a great deal of support and encouragement and gradually this support is withdrawn until they can cope with not only the cooking of the food, which we find is the easy task, but also the planning of a good diet and organising their finances to be able to meet their needs until the end of each week. It would be fair to say that this scheme is a resounding success in that it is an excellent learning situation and it is thought, by the majority of boys, to be worth doing, therefore having the greatest chance of success. There have been boys who have found it very difficult at first but it has never been an insurmountable problem.

The most recent of the advances is perhaps the most exciting, in that we found it to be a problem that when boys left "43" some of them found great difficulty in adjusting to life in bed-sits and flats. We are fortunate in being able to provide a two-boy bed-sitting unit with a bathroom and kitchen and their own entrance. This gave us the chance of trying out boys in the situation of total independence while having the support, albeit in the background, of the staff of "43". The boys who use the flat have to use the local facilities while paying a realistic rent of £10 per week based upon the charge explained earlier. The idea of providing all the facilities for adolescents to make the transition from care into full independence with every chance of success is very important. In many ways part of the success of "43" is that we are providing something that the young people who are in care want; therefore it is, in the majority of cases, assured success in being able to help them to make a life of their own and without the support of outside agencies.

What for the future? It is envisaged that a trust fund may be willing to buy a large house that can be converted into bed-sits to provide a service that is not met by local authorities or private organisations and where people in need of accommodation and a very limited degree of support can live. The provision of residential support for adolescents is an area of development, yet there are certain regions where there is still very little support for this age range. It is important, if any success is to be achieved from a period in care, that the opportunity is provided for the people in care to make their own way in life so that they do not repeat the pattern of delinquency that is evident from their background.

Further Reading

CARLBACH, J., *Caring for Children in Trouble*, Routledge & Kegan Paul, 1970.
DUNLOP, A., *The Approved School Experience*, Home Office Research Studies, No. 25, HMSO, London, 1975.
MAY, D., Delinquency control and the treatment model, *British Journal of Criminology*, **11** (4), 1972, 359–70.
MILLHAM, S. *et al.*, *After Grace—Teeth, A Survey Of Eighteen Approved Schools*, Chaucer Press, 1975.
PARSLOE, P., *Juvenile Justice in Britain and the United States, the Balance of Needs and Rights*, Routledge & Kegan Paul, 1978.
POWER, M. *et al.*, Delinquency and the family, *British Journal of Social Work*, **14** (1), 13–33.

SPARKS, R. F. and HOOD, R. G., *The Residential Treatment of Disturbed and Delinquent Boys*, University of Cambridge, Institute of Criminology, Cropwood Round Table Conference, 1968.

TROJANOWICZ, R. C., *Juvenile Justice, Concepts and Control*, Prentice-Hall, 1973.

WALTER, J. A., A critique of sociological studies of approved schools, *British Journal of Criminology*, **17** (4), 1977.

WEST, D. J. and FARRINGTON, D. P., *The Cambridge Study In Delinquent Development:* Vol. I (1969) *Present Conduct and Future Delinquency*; Vol. II (1973) *Who Becomes Delinquent*; Vol. III (1977) *The Delinquent Way Of Life*.

There is a wealth of literature in general on delinquency and a fair amount on the residential treatment of adolescent boys in Britain. The titles above are a very selective list: Carlbach (1970) puts the development of residential provision for this client group in its historical perspective, whereas Parsloe (1978) traces and compares the development of Juvenile Courts in England and Wales, in Scotland and in the USA. Sparks and Hood (1968), Millham *et al.* (1975), Dunlop (1975) together give a picture of the existing provision, whilst May (1972) and Walter (1977) give a critical analysis of the system. Power and Trojanowicz (1973) along with West (1969–79) address the issues around the causes of delinquency. Further references are to be found in most of these works.

INTRODUCTION

Any residential establishment is a complex environment where residents who, except for their social circumstances may well have chosen not to be there, live with staff who may have a variety of care or treatment functions. The patterns of relationships and social structures which exist in the smaller single unit are intricate enough, but in larger single establishments or a complex of buildings within a defined campus, the structures and relationships are vastly more complicated and varied. This section aims to examine some of the problems and methods of dealing with organisational and management issues. The underlying assumption is that the organisational structures and management process are intimately related to the quality of life and ability of staff to work with and on behalf of residents.

Organisation and management issues can be dealt with at the agency level, where residential care may form the whole or a part of the agency's services (as in a social services department) or at the level of a particular home. Because of our focus on practice we have tended to concentrate at the level of the individual establishment, whilst recognising that for the particular establishment the wider agency constitutes a part of its external environment which may have a strong influence on internal processes. The contributions in this section illuminate the key management task which is to structure a physical and social environment for residents which maximises their quality of life. Buildings and staff are a major part of this environment. There is plenty of evidence to show that in the past buildings and staff contributed to an institutionalising process. The following contributions try to take a different stance, examining ways in which physical and human resources can be directed most effectively to the welfare of residents.

CHAPTER 16

SOCIAL SERVICES DEPARTMENT STRUCTURES AND THE ORGANISATION OF RESIDENTIAL SOCIAL WORK

RODNEY BULL

Introduction

Although the Seebohm Report, as the basis for the 1970 Local Authority Social Services Act, was speaking of services for the elderly when it said (para. 305), that "Local authorities are the major providers of residential homes. . . ."[1] the same could be said for other client groups or areas of need across a range of problems relating to a variety of residential settings. It is for this reason that the focus here will be on the local authority Social Services Department (SSD) structure and organisation of residential social work (RSW).

In what follows it has seemed important to locate the discussion within a loose framework drawn from organisational studies in the field of management and administration, various sociological literature and some of the relevant material available from social work itself. Inevitably, in view of the depth and breadth of the area, it will be necessary to concentrate on particular aspects of structure and organisation and, given the space available, to sacrifice some detail in order to present some main points.

Perhaps the largest theme running through this presentation relates to bringing back the presence of the residential social worker into a discussion of organisational structure. Sir Harold Wilson said of unemployment statistics that for the person out of work unemployment is 100%. Similarly, we might say that for RSW staff employment or work envelopment is also total; not in the literal sense of a weekly 40 hours plus overtime ($37\frac{1}{2}$ in the field!) but where the general requirement to provide full continuity of coverage within an establishment or centre seems to both need and generate full involvement. Because of this, emphasis will be given to organisational support particularly for the "Head of Centre", "Head of Home", or residential social worker in charge (RSW i/c). The obverse is also required and suggests itself, namely the support given to the structure by organisational members. First, it is necessary to look at some of the ways in which managers and management have been described and discussed.

Management Types and Management Styles

Burns and Stalker have viewed management in terms of two "ideal types": "mechanistic" and "organic".[2] The mechanistic form, which resembles Weberian bureaucracy, is characterised by a clear hierarchy, strict specialisation and vertical communication.

It will tend to emerge in stable conditions. An organic form will not have a clearly defined hierarchy and will engage in continual redefinition of roles (therefore fewer formal job titles) and will have lateral communication between organisational members. With co-ordination occurring via regular management meetings these individuals will be expected to relate their own activity to the aims of the organisation. Such a form is more relevant in unstable conditions because of its use of advice-giving, consultation and easy information flow rather than the "mechanistic" instructions and decisions being handed down.

The argument is that neither form of management is "best"—neither the "mechanistic" with its emphasis on job titles and job descriptions, on exactly who is going to do what, and how each organisational role is fitted together to form the desired organisational pattern, nor the "organic" type with its smaller emphasis on specific titles and descriptions and greater on organisational members arranging themselves and the work into a commonly purposeful, relatively fluid and flexible form responding "organically" to environmental changes.

In relating a type of management to a particular situation or set of circumstances the question arises as to what actually constitutes changing or stable conditions in various areas of social work. Thus, within any one RSW establishment there will be at any one time a finite number of beds. Once all currently available bed spaces have been allocated, then an upsurge in need or demand will filter through to the RSW i/c in particular ways. For example, extra beds may be provided and a requirement made that either an unused or a "daily living" area be redesignated as a bed area or bedrooms. Or again, there may be pressure to complete "due process"—as in an assessment centre—more swiftly. Generally, these moves, or at least in the short term, result in extra demands being made on a finite number of staff. However, it is quite uncertain just how outside change is perceived in RSW and how it takes effect compared with, say, the effect of an increase in referral bombardment on an SSD area office.

Whether a participative rather than authoritarian form of SSD management is more appropriate is not easily resolved. In the absence of profitability and a pricing system on which to base considerations of efficiency and effectiveness, indexing the relationship between management type and environmental conditions is bound to be problematic. However, it seems likely that low staff morale will influence the quality of work in client contact. This is particularly so in a residential setting with its close and ongoing nature of contact between residents and staff. Further, that participation and consultation are likely to increase loyalty to the organisation and to reflect the role of those professionals working within it. It also seems likely that this form of management may be closely related to the conception of management as a learning process.

J. D. Stewart distinguishes between two differing processes of management: the static process and the learning process.[3] In a static process, management is primarily concerned to carry on with the existing pattern of activities. Performance is evaluated on the basis of whether existing targets are met, but the targets themselves are not reviewed. Static management can be sustained by (a) the necessity to "carry on" (but not necessarily, of course, exactly in existing form) given the possibility of various unforeseen costs, not just financial, in making change. One recalls Columbus's advice to his cartographer: "Where unknown, there place 'Terrors'." In the same vein a local authority SSD research officer has discussed with me what he terms "the inbuilt inertia factor" in local government. Donald Schon, in the 1970 Reith Lectures, got much nearer the heart of the matter by moving away from the essentially passive metaphor of inertia—drawn from physics and referring to the property of an object to tend to remain where it is unless a force is exerted upon it. Schon proposed instead that organisations are "dynamically conservative",[4] that is to say, they fight very hard to remain the same!

The process remains static also because of (b) "management by intuition",[5] usually referred to as management by experience—with various individuals' length of service often being mentioned. The possibility exists that, at least hypothetically, 10 or 20 years' experience can in practice mean the experience of 1 year repeated 10 or 20 times. It is worth noting that use of the term "professional judgement" as a reason or justification for action or inaction is open to abuse. As with intuitive management it may see the suggestion of a need for discussion as a challenge to ascribed "excellence", a challenge which if avoided may reduce the possibility of change. This issue will be returned to in a later section.

Stewart considers that when management is viewed as a learning process, the concern is not simply with "carrying on" but with improvement, so that the starting point is not a target itself related to the output from immediate activity but the reason for undertaking the activity in the first place, for setting the objective that activity is designed to realise. Management would then resume with the replanned objectives, examine and evaluate the alternative ways, including the current one, of meeting them, decide on a course of action and then set targets on the way to meeting those objectives. Review would occur fairly regularly—although Wildavsky has written about the difficulties in developing a self-evaluating organisation[6]—and the views of individuals working within the organisation will often be taken into account.

Organisational Descriptions

Before turning to look at models of SSD organisation it is necessary here to place aspects of that later discussion in a humanising context: the needs, perceptions and interactional positions of organisational members, of workers in a service organisation, have to be taken into consideration and are often ignored to the cost of that service. The formal organisational "blueprint" is only part of the picture. Manning points out that ". . . features of organisational settings are not exhausted by structural characteristics. To ascribe to this view is analogous to believing that language behaviour can be understood by a close study of a dictionary."[7]

For any particular organisational setting or situation there are, then, four possible different descriptions:[8]

(1) Manifest —the situation as described formally, displayed, codified, written down.
(2) Assumed —the situation as it is assumed to be by the various individuals in that organisational setting. These assumptions might not coincide with the manifest position or even with each other. This is important because, in the words of W. I. Thomas's dictum, "if men define situations as real, then they are real in their consequences".
(3) Extant —the situation as revealed by careful and systematic study. Inevitably, it can never be completely known. An example of the difference between manifest and extant descriptions would be where a mental health consultant's executive responsibility for admissions to a mental handicap

hostel is revealed to have been delegated to the RSW i/c on the basis of the latter's level of skill and expertise.

(4) Requisite —the situation required, given a set of objectives or a context of needs to satisfy or realise those contextual properties in the most appropriate manner. This fourth description does not have to be an idealistic "ought" statement in the form of an imposed "best" structure: aspects of a requisite form can suggest themselves from existing structural difficulties and the proposed resolutions thereof in an incrementalist progression.

The ideal—in the sense of balance—situation will have the four different possible descriptions coinciding or as close as possible. There will, however, because of the processual nature of organisations, always be a tendency for the four to keep moving out of line.

The importance of organisational members in what sort of organisational structure exists is heavily implicit in the above comments. Members who by way of their own interpretations, endorsements and acceptances, denials, misunderstandings or part-understandings help create a textural complexity; members who contribute to the existence of multiple understandings of a situation or organisational relationship—a multiplicity which continues to exist because it may never be fully challenged; members who, in effect, "pull" small parts of an organisation into a more acceptable relationship for daily working purposes; or members who informally fill in various gaps and deficiencies in the formal structure: members who may, in all these ways and more, either prop up or lay seige to formal structure.

The significance of all this resides in the fact that it is usually a formal structure which is originally proposed as the "best" way of meeting aims or requirements, and yet that manifest existence may only manage or not manage to do so because of these other realities. Evaluative assessments, in view of this, need to consider all these aspects when trying to decide on the appropriateness of any particular organisational structure.

To provide a balance for these statements about the importance of individual interpretations and assumptions, and before finally moving on to the main models of SSD organisational structure, it is essential that we consider briefly one further argument, that about reification.

Reification

The basic feature of this standpoint is that designations, titles, roles and structures tend to be seen as developing an existence which becomes independent from the people who have or relate to those titles and work within, or who are otherwise affected by, those structures. There is, in effect, a tendency to view both role and structure as non-human facticity—for them to become reified.

Berger and Luckmann have expressed it thus:

> Reification is the apprehension of human phenomena as if they were things, that is, in non-human or possibly suprahuman terms. Another way of saying this is that reification is the apprehension of the products of human activity as if they were something other than human products—such as facts of nature, results of cosmic

laws, or manifestations of divine will. Reification implies that man is capable of forgetting his own authorship of the human world, and, further, that the dialectic between man, the producer, and his products is lost to consciousness.[9]

Now, of course, organisation and process require structure, and continuity is required for the implementation of any policy—but not a continuity of complacency without regard to improvement. How often have we heard that "that is not possible in the existing structure" or seen a present difficulty or dispute "resolved" by referring (it) to the established framework? Certainly, all things are not possible; one cannot have infinite flexibility. But somewhere in the middle ground between the extremes there are managers, workers and residents who are or could be operating on the basis of "we won't know unless we try".

I am reminded of the series of hurdles an ex-colleague had to overcome to establish a licensed bar in a Part III Home. This example of tenacity serves to remind us that very probably there will be differences between workers in what they consider as "reified" or not, so that elements of both arguments in this section may apply within any particular organisation.

Models of Organisational Structure

Although there is no countrywide uniformity of SSD organisational structures they can nevertheless be considered to loosely correspond to one of two models.

A model can be presented as a network or series of relationships between items and is useful depending on its "representation of structure"—that is, manifest structure—thereby enabling us to examine aspects of some large and complex phenomenon, in this case SSD structure, without too much difficulty. Needless to say, any one Department will not necessarily coincide exactly with the state of affairs represented by one model but there are likely to be large approximations for which the linkages and relationships shown on a model will provide food for thought.

Both models will be briefly described and then compared and considered with particular reference to residential social work.

(1) *The Function Model* (Fig. 16.1)

This represents a SSD divided primarily according to function—for example, residential and day care, fieldwork, research and administration. It has been termed Model A by the Brunel research team[10] and also refers to what has been described as a "centralised" department because, beneath the Director, and possibly also a Deputy Director, there will be a number of Assistant Directors (AD), headquarters (HQ) based, each heading and managing one of the functional divisions of work area. Some local authorities will have an AD for domiciliary and day care services, while others combine fieldwork and domiciliary work as the responsibility of one AD, while another AD takes on residential and day care provision also on a combined basis.

Below HQ level, fieldwork services are provided through a number of Area Offices, on a basis of geographical area, each headed by an Area Officer (AO). Since each office

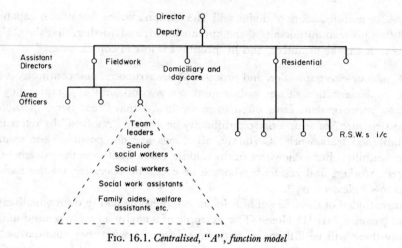

FIG. 16.1. *Centralised, "A", function model*

is the main link between potential "clients" and the SSD it will usually be the first point of contact for the provision of residential or day care resources.

(2) *The Geography Model* (Fig. 16.2)

This is also termed "decentralised" or (Brunel) Model B. An SSD is divided, primarily on a basis of geographical area, into a number of Divisions each headed by a Divisional Director (DD) (and possibly further subdivided into Areas with Area Officers or Divisional Officers [DOs]) and in which residential and day care services and facilities are used and managed by geographically localised offices also providing the full range of other services for the area. These Divisions can be loosely regarded as smaller departments within the larger department with each DD accountable to the Director of Social Services and responsible for all the services (domiciliary, day care, residential, fieldwork) within the Division. The locus of control over budget allocation and use is crucial here but as those details are not central to the aims of this discussion they will not be directly included.

Kogan and Terry make a distinction between what they term the "non-operational activities" involved in economy, clarity of organisation, efficiency, output budgeting, co-ordination and other "management virtues" and the operational activities of "promoting better relationships between professional and client and a better responsiveness to the needs, sentiments and participation of the consumers of the service".[11]

Within this geographic model, because of decentralisation, the non-operational senior level posts, at AD or near level, become particularly important in the effort to co-ordinate functional activities, although none would have a managerial accountability for the delivery of operation services.

There can be terminological problems in discussing these two models. For example, when using "division" we need to be clear whether it is being used in the sense of work division and task responsibility demarcation as in the function model, or whether as a "division" on the basis of geographical separation. Also, in the use of "Area Officer" and Area Office we have to be careful because in some SSDs geographical Areas are termed

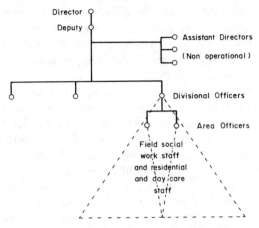

Fɪɢ. 16.2. *Decentralised, "B", geography model*

Divisions (as in the geographic model) even though there may be a virtual centralisation of responsibility for functional service areas in the form of HQ-based ADs (as in the functional model).

For convenience, and to avoid other terminological difficulties, the Brunel use of letters of the alphabet will also be followed here. However, even this is not free from problems: since a number of SSDs have changed from Model A to Model B this alphabetically natural sequential progression can be value-laden in that it is often taken to represent this "progress" and all that that concept implies.

Implications for Residential Work: Some Arguments

The following will be stated in a fairly straightforward manner so as to convey the main issues. Some of the arguments even for the same model may appear as in real or potential conflict, but this seems to accurately represent the confusion which exists. Also, inevitably, some overlapping will occur. During this section the arguments for and against each model will be seen to gradually extend and build up to the current turbulent and complex state of affairs. The discussion from earlier sections needs here to be borne in mind.

(1) The Model A segmentalisation of resources under the various ADs is held to lead to fragmentation: disagreements or lack of co-ordination can develop between the functional divisions of work such that less than comprehensive service planning occurs. Since operational co-ordination is not structurally inbuilt often numerous discussion groups or working parties are set up which then attempt to develop linking procedures and practices.

The Model B organisational structure can make it possible for each geographical division to develop, co-ordinate and make more flexible all the available resources including residential and fieldwork to meet local needs.

(2) In Model A the ADs, by concentrating on one functional work area, can develop their expertise and so make more efficient the use of specialised resources.

In Model B, DOs, almost invariably with fieldwork backgrounds themselves and based in fieldwork area or divisional offices, do not have the interest, specialised knowledge or time to adequately represent the interests of residential social work. The psychological truism that "valuation precedes cognition" is highly relevant here; without the focus or orientation there will be less than full appreciation or understanding or even apprehension of difficulties and needs.

(3) In Model B what tends to happen in practice is that within each Division there is a further breakdown or separation into the "functional" pattern of separate disciplinary areas (as in Model A) but without the combination of executive authority and relative expertise in the form of the relevant ADs. In view of the predominant fieldwork perspective in a SSD this absence has particular importance for residential work.

For Model A, in any one Divisional Office, several ADs each have an equivalent superior executive authority over the DO for their individual spheres of work so that local resource co-ordination will depend on an interplay between the DO and each AD and between those latter worthies themselves at headquarters meetings; less than rational factors may operate and the DO is in an ongoing potentially problematic position *vis à vis* this group of ADs.

(4) In Model B, without ADs responsible for operational objectives, in order to achieve some consistency of work standards and service planning within the whole SSD boundary there needs to be someone who can monitor divisional consistency: various "Consultant", "Adviser" or "Consultant Adviser" (CA) posts have been created. These posts are usually on the basis of client-group specialism. The status of CA is that of expert in a "narrow field"—narrow in that, for example, each CA would see it as legitimate to attempt by various means to ensure as large a "slice of the cake" as possible for their own client-group specialised area of work. Because of the client-group specialisation there will usually not be a CA for residential social work and each specialist would be expected to advise on residential, day care, domiciliary and fieldwork services. The post of CA carries a duty to advise the Director and so the direction of flow is upwards rather than downwards, although the intention is that an "advised" Director will initiate the required action.

In Model A any RSW i/c within an Area Office area has a routine direct line of communication to the AD (Residential) who is at an executive level only once removed from the Director and his Deputy and who could thus directly initiate action to resolve a difficulty.

(5) The Seebohm Report stated (para. 524) that ". . . we are clear that there ought to be someone, at both headquarters and area team level, with a particular responsibility for helping with the problems of residential institutions. . . ."[12]

In Model B the authority of the CAs may be more assumed than manifest and is based on them being headquarters-based. This provides access to central incoming information and data, thereby facilitating a more wide-ranging perspective and knowledge, and gives them an assumed headquarters sphere of influence. It is interesting that current aggravations relate variously to the CA not doing his job properly and to a CA in the post not being able to undertake the necessary work, i.e. the arguments sometimes confuse failure of the role incumbent's performance with failure or inadequacy of the organisational role itself to relate to what is required (assessed by whom?).

In Model A, an AD (Residential) will be both headquarters-based (with the "ear" of the Director) and have executive authority at Area Office level.

(6) The nature of the advice and consultancy is important: does a CA post have

responsibility without authority? Perhaps it can persuade but may not be allowed to direct. Does a consultancy post act as the linchpin of a residential communication network facilitating the exchange of information and ideas between establishments—or should this be inbuilt elsewhere in the structure? Does it have routine RSW i/c contact or act primarily on a "cry for help" basis? Does it offer advice in the "Godfather" manner of "making an offer that cannot be refused"? What are the consequences of not taking the advice?

In Model B the argument generally would be that a CA, who will usually be at Principal Officer level—say at PO1 compared with a slightly higher level of PO2 for the DO—is not in the main line of executive authority delegated down from the Director. Thus, a CA will not have executive authority over a RSW i/c because (a) by the very nature of the post the RSW i/c has responsibility for the establishment, and (b) he can realistically only be accountable to one person, namely the DO, and (c) such authority would change the relationship between the CA and DO which would effectively reduce the possibility of the latter's control, co-ordination and development of services within the Division.

In Model A the AD (Residential) would have the expertise, interest and decision-making capacity but, because of the number of establishments within the whole SSD area, the closeness of contact with any one RSW i/c will be limited—although there may be various posts at, say, Principal Assistant level giving extra coverage. These latter posts may be charged with the requirement to liaise, filter or "maintain a presence at the front". They would almost certainly act for the AD rather than as the AD and this may produce an extra hurdle for a RSW i/c to negotiate. Attempts by a RSW i/c at circum-navigating this hurdle and going directly to the AD would almost certainly be discouraged.

(7) In SSDs which have moved from Model A to Model B residential staff have found themselves attached to or superimposed on a Divisional Area which is predominantly fieldwork orientated.

In Model A they existed with others (fieldworkers etc.) as integrals of a cohesive organisation. Notice again the importance of terms: integral does not necessarily mean equality or equivalence and many RSWs i/c would assert that disparity was extant but never "spelled out".

(8) In Model B there is a need for RSWs i/c to have someone they can identify with and who has executive authority to actually get things done on their behalf; in other words, for the direction of flow of work and communication from the RSWs i/c to be as well represented structurally as the work-flow towards them. Manifestly, the "someone" exists in the form of DO but there seems at present a significant gap between manifest and extant descriptions. It must be said that this gap is wider in some Division than others—so pointing us either to examine DO role-performance difficulties or to question the structural expectation that one role incumbent can achieve what is required.

It may be that DOs require explicit assistance in the personal development of their RSW knowledge and focus, together with being charged with a far greater detailed residential service accountability to the Director in order to achieve the integration suggested by Model B. Specific in-service training seminars may be necessary for these DOs to assist in their relationship with RSWs i/c. There is little point, for example, in "Heads of Home" meetings with the DO every month or so if all that is meant to occur is generalised comment. This can easily smack of a ritual of ventilation which the RSWs i/c may respond to by voting with their feet, i.e. staying away, so leading the DO to a self-fulfilling consequential conclusion of even less interest—"if they can't be bothered . . .".

As there is not the daily visibility of each other's work to ensure work consistency between RSWs i/c, so co-ordination or comparability of quality between the activities of different establishments would be made even more difficult by this, to use Merton's term, "retreatist"[13] response to the gap between means and goals; routine practical needs can be satisfied through the submission of requisition orders etc. to the appropriate administrative section at Division with any detailed discussion of the social work development of individual establishments being left more or less in abeyance.

Incidentally, it is worth mentioning here the (outdated?) mechanism whereby separate house committees of elected members of the local authority used to exist for the purpose of overseeing the affairs of individual establishments. The Chief Officer and Head of Home used to be present at such meetings which, typically, dealt with staffing issues, complaints, purchases, activities, care programmes and so on. The residential staff felt that they had occasional direct access in a business setting to elected members and their own Chief Officer—and the views of clients could be directly advanced. Further, decisions were directly seen to be taken. Arguments about waste of professional time and infringement of professional roles and responsibilities under such a scheme might be countered by the present failure to provide a similarly direct and effective mechanism.

(9) It has been suggested that, in Model B, to ease the DOs burden of work an extra post at divisional level be created so that that person can relate on behalf of the DO to the residential service. What would be important is the level of executive authority attached to the post: if only at a low-authority, liaison level without being able to make decisions this would, effectively, introduce one more layer for RSWs i/c to get through before reaching an extant decision-making level—the person in that post might simply be, as one RSW i/c has speculated, "just a messenger for the DO".

The Brunel researchers say that "All the evidence points to the need to create in departments of medium or large size new posts under some such titles as 'residential group manager' or perhaps 'residential manager' to fill what we have come to call the missing level in residential management."[14] They also speak of various "central staff" staff-officer or service-giving roles being needed to supplement the main structure of managerial roles in both Model A and Model B departments. These latter roles would be "non-operational" and not in a managerial relation to RSWs i/c. There is, as already mentioned, a difficulty with the former posts—if established in Model B there is a risk of RSW compartmentalisation, particularly if the posts are at approximately Area Office level beneath the DO; if, in Model A, the posts are also at Area Officer level they would, if without effective powers of decision-making, introduce one extra barrier between AD (Residential) and RSW i/c; therefore their executive authority would need to be comprehensively defined before an evaluation could occur.

Interaction between Field SW and RSW

At this stage in the argument I should like to focus briefly on aspects of the routine contact between field social work staff (FSW) and RSWs i/c. Bromley speaks of a widespread "prescriptive" model[15] in which field staff believe, on the basis of skill disparity and because they are better able to identify the range of resources that can be used to meet client need, that they should control residential entry, the nature of treatment and care during residence, and when there should be a return home, i.e. they prescribe the context of residential work. This is contrasted with a "collateral" model, without prescription and where, instead, agreement is required between the residential and fieldworker on who is admitted, the treatment and care plan, and on departure. In reaching this agreement it is felt that the negotiation, discussion and exchange of ideas is likely to lead to an understanding of each other's perspectives and specialist knowledge—which is one strand in the development of a unified approach. However, such agreement is problematic given the general dominance of fieldwork and the assertions of skill disparity. It is well known from sociological material that the definition of a situation by the most powerful "actor" in it is likely to prevail. The latest CCETSW estimates of qualified workers in the future are that only 30% of residential and day care workers will be qualified towards the end of the 1980s compared with 80% of field social workers by 1985. Any one qualified RSW i/c may have to contend with the general assumption of "superiority" by field staff and it is not surprising that a residential worker may feel on shaky ground in a boundary dispute since a fieldworker will often reach right inside the establishment to control treatment plan and so forth.

There is another aspect to boundary issues which is more represented by an absence than a presence. For example, following a Part III Home for the Elderly admission it is usual for the field social worker to "close" the case immediately or after a short period. This then effectively transfers responsibility to the RSW i/c. If a care and treatment plan results, say, in the possibility of transfer to sheltered accommodation the RSW i/c will not be encouraged and may actually be discouraged from making contact with the Housing Department Welfare Section because any such contacts routinely occur through the Area Office. The case has, however, been "closed" by the FSW and since no channel may exist for dealing with this and other problems the RSW i/c often feels the second-class worker of a SSD. Needless to say, as in this example, a resident may receive less than full consideration.

In Model A or Model B the way in which fieldwork is organised within any one Area Office is likely to have a bearing on the possible integration or otherwise of residential work. In this writer's experience, a system of geographical "patch" fieldwork teams has more potential for such integration than an office organisation of work into an Intake Team and several Long-Term Teams. Within a patch the RSWs i/c can, *ceteris paribus*, identify with and even possibly be attached to the team for the purpose of joint education and shared knowledge about local conditions as well as positive discussion about organisational problems. However, this does not resolve the need of the residential service to have someone able and willing to take executive decision on their behalf.

Further Discussion

In an article which examines what actually is organised within an organisation Haire asserted that ". . . two questions seem to me to be absolutely essential in organisation theory: "What are we trying to do with the organisation?" and "How do various aspects of the organisation structure affect the various goals?"[16] These questions are essential not only for Model A or Model B SSDs but also particularly when considerations are being voiced about possible transition from one to the other.

There are likely to be some "grey areas" in any organisational structure: relationships and areas of work which are either ill defined or not defined at all even on a manifest level. The problem arises when there are so many patches of grey that a structure looks definitely decrepit, and, to carry on the metaphor, when attempts to clarify and refine can look like poor "retouching" jobs. There is also a difficulty in trying to decide to what extent organisational problems arise from various structural difficulties and lacunae, or whether they have developed from manifestations of the perennial social work organisation phenomenon of "personalities" and idiosyncratic role performances—after all, individuality and the development of personal characteristics are encouraged in social work and yet some of those same individuals when moving up the management ladder are expected to constrain some of those earlier attributes and keep within certain bounds which, because never made fully explicit, are often not effective.

It can be argued that there is a conceptual danger implicit in Model B in the assumption of integration, adaptability and responsiveness of the whole service through geographic decentralisation and direct delegation of executive authority from the Director to the Divisional Officers. In some sense the issues involved are confused with parallel trends in social work—parallel but of a quite different nature. These are, briefly, emphasis on "transferable skills"—transferable across different work settings, client groups, and a range of different problem areas; a change from considering an RSW establishment or centre as a part of social work methodology (as one of the "traditional four" of casework, groupwork, community work and residential work) towards a view of it as a setting for work practice skills; and finally, a predominating promotion of the unitary or integrated approach in social work whereby each worker is expected to be able to utilise a range of methods and skills in an embracing system approach to social work intervention.

In conclusion, it has been shown that a move from Model A to Model B has been for the residential service a "tyranny of progress". Residential social work loses out in Model A but loses even more in Model B. A number of SSDs took the opportunity presented by the local government re-organisation of 1974 to re-organise from A to B and others have done so since. The time has come, however, for all SSDs to seriously examine the extent to which residential social work remains their "Cinderella". Such examination can only occur with the direct participation of residential staff themselves without mediation through the fieldwork service.

References

1. *Report of the Committee on Local Authority and Allied Personal Social Services* (Seebohm Report), Cmnd. 3703, HMSO, 1968, para. 305.
2. T. BURNS and G. M. STALKER, The Management of Innovation, Tavistock, London, 1961.
3. J. D. STEWART, The Analytical Approach to Decision-Making, in A. GATHERER and M. D. WARREN (eds.), *Management and the Health Services*, Pergamon, London, 1971, Chapter 3.
4. D. SCHON, Dynamic Conservatism, Reith Lecture No. 2, printed in *The Listener*, 26 Nov. 1970.
5. STEWART, *op. cit.*, see also J. ALGIE *Six Ways of Deciding*, BASW Publications, 1976.
6. A. WILDAVSKY, The self-evaluating organisation, *Public Administration Review*, **32** (5), 1972, 509–20.
7. P. K. MANNING, Talking and Becoming: a View of Organisational Socialisation, in J. D. DOUGLAS (ed.), *Understanding Everyday Life*, Routledge & Kegan Paul, London, 1971.
8. W. BROWN, *Exploration in Management*, Heinemann, London, 1960.
9. P. L. BERGER and T. LUCKMAN, *The Social Construction of Reality*, Allen Lane, London, 1967.
10. BRUNEL INSTITUTE OF ORGANISATION AND SOCIAL STUDIES, Social Services Organisation Research Unit, *Social Services Departments: Developing Patterns of Work and Organisation*, Heinemann, London, 1974.

11. M. Kogan and J. Terry, *The Organisation of a Social Services Department: a Blue-Print*, Bookstall Publications, London, 1971.
12. *Report of the Committee on Local Authority and Allied Personal Social Services. op. cit.*
13. R. Merton, *Social Theory and Social Structure*, (revised ed.), Free Press, Glencoe, Illinois, 1957.
14. Brunel Institute of Organisation and Social Studies, Social Services Organisation Research Unit, *op. cit.*
15. G. Bromley, Interaction between field and residential social workers, *British Journal of Social Work*, **7** (3), 1977.
16. M. Maire, What is Organised in an Organisation?, in M. Haire (ed.), *Organisational Theory in Industrial Practice*, Wiley, New York.

CHAPTER 17

MANAGEMENT ISSUES IN AN INDIVIDUAL HOME

GORDON M. GENTRY

In deciding quite how to approach the management issues in a comparatively short paper the writer has to determine whether to identify a few and study them profoundly, or endeavour to give the reader as broad a picture as possible of management issues in the residential home. "Residential Social Worker" can be an apt nomenclature for those involved in group living, but experience shows that it can be misleading to the uninitiated. Some workers entering the residential sector feel that the name implies that RSWs carry out a fieldwork style job in a residential setting. This is far from an accurate concept of the total task. In the past decade some of the work undertaken by RSWs has been advertised under such headings as "Houseparent", "Residential Child Care Officers", "Group Worker", etc. In this paper, to try to prevent perpetuation of the misconception, the writer has decided to give as full a picture as possible of the management issues and range of work impinging upon all residential workers rather than examining a few in depth. The reader may then have a fairly complete view of what residential management involves in its broadest sense.

It should be understood that I am now in senior residential management within a large institution. Though issues discussed are generally seen from that viewpoint, they will impinge on all workers associated with the working in various homes and very much affect the lives of their residents. Heads of Homes have normally worked their way through various grades and experienced the problems that beset the whole range of residential workers.

There are common core issues in residential management that apply to the very wide range of establishments. Firstly, we have to take into account the generic view of social work and the vastly diverse groups of clientele catered for in homes for mentally handicapped, old folks, children, the disturbed and delinquent, etc. Secondly, we are considering homes catering for from 6 to in excess of 100 residents. The magnitude of the issues and the proportionate time involved will vary very considerably from one institution to another. The residential worker can be one of a staff of 3 up to say 60 professionals. The amount of ancillary and other assistance will also vary very considerably. It follows that degrees of emphasis in management issues will vary. In joint meetings of Officers-in-Charge of a variety of establishments in a Local Authority, it is clear that there are distinct common areas in management issues, but the emphases are often quite different.

It would be helpful at this stage to identify the wide range of issues affecting the residential manager and this may best be tackled by listing many of the tasks and areas

197

coming within his remit. As already indicated, the percentage involvement in each area will vary from home to home. The manager needs:

(1) To understand the dynamics of residential living.
(2) To propound theoretical and conceptual bases for the *modus operandi*.
(3) To be a leader, enabler and supporter.
(4) To be a reasonable forward planner.
(5) To be capable of exercising control.
(6) To be a confidant, mentor and counsellor.
(7) To be an educator.
(8) To be a specialist in his own particular field of work.
(9) To be a credible model.
(10) To be a responsible administrator.
(11) To be capable of handling budgeting issues.
(12) To be a reasonably lucid writer.
(13) To be a public relations officer.
(14) To have the ability of working with outside management in his Local Authority or voluntary body.
(15) To have an ability to establish a communication network.
(16) To have some skill in staff selection.
(17) To be, to some degree, flexible and adaptable.
(18) To have knowledge of areas of work likely to affect the management of a home, such as grievance procedures, legal procedures, specialist and support services, legislation relevant to his home.
(19) To have some knowledge of such practical matters as furnishing, maintenance of fabric, and general hotel practice.
(20) In many homes to have some knowledge and ability in fund-raising.

This list does not claim to be exhaustive but will indicate that management issues are very wide ranging. No person would claim, or realistically expect, that a Head of an establishment should be proficient in all of these areas. It is, however, helpful if he has the ability to identify strengths in his staff in order that in the shared task all the above areas are catered for. The possibilities of coping adequately will again vary very much depending on the staffing establishment which with ancillary staff could be any number from 8 to 80.

It is evident from the above that management issues fall into various broad categories, some of which are conceptual and theoretical and others of a more practical and down-to-earth nature. A management skill is to bring the whole together in forming a living and dynamic community with a recognisable ethos. The visitor with no previous knowledge of an establishment can soon discover whether this ethos exists. To establish it is not easy and experience shows that it cannot be done from a purely theoretical stance or just by having efficient administration and material provision.

A fundamental issue in management is the definition of the task. It is not uncommon in homes to find that both staff and residents are very vague if questioned about this. It is not always easy to clearly define the task but essential that one is able to do so. In my own experience questions from visitors, and indeed from residents, have not always been easy to answer in terms of finding lucid and clear definitions. Management need to frequently pose questions to themselves in terms of the task, objectives of the establishment, aims, and generally what purpose is being served or should be served. Throughout all this it is important to maintain a good degree of objectivity which is not easy for those involved in the living situation. Constant reviewing and re-examination is essential employing whatever degree of staff and resident involvement the style of management in the home indicates.

In some homes the type of resident changes as the months and years go by, sometimes almost imperceptibly but to a significant extent. This will perhaps depend on current demands from Local Authorities and changing social climates. It is not always easy to recognise these changes and one can carry on over the years without any redefinition, rethinking and re-adjustment. In my own experience I have an incident where this could easily have happened and indeed did happen to a certain extent. In a Community Home for disturbed teenagers there was a major change by introducing senior girls. It so happened that at that time a number of older boys left the establishment and a younger group of boys was introduced. Many groups, seminars etc. were held to discuss the likely effect of introducing girls and, in the process, the fact that the age range of the boys had changed was nearly overlooked. In contact with a variety of homes it is not difficult to find parallel cases, even in dealing with old people where one might easily gain the impression that things never change. One of the dangers here is that we become insular and not always totally aware of changes in society around us. A regime can be established and a basic approach defined and it is easy for this to become rather inflexible and unadaptable. Essentials in residential social work are continual reviewing, re-assessment and re-evaluation leading to positive forward planning.

Having defined the task, clarified aims etc., there is the essential need to establish what type of regime is going to operate in the residential community. It seems to be widely accepted that the style will depend firstly on the philosophy and, to a degree, on the personality of the Officer-in-Charge. In some cases a regime and style of management is imposed on the residents and staff. This can lead to a lack of satisfaction, i.e. frustration. The good leader will use all members of his community in developing the style of management and enable a general feeling of involvement amongst staff and residents. This is easier to operate in some types of regime than in others. Leadership regimes are labelled under such headings as, "authoritarian", "hierarchical", "democratic", "paternalistic", "*laissez-faire*". A whole thesis can be written on styles of management and leadership, but here we can only briefly consider them. The style adopted will have a direct effect on the functioning and involvement of the staff and residents. It is easy to see that this is a crucial management issue.

In the authoritarian regime there is very little opportunity for staff or residents to make their own decisions and effect policy changes; whilst in the *laissez-faire* regime there is an expectation that the latter will redirect as they feel appropriate. The democratic system of management falls somewhere between the two, with varying degrees of authority and manipulation from the Head.

It is possible to have hierarchical structures in various management regimes and many staff and residents find this desirable. If questioning the Heads of a variety of homes about their type of regime, one can come up with a vast number of permutations and combinations of the elements in the more clearly defined styles. It also sometimes becomes evident that the style proposed by management is not, in practice, quite what exists, though one has to bear in mind that senior management in homes easily become the subjects of rationalisation and can be scapegoated when things are not going the right way.

It is essential that staff and residents have a fairly clear idea of the type of management in their home and to what degree they are able to make their own decisions and involve themselves in change. It can be extremely confusing for them if they are unaware of their freedoms in these matters.

The system of management adopted can be to a certain extent dictated by the category of resident that the establishment caters for. It has already been seen that this varies tremendously in a group of homes in any area. Some types of residents would benefit from a highly structured day-to-day living situation which may be easier to effect under a certain type of management style. Other residents need a very considerable amount of independence and freedom for personal decision making. A management skill in some homes is to enable their residents to move from a high level of dependence to a considerable degree of independence, e.g. in homes like half-way houses for the mentally ill and homes for disturbed and delinquent youngsters.

The management style has also to take cognisance of the change in social patterns, growth in social work styles, changes in emphasis on rights of residents, changes in legislation, Local Authority policy etc. Workers who have been in the residential field for a number of years, if able to examine their styles, will find that they have had to adapt and, in many ways, "move with the times". Social work is open to constant change and the effect of new trends. Not all of these are lasting and can be transient. It is easy to get on a "bandwagon". At the time of writing, there is much emphasis on terms such as "integrated social work", "keyworker", etc. It looks as though these could stay. Groupwork and group dynamics became the "in thing" about a decade ago to such an extent that most establishments felt that they ought to get involved. This was not always beneficial. It receded in magnitude and is now mainly used by people who believe in it and know what they are doing. Then one could become preoccupied with systems such as family fostering. No good social worker could disagree with it, but some become carried away to the exclusion of other good alternative methods of care. Residential management has to be aware of all change, take account of it and try and assess which is of a permanent nature, to what degree it should be taken into account and where one needs not to take it too seriously in the establishment.

It has to be remembered that at the time of writing Social Services Departments have been in existence for less than a decade. They are, to a large extent, still finding their feet. Training has been inadequate, particularly in the residential field. Real expertise is in short supply. The Departments have already carried out tremendously valuable work but in view of some of the above, there has been a danger of losing some of the extremely good elements of long-established systems in an effort to update our social work methods, "to throw out the baby with the bath water". We are getting to the stage of being able to identify and introduce new ideas that are of a lasting nature. It is important that residential managers take note of these developments and update their approach. Examples would be helpful:

Traditionally, residential establishments worked almost in isolation from colleagues in the field, whilst very often the fieldworker maintained the nominal position as the responsible person. It has become increasingly clear that it is more in the interests of the resident to have a joint involvement between residential and field social workers and a much closer and integrated teamwork approach. The development of the idea of integrated social work can very much benefit those in care, whether legally or voluntarily. This is a major issue in residential management in breaking down barriers and accepting what is in the best interests of the client. There has been a traditional view that the "keyworker" for a person in care is somebody based in a fieldwork office, even though contact with the client is nominal. There is now a recognition that some member of staff living with the client in a home would more aptly be designated the "keyworker". This again is a change that needs to be acknowledged by all social work colleagues whether resident or in the field.

In considering general concepts and basic management issues outlined above, the whole question of staff selection arises. It is reasonable to assume that the type of resident we take in our homes is broadly dictated to us and we have only a limited amount of choice. At the time of writing one may argue that there is only a limited amount of choice in staffing. This to an extent is true, but it is due to availability of suitable staff and suitability of available staff. Developing staff selection techniques is a most important part of management training. Methods of staff selection vary tremendously but there appears to be a grouping into patterns over the last few years. The days of facing 30 members in a Council Chamber have nearly passed. Informal visits to homes, sometimes including a brief stay, are much more general. The main interviews are less formal, but nonetheless searching. Sometimes a special exercise is included. Even with new techniques it is still extremely difficult to identify the right staff and this presents tremendous problems since the quality of staff affects the stability of the whole establishment. It is most important in the interviewing process that staff in management positions in homes are very closely involved with interviewing and are not easily overridden by advisers from the managing Authorities.

A vital part of the selection process is to see that candidates are given as clear as possible a picture of the aims, objectives and tasks, and of the type of regime. The first part is often covered reasonably adequately whilst the second can be left rather open. It is pointless appointing staff committed to a *laissez-faire* style of work in an authoritarian type establishment. Square pegs in round holes lead to major problems. The management's task is to indicate as accurately as possible to intending applicants, the type of regime and to develop skills in assessing the likelihood of their obtaining job satisfaction in that regime. Most Heads of Homes find staff selection an extremely difficult task. There are peculiar problems in the large establishments where the Heads of separate units or team leaders are looking for autonomy whilst the overall structure and strictures of the total establishment can infringe upon this.

Staff and staffing produce numerous management issues. If the staff are happy and work well together, the foundation of a successful community is laid. If they are unhappy and lack job satisfaction, staffing becomes unstable and so then do the residents. As with many areas mentioned in this thesis a whole chapter could be written on staffing issues. Some of them will be identified here and discussed briefly. Again we may be thinking in terms of homes with a few staff or one like that in which the writer works, where there are over 50 staff for 57 children.

Management cannot help becoming involved with every aspect of staff life and work. Basic day-to-day matters are as important as the theoretical perspective. At the very beginning, careful thought should be given to the arrival of staff. If they are resident, is their accommodation comfortable, have suitable arrangements been made for welcoming them, has some person been allocated to talk about duty rotas, holidays, social life and all such topics that give rise to initial anxiety? In some homes a great deal of thought is given to the admission of new residents whilst forgetting that new staff experience similar fears and anxieties and indeed the opposite could be true.

Then managers need to have a carefully thought-out induction programme for new staff, with opportunities for them to see how the home operates, to learn about routines, to assimilate some of the rules that exist in most homes etc. New staff are always open to manipulation by residents who are only too aware of their lack of knowledge of the home, and this can lead to unhappy early experiences in the new job. All levels of staff can be involved in the induction process. In the small home, line managers will be officers-in-charge or deputies but in the larger home it may well be some kind of team leader.

All staff in residential communities experience stress. Managers must have some expertise in identifying this and the time or facility available for dealing with it. Clearly, Heads of large establishments cannot have too regular contact with all staff but they need to see that their organisation allows for somebody in the management structure to have an awareness of the feelings of each member of staff and that their feedback is sufficient to allow for some form of intervention. Staff support, counselling, reassurance etc., occupies a large portion of senior staff time. Identifying stress is a vital part of a good communication network and indeed communication in all areas is an essential ingredient in the positive residential process. It is vital that staff and residents give thought to their methods of communication and establish the best possible system for their particular home. Poor communication gives rise to many problems and frustrations.

Whilst clearly there is a skill in identifying and assessing individual stress, it is equally important to be able to assess the atmosphere in various groups whether staff or resident or both. With some managers this is almost an inborn skill, but more generally it is an expertise developed over a period of time. Those experienced in residential work acknowledge that it is important to be able to "get the feel" of the group. Failure to correctly assess the mood of the group can lead one into quite serious difficulties. Good managers are able to use their skills in handling staff groups and this is an excellent learning situation in dealing with client groups. It is not always possible to get staff to acknowledge this and indeed some staff take exception when staff groups are compared with client groups.

Management in the individual home appears to operate most successfully where staff and residents are involved in policy making, decision making, forward planning etc. Authoritarian regimes make this more difficult and this is probably why over recent years this type of regime has receded in the social work field. It was not uncommon a decade or so ago to find homes which seldom held staff meetings, group discussions etc. Specialists such as visiting psychiatrists were the jealously guarded possessions of Heads and Deputies. Members of the residential community were, to a large extent, directed. However, experience has shown that by organising good channels of communication, building in opportunities for staff discussion and participation in all aspects of the home's life, job satisfaction is enhanced and ultimately the residents benefit. It is essential that all groups in the home are involved in staff meetings. This latter has again been a developing area and fears over confidentiality and professionalism, whilst needing to be stressed at all stages, have very often been unfounded. The various types of meeting indicated above are excellent training situations for staff.

Elsewhere in this book there are complete articles on training. The attitude of the Head in a home towards training can have a critical impact on training issues. Management need to offer encouragement and point out possibilities to their staff whilst having the ability to identify training needs. They can start off with staff induction, and progress through in-service training to full qualifying courses. It is helpful in homes to have a regular flow of students from training centres, not only from the students' point of view but because they introduce current issues. Very often members of the home's staff make excellent student supervisors and management can help by making time available for them to carry out this work.

Whatever the manager in the home tries to do to help maintain a good morale and improve the circumstances of the staff, he will from time to time have to deal with complaints, grievances and bad practice. Most employing Authorities have guidelines for dealing with these matters and the Officer-in-Charge should see that staff are fully conversant with them. He needs also to advise his line managers on how to deal with the early stages in these matters and possibly terminate them at this stage to everybody's satisfaction. Handling grievances and bad practice is a skilled job and calls for very careful judgement. The Head has to be able to decide whether matters should go outside the home campus. He may be able to skilfully resolve them himself but in cases of dissatisfaction it is necessary to involve the outside Authority. Very careful, accurate and witnessed recording is essential in order that the facts may be transmitted exactly. The Head of a home needs to have access to, and if possible a certain background knowledge of various forms of legislation, adding again to his multitude of tasks. There are currently eight Acts of Parliament affecting employment relations, for instance. These affect matters of redundancy, pay, contracts, rehabilitation of offenders, trade union labour relations, employment protection, sex discrimination and race relations. Grievance procedures can lead to extremely serious consequences, even dismissal, and it is not, therefore, difficult to see why the management's judgement is so important.

Although the residents have been mentioned from time to time so far, not a great deal has been said about them in connection with management issues. Social work exists for the clients' benefit. One frequently hears complaints that as much of the social worker's time is spent on administration as on client contact. Research has shown this to be true in the fieldwork situation and it can also be the case in residential work. Many who have been in the profession for some length of time have seen homes which are staff-orientated rather than resident-orientated and special studies have been undertaken on this. The skilled manager creates a total living community with staff and residents forming a positive homogeneous whole.

Developments over the last decade have led to far greater resident participation and this has improved the quality of life for the resident and, in many cases, helped them to maintain a reasonable dignity. The residents' rights have been given far more attention. Some of the matters involved have been quite mundane but important; for example, the right of residents in an Old Folks' Home to brew tea in the home's kitchen and to vary their meal times occasionally.

In the section above mainly relating to staff matters, the word resident could be substituted in many of the cases, and in connection with a number of issues, e.g. arrival and admission procedures, involvement in decision making, positions in the communication network, detection of stress, availability of support, counselling etc., arrangements for meetings, dealing with complaints and grievances. It is not really necessary to expand on these again but it would be a useful exercise for the reader to compare and contrast issues in management from staff and resident points of view.

A fundamental part of staff development is for them to be able to understand from their own experiences some of the feelings of a resident. This is sometimes an acquired skill. In contrast to the case mentioned earlier, there was the example of a new member of staff who complained at considerable length about the poor arrangements for his arrival and induction but had a totally inadequate and insensitive admission procedure worked out for the newly admitted child in the home. This fact was used from a positive experiential point of view and led to the production of a first-class admissions procedure for new children. It can often be useful for managers to direct attention to the normal lives of their staff and the community at large when considering the needs of residents in their homes. It is easy to be inconsistent in approach to the day-to-day living of the residents and that of people living in normal society. For example, lack of privacy in the residential home can be quite easily accepted by people who would find it intolerable in their own life-situation. Whilst it is unrealistic to expect institutions to be the same as normal homes, every endeavour should be made to de-institutionalise unless there is a definite policy against this, e.g. in a corrective institution. In some ways, life in a home, particularly in an Old Folks' Home, can be more like that in a hotel, and, whilst accepting that there are administrative similarities, the hotel atmosphere needs to be skilfully dissipated.

It is important that staff groups and the total group frequently review the needs of their particular residents. Again, the reader could identify these and expand on them, setting up particular problem areas. Some examples considering a range of homes and client groups would be, what level of staff/resident contact is required, what are the relative merits of individual and group casework, how important is routine and to what degree is it required, how structured should the establishment be, what degree of contact should be maintained with families and relatives, how important is total family involvement, is a reasonable degree of consistency being transmitted to the resident in day-to-day living, what measures of control are required in the lives of the residents etc.? The nature of each individual resident's own problems and needs must never be forgotten in the group living situation. It is so easy to lose sight of the fact that every member of the group in the home is an individual and that, whilst involved in living together in groups, the dignity and rights of the individual can never be allowed to take second place.

However much one is attempting to supply a service for residents and cope with the specialist social work task, and however social work orientated one attempts to be, the more mundane organisational and administrative work of the institution cannot be avoided or neglected, neither can the material problems that beset our establishments all too frequently. We expect to be concerned with material comforts such as food and clothing as essentials in the caring process, but one often fails to appreciate the more extended administration. In the larger home there are usually maintenance and administrative staff, but in many smaller homes there are none. Planned casework on a day's programme can often be totally disrupted because of such simple matters as broken-down boilers. Senior staff may then spend a totally disproportionate amount of time on the telephone trying to locate engineers etc. This example can be multiplied many times.

It is an essential part of the caring process to have good practices in administrative and organisational aspects of the home. Recently, a job description was compiled for an Administrative Officer for a home and this indicated a full-time appointment. This is amazing when one considers that in many homes there is not even a part-time officer and the work has to be covered by social work staff, and can often be completed only by "burning the midnight oil". Although space is limited it might be helpful to indicate some of the tasks.

(1) Putting into practice administrative memos from the Local Authority or governing organisation.

(2) Exercising control over expenditure and annual budgetry together with preparation of budget estimates.

(3) Monitoring maintenance of buildings, equipment and grounds.

(4) Documenting appointments of manual staff and drafting advertisements for other staff.

(5) Stock control.

(6) Maintaining inventories.

(7) Keeping good records of residents' financial affairs, valuables, etc.

(8) Assisting with residents' personal monies, such as old age pensions, pocket money, etc.

(9) Attending to accounts.

(10) Producing weekly wages returns and paying out wages.

(11) General clerical work including correspondence, staff records, minutes of meetings, filing, etc.

(12) Handling numerous telephone calls, etc., etc.

It is not difficult to see that neglect of such areas can lead to discontent and will ultimately affect social work processes.

In many homes the preparation of duty rotas alone is a major task and these continually need re-adjustment due to illness, staff changes, etc. In my own Local Authority there is a move at the moment to give all homes some form of clerical assistance and one hopes that this will become widespread within residential establishments.

Another issue that is sometimes forgotten, is fund-raising. There are always items that a home requires that cannot be obtained through official expenditure and most homes have some form of voluntary amenities fund. Fund-raising is very good for staff and residents, but highly time consuming. Sometimes the local community can be involved in this. Indeed, community relations are another major issue in residential management. With some Children's Homes and Old People's Homes it is not difficult to establish good relations, but it is not such a simple task for homes catering for the more difficult elements in society that many of the public are quite happy to see kept out of circulation. In my own establishment the residents from time to time involve themselves in burglaries and car stealing in the locality. The local community are very often surprisingly co-operative and helpful in the face of difficult circumstances.

Staff in the residential home have, of course, to be able to work with a range of professional colleagues at all levels, both from their own Authority and other agencies. Depending on the size of the home a varying degree of autonomy operates and accordingly the main link at Head Office will also vary. One cannot refer to the link person by a specific name as there are such a variety of terms in use, e.g. Homes Advisers, Residential Advisers, Principal Social Services Officers, Residential Co-ordinators, etc.

Working successfully with whoever happens to be the link person is, however, an essential part of establishing good social work patterns in the home. Many decisions are made jointly and some have to be ratified by Head Office. Further to this the Head of an institution has also to be able to work with a number of specialists and agencies such as psychologists, psychiatrists, medical consultants, field social workers, etc. The ability to work with a range of disciplines is an asset in residential management.

One could continue to expand the number of issues in the management of a residential institution and the reader will doubtless wish to identify some of his own. One would always like to develop other issues and expand on those that have been mentioned. It is hoped that this paper will pose many questions in terms of residential management issues. Many have been with us for decades, some remaining unchanged, some changing, whilst others are issues that have arisen during the last decade. Managing a residential institution is involvement in a dynamic and ever-changing situation. The managers have often little opportunity for management training and depend very much on experience and what professional advice they are able to obtain. On reading this chapter this may seem almost unbelievable, and possibly over the next decade management training may be one of the improvements in our social work service. Certainly it has started in my own Local Authority and is proving most helpful. Other Authorities are also instituting some training, but we have a long way to go.

Further Reading

There is very little reading which focuses specifically on the management task in residential homes, but some of the following titles drawn from the wider social work and business organisation literature discuss *ideas which can then be applied in the residential setting* by the reader.

BLAU, P. M. and SCOTT, W. R., *Formal Organisations*, Routledge & Kegan Paul, 1963.

BRIDGE, J. and DODDS, J. C., *Managerial Decision-Making*, Croom Helm, 1975.

BUTLIN, E., Institutionalisation, management structure and therapy in residential work with emotionally disturbed children, *British Journal of Social Work*, **5** (3).

DOCKAR DRYSDALE, B., *Consultation in Child Care*, Longman, 1973.

EDWARDS, W. and TVERSKY, A. (eds.), *Decision Making*, Penguin, 1971.

ETZIONI, A. (ed.), *A Sociological Reader on Complex Organisations*, Holt, Rinehart & Wilson, New York, 1969.

HARDY, C. B., *Understanding Organisations*, Penguin, 1976.

JONES, H., The Approved School: a theoretical Model, in MAYS, J. B. (ed.), *The Social Treatment of Young Offenders*.

LYDEN, F. J. and MILLER, E. J. (eds.), *Planning, Programming, Budgeting*, Markham, Chicago, 1972.

MENZIES, I., *The Functioning of Social Systems as a Defence against Anxiety*, Tavistock, 1970.

NORDSTROM, C. E., The Unique Challenges of Institutional Administration, in WEBER and HABERLEIN (eds.), *Residential Treatment of Emotionally Disturbed Children*, Behavioural Publications, 1972.

PUGH, D. S. (ed.), *Organisation Theory*, Penguin, 1971.

RESIDENTIAL CARE ASSOCIATION, Manpower Problems in Residential Social Work—The Dalmeny Papers, RCA, 1976.

ROWBOTTOM, R., HEY, A. and BILLIS, D., *Social Services Departments*, Heinemann, 1974.

SMITH, G., *Social Work and the Sociology of Organisations*, Routledge & Kegan Paul, 1970.

WARHAM, J., An Introduction to Administration for Social Workers, Routledge & Kegan Paul, 1967.

WARHAM, J., *An Open Case*, Routledge & Kegan Paul, 1977.

CHAPTER 18

TOWARDS CARING THROUGH DESIGN

ROBERT SLATER AND ALAN LIPMAN

Introduction

These comments arise from our research concerning the architectural design implications of residential homes for old people.* This focussed on 12 homes—chosen for their divergent design—from a sample of 60 (Barrett, 1976) which represented (in terms of date of erection and geographical location) all purpose-built homes opened under the "Part III" legislation of the National Assistance Act, 1948. The 12 comprised: three "large" homes (50 or more residents) of an institutional design (principally, where the communal sitting spaces are large and centralised); three "small" homes (35 or fewer residents) of similar design; three "large" of a "domestic" or "family" design (principally, where communal sitting spaces are small and dispersed in bedroom wings); and three "small" "domestic" homes. Eight of this sub-sample were chosen for further study to maximise differences in proportions of "confused" to "rational" residents: each design type was represented by a home with a relatively low ratio of confused to rational residents, and by another with a relatively high ratio (Slater and Lipman, 1977).

A 2-week period of participant observation—during which the research personnel worked as Care Attendants—was spent in each of the eight homes. This was followed some 3 months later by a period of structured observation in the sitting spaces of the homes. These 34 communal spaces were observed for a total of 6 hours each throughout the day and evening. Verbal exchanges between the occupants of the sitting spaces, together with other data, were recorded on field logs (Harris, Lipman and Slater, 1977). In what follows we shall be drawing on the experience of life in the homes gained from these research procedures. On the basis of this experience we have identified a number of "themes" in residential care that appear pertinent to design decision making. For convenience, these themes are examined by referring primarily to the conditions we encountered in one of the homes.

Themes in the Residential Care of Old People

To afford a better quality of life for residents of old people's homes, consideration must be given to several issues that have recurring implications for individuals, physical settings and particular circumstances. These we have called "themes" or "evaluative dimensions" (Slater and Lipman, 1976). We have found that, with these themes in mind,

* This research was funded by the Social Science Research Council (Grant HR2548); a Final Report to the SSRC is available on loan from the National Library, Boston Spa.

207

examining a building that is occupied, or one still in the design stage, may not only highlight potential problems but also lead to design innovations (Lipman and Slater, 1977). The following, we consider, are the most salient of these themes:

Choice

Certain aspects of choice in the lives of residents are obviously thwarted by their physical condition—few may be capable of going jogging, for example. In addition, however, administrative and design features can limit the ranges of choice residents can exercise in the main aspects of their daily life—eating, sleeping, sitting, toileting and bathing. Here we will consider instances in which physical design impedes choice, but the limitations of choice purported to be imposed by the mental and physical frailty of residents, and the interpretation of this in the administrative context of running a home "efficiently" should also be taken into account (Slater and Greenfield, 1979). Clearly these considerations are interdependent. For example, do long corridors encourage residents who use walking aids to be, say, taken to bed in wheelchairs because (a) they are too frail to manage the journey or (b) it is easier for staff?

Independence

The use of wheelchairs suggests that residents may become dependent on staff as a consequence of a specific aspect of design—for instance, in the design of circulation spaces, of corridors. But independence can also be reduced by matters such as inappropriate bathroom equipment, or light switches awkward for people who are arthritic— features that might be circumvented by reference to a standard work on designing for disabled people (Goldsmith, 1976).

Convenience

We question the commonly expressed notion of "therapeutics through inconvenience"; of, for example, long corridors that "force" people to exercise in moving from one place to another. Like design for independence, good design is usually design for convenience. Thus it is plausible to suggest, for instance, that the inconvenient siting of communal toilets may exacerbate the "problem" of incontinence in homes.

Privacy

The extent to which design militates against the ability of residents to live private lives, yet voluntarily to engage in social and public activities, is a dilemma that calls for resolution. Privacy, we insist, is a right, not a privilege. Further, opportunities for personal and social privacy—for being alone or with chosen others—are, if exercised, likely to be beneficial for the socio-emotional well-being of residents (Schwarz, 1975; Pastalan, 1970).

Comprehensibility

We take this term to include the closely related notions of familiarity, complexity and conventionality. The more residents are able to personalise their rooms—by their own furniture, knick-knacks, paintings, etc.—the more domestic and so familiar the environment they recreate around them. Indeed, loss of contact with familiar objects and surroundings may increase disorientation for people whose sensory acuity is poor or deteriorating (Lipman and Slater, 1976). In a similar manner the layout of homes may be confusing and help foster the spatial disorientation commonly taken as a potential symptom of senile dementia (Slater and Lipman, 1977). Furthermore, the provision of specialised equipment of an unconventional nature—mechanical hoists for lifting residents into baths, for example—may make them more dependent on staff because they, the residents, are unable to use the equipment.

An Example: a Home of "Conventional" Design

The manner in which these themes can be brought to bear when evaluating the design of homes can probably best be illustrated by a detailed discussion of a specific case. To this end, we have selected one that may be regarded as being of conventional design (see Figs 18.1 and 18.2). Before this, however, it is necessary to provide a "pen-picture" of conditions in the home. The following descriptions are taken directly from notes made during our participant observations.

The Dining room

"The parquet floor has been sealed and now has a glossy surface that produces glare. There is a strip of carpet along the length of the room adjacent to the folding room-divider that separates the dining from the sitting room. On the wall there is the odd picture, and the windows are curtained. At meal times no tablecloths are used and the kitchen area can be observed when the sliding hatches, through which food is served, are open. At each table there are individual place settings, but no teapots for each person or even for each table. Meals are served centrally at the hatch and are taken to residents by Care Attendants. The menu is fixed—there is little choice. Staff decide who has what, and whether they will comply with residents' requests. Generally, liquid intake is not encouraged because of the incontinence consequences and the residents are not allowed more than two cups of tea at any one meal. The tea is made centrally in two big pots, one with sugar and one without, and taken around the tables; particular residents who finish their meal early often have to wait for cups of tea because tea is served towards the end of the dining period.

"The plates on which food is served are generally not warmed, although there is a hot-plate. The food is handled (i.e. without utensils) by the matron, even though she chides others for doing so. Aprons are tied round the necks of many of the women like bibs. Medicines are given out in the dining room after meals while residents are still sitting at the tables. No medicine records are used and bottles are brought in a large tin and apparently given out as per instructions on the bottles. I heard residents asking a

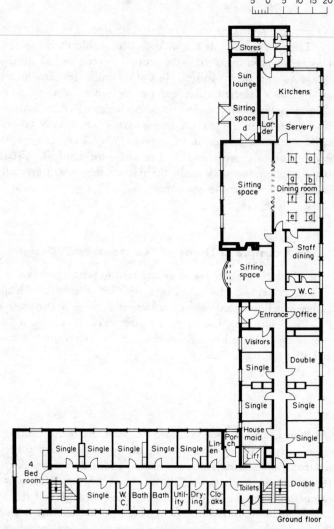

Fig. 18.1. Ground floor plan of a home of "conventional" design.

number of times, "Where are my pills?"—who obviously had been missed out. Medicines are removed from residents whenever found."

Sleeping areas

"All upstairs bedrooms have faded carpets, as does one downstairs—the other bedrooms on the ground floor have lino with bedside rugs. All bedsitting rooms have curtains at the windows but whereas the upstairs bedrooms have wallpaper on the walls the downstairs ones have an institutional paint finish. Upstairs the bedspreads are fitted nylon ones whereas downstairs they are candlewick throw-overs. None of the bedrooms

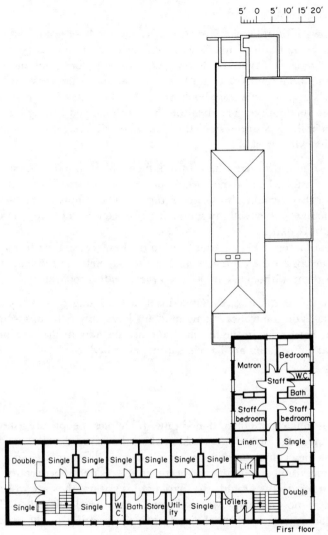

FIG. 18.2. First floor plan.

have pictures in them and few have ornaments, etc. Bed making is generally badly done—the sheets are left wrinkled and the rubber incontinence sheets under them are poor and the rubber has some leaks. All residents have rubbers on the beds whether they are needed or not. Blankets are often not big enough. The sheets are changed regularly and when needed, but turning back the beds in the evening usually undoes much of previous bed making. When the lockers are cleaned, about once a fortnight, all things are removed from them and from the drawers in the dressing tables, and placed on the beds. The lockers and drawers are then washed out, dried, and the things put back—anything considered to be rubbish is thrown away. All this is done regularly with no permission obtained from the residents for either cleaning or throwing things away."

Sitting areas

"The windows of both lounges are curtained and the floor is covered by large carpets although these are not quite fitted. There are some cushions on most of the chairs, which are the usual "geriatric" type. Each lounge has the odd foot-stool and small table, but additionally the large lounge has a TV and piano and a bookcase, whereas the small lounge only has a virtually empty bookcase and just a radio. There are few pictures or knick-knacks in the lounges. The furniture has not changed during our study, and has probably been in these positions since the home opened. The same people always occupy the same chairs. Matron said:

> I take them to the lounge where I think they will fit in best. The small lounge is for the more sensible. I think they need a place of their own. If I left them to find their own place there would always be argument. The confused are excluded from the rational lounge—they will say something like 'Get out of here, you don't belong in here, you talk daft'.
>
> Residents accept a person that I put in the lounge, i.e. they accept my judgement of that person. In the dining room I try to put helpless residents with those who will help them, although I try to keep messy eaters separate.

"Drink, coffee in the morning, is handed out in the lounges from the trolley, sugar is added to the cups on the trolley. Some residents have only half cups, some are given no saucer. It is always coffee in the morning and always milk in the evening, and the only things to eat at coffee times are leftovers from yesterday's tea."

Toileting

"Toileting is much more often done at night. Helpless people are asked if they would like to go to the toilet or are often taken when they ask. Usually, residents are taken individually as they come and go to either lounges or dining room—in particular before meals. This supervision of toileting also occurs in the residents' bedrooms. Three residents are commoded regularly at night: the main light is put on, they are woken up, lifted out onto commodes—no dressing-gown or slippers—then put back to bed. The light is put on even in double rooms when obviously this is upsetting to the resident not being commoded."

Bathing

"Every resident gets a bath weekly, plus hair washing one week then nail cutting the next. No-one is ever left on their own in a bathroom. Downstairs the residents have two Care Assistants to help them, upstairs one. Generally, the residents are fetched individually but upstairs sometimes two are taken at once, in which case one must wait as there is only the one bathroom on that floor. The residents on the ground floor don't bath themselves—just their private parts. Residents in the bedrooms upstairs do bath themselves but with a Care Attendant present. Clean underwear and often clean top clothes are given after a bath—these are normally labelled with the resident's name. Communal underwear is very occasionally used but communal bath towels, sponges, flannels, soap, talc and combs are used downstairs. Upstairs residents tend to bring their own things to the bathroom and take them back afterwards. The bath is not usually washed out between residents and there is no choice about bath times—residents have their bath when they are told to do so. Matron said: 'We mùst have a Care Assistant present when they are being bathed because of risking falls. Wouldn't like them to fall— don't think it would be right. Would be a stigma.' She went on to explain that relatives and the population at large would lay blame on the home for falls in bathrooms whereas falls in a corridor, for example, are excusable: 'It's just one of those things. There aren't enough staff to watch all the time, so they may fall in the corridor or lounge—this is justifiable, but it's not justifiable for them to fall and be hurt in the bath.' "

The setting

"The home is situated in a local authority housing area—a council estate—on the outskirts of S—— [a small northern industrial town]. The home itself is at the end of a short (80 yards deep) cul-de-sac and is flanked on either side by council houses with the same red brick facing. Despite being larger than the surrounding houses, the home does not seem at all out of place because of its size. This is partly due to one wing of the L-shape being single storey—the other being double storey—but also because the site slopes downward. This brings the level of the home's roof almost into line with those of the houses (Fig. 18.3). A glance into the cul-de-sac shows that the building at the end [the home] looks like a council house.

"The home is not on a direct bus route and the nearest bus-stop is some 300 yards away. The nearest shops are just over a quarter of a mile walking distance. They contain most of the shops one expects to find in the central shopping area of an estate. The route between the home and the shops is on a long incline; in general the whole area is hilly, but slopes are gradual rather than steep.

"Despite the fact that the home 'fits in' physically with its environment—because of the domestic appearance of the sitting room with a large bay window—nevertheless the degree of contact between the home and people outside is slight. As Matron told me: 'The surrounding houses act as though they do not want to know there is an old people's home here.' But when a little girl came to ask if she could see the 'old ladies' she was told she couldn't, and an excuse was made about them being asleep. In explaining this to me Matron said: 'They come for what they can get from the old people, who give them money and sweets. They're dirty and might pass things on to the ladies. We always make excuses.' "The 'things' she was referring to were nits."

Daily routine

"All residents are up, washed and dressed ready for breakfast by 7.00 a.m. An hour later breakfast is served and some residents needing help are taken to the toilet on the way to or from breakfast. Medicines are put on the breakfast tables. Following breakfast the beds are made. The bedrooms are tidied and commodes are emptied and cleaned. At 10.30 a.m. staff have coffee, and half an hour later the residents are served theirs. At 11.30 bathing starts for some residents, while those Care Assistants not involved in bathing deal with the laundry, or clean out residents' lockers.

"At midday lunch is served in the dining room and again residents wanting help with going to the toilet are taken there on the way either to or from the dining room. At 1.00 p.m. staff have lunch and an hour later start on their afternoon duties, the same as those begun before lunch: namely, bathing, laundry work and locker cleaning. At 4.00 p.m. residents are given tea, some are taken to the toilet, bedroom windows that were open are shut, the beds are turned back and the commodes are taken back to the bedrooms.

"At 5.30 staff have their tea break; half an hour later some of the residents are taken to bed 'early'. At 7.00 an evening drink is distributed to residents in the lounges. By 7.30 the rest of the residents have been put to bed. From 8.00 p.m. onwards the staff still on duty busy themselves by tidying lounges, washing plastic covers on the chairs, and continuing with laundry work. At 10.30 p.m. the night staff come on duty and are given reports about noteworthy incidents of the day.

"During the night, staff make once-hourly visits to all residents' rooms. In addition they put on the commode those residents who are known to require it—this is done as often as is considered necessary for each individual. In addition, night staff answer all call bells. Apart from this, they busy themselves by doing ironing and mending clothes, etc. At 6.00 a.m. they start waking and dressing those residents who require such help. By 6.30 a.m. they have made sure that all residents are up. The daily routine commences once again."

The Design of the Home: an Evaluation

Several implications for design can be deduced from the above short pen-picture of a home. The following are worthy of comment: shiny floor surfaces; lounges with few and bedrooms with no paintings on the walls or places where knick-knacks can be put; the "cafeteria-type" dining room; "institutional" paint finishes on walls; inappropriate light fittings in double bedrooms; the distance of the home from a bus-stop; and the location of the home on a hilly site. Do floors have to be shiny? Do rooms have to look institutional? Can convenient light fittings not be used in double bedrooms, i.e. at least two lights each with a dimmer switch. Obviously bedrooms ought to be designed so that paintings and posters, etc. can be put on walls; so that knick-knacks can be put on shelves; so that the lighting can be controlled so as to have it at desired levels.

Our evaluation of this home refers to the themes we outlined earlier. These are taken as reference points for describing ways in which we observed the spaces to be used during our study. Thus the evaluation is not made solely in design terms, rather it draws heavily on our understanding of how the homes were actually used. The factors we examine are those associated with the five daily activities we have mentioned: eating, sleeping, sitting, toileting and bathing.

Eating areas

As shown in Fig. 18.1, the home has one eating area (the dining room) to cater for all residents. This contains eight tables, each seating four residents. In addition, reference to the plan indicates that the dining room is peripheral in terms of the circulation route on the ground floor: it is near sitting spaces and a toilet, but far from the sleeping areas.

FIG. 18.3. The home in its surroundings.

FIG. 18.4. The servery and dining room furniture.

FIG. 18.5. A bedroom corridor.

FIG. 18.6. The large sitting room, looking toward the sun-lounge.

In this home, then, the residents are offered no effective *choice* as to the areas in which they might eat. They do not, for example, have kettles in their rooms. Food, prepared on their behalf, is served at the tables in the dining room. A reading of the plan suggests that the building was designed to keep residents out of the food preparation area. This is separated from the remaining accommodation by the servery to the dining room (Fig. 18.4). And we observed this physical barrier to work in practice: residents seldom, if ever, participated in food preparation or indeed in serving their fellow residents. In the exceptional cases when they did so, this was a concession accorded to privileged residents.

Obviously residents do not have the opportunity to exercise the *independence* of being able either to prepare their own food or, since they are served at the tables, to select the types and amount of food they individually prefer. All residents come for their meals at specified times, presumably at the convenience of the staff. Thus, residents had no *choice* as to when they might eat. Such "choice" as did exist was confined to arriving in the dining room for breakfast an hour or half-an-hour prior to this meal being served.

No *privacy* is afforded to eating, and such social contact as might flow from the dining arrangements must be regarded as less than voluntary. True to the spirit of the "hotel model" of the 1948 National Assistance Act (Harris, 1977), the dining room does not permit privacy with regard to eating. Unlike people living in their own homes, residents must take all their meals in public. No doubt, from when they ate in cafeterias, some residents may be *familiar* with sitting on bulk-purchased, premoulded chairs at formica-topped tables whose spindly legs rest on a high-gloss parquet floor (Fig. 18.4); it is an open question, however, whether an institution-like experience of this nature is desirable in an old people's home.

The dining room is obviously *convenient* in terms of distance from the home's sitting spaces; it is adjacent to both of them. Further, it is close to a toilet. But it is some distance from the sleeping areas; in particular, from the bedrooms on the first floor. The lifts and stairs are at the junction of the L-shape plan, and are thus at least half-way (some 80 feet) along the internal corridor on the ground floor.

The layout, the plan form (Figs 18.1 and 18.2), of the home is simple, it is *comprehensible* and the relationship between the dining room and the sitting spaces is direct, even to the extent of one of the sitting spaces opening off the dining space via a folding "wall" —something, however, with which residents may not be *familiar* from their own homes.

Sleeping areas

Of the 32 residents in the home, 20 occupied single bedrooms, 8 were in double rooms, and 4 shared one room. If the *choice* of occupying single, double or four-person bedrooms is regarded as advantageous, on this count the home could be rated highly. However, choice of a four-person room seems a dubious advantage. The most beneficial situation would probably be one where there are spare multiple-occupancy bedrooms. This would enable all residents to have a single bedroom and, in some instances (i.e. married couples, relatives or close friends) the opportunity to share double or even larger rooms. In other words, the existence of four-person rooms is a count against a home unless all residents can have a single room from *choice*. Patently, in addition to single or multiple occupancy, there are other types of choice about sleeping areas in homes.

These range from those, as in the home we are discussing, where bedrooms open off each side of a corridor to those in which bedrooms are clustered about sitting, dining and abluting facilities.

Consider yet another avenue of choice: if residents had been able to select the sleeping area in which their bedrooms were to be located, this would still limit their options. There are few physical differences between the bedroom zones and thus few criteria on which to base their choice.

As the plan indicates, the bedrooms are in two wings of an L-shape, and open off the corridor which runs through both wings. *Choice* in the selection of either bedrooms or sleeping areas is lacking, primarily for two reasons: (1) there are no spare bedrooms; and (2) the staff allocate residents to bedrooms. Since each single bedroom is in design identical to all other single bedrooms, residents can exercise no *choice* in terms of shape, size and internal layout when allocated their rooms. Apart from the few personal possessions that residents do have, we found them to be identical in both appearance and in furniture arrangement.

Perhaps the most important aspect of residents' *independence*, as far as bedrooms are concerned, is their ability autonomously to care for themselves and their surroundings in the manner in which they might wish to do so. The uniform design, layout, and the standard equipment and furniture in the home do not appear to facilitate exercising *independence*. On the contrary, such standardisation eases the work of staff rather than allowing residents to express idiosyncratic wishes. Each single room has a fixed basin, radiator and a light placed centrally in the ceiling. Each room is supplied with an identical bed, wardrobe, dressing table, hard chair, commode and locker. In the multiple occupancy bedrooms it was found that often all these items were not available for each individual. Only one of the 32 residents in this home had brought in her own article of furniture, an easy chair.

All these factors exemplify the hotel-like care which pervades the home. Residents cannot readily entertain visitors in their rooms, they do not readily eat in their rooms, and the limited space in the rooms scarcely allows for individual pastimes or hobbies. Thus, little opportunity is given for *private* social intercourse to take place within the confines of the rooms.

All single bedrooms, indeed all bedrooms, open directly onto the corridor. Unless doors are in a completely or slightly closed position, a direct view is afforded to anyone passing down the corridors. Little sense of *privacy* may be obtained in this arrangement.

Inadequacy of the rooms for social intercourse, together with the existence of communal sitting rooms, suggests that the home was designed with the expectation that social contacts among residents would occur in the public sitting rooms rather than in the privacy of their own bedsitting rooms. As can be seen from the plan, the four sleeping areas are, in the main, somewhat distant from the centralised sitting spaces, dining room, kitchen area and entrance. However, as was noted above, all bedroom zones are near a toilet, whereas only two of the four are near a bathroom. It would seem, then, that the bedroom zones are inconveniently located for all but toileting activities. And data from our participant observations showed that the staff were running the home in a manner consistent with this situation: residents were bathed by members of staff in accordance with a weekly rota. Furthermore, given the distances between the sleeping zones and the centralised facilities, it is not surprising that the majority of the residents spent most of their time sitting in the centralised lounges rather than in their rooms; a situation which was reinforced by the staff's reluctance to let residents spend substantial periods of time in the "seclusion"—the *privacy*—of their rooms.

Apart from items such as family photographs, calendars and ornaments, the residents were unable to accommodate personal articles in their rooms. Even the most cursory tour of these rooms indicated that the standardisation of furnishings and decor militated against residents establishing *familiar*, individualistic surroundings for themselves. Our participant observation notes report: "Very little evidence of personal possessions in bedrooms, except for the odd photograph; no pictures whatsoever in bedrooms; no evidence of any personal radios and certainly no TVs; no cups and saucers; very few ornaments."

Far from being complex, the layout of the bedroom zones in this home is a simple L-shape—unlike others we have studied. Nevertheless, the corridors are long and are more or less identical. For a mentally frail resident, particularly one who is spatially disorientated, the task of finding his or her room—namely one door in a whole row of fairly identical doors—may not be easy (Fig. 18.5). As the Matron pointed out, despite the fact that WC doors were painted a different colour from bedroom doors, "quite often confused residents can't find the WC, and wander in and out of other rooms". Furthermore, the similarity of the internal layout of bedrooms tends to make most single rooms appear alike when viewed from the corridor. So, despite the home being simple in layout, the task of finding specific rooms within it may not be straightforward.

Sitting areas

As the plan indicates, the two sitting areas are grouped together at one end of the L-shaped ground floor circulation route. Thus, they can be said to be adjacent to the dining areas, near a toilet, near the food preparation area, but distant from the sleeping areas. Accordingly, 32 residents have the notional *choice* of sitting in either one or the other sitting space. One of these contains 23 chairs, 19 of which are usually occupied, and the other contains 10 chairs, all of which are habitually occupied. In addition to these two sitting spaces, there is a sun lounge (Fig. 18.1). Our observations, and statements made by the Matron, indicate that this had not been used since it was built—some 3 years before our study commenced.

Chairs in the sitting spaces were found to be arranged around the walls of the room, and in addition, in the case of the larger, in two rows of paired chairs in the centre (Fig. 18.6). Some grouping of the chairs had taken place in the latter area. Consequently, residents who use the larger room have the opportunity of sitting in more than one group of chairs. However, throughout the 2-year period of study, it was noted that residents occupied the same chairs in the same positions. Though a *choice* of chair may exist it is certainly not implemented. The pattern in which the chairs in the two sitting spaces is arranged is maintained; thus residents do not appear to have the *choice* of varying the orientation of their seats. As was the case with the furniture in the dining room, the types of chairs provided in the sitting spaces are standardised.

The residents are not able to select their chair positions *independently*. In this home, as in the others we have studied, chairs are allocated by the staff and the residents remain in these chairs regularly. This procedure—whether so intended by staff or not—enables them to maintain surveillance of the residents. This is facilitated by the entrance doors to the sitting spaces being glazed in clear glass. The staff know where individuals sit and can locate them at a glance. The size and number of chairs precludes individual or small group *privacy* in the sitting spaces. Since residents habitually occupy specific chairs, the range of individuals from whom they can select friends (in terms of immediate seat-to-seat contact) is restricted. Here, then, residents' sociability can be described as enforced. As both the sitting spaces face the same direction (i.e. the front garden of the home), a *choice* of view is not available. They are also, of necessity, on view from the outside, giving little opportunity for residents to see and not be seen. As well as being easily on view from outside, the residents are also easily on view from within.

The two sitting spaces and the unused sun lounge are *convenient* for getting to the dining room, to the entrance of the home, and to a WC. This is not the case for access to bedrooms—the sitting spaces are some 80 feet from the lift and from the closest flight of stairs. However, their proximity to the dining room means that they are close to the major centre of staff activity in the home; indeed, the staff dining room is directly across the corridor from both sitting spaces.

As well as being unfamiliar in terms of their size, the sitting spaces do not contain other features which might be considered *familiar*; features such as personal photographs, ornaments, family mementos and furniture—foot-stools, etc. Further, the type of "modernistic" decor of the rooms is probably dissimilar to that which most of the residents would have chosen for their own homes (Wilkins, 1978). The only object that residents regard as personal is "their" seat. This is the ubiquitous "geriatric chair"—a plastic-covered upright, fairly rigid chair with wooden arms and raised seat to enable residents to lift themselves into and from it.

Toileting areas

The majority of toilets are far from the sitting and dining rooms but are close to the bedroom areas. Two open directly onto a corridor, and six do so indirectly. On the ground floor there are two pairs and one single suite of toilets: on the first floor there are one pair and one single suite of toilets. There are 8 toilets for 32 residents. A toilet–resident ratio of 1:4 is, in the context of the development of purpose-built accommodation for old people, surprisingly favourable for the period (the 1950s) in which this home was designed (Barrett, 1976). This ratio is the same as that found in homes built in the 1970s (DHSS, 1973). Since there are no special WC compartments large enough and equipped for wheelchair users, such residents are forced to depend on staff or others for assistance. The remaining residents (i.e. those able to care for themselves in this respect) may exercise their *independence* by using the WC closest to their bedrooms and/or closest to the sitting and dining spaces.

Unlike the Matron's flat, none of the residents' bedrooms has a private toilet; they must either use a commode in their bedroom or the shared WCs, access to which is public. Furthermore, the opaque glass panels of the lavatory doors—whilst facilitating surveillance by staff—minimises residents' *privacy*. Although the WCs are *conveniently* distributed amongst the various zones of the home, the fact that there is only one toilet adjacent to the communal areas—in which the majority of residents spend most of their time—means that this toilet tends to be used disproportionately.

Despite the fact that the toilets are *conveniently* distributed throughout the bedsitting areas, the ease with which they are recognised by "confused" residents is open to doubt. To quote Matron:

> Confused residents find bedrooms sometimes by numbers on doors. They can find toilets sometimes if the doors are open. Often they know the direction vaguely, e.g. down the two steps, but don't know which room unless the door is open and they see the WC inside. The WC doors are painted different colours but it is not obvious and residents don't seem to notice the colours.

Bathing areas

The home has three bathing areas—two grouped on the ground floor and one single bathroom on the first. None is in the vicinity of the communal sitting areas, they are mainly near sleeping zones. On the ground floor, residents could choose to use one or other of the two bathrooms, whereas on the first floor there is no *choice* available. In practice, residents are bathed by staff once a week according to a fixed rota—thus *choice* is virtually non-existent. Similarly, residents are afforded no *independence* or *privacy* as far as having a bath is concerned. On the ground floor two bathrooms are situated next to each other and are convenient for one bedroom zone, although not for the other. On the first floor there is only one bath, which is placed centrally in the bedroom zone.

Concluding Comments

The themes we have outlined suggest that residential accommodation be planned with reference to a number of guidelines. The fundamental principle should be that the physical settings in which people live furnish opportunities for residents to be and to remain independent and autonomous, to maintain social contact, and to find privacy, in a manner consistent with the maximisation of their quality of life. Such a principle would, for example, presume a commitment to include design elements that maintain abilities to remain active and mobile. At minimum, residents' surroundings should not prejudice objectives of this nature.

In examining many purpose-built homes for old people from this viewpoint, we have found them defective on the following counts. Though often referred to as "bedsitting" rooms, the rooms are insufficiently large to use for anything but sleeping. Their plan forms often preclude *choice* in furniture arrangements. Homes have toilet and bathroom accommodation arranged in centralised blocks, so minimising residents' opportunities to use them *independently* and in *private*. They have centralised communal dining rooms, and food preparation areas to which access is not customarily available. They have lengthy internal corridors that inhibit mobility (often residents get unnecessarily wheeled to bed) and so reduce *independence*. They are unfamiliar, lack easy *comprehensibility*, and may well contribute to spatial disorientation.

Considering one issue in detail—door locks. Few of us leave our front doors unlocked or open, or sit with ease on a lavatory behind a door we cannot bolt. The door lock is a bastion, a symbol, of our right to privacy. Yet many homes have, or once had, locks on bedroom and lavatory doors that are removed or do not operate. And in home after home we have found that residents are not given keys to lock their bedroom doors. Why not? "Well, they might collapse behind the door and then we'd have to break in through a window . . .", so the argument goes. Should a probably lifelong right to privacy, especially in sleeping and toileting, go by the board because money has not been provided for doors which can open outward in an emergency, or be tilted off their hinges, or for locks that can be "overridden" from outside?

We contend that new as well as rehabilitated residential accommodation should be studied to see that it at least enables individuals to:

(a) exercise choice about the use of their personal rooms as sitting rooms;
(b) maintain dignity when bathing and toileting;
(c) exercise independence and self-care by preparing at least some of their own meals; the accommodation should also
(d) help minimise the occurrence of spatial disorientation, and
(e) preserve privacy by screening personal accommodation.

We have suggested a checklist of questions—by no means exhaustive—which should help designers to focus on the desired outcomes for particular design elements (Slater and Lipman, 1976); for instance:

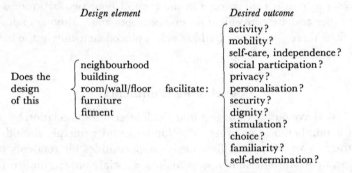

Design element			Desired outcome
			activity?
			mobility?
			self-care, independence?
	neighbourhood		social participation?
Does the	building		privacy?
design	room/wall/floor	facilitate:	personalisation?
of this	furniture		security?
	fitment		dignity?
			stimulation?
			choice?
			familiarity?
			self-determination?

Obviously not all design elements relate to each and every desired outcome: the design of a teaspoon may have little to do with privacy! It has, however, to do with self-care (being able to feed oneself) and hence to *independence* and self-determination; and perhaps a feeling of security. And if it is "your" teaspoon it may well relate to the personalisation of your circumstances and to *familiarity* with your eating implements. And it could relate to *choice*, one might have a preferred teaspoon for boiled eggs, and another for stirring tea! Similarly, it may seem inappropriate, for example, to ask how the design of walls can facilitate mobility, and yet . . . a person may fear getting lost because all the rooms and corridors look the same—to which feeling the wall surface may contribute. They—the walls—may discourage one to be active in personalising them; because they are all the same they may be unstimulating, boring, unfamiliar.

Reference to research studies of other built forms—such as grouped housing (Page and Muir, 1971), and "granny annexes" (Tinker, 1976)—suggests that, like old peoples' homes, they too are deficient on a number of scores. Judging by our experience, efforts to bring a design philosophy, a set of principles, to bear in examining these and other types of residential accommodation may lead to design innovations. But clearly the themes, the principles, we have taken as basic to a design approach do not necessarily coincide with those considered relevant by the present and future occupants of residential accommodation. It would seem appropriate to base an adequate design philosophy on residents' self-perceived needs concerning the quality of life they wish the built environment to afford them. And this requires research techniques that can get beyond the "well, you get used to anything in time, don't you, dear" response; techniques of a more qualitative case-study or action-research nature that require participation and in-depth interviewing (Fairhurst, 1976).

Further Reading

BARRETT, A. N., User requirements in purpose-built local authority residential homes for old people: the notion of domesticity in design, PhD dissertation, submitted in the University of Wales, 1976.

DHSS, *Residential Accommodation for Elderly People*, HMSO, London, 1973.

FAIRHURST, E., Sociology and ageing: an alternative view, *Concord*, **6**, 16–19, 1976.

GOLDSMITH, S., *Designing For the Disabled*, Royal Institute of British Architects, London, 1976.

HARRIS, H., Workhouse? hotel?—it's just the bleedin' same, *Social Work Today*, **9**, 13–15, 1977.

HARRIS, H., LIPMAN, A. and SLATER, R., Architectural design: the spatial locations and interactions of old people, *Gerontology*, **23**, 390–400, 1977.

LIPMAN, A. and SLATER, R., Building high to avoid confusing the elderly confused, *Health and Social Services Journal*, 11 Sept. 1976, 1634–5.

LIPMAN, A. and SLATER R., Homes for old people: towards a positive environment, *The Gerontologist*, **17**, 146–56, 1977.

PAGE, D. and MUIR, T., *New Housing for the Elderly: a Study of Housing Schemes for the Elderly Provided by the Hanover Housing Association*, National Corporation for the Care of Old People, London, 1971.

PASTALAN, L. A., Privacy as an Expression of Human Territoriality, in PASTALAN, L. A. and CARSON, D. H. (eds.), *Spatial Behaviour in Older People*, University of Michigan Press, Ann Arbor, 1970.

SCHWARZ, A. N., An observation on self-esteem as the linchpin of quality of life for the aged, *The Gerontologist*, **15**, 470–2, 1975.

SLATER, R. and LIPMAN, A., Accommodation options for old people—towards an operational philosophy, *Design for Special Needs*, **11**, 10–15, 1976.

SLATER, R. and LIPMAN, A., Staff assessments of confusion and the situation of confused residents in homes for old people, *The Gerontologist*, **23**, 390–400, 1977.

SLATER, R. and GREENFIELD, R., *Collective Care: Unit 13 of An Ageing Population*, Open University Press, Milton Keynes, 1979.

TINKER, A., *Housing the Elderly: How Successful are Granny Annexes?* Department of the Environment, London, 1976.

WILKINS, L., Old for new, *Building Design*, No. 423, 15, 1978.

CHAPTER 19

EVALUATING RESIDENTIAL CARE AS A METHOD OF SOCIAL WORK INTERVENTION

RON WALTON

Social workers have a love–hate relationship with research. This is no less true of residential social workers than of social workers in community-based settings. They wish their help to be effective and therefore should be keen to use research to improve the effectiveness of their practice. Yet simultaneously they are frightened that the research will reveal that their help is marginally effective at best and at worst actually damaging to residents. Researchers can calmly discuss the fact that a particular form of residential care is, according to both commonsense and research criteria, failing to change significantly the attitudes and behaviour of residents. For the residential worker this detachment is not possible. He or she is struggling with a difficult task which demands emotional and physical stamina; to be informed that once approved schools (community houses) are robbed "of those whose behaviour they can improve . . . who can as successfully be dealt with by less drastic curtailments of personal liberty, the schools are unable to deal effectively with the remainder"[1] is challenging to professional and personal morale. How is the residential worker to assimilate findings such as these without resorting to defensive rationalisation, or having a crisis of confidence in all he is attempting?[2] Facing up to research and evaluation of practice requires courage and a willingness to change. However, as has been discussed in earlier and later chapters residential staff have been ill-equipped to confront the challenge of research by lack of training opportunities. Even where workers have had the opportunity of professional training, there is no evidence that most courses have been able to incorporate successfully research components which enable practitioners to evaluate social work research and its implications for practice.

Research is often surrounded by a mystique of science and sophisticated statistical prowess. But practitioners too easily forget that research is grounded in curiosity and a desire to find out. How do things work? Why does this happen when I do·this? A large part of a child's life is research in the sense of playing with and exploring the world, discovering how reality is constructed. Unfortunately, formal education too often stifles curiosity and questioning, although most of us can remember gifted teachers who encouraged this capacity. Research in adult life is an extension of this drive to explore and understand and is grounded in the ability to ask imaginative questions. Asking questions is the starting point of useful research and this is where we must start in considering how to evaluate residential care.[3]

"Is residential care effective?" is an example of a poorly formulated question. It is as meaningless as the question "Is social work effective?" or "Is medicine effective?" Residential care is of many types, serves many purposes and is used as a part of the service for many groups of people. Therefore, questions of effectiveness must relate to particular types of residential care designed to meet the needs and problems of a specified group. In the past the question of effectiveness has been subsumed under the global question, "Is residential care good or bad?" Many investigators have described conditions, processes and treatment in residential care which are damaging to people, the inference being drawn that residential is necessarily bad. Whether the research has been into institutions for children, the elderly, the mentally handicapped or mentally ill, features such as batch living, lack of privacy, depersonalising admission processes, poor physical conditions, separation of the sexes and infringements of liberty have been found. The titles of the books describing research findings speak for themselves—*The Last Refuge, Asylums, Put Away, A Life Apart*.[4] It is an inescapable fact that for the institutions surveyed and described, residential life has been degrading and damaging for both residents and staff who have been the victims of physical and social structure, which imprison mind and body. In a civilised society all would agree that dehumanising practices should be abolished and that we should move towards the point where residential care is not simply unharmful but actually beneficial to residents. The research of dysfunction since the last war has been essential, in that with the passing of the Poor Law in 1948 it had been too easily assumed that all the deficiencies of institutional care had been corrected— somewhat similar to the manner in which poverty was assumed to have been abolished in the 1950s. Research which exposes gross neglect and maltreatment will always be valuable as long as the basic conditions for satisfying group living remain unmet. Yet for research to be solely preoccupied with this kind of question is unacceptable. Increasingly, other kinds of research which evaluate residential living alongside other forms of alternative social care will be needed in the future. Even if particular forms of residential care are shown to be beneficial, it is vital to know whether the same benefits or improved benefits would accrue from other types of provision.

In asking questions about residential care, a common deficiency has been to confine the questions to the residential establishment and to pay too little attention to the periods before admission and after discharge. Residential life has a laboratory-like quality. Its self-containment, with an identifiable boundary, has proved attractive to social scientists. Social work is frequently criticised for a lack of research, yet in residential care there is an abundance of studies, though often negative in character.[5] Just as residents have been scapegoated by society, so residential care has tended to be scapegoated by researchers who search for the harmful rather than the helpful aspects of care. In searching for explanations of this phenomenon, one must take account of the fact that residents have often been passive objects of the researchers' trade, captive subjects for the imposition of tests and observations, given little or no choice in the matter. In addition, there is an implied idealisation of community living. Punitive structures, inhumane treatment and neglect, if shown to exist in institutions, are assumed to be a property of residential life and not of the wider community. In contrast to this view we can ask whether the treatment of some people by the Supplementary Benefits Commission, housing departments, Social Services Departments will be proved any less coercive, degrading and neglectful. This point can be developed by arguing that many critiques of residential care are based on failure when a resident is returned to the community.

Statistics of recidivism and breakdown are used to attribute failure to the residential system. These arguments may be invalid, unless full account is taken of the damaging influences experienced by the resident before and after a period of residential care. It makes no sense to blame residential care for the breakdown of a mentally ill person who is isolated on discharge to the community, cannot find work and has inadequate accommodation. The same argument applies to reconviction rates of delinquents. That high reconviction rates are shown for community homes with different philosophies, structures and treatment methods does not demonstrate that they are equally ineffective. It is equally possible that delinquent young people experience the same environmental disadvantages on release to the community, adding to an accumulation of social disadvantages where effects have frequently been built up since birth.

An important issue which also confuses and complicates research into residential care is the lack of clarity about objectives which may be acute with delinquents and the mentally ill. Stated (manifest) objectives may focus primarily on treatment and care, whereas the underlying (latent) objective may be custody and punishment—deprivation of liberty may be considered as protecting the public and punishing the individual—then residential care might be viewed as successful in meeting the latent objective even if unsuccessful in achieving stated objectives. Research into residential care cannot ignore issues of public attitudes and policy-making which cloak aims of custody and punishment in the language and ideology of treatment.[6]

So far, more general issues relating to the value and significance of research have been examined. But residential social workers have more immediate concerns when they are dealing with residents. What kind of regime is most helpful? Which methods can I use? Which approach is best for a particular person? Clues and indications about appropriate practice can be drawn from existing research but this remains a neglected area; before embarking on and pleading for new research we should apply the results of existing research. "If even half of what is now clearly known were accepted with feeling and carried out with understanding by all, the picture of residential child care would be transformed. Of course we need to know more. But meanwhile we need not, indeed cannot afford, to wait. The immediate and major problem is to will the means to translate into action what is already known."[7] This was written a dozen years ago but is still true and not only for children. A list of some of the major results from research can show the potential for applying the results of research:[8]

(1) Large, separate establishments tend to create depersonalised batch living:[9] smaller and more medium-sized establishments create the potential for more personalised care. The Literature of Dysfunction has its positive dimension in suggesting alternatives to harmful features of residential care. It is essential to note that the size, of itself, is not a critical factor in determining the quality of life but only a more or less favourable context for good practice.[10]

(2) Clarity about the aims of establishments and their place in the overall pattern of care is essential if conflicting and often irreconcilable demands are not to be made on staff and residents. This point is based on the evidence of very different views of the aims of an establishment which often exist between the staff groups and residents.[11]

(3) Quality of staff and leadership are related to the quality of care which residents experience. This is not necessarily always related to training but the quality of

leadership seems to be of special importance in determining the ethos and general climate in a residential establishment.[12] Democratic styles of leadership seem to be more effective than authoritarian or permissive styles.

(4) So far, residents play a relatively small part in determining the pattern of group living. This has implications for the management structure of establishments and the roles of staff.[13]

(5) Residential care often appears to fail because of inadequacies at admission and discharge. Residential care considered in isolation from a resident's pre-admission and discharge experience is likely to be ineffective. The degree of change of a resident in institutional care is not a good guide to whether successful rehabilitation will take place.[14]

Attention to research findings such as these do not vitiate the need to evaluate different methods within an establishment, but indicate that unless sufficient action is taken in the areas of pre-admission work, the overall structure and climate of the home, and to secure a favourable environment after discharge, it is likely that the effects of different methods will tend to be swamped or distorted. But it is possible for residential social workers to evaluate their home in a variety of ways which may help them to become more effective.[15] Most of the studies which have influenced attitudes to residential care have involved full-time research teams over a period of years. But there is much evaluation which can be undertaken by practitioners without such resources, or by forming links with research staff in their own agencies, with teaching staff on social work courses and with social work students.[16]

The kinds of questions which the staff of an establishment need to answer if they are to begin to evaluate the work of a home are: What objectives does the home serve? What is the process by which residents are selected and admitted? What are the characteristics of the residents? How is any special treatment or care defined? How long do residents stay? How are decisions about discharge made? What happens to residents after discharge? In finding answers to these questions there are many sources of data-records; observation and participation in the life of the home; the views of staff and residents; the views of staff outside the establishment. It is a fairly common experience that what actually happens in a home differs from the picture drawn by different staff and residents. Thus, beginning to ask such questions, to gather basic information, and to discuss the results can be a fruitful source of change and aid a more general critical attitude to the purpose and functioning of the establishment. If a particular change—for example, the introduction of formal group work or individual counselling sessions—is under consideration, its purpose and method can be clarified with a plan to record changes and review the operation of the method after intervals of, say, 3 to 6 months. One kind of expected change from the introduction of groupwork would be improved communication skills among residents and also greater perceptiveness of and identification with the objectives of the home. A record of the general level of communication skills and of those for individual residents would show whether these expectations had been achieved. Similarly, it would be necessary to detail the expected effects of introducing counselling sessions with residents and to make some attempt to measure any changes in, say, attitudes to relatives, or a reduction in anxiety. Help in planning the monitoring procedure may be forthcoming from a variety of sources but advice and collaboration should initially be available from the research section of a Social Services Department.

As well as evaluating parts of the residential programme every effort should be made to monitor the progress of residents. This involves establishing a baseline of data for the resident at a particular time and noting changes. Skill training is particularly suited to this type of evaluation, but attitudes and other behaviour are equally amenable to this approach. A key element in evaluation of this kind is the identification of objectives and tasks with the residents and evaluation should be on a shared basis and avoid the atmosphere of marking time or being in a limbo. Individual evaluation also encourages individualising of objectives within an overall programme which must then be flexible enough to cater for individual needs.

Research of this kind, undertaken by practitioners with possibly a limited amount of external help, may be research evaluation with a small "r", but is nonetheless essential in improving the quality of residential care. It is, however, dependent upon clear and systematic record keeping, whether written, tape-recorded or in video form.[17] Residential staff are frequently hindered in the task of evaluation by lack of information at admission and poor feedback after a resident has left the establishment. At the same time residential staff are sometimes reluctant to record systematically. Strengthening the record system in partnership with residents improves the communication system within the home and leads to far greater openness and less distance between staff and residents.

It is clear that the questions raised about residential care can be tackled with varying degrees of rigour and complexity. After a certain point paid specialist researchers would be vital to give validity to the research findings; they would be needed to design the research, formulate questionnaires and undertake a complex analysis. Studies requiring special resources would be:

(1) In-depth study of the life of an individual home or of a small number of homes using participant-observation techniques as well as other methods of data collection.
(2) Comparative evaluation of different establishments or treatments serving the same group.
(3) Comparative evaluation of forms of residential care with other alternatives such as day care or fostering.
(4) The demonstration project. Establishing a residential service markedly different from existing patterns and evaluating its effectiveness.

Fortunately psychologists and sociologists, as well as social workers, are becoming increasingly interested in applied research in the field of personal social services and there is a great need for academic researchers to join with departmental researchers, practitioners and residents to sharpen up the most productive questions and the most economical and appropriate methods of investigation. This is likely to avoid research for its own sake rather than as a contribution for improving service; it will also ensure co-operation from staff and residents.

A possible confusion exists about whether residential care is a method of social work. Sometimes residential work is considered as a fourth method in addition to casework, groupwork and community work. At others residential care is conceived of as a special setting for personal social service within which a variety of methods can be used. Both interpretations have a certain validity. When residential care is taken to mean a therapeutic community, it can be considered as a method if the whole structure and philosophy of the community is held to be the therapeutic agent. The other view, that residential care is a particular kind of environment, within which particular helping methods may be used, also has much to commend it and it can be of value to use both meanings provided that the context is clear. Even within a therapeutic community, there are many components of structure and methods which can be evaluated with a degree of independence.[18] The alternative viewpoints highlight, however, the complex nature of the task in evaluating residential care. The range of variables is vast, as the following list illustrates.

Resident variables

Resident characteristics
   (physical, social, emotional)
Family structure
Pre-admission experiences
Criteria for admission

Length of stay
Discharge situation
Contact with family, friends
Criteria for discharge

Institutional variables

Leadership
Staff numbers and training
Staff attitudes
Communication staff/staff

Communication residents/residents
Communication staff/residents

Objectives
Type of regime
Internal groupings
Programme components:
   Education
Counselling
Groupwork
Psychiatric
Contact with community

This list is not comprehensive and each heading may be subdivided many times. The pitfalls of comparative evaluation should not be underestimated, and the research conducted at Kingswood School in the late 1960s contains many examples of the kind of problem which may be met in research of this kind.[19] The Kingswood research attempted to evaluate a therapeutic regime—one house unit compared with a traditional regime in another house. There were no significant differences in the rates of delinquency after discharge, but because post-discharge variables were less well monitored and there were changes in staff in the units whilst the experiment was in progress, it was difficult to interpret the results. There was some degree of contamination between the units as boys had some common activities. Therefore, the authors of the report relied substantially on the fact that the rates of post-discharge delinquency were not markedly different from the general pattern for all approved schools, and that, as these were much worse than for fining, and for offenders with previous convictions—about the same as for discharge, or probation—the effectiveness of the whole system should be seriously questioned. A later research report into the staff of community homes (formerly approved schools) gives a rather different slant to interpreting the results.[20] It indicates that tensions between the functions of control and treatment, rapid turnover of staff, differing philosophies in the educational and house sectors of schools, comparisons in role and task of house staff, and problems of leadership and management seriously undermined effective working. It must be presumed that these factors were present as much in Kingswood as elsewhere and thus throw a measure of doubt upon the results of research of similar design to that at Kingswood. Research into methods must take full account of the agency framework and functioning if more valid conclusions are to be reached. To follow this line of argument further, it makes no sense to undertake research into method: in establishments which are known to have basic deficiencies such as poorly-trained staff, poor staffing ratios, poor morale, or severe staff conflict. This would be rather like conducting medical research with sophisticated surgical or drug treatments in hospitals which were unhygenic, understaffed and with few trained nurses; we know, in fact, that medical research is generally conducted in wards with good standards of basic care, and well-trained staff; teaching hospitals, which are centres of research, absorb a much higher proportion of resources than non-teaching hospitals.

Residential care, despite the fact that it absorbs such a high proportion of personal social service resources (and is likely to in the future, even with extensions in community care) does not yet receive a proportionate investment of research resources, and only in the mid-1970s did local authority departments begin to focus rather more on, for example, research into the residential care of the elderly.[21] Research has its fashions, intermediate treatment being one at present—but there is a strong case for a regular investment of research resources into improving the quality and effectiveness of residential care as well as researching the various forms of community care. But in future the research priorities should be into positive functioning rather than dysfunction. The knowledge we already have indicates that the following areas of residential care may be fruitful in terms of improving the welfare of residents. Firstly, further work is necessary on the pattern of admission and discharge which are most likely to ensure that residential care is used constructively for residents. Secondly, which internal structures and processes (including particular methods of helping) are most likely to benefit particular groups of residents—an aid to differential practice will be the handicapped, mentally ill, the elderly and children. Thirdly, research into the place of residential care within the whole spectrum of services will be an increasingly fruitful area of investigation, as we continue to assimilate the insight of recent social policy thinking.[22] Fourthly, the area of linking residential care with other kinds of service—the development of new hybrid services combining residential, day care and other community service elements—will demand careful evaluation to sift out the most helpful blends of service provision. Fifthly, the involvement of residents in the process of developing better residential services may set a precedent for other forms of personal service research.

The above discussion has not attempted to give a full survey of residential research or to give a systematic account of research methods. Its main focus has been on the value of research in improving practice. This can take the form of incorporating the results of existing research into practice, undertaking internal evaluation of an establishment's functioning and of residents' development, or of fully fledged research projects with full-time staff. The dominating assumption is that research is not a remote activity whose only function is to produce reports which gather dust on library shelves, but that research is something which we can all engage in. The practitioner is a researcher to the extent that he makes an effort to monitor his own work and that of the establishment he works in and has a receptive mind to the findings of research conducted by others. Residential workers should be making known what they think are the questions which need answering by some form of research evaluation. Only in this way will more progressive and effective innovation be achieved. Without continuing research into residential care, we remain shackled alternately to tradition and fashion in determining practice.

References

1. D. B. CORNISH and R. V. G. CLARKE, *Residential Treatment and its Effects on Delinquency*, Home Office Research Study No. 32, HMSO, 1975, p. 68.

2. P. Cawson, *Community Houses: a Study of Residential Staff*, DHSS Research Report No. 2, HMSO, 1978, p. 169.
3. See N. A. Polansky (ed.), *Social Work Research*, University of Chicago Press, 1975, for an introduction to social work research methods; and T. Tripodi, P. Fellin and I. Epstein, *Social Programme Evaluation*, Peacock, 1971, for an outline of evaluative techniques.
4. P. Townsend, *The Last Refuge*, Routledge & Kegan Paul, 1962; E. Goffman, *Asylums*, Anchor Books, 1961; P. Morris, *Put Away*, Routledge & Kegan Paul, 1969; E. J. Miller and G. V. Gwynne, *A Life Apart*, Longman, 1972.
5. See, for example, in the field of residential care of children: R. Dinnage and M. K. Pringle, *Residential Care—Facts and Fallacies*, Longman, 1967; H. Prosser, *Perspectives in Residential Care*, NFGR/National Children's Bureau, 1976. Useful references to research with the elderly are to be found in C. P. Brearly, *Residential Work With the Elderly*, Routledge & Kegan Paul, 1977.
6. Cornish and Clark, *op. cit.*, pp. 50–1.
7. Dinnage and Pringle, *op. cit.* See also T. Tripodi, P. Fellin and H. J. Meyer, *The Assessment of Social Research*, Peacock, 1969.
8. R. Walton, Research for practice, "In Residence", *Social Work Today*, **9** (22), 1978.
9. Townsend, *op. cit.*
10. R. D. King, N. V. Raynes and J. Tizard, *Patterns of Residential Care*, Routledge & Kegan Paul, 1971.
11. Cawson, *op. cit.*, Chapter 4.
12. Cawson, *op. cit.*, King, Raynes and Tizard, *op. cit.*
13. R. Paige and G. A. Clarke, *Who Cares?* National Children's Bureau, 1977.
14. D. A. Taylor and S. W. Alpart, *Continuity and Support Following Residential Treatment*, Child Welfare League of America, 1973; I. Shaw and R. Walton, Transition to Residence. An evaluation of Selection and Admission to Homes for the Elderly, in *Residential Care Association Annual Review, 1979*.
15. N. Manning, The Politics of Survival: The Role of Research in the Therapeutic Community, in R. D. Hinshelwood and P. Manning (eds.), *Therapeutic Communities*, Routledge & Kegan Paul, 1979, Chapter 27.
16. A good example of the use of students in research is J. Berry, *Daily Experience in Residential Life*, Routledge & Kegan Paul, 1975.
17. D. Elliott and R. Walton, Recording in the residential setting, *Social Work Today*, **9** (32), 1978.
18. N. Manning, Evaluating the Therapeutic Community, in R. D. Hinshelwood and N. Manning (ed.), *op. cit.*, Chapter 29.
19. R. V. G. Clarke and D. B. Cornish, *The Controlled Trial in Institutional Research*, HMSO, 1972. A valuable critique of research and its findings is given by J. Burns, The socialisation of research data and the orientation of results papers: a commentary on residential treatment and its effects on delinquency, *Community Home Schools Gazette*, Dec. 1976.
20. Cawson, *op. cit.*
21. A. Leigh, The work of social services research and its impact on policy, *Social and Economic Administration*, **11** (2), 97–116, 1977.
22. See the useful discussion by J. Murphy, Alternatives to residential care: a review of developments in North America this decade, *Community Home Schools Gazette*, **72** (9), 1978.

PART II: QUESTIONS AND EXERCISES

1. What are the advantages and limitations of assessment in a residential setting?
2. Identify those professions which have a contribution to make in the assessment of a client. Say what you think that contribution involves in each case. How far are their judgements likely to differ from or match with those of a field or residential social worker?
3. How can clients become more involved in their own assessment than they are at the present time?
4. What does "labelling" mean?
5. (a) The grid identifies some roles and activities common in the practice of residential work. At the end of a typical working day, tick the number of times in which each of these roles or actions has been carried out.
   (b) Add further headings as might be appropriate.
   (c) Analyse the implications of the scatter shown by the ticks.
   (d) Ask one or more of the residents to indicate their view of the staff role by completing the grid.

Activities											
Encourage											
Support											
Physical contact											
Shared experience											
Indicate pleasure											
Reward											
Arbitrate											
Initiate											
Give advice											
Discourage											
"Tell off"											
Act aggressively											
Control											
Direct											
Appear angry											
Become angry											
Punish											

Roles													
Servant													
Domestic													
Counsellor													
Enabler													
Companion													
Friend													
Adviser													
Advocate													
Provider													
Nurse													
Teacher													
Manager													
Supervisor													

6. How important are theoretical frameworks to the practice of residential care in an individual establishment? Discuss the relative contribution of psycho-dynamic and behavioural theories to the practice of residential social work.

7. The application of an integrated approach based on systems theory offers a positive model for interpreting and extending the functions and practice of residential social work. Discuss.

8. What opportunities does the residential setting offer for the application of social work knowledge and skills?

9. (a) Identify skills associated with the practice of residential care with a particular client group, but which might be applied to work with other client groups.

   (b) Having identified those skills common to work with all client groups in the residential setting, discuss how far these have relevance for social work in other settings.

   (c) What skills do you think social workers in other settings have which might be usefully acquired by residential workers?

10. Discuss the nature and importance of relationships in residential care, in relation to other factors which affect the quality of care available to a client in the residential setting.

11. It is not possible to be an effective residential worker without a knowledge of group functioning and skills of working with, and intervening in, group situations. Discuss this statement using illustrations from practice.

12. Identify the management skills in running:

    (a) A Home for the Elderly.
    (b) An unstaffed Group Home.
    (c) A Secure Unit.
    (d) A Hostel.
    (e) A Hotel.

Discuss how far common management skills are needed in running these establishments, and where specialised skills might be necessary.

13. In what ways does the quality of management in a residential establishment affect the lives of residents?

14. What does the role of a residential adviser involve?
What kind of social work experience and knowledge does he/she need to fulfil this role?

15. What changes in the design of residential homes should be considered to meet the needs of a changing pattern of residential care?

16. If a grant were available for a research officer to be attached to the home in which you work, or of which you have some knowledge, how do you think his/her time over 2 years might be most profitably spent?

PART III

Ethical Issues in Residential Care

INTRODUCTION

All social work involves a reciprocal relationship between ethical principles and methods of working. For example, the philosophy of community care embodies an ethical assumption that it is better for people to be sustained in the normal pattern of community life than to be segregated into institutions. But such a moral assumption also places an obligation on the community to provide effective help and support in the community situation, i.e. the community situation should in reality be better for a person than life in a residential community. Conversely, admission to residential care is based on the moral belief that the person admitted will experience an improved quality of life than if he were to remain in his community situation.

This kind of argument leads us to deduce that neither residential nor community care is necessarily good or bad. Each setting and the methods used must be judged by other criteria, the primary one being that individuals should be dealt with as human beings whose individuality and integrity should be respected. We have seen in earlier chapters that the Literature of Dysfunction was based on evidence that in some institutions, at some periods, patterns of residential life violated the rights and integrity of residence. Lack of contacts with the community, segregation of the sexes, brutality and regimentation are examples of violations against the humanity and rights of residents. In this section the centrality of ethical considerations to residential practice is underlined by discussions of the rights of residents, control and freedom, and dilemmas of sexual relationships. An important factor distinguishing man from the rest of the physical and animate world is the capacity for making a wide variety of moral choices. It follows that in residential care, as in all other forms of human service, a prime aim is to encourage and develop within the particular form of service the possibility of choice, understanding of the implications and consequences of making choices, and the capacity of individuals to act on their choices, accepting responsibility for their own attitudes, relationships and behaviour. Once accepted, this principle entails that rules and regulations are not absolute but open to question and negotiation. Staff cannot presume that their own values are sacrosanct and have to be imposed on residents. Neither can residents avoid the responsibility of examining the consequences of their own actions and attitudes for other residents.

Thus residential living is an area in which many conflicting values have to be worked out in a form which is constructive rather than destructive, posing both opportunities and challenges for staff and residents. Each contribution in this part illuminates a particular aspect of moral choice and dilemma, which, without denying the conflicts and problems, demonstrates the positive features of engaging the fact of morality implicit in all human activity and relationships.

CHAPTER 20

CHARTER OF RIGHTS: THE END OR
THE BEGINNING?

RON WALTON

People in institutions do not have a code of rights at present. Neither do citizens in the community. Such rights as do exist are encompassed in an assorted array of specific legal provisions and regulations governing appeals against arbitrary executive action by state and welfare bureaucracies and protecting the individual from arbitrary arrest and treatment by the police and courts. Because residents in institutional care are in a less eligible position than most citizens arguments for a Bill of Rights for the citizen are mirrored in the demand for a statutory statement of rights for children, the mentally and physically ill, prisoners and the elderly who live in institutional care.*

The question needs to be asked—will a statutory code of residents' rights be the most effective way of improving the quality of life for residents? To answer this, the most common forms of violation of residents' dignity as people need to be detailed and the likely effects of a statutory code explored. The most common areas of infringement of natural rights are:

—opening and screening of mail and restricted communication;
—rules and regulations imposed by staff and agencies which restrict the liberty of residents to go out, have control over their money, etc.;
—punishments, which may be unfair or undignified, imposed by staff;
—non-involvement in decision making affecting key aspects of their lives;
—absence of any properly constituted appeal procedure if a resident feels that he has been treated unfairly;
—compulsory or secure detention without adequate recourse to appeals procedures.

Not all of the types of violation listed occur in all institutions, but few residents would not have experienced one or more of these violations. It is for this reason that the Council for Civil Liberties has become active in this field in recent years—within the penal system, on mental hospitals and latterly with children in care. Similarly the world-wide growth of the "participation" movement has begun to sensitise residents of institutions to systematic infringements of dignity and freedom.

Children in residential care are just becoming aware of the Children Act 1975 which gives them a right of consultation about decisions affecting their welfare. They are marching in the streets claiming their rights and some have resorted to direct action in barricading themselves in a home due to be closed. The Year of the Child is bound to

---

* For a discussion of rights in social welfare, see M. Cranston, Human Rights, Real and Supposed, Chapter 5 in Talking About Welfare, (ed. N. Timms and D. Watson), Routledge & Kegan Paul, 1976.

strengthen the demands for legislative measures protecting children—not against environmental disadvantages in the community but against the very agencies whose duty it is to provide substitute care.

Imagine that present pressures are successful and notwithstanding the difficulties of an election year and a new Parliament—new legislation is enacted stating residents' rights much more unequivocally. The first fact to remember is that the residents, the staff and the buildings in existence now will still be there—largely unchanged. Attitudes and resources will not be magically transformed. As with the Children Act 1975 and the White Paper on *Violence to Children*, for example, there is no sign that the Government is willing to give more resources to welfare than it can avoid without major scandal.

Two scenarios are possible in this situation. The first is for legalistic battle lines to be drawn between residents and staff in a painful war of mistrust and attrition. Such a possibility though perhaps yielding short-term gains for residents will not benefit them in the medium and long term as it will inevitably lead to demoralisation, cynicism and depressiveness on the part of staff who would tend to fulfil the letter of the law and no more. The unintended consequence could be precisely that division of staff and residents vividly portrayed by Goffman and other analysts of residential care, characterised by distance and restricted instrumental communication.

The alternative scenario is a new alliance between staff and residents to alter the management and decision making of their agencies, combined with a variety of actions to press for better resources and opportunities. What might tip the balance towards this second, more progressive scenario? The first hopeful indication is that many of the rights being advocated are congruent with good professional practice. Any casework or residential text recommends the movement of the person in difficulty in the process of identifying the nature of the difficulties, possible solutions and participation in decisions and their implementation. None of this should run counter to the trend toward emphasising residents' rights and their responsibility for managing their own lives.

A second pointer is the support of RCA for the present campaign for children's rights. Unfortunately the vast majority of residential workers are not RCA members and their reactions cannot be predicted as certainly. Similarly, with the low levels of training, consequence of the rights movement with good professional standards may be a factor of limited impact. A more difficult indicator is the attitudes of senior management in agencies and elected members whose interest may be much more in the area of control and regulation, than more open-ended, unpredictable care situations which the rights movement will generate.

Which scenario develops will depend also on a more mundane but essential factor— the form in which rights are expressed. Law and regulations will necessarily be general but there are many issues of detail which may be crucial. Should provisions deal with issues like attendance at case conferences, obligations to provide the placement deemed to be best, management of money, independent advocates and legal representation? What methods of arbitration in cases of dispute will be provided? These and many other matters of detail will need considerable skill and time if humane formulations are to be arrived at—formulations where the law remains the last rather than the first resort.

It may seem begrudging to raise some of these issues when a spirit of enthusiasm and hope is abroad. But the UN Charter and the American Constitutions are evidence enough that problems are not automatically solved by Charter of Rights. Charters are important because of what they symbolise as much as what they say. As such, statements of rights are a key part of a much longer-term programme of development and improvement. The danger is that the achievement of a Charter of Rights for Residents might be seen as an end rather than a beginning.

With or without a Charter of Rights the participation movement will gather momentum and the problems sketched above will have to be resolved. If rights are expressed in law and regulation let the achievement be seen as a limited gain, a bridgehead from which a long, hard battle will need to be fought to turn ideals into reality.

A final question remains. Is the long-drawn-out resistance to residents' claims for rights inevitable? Much bitterness and frustration could be avoided if the management of social services agencies and the staff of homes were to take the initiative in opening up the question of rights with residents. Not all conflicts would be resolved by this approach, but they would be set in a climate of greater trust and constructive effort.

CHAPTER 21

RESIDENT PARTICIPATION, A CONSUMER VIEW

A personal opinion of Brian F. Line,
a Resident of The Leonard Cheshire Foundation Home, Le Court

Visitors to Le Court look at me with horror and dismay when they learn that I have lived here, in care, for 20 years. Yet most people live in the same place for similar periods of time. The big difference is that most people can, if they wish, move away but I cannot because there is no suitable alternative. Le Court today is, I believe, the best residential home for the disabled in the country: there are few homes where the residents have as much freedom, as much involvement in the running of the home and as much independence, as we have here. I was from my earliest days at Le Court impressed with the attitude of residents to their disability; their acceptance of it and their refusal to be classed as second-class citizens because they were handicapped. But I am going to describe some of the trials and tribulations of life in care at Le Court in its early days, in order to illustrate the evolution which has made the home what it is today. Despite their difficulties each resident has over the years achieved many things not thought possible before discovering this home—the first of its kind.

The Leonard Cheshire Foundation has always tried to do more for the young disabled than just keep them warm and fill their bellies. At the Foundation International Conference in 1970, the Singapore Cheshire Home described the aims of the Foundation in a Charter:

> A Cheshire Home should be a place of shelter physically, a place of encouragement spiritually, a place in which residents and staff can acquire a sense of belonging and of ownership by contributing in any way within their capabilities to its functioning and development, a place to share with others and from which to help others less fortunate, a place in which to gain confidence and develop independence and interests, a place of hopeful endeavour and not of passive disinterest.

This Charter was the first proper written expression of our aims.

Before I arrived, when money had been donated to the residents of the home, they had asked for it to be handed over to them. With it they formed a Resident's Welfare Association. The money, they realised, was the key to independence if ever it was to be won, but first they had to prove to the Management Committee that they could manage their own affairs. One early resident, now 91-years-old, set about doing this by using the donated money to open a residents' shop. This sold all the one hundred and one things needed from day to day—shampoo, soap, notepaper, stamps, newspapers and sweets—and with careful management they were able to build up a profit each year which would subsidise running the ambulance and the cinema, the first small steps towards a greater freedom.

It seemed that the longer the home was in being the more conscious residents became that they were the only permanent element in the home, and that it was most of the staff, the Administration and the Management who were the ships that pass in the night. This feeling was aggravated by the distrust which existed between the residents and Management Committee, which resulted in their misunderstanding many of the decisions taken by them. This distrust also erupted from time to time between the residents and care staff, sometimes with disastrous results.

Apart from the paid Matron, SRNs and Auxiliaries, there was an army of devoted voluntary helpers. In those days we affectionately called them slaves. These were kind people with big hearts who naturally had little knowledge of professional care work, but who showed their willingness to help by descending on Le Court at weekends and holidays. There would be an influx on Friday nights and an exodus on Sunday evenings. Some would be carpenters and engineers, BBC producers, film makers, writers and teenagers wanting to do something to help other people. There were also some local housewives who came on a regular basis to bath the residents. Some of them would be influenced by the Matron-in-Charge and the staff and the attitudes which they found in their colleagues as to how to look after the handicapped. In those days of isolation, 7 miles from any town and having virtually no means of getting out except occasionally in the old bus, they brought in a welcome breath of fresh air.

The staff, on the other hand, had reasons for coming here which were sometimes much more complex, maybe unfulfilled ambitions to be a Matron or a Doctor, or perhaps a general liking for the discipline of an institution. For Auxiliaries it could be to look smart in a white coat, a passing interest in medicine, and a desire to make people happy and put the world to rights. Some professional nurses have a tendency to wish to dominate the people they care for and to make unnecessary petty rules, but it must be remembered that in those days the emphasis was perhaps more on nursing than on care, and for us it was the latter which was the more important.

In the early days wards were of four to two beds; the single rooms which we have now were an undreamed-of step forward for the chronic sick. One of the objects of the Cheshire Foundation is to enable disabled people to be free to live their own lives and to develop their own interests and talents as much as their disability allows. To do this we had to struggle and it seemed at times that we would take two steps forward to one backwards. One of the first issues we took up was that we thought it was not a good thing to be changed into night clothes at tea time. Not succeeding in persuading those in authority by reasonable means, a few of us decided to change—as ordered—but still go down to the village in the evenings. Soon complaints were received from the village about residents riding around in their outdoor electric wheelchairs—in pyjamas! We were "on the carpet" and despite our arguments nothing was achieved. Finally the Committee of the Residents Association put forward the views of the whole house, and so we were allowed to stay in day clothes until after 7.30 if we had outdoor electric wheelchairs. A small victory perhaps, but a great step forward. I use this as an instance of the many petty little things which had to be negotiated by our residents. In those early days there was only one night nurse; today we have four and can go to bed when we like.

At about this time Matron decided that our morning coffee get-together in the BBC lounge should be stopped. The residents were very upset by this, feeling that it was a step towards turning Le Court into a hospital, and sent the staff to "Coventry". At the end of 3 weeks, during which time we had only asked politely for whatever we needed, we were told by the Matron and the Warden that the coffee break would be replaced by a short tea break.

A subsequent Matron was given to being unnecessarily rude to visitors and residents' relations. This became so unbearable that the situation was reported by the residents to the Founder, Group Captain Cheshire, himself. Following this, questions were asked and six residents who were attached to the Admissions Committee at that time were called in front of the 20 members of the Management Committee, and told that we were the ringleaders of all the trouble in the home and that this had got to stop. Like school-children we sat in a row and were told that we were given 1 month to sort out the trouble and to make sure that the discontent in the home should cease. We were also told that we were no longer suitable for being attached to the Admissions Committee. If peace was not restored to the home when the Management Committee met in a month's time, we would be transferred to six different homes in the Foundation where we could cause no more trouble. This was incomprehensible to us. We left the room dejected and bewildered—what had we done? Nothing but complain about the inhuman way people were being treated, befriend those who could not speak for themselves, and speak up when somebody who had been put in charge was falling down on the job, and now we were made to feel outlaws.

We discussed the matter and decided on action. To go to the newspapers could be too sensational and damaging to our home. We felt that it was better to speak to people whom we knew, or whom we thought were already giving us financial support and let them know what was going on. Within a fortnight the pressure was being felt in the office, the Warden was receiving telephone calls and letters from people outside the home, asking what was going on. When they heard the explanation given by the Warden, they said they did not believe that it was necessary to move someone from their home. One went so far as to say that if it happened he would cease to support the home—both in kind and in money.

As the end of the month came nearer, naturally we all became more and more worried. Only a week before the Management Committee meeting we heard that the Founder himself was coming down, and then it all seemed to be over. At the next meeting we were told to our relief that under no circumstances would anyone be moved elsewhere, and we could sleep with the knowledge that we would not be asked to leave. Needless to say, this event led to changes in the senior care staff. It appeared that our standing firm as a group supported by all residents had brought the Management to a new understanding. They had investigated and for perhaps the first time made real personal contact with us.

Why were the six of us who were hauled up before the Management Committee branded as troublemakers? To understand this we have to realise that at that time the Management Committee and Administration saw anyone who criticised and challenged authority, without in their eyes any right to do so, as a troublemaker. This attitude prevailed, even though criticism was constructive. It was because of this that we, the managed, came into conflict with the Managers.

Our next Matron was an SRN who had worked at the home since the early days and was already a supporter of residents' rights and believed in giving them freedom and responsibility within the home. She was greeted with joy by everybody; she was a motherly person whom we all knew, respected and loved, and during her reign we made many definite strides forward. Unfortunately, her organisational abilities appear not to have matched her love, compassion and understanding for the residents and finally the strain made her ill which led to her resignation. Fortunately, our present selection procedures for senior staff are, as will be seen later, much more effective.

At about this time two important developments took place. The first was that the Trustees decided that as Le Court was the first home it was to become *The* Cheshire Home, the spearhead of the Foundation, the model for other homes, and the showplace to which visitors would be taken. Indirectly Le Court has, in fact, become the model, although it was felt at that time that what was right for Le Court would not necessarily be so for other homes. People come to visit from all over the world; in recent times those interested in opening new homes have come from as far afield as America, Canada, India, Japan, Portugal and South Africa. The second development was that a Chairman was appointed to the Management Committee, who had a completely new and enlightened concept of what the role of a Management Committee should be.

One of the principal aims for the Management Committee under its new leadership was that it should be fully representative of the home as a whole. Gradually, and not without some opposition and much conditioning of minds to accept change, the Committee became fully representative. Today it is composed of three resident members, the Chairman, Vice-Chairman and Secretary of the Residents' Association as it had been renamed; and three members of the staff, who comprise the Staff Committee. The balance of the Management Committee is composed of 12 outside members. Resident and staff membership is determined by annual elections from among those they represent. The outside members are elected by the members of the Committee as a whole. All these elections are by secret ballots.

The Wardon and the Matron, now designated Head of the Home and Head of Care, are not members of the Management Committee. They are normally expected to be "in attendance" at meetings of the Committee, which take place monthly, at which they are free to express their views. They are responsible for implementing the decisions of the Committee, day-to-day running of the home in detail, and reconciling the wishes and needs of both residents and staff. In all this they are given a wide measure of discretion and freedom of action whilst being wholly accountable to the Management Committee.

Complementary to the Management Committee is a monthly meeting of residents with the Committee of the Residents' Association. Residents' meetings had taken place for years, but until this time they were far from complementary to the Management Committee. A weekly meeting now takes place between the Head of Home, Head of Care, the Residents' Committee and a member of the Staff Committee. In addition, there is almost daily contact between the Head of Home, Head of Care, the Residents' Committee and individual residents. In this manner a two-way flow of information and communication is established which facilitates swift solutions to problems and attention to complaints and suggestions, and which generally serves to contribute to the smooth running and happiness of everyone in the home. A far cry from the way things used to be.

The Standing Orders for the Management Committee make provision for the Committee's business to be conducted in two parts: Part I for general business, and a Part II, from which Resident and Staff Members withdraw when matters of a confidential or personal nature concerning any individual resident or member of staff are to be discussed. When this system was first introduced Part II sessions were fairly frequent, but significantly they are now a rare occurrence, largely because matters previously reserved for this part are, in the main, solved within the framework of the normal system of day-to-day management. It is, therefore, very rarely necessary to refer such matters to the Management Committee.

Another very important feature which has evolved is that any resident or member of staff may attend Management Committee meetings as observers. This has proved to be a tremendous advantage to everyone. It provides an opportunity to see Committee members in action, to become acquainted at first hand with decisions that are taken and the reason why, and it facilitates more informed discussion among residents and staff in that they all have a better knowledge of what they are talking about.

Resident and staff membership of the Committee, and the facility for anyone to be present in attendance at Management level, has helped enormously in increasing the feeling of mutual trust and understanding between Management, residents and staff— for the simple but fundamental reason that the system enables everyone who wishes to be involved to hear each other's point of view. The results of this were that gradually the attitude of residents changed from being on the defensive to one of working in unison with those in charge. Outside members of the Management Committee also became more deeply aware of the nature and importance of all the things done by residents in a way which had not been possible before. It was, for example, seen and acknowledged how successfully and efficiently residents had been running the workshop, the shop and the welfare car, and that there were other areas in which more responsibility could be given to residents than previously. A field in which residents were particularly effective was, and still is, fund-raising. This included personal fund-raising projects, flag-day selling, contacts with Church organisations, solicitors, and public houses, sponsored wheelchair walks to London, round an aircraft carrier and an aerodrome. We were members of an Appeal and Development Committee which was formed to cope with the formidable task of launching a major appeal for the building of the west wing.

I referred earlier to the question of selection of senior staff. The need to obtain, in particular, Wardens and Matrons of the right calibre was recognised as being of paramount importance if the system of management which we had evolved was to be fully effective in the executive field. Equally, it was realised that if we were to keep senior staff of calibre and quality then the system had to be such that they would be given a reasonable measure of freedom to act within the sphere of responsibility delegated to them by the Management Committee. We were helped greatly in our thinking in this respect by a team from the Tavistock Institute who came and worked for a period at Le Court, as part of a study on residential care for the physically handicapped in Regional Hospital Board, Local Authority and Voluntary Homes. They also assisted us in devising a much more selective procedure for appointing Wardens and Matrons.

A Selection Sub-Committee was formed which included resident membership to select and appoint Wardens and Matrons. This Sub-Committee has operated most sucessfully since it inception. Briefly it functions in the following manner. The job is advertised in the press, and the resulting applicants receive a job description, and this reduces considerably the number of people who wish to continue in their application. Candidates are shortlisted and come for an interview which spans almost the whole of the working day. There is an initial interview with the Sub-Committee, followed by an informal meeting with the staff; a 2-hour tour of the home conducted by a resident, meeting and talking with other residents and staff; a buffet lunch at which selected residents, staff and members of the Management Committee are present. After lunch, the selection process continues in the form of a formal and searching interview with the Selection Sub-Committee. Applicants are in this manner subjected to a very comprehensive and varied form of scrutiny. Before final decisions are made the opinions of a very wide and representative body of the home is taken. It is an interesting fact that on the last occasion the general opinion coincided with that of the Sub-Committee.

This selection process has made it possible to find men and women far more suited to the purpose of the home than ever before. Recent Heads of Home and Heads of Care have been tremendous assets and successes. Le Court has not only benefitted materially from this by having new wings added, single rooms provided for all residents, and the dining room extended; it has gained enormously in the quality and efficiency of its administration and, above all, in its cohesiveness of operation on the basis of co-partnership. These men and women brought to their work a real personal humility and the realisation that a new job had to be learned. They are more enlightened people willing to be receptive to the ideas of residents, showing respect for individual freedom of choice, a readiness to listen and consult and then take sensible decisions when decisions are necessary. All this has made it possible to develop many of the philosophies which I believe have made Le Court unique in its field.

Residents play a full and vital part in the work of the Admissions Sub-Committee. The application of the admissions policy is probably one of the most difficult and exacting tasks which face any of the Committees involved in the functioning of Le Court. The Sub-Committee has a heavy burden of two-way responsibility, one to prospective residents and the other to those already resident at Le Court. Principally for this reason two members of the Sub-Committee are residents. The Admissions Policy is selective, and must be in order to regulate and maintain a proper balance in the atmosphere and environment of the home, thus meeting the needs of the people who must live in residential care.

One major philosophy that attracts me to Le Court and keeps me here is that of work. When we first came here we had a paid Occupational Therapist, and we found her ideas rather restricting, so when she resigned we did not replace her. Since then our Workshop Manager, a resident, has trained housewives to do the job for us. He initiates them into how to make baskets, trays and many other things; but they have a natural bent for handicrafts and are soon eager to introduce their own ideas. In the Le Court workshop if you want to make baskets you can, and if you want to start your own printing business you can. If you need the money to start your own venture, you can get a loan from the Workshop Fund.

But not all of us want to work in the workshop because, in our philosophy, work gives us a dignity and a reason for existence. It is more than the mere earning of money, which seems to me to be, fundamentally, a wrong approach. Work is an integral part of life and we have to work to live, but there are two kinds of work, one that demands physical energy and the other mental energy. Some of our work is paid and some is not. To get the most satisfaction from work at a place like Le Court and to make it really meaningful and not just an occupation to pass the time, it is essential that we accept the fact that we need help to avoid wasting precious energy in trying to do things beyond our physical powers. If a man works in the Le Court workshop and makes a basket he gets 50p. He is working and the money goes into his own pocket, and the basket is sold for the Workshop Fund to cover the cost of materials. If the same man also runs a fund-raising project for the home and that project raises £500 he is also working, but he has a different kind of job satisfaction without any financial gain. In the first case he is able to make a basket if somebody sets it up first for him, leaving only the weaving to do, and this help is accepted as normal for the handicapped. On the other hand, what is not always generally accepted as normal, is for the same man to use his mental rather than physical energy, to run a project for which he needs somebody to type the letters or to drive him around his contacts. In many homes this is not considered suitable work because he cannot do it alone, and help is not provided. At Le Court where, for example, there is a need for someone to undertake fête publicity, this could be done by the Fête Secretary. If, however, a resident has a flair for publicity, posters and advertising, he is encouraged to volunteer to take this on and is offered the services of the Fête Secretary to help him. She may not be trained in publicity and so the two of them, able-bodied and disabled working together, make a success of it. There is not a shortage of work at Le Court for those who are willing and able to do it.

Another major philosophy binding me to Le Court is the more realistic approach, by both residents and the Head of Care, to the taking of reasonable risks involved in our new freedom. The residents can always discuss a risky situation with the Head of Care, who is ready to offer advice without any obligation. For example, there is a general feeling throughout society that it may not be wise to drink if you are taking too many drugs and in many homes drinking is banned. Here, in 1976, the residents installed their own bar and it is left to our discretion whether we drink or not. This has worked well and without detriment to anyone.

People go on holidays to Denmark, Holland, Spain and France with only 20-year-olds to look after them, and on day trips to London for shopping or the theatre. Residents drive down the steep hill of our drive-way, around the neighbourhood in their invalid cars, and we have had minor accidents and difficulties which the residents have accepted and so have the Administration and Management.

Earlier I said there was no other place to which I would be willing to go. All life outside Le Court is founded on the same dignities which we hold dear at Le Court, that of freedom to choose and freedom to create one's home. If the Management at Le Court had said "No" to the kind of evolution I have tried to describe, it would have done far more than anything else to promote a feeling of being a second-class citizen, but that is certainly not what any resident can be called here.

I do not believe that it is pure coincidence that we have obtained the calibre of senior staff we now have. I believe that the evolution which took place at Le Court was a reflection of what was taking place in society. The introduction of the Disabled Persons Act and pressure from groups such as DIGG, together with more and more of the handicapped coming out of their back rooms into society has helped to push forward the ideas which had already been advanced by residents.

As far as Le Court is concerned, it has certainly changed since I came to live here. It is a bigger community—it is less overbearing. We now have three married couples with both partners disabled, and the rest of us have single rooms. We no longer wake in fear of reprisals by Heads of Care, Heads of Home or staff. Complaints against residents or staff are fairly investigated. Away has gone the award and punishment system, and away have gone the minor mental cruelties which were prevalent in the past. The big reward that one has in Le Court is that which one gets out of doing things for oneself and for other people. Most of us have a community job as well as our personal job and that community job gives us our own rewards. The rewards are greater or smaller according to the type of job we do. In fact, the range of jobs—there are over 80—and the role the residents play in the home is far greater than it was 20 years ago. In the early days it was the small jobs like running our own bus and our own shop, giving out the post and the newspapers, and sitting on our own committees. These, of course, are still done but now the responsibilities are far heavier. Residents serve on the Appeals Committee, the Admissions Committee and the Management Committee. Whenever a sub-committee is set up to deal with any specific subject or problem which requires a lot more time than the Management Committee have available, the residents are always invited on to it, examples being major projects such as building the new wing, the new dining room and the bar.

The nature of Le Court is that an atmosphere is created in which one can grow and mature mentally and emotionally. In such an atmosphere there is encouragement to become an independent thinking individual, capable of making decisions, contributing to the life of the home, living a life of one's own and of taking one's own risks. In short, we are a living, breathing, interacting community which places high values on the standard of life, in acknowledgement of each person's entitlement to be himself. This atmosphere is not one which is created by management or staff or residents alone. It is attained by all these acting and striving together in mutual trust and understanding, which in turn breeds the strength to withstand the many ups and downs which any community is faced with. This, I feel, should be the case in all residential homes for the care of the physically handicapped.

Appendix 1

*Resident Involvement and Contribution
to the Le Court Community**

Activity	Number of residents involved
Residents' Association Committee and members of Management Committee	3
Treasurer, Residents' Association	1
Admissions Sub-Committee	2
Le Court Association Executive Committee	3
Appeal and Development Committee	3
Staffing Sub-Committee (Selection of Head of Home, Head of Care and Senior Care Staff)	3
Fête Committee	4
Bar Committee	4
Workshop Manager	1
Shop Managers	2
Caravan Administrators	2
Outings Officer	1
Publicity Officer and Newsletter Editor	1
Newsletter distribution	1
Newspapers: Distribution,	1
Ordering & Accounts	1

* This list is based on 52 residents.

Activity	Number of residents involved
Post distribution	1
Welfare car management	1
Talking books	1
Green Shield Stamps	1
Weekly Shopping Trip Organiser	1
Ladies' Hairdressing Room Supervisor	1
Gentlemen's Hairdressing Room Supervisor	1
Fund-Raising for Katpadi (India) Cheshire Home	1
Voluntary Helpers' Co-ordinator	1
Librarian and Liaison with County Library	1
Red Cross picture rotation	1
Clothes marking	1
Official Photographer and Photographic Processor	1
Public speaking	5
Visitors' guides	10
Terrace gardens	1
Upper gardens	2
Red feathers	1
Cheshire Smile and Historian	1
Independence Boys—Liaison	1
Cheshire Voice Talking Magazine	4
Ladies Shopping Roster Organiser	1
Disabled Foundation News-sheets	1
Chapel Committee	3
Secretarial and Typing	2
Bar duty	9
Fish tanks	1
Disablement aids	1

Age, Sex and Disabilities

Age Structure

Age:	90+	80+	70+	60+	50+	40+	30+	18+	
Numbers:	1	—	1	6	13	17	10	4	= 52

Note: The majority of residents (30) are in age groups 40+ and 50+.
Proportion men/women: Men: 28; Women: 24.

Nature of Handicap

There are some 30 different natures of handicap, the 3 largest being:
Muscular Dystrophy: 7
Handicap following accidents: 8
Multiple Sclerosis: 10.

A significant factor of Le Court is the high percentage of residents who are in the high-care load category—60%. The remaining 40% is divided between the medium- and low-care load categories. Of the above percentage 6 are usually confined to bed. There is a large number who need to have their food cut up or be fed—50.

We have in the home 13 with a static handicap and 39 degenerative; those who have difficulty in communicating—9.

There are 4 walking; 16 have self-propelled wheelchairs and 26 have power wheelchairs.

CHAPTER 22

SECURE PROVISION FOR CHILDREN AND YOUNG PEOPLE

WILLIAM H. GREGORY

Evil is he
Who holds the key
To someone else's liberty

This piece of doggerel may be unpoetical but it is not meaningless. It is to be seen in various parts of a secure unit for boys and was printed on card by boys in the printing workshop, one of the unit's activity rooms. The three lines focus attention on a major problem that confronts all those who are concerned with secure establishments for children: can the locking up of children be justified?

Small wonder it is that this question is perpetually being brought to the fore. It embraces many questions for which there are no easy answers, questions that ebb and flow as our society shifts and adapts to changing circumstances in an effort to maintain some form of equilibrium, questions that maintain the conflict between the rights of the individual and the demands of society.

Our society invests a great deal in the notion that a happy family life is the most important of a child's needs. In the words of Richard Titmuss, "Without affection, life has little meaning for most people and none at all for children." In spite of the rising divorce rate it is still the case that the majority of our children grow up within the family setting and the majority of our children reach adulthood without too much friction. Society is ensured of satisfactory recruits. Because this child-rearing pattern works satisfactorily every effort is made to depart as little as possible from it when children are deprived of family life. The child may be deprived of family care for long periods because of special personal need or handicap, temporarily because of such things as mother's illness, permanently because of death of parents or desertion by parents, and temporarily but perhaps on a long-term basis because of misbehaviour or because home conditions are detrimental to his moral and physical development. Because our society values good, dedicated parents it seems logical to argue that the further away from family care the alternative form of care is seen to be, the less desirable that form of care will be regarded. For example, fostering would be regarded more highly than institutional care. Now, what form of institutional care would be seen as furthest removed from family care? Surely, the form of care occupying the position on the continuum of forms of care furthest away from family care would be that which takes place behind bars and locked doors?

Over the centuries the notion of maximum security has been linked with punishment. Punishment! What a nasty word! One meaning of the word is "that which causes an offender to suffer". Who in the field of child care wants a child to suffer? Have the psychologists not informed us that the carrot is mightier than the stick? One need not wonder about the fact that there is much emotion expended on the idea of incarcerating human beings in secure establishments, and naturally emotion is heightened when those human beings are children and young people. It is a commonly held view that rehabilitation is possible only in conditions of freedom.

For over a thousand years—since the time of Æthalstan—imprisonment as a form of punishment for various crimes has been used. However, it was in the 1840s that most of the prisons which exist today were built in this country. The prisons still hit the news headlines and whatever happens in them will be criticised by a section of our society. Increased security will be welcomed by those who hold dearly the well-established ideal of law and order, who believe in the value of punishment as a deterrent and retribution as a just consequence of law-breaking. The same measure will be anathema to those who believe the main objective should be the rehabilitation of the prisoner.

The Howard League for Penal Reform is still active on behalf of those unfortunate enough to find themselves locked up in prisons. It was John Howard, the Bedfordshire landowner and County High Sheriff who, in his work in 1777, *The State of the Prisons in England and Wales*, brought the subject before the public eye. Hibbert[1] tells us of the revelations of Howard's work. Howard was a deeply religious and thorough man who took his work seriously. He used to accompany the judge at the assizes and he also visited the gaols. He was horrified by what he saw and was particularly concerned when he discovered that the gaol officials received no salaries and had to extract what they could from the prisoners by levying fees. He demanded that the county should pay salaries to these officials. The justices refused to accede to this demand unless a precedent could be found. To find such a precedent John Howard searched throughout the country. His search uncovered cruelty, injustice and squalor, and the link between incarceration and punishment was well established. In no sense was imprisonment conceived to make the prisoners better people or to cure or rehabilitate. It was used to help the owners of the prisons make money out of the prisoners. "With insufficient water and ventilation, with vermin and insects crawling everywhere, without proper food or light or sanitation, shivering half naked in the winter and suffocating in the summer heat, most prisoners lived out the days and nights in unutterable misery."

Such descriptions were made credible by factual reports. For example, more people died of gaol fever in 1773–4 than were executed. Physical deterioration in prisons was certainly revealed by Howard's work and a previous writer, Henry Fielding (1707–54), had stressed the harm to character development suffered by prisoners. "For prisons were not only prototypes of hell, as Fielding described them, they were not only the most expensive places on earth to live in, they were also schools of crime and of profligacy."

Charles Dickens, 1853, also touched on an effect of prison life—an indefinable effect which was the more terrible for being so: ". . . something of that strained attention which we see upon the faces of the blind and deaf, mingled with a kind of horror, as though they had been secretly terrified."

It can be seen that for many years there has been opposition to the locking up of human beings, as there has been to the keeping of wild animals in cages. The idea that rehabilitation and deprivation of freedom do not mix is reinforced by literature. Behan's *Borstal Boy*[2] described aspects of life in Borstals as seen through the eyes of an inmate which by no stretch of the imagination could be described as therapeutic, and Sillitoe's

The Loneliness of the Long Distance Runner highlighted the psychological distance that can exist between staff and inmates and draws negative treatment implications.[3] Several incidents of great historical significance have indicated the strength of public feeling against prisons. An example is the storming of the Bastille. Admittedly there were fire-arms stored there but "the building had typified the old order of things and its fall seemed like a portent of change".

Up to 20 years ago sociologists' work on penal institutions was mainly concerned with the informal life of the inmates, on similarities between institutions, on internal structure and on the stable aspects of institutions. From much of this work it was concluded that little treatment was possible. Clemmer[4] emphasised that during their stay in prison inmates are to a greater or lesser extent socialised into a deviant, criminalistic subculture. Clemmer introduced the concept of "prisonisation". By this he meant the taking on of the norms, customs, values and culture in general of the institution. He hypothesised a negative association between degree of involvement in the inmate culture and adjustment after release. More recently many of the assumptions of the sociologists of 20 years ago have been challenged, but the effect of their work is still with us and it is a commonly held view that the oppositional cohesion of the inmates in secure establishments enables them to withstand the pains of imprisonment but prevents treatment.

Many people living today have experienced life in prisoner of war camps and in concentration camps. They are, understandably, quick to identify with those who are incarcerated in secure establishments and quick to believe that treatment in such places is impossible.

Sydney and Beatrice Webb (1922) stated their views on the possibility of treatment in prisons: "The most practical and the most hopeful of prison reforms is to keep people out of prison altogether."

Sir Alexander Paterson, who contributed so much to the Borstal system, was well known for his belief that "you cannot train men for freedom in a condition of captivity".

Thouless[5] supports this view: "It is found by psychologists working with criminals that remedial treatment cannot be successfully applied to the criminal who is suffering a prison sentence."

The idea of imprisonment, then, is repugnant to many who concern themselves with treatment and reformation. It is linked more closely to the concepts of deterrence and retribution than to rehabilitation. In residential work with children the objective of most effort has been to keep children out of prison. In *The Romance of Child Reclamation* Spielman, who was one of HM Inspectors of Reformatory and Industrial Schools, tells us of the work of the pioneers of the approved school system.[6] During the early part of last century Buxton successfully aroused public indignation against prisons and prison discipline—"the nurseries and hotbeds of crime, the almost inevitable ruin of all who entered their walls." The pioneers preferred the idea of open schools for wayward children. Pounds founded the Ragged School, the precursor of the Industrial Schools, in 1818. In Edinburgh similar work was done by Guthrie in 1847. Mary Carpenter, born in Exeter in 1807, was an ardent campaigner against the practice of imprisonment for children. Her book *Reformatory Schools for the Children of the Perishing and Dangerous Classes and for Juvenile Offenders* was published in 1851 with the purpose of showing that "the prison system, even as best conducted, is proved ineffectual as a preventive and reformatory measure for children".[7] This book, which incidentally gave birth to the term "little perisher", made a valuable contribution to the enactment of the Juvenile

Offenders Bill in 1854 which legalised the position of Reformatory Schools. Convinced that "a child will never behave well in prison from a moral sense" she established a Reformatory School at Bristol. It is paradoxical that after all this work to keep young people out of prison it was at this very school that the first special unit, a secure unit for boys, was opened, in October 1964.

In view of all the evidence and strong feeling against incarcerating people surely there had to be good reasons for setting up a secure establishment for adolescent boys as part of the approved school system? Currently the secure establishment in question is a community home, a special facility in the public system of community homes, but, when instituted, it was an approved school. In 1964 it was opened to provide for those boys who, because of persistent absconding and unruly behaviour, were unable to benefit from placement in existing approved schools which had no secure accommodation. Soon after the first classifying school was opened in County Durham in 1942 it was discovered that there were some boys who would be misfits in any approved school and would need special provision. Efforts to manage these boys failed and the concept of closed provision was discussed. A working party of Home Office inspectors and others was set up to consider the problem. The working party's deliberations did not produce action and the work of approved schools continued to be adversely affected by a small number of persistent absconders and otherwise disruptive children who damaged relationships between the schools and the local communities, and whose need for time and attention prevented the approved schools from working effectively with the majority of the children who were capable of responding to the training. Action did come, however, as part of the aftermath of the disturbances at the Carlton Approved School on 29 and 30 August 1959.

Carlton Approved School was remotely situated in rural surroundings on the outskirts of Carlton village in Bedfordshire. The school catered for 96 senior boys, that is, young men aged from 15 to 19 years. The school was thought to be suitable for the training of the more robust and vigorous boys and also for boys of low intelligence and educational attainment. It had not been considered an appropriate school for disturbed and difficult boys but it had in its population a proportion of such boys because there had been an increase in the demand for vacancies for such boys in senior approved schools and Carlton School had taken its share. The disturbances at the school took the form of mass disobedience, that is, a refusal by all boys to carry on with the daily routine. There was some violence and destructive behaviour and mass absconding. The police and the press were involved and an official inquiry was conducted by Mr Victor Durand, QC. The report of the inquiry was presented to Parliament by the Secretary of State for the Home Department in January, 1960.[8] Recommendation number 11 of the Durand Report stated: "The establishment of one or more schools (as necessary) with closed facilities should be considered for boys not essentially unsuitable for approved school training but who need to be held securely for a period in order to achieve progress with their training."

In October 1960 the Report of the Committee on Children and Young Persons, known as the Ingleby Report, was presented to Parliament.[9] This report endorsed the recommendation of the Durand Report that closed facilities should be provided within the approved school system but added that the closed blocks should be associated with the classifying approved schools where the specialist facilities existed and could be shared.

These recommendations were duly implemented and special secure units were established at Kingswood in 1964, at Redhill in Surrey in 1965 and at Red Bank School in

Lancashire in 1966. It can be seen that secure units carry out the task of managing particularly troublesome youngsters for a period of time, that for this period of time the public is being protected from their troublesome and sometimes dangerous behaviour, that some youngsters are being protected from their dangerous behaviour towards themselves, and that open institutions are being relieved of the need to look after this group. It cannot be said that secure units are any more successful than other forms of care in reducing adolescent recidivism; they are very expensive places to run, so where is the justification for having them? Children have rights—the right to be properly looked after and the right to have their developmental needs met as well as possible. Just as a dependent baby must be looked after in every way, so those adolescents, who have suffered privation or have been deprived of experiences necessary to their overall development or have been brought up in a delinquent life-style so that their behaviour can be dangerous to themselves or others, must be looked after. For a small proportion of youngsters in care secure provision is necessary.

Depriving a young person of freedom removes to a large extent the possibility of learning by natural experimentation. Consequently the learning by other methods must be of good quality. Incarceration of children and young people can only be justified if, taking everything into consideration—and this includes taking into account the consequences of continued law-breaking—life for them is improved. How can this be accomplished?

Secure units providing long-term care and education for young people must have good-quality staff providing a high staff/child ratio. West, 1967, gives the justification for this:[10] "The task of alleviating social handicaps and character defects calls for much more sophisticated techniques of educational and psychological training than are generally available", and "it is the worst cases who should get the best attention".

It is probably true to say that there is no method in residential child care for disturbed/delinquent adolescents which is more important than the people engaged in the work. Therapeutic communities seem to have lost ground as a helping technique and token economies are coming into favour. A method or technique can be helpful provided that it is operated by dedicated and committed staff. Unfortunately, basing residential work with children on one method usually embodies the notion of selection and consequently rejection of candidates. As this is not possible in a secure unit (after all, one important criterion for admission can be the negative one of inability to find an alternative form of care), it has been found best to have an eclectic approach and to base the work with each child on a belief that in every case there is the possibility of development.

The approach that will be described is interdisciplinary, involving the formation of a staff team made up of field and residential social workers, nurses, teachers, psychologists and psychiatrists.

In a secure unit it is possible for a feeling of worthlessness to pervade the total adult/child group. The children may have been regarded by those who had been unable to help them in open establishments as unhelpable, and consequently may see themselves in this way. It is essential to construct goals which stress the positive. The work satisfaction of the residential workers will be provided only if the frustrations imposed by security are kept to a minimum and staff are able to use their various skills to help the children as developing individuals and group members. Clarification of the task, which is a function of the needs of each young person in the unit, serves the double purpose of ensuring that the children's needs are given careful consideration and also of demonstrating to staff that caring, education, treatment and control are possible.

The weekly case conference is the instrument that knits together the staff team representing the different professions; this is the task-orientated staff group which breaks down resistance to co-operation caused by different backgrounds, different kinds of training, different perceptions, different organisational structures, different jargon and different salary scales. This group must be seen by staff to be of the utmost value. From the deliberations of this group are evolved the individual programmes on which the everyday work of the unit is based. Members of the different professions join together in a common task and learn to appreciate each other's contributions. Unhelpful attitudes and hostile feelings (for example, between field and residential workers or between teachers and care staff) can all be worked through if the staff group in the form of the case conference is conducted along the lines formulated by McGregor in 1960, when he characterised a well-functioning, effective, creative group.[11] In this group the atmosphere tends to be informal and relaxed and almost everyone takes part in the discussion which remains pertinent to the task which is well understood and accepted by the members. The members listen to each other and every idea is given consideration. The people are not afraid of appearing foolish, and disagreements are talked through. Decisions are reached by a kind of consensus and when action is taken clear assignments are made and accepted. The chairman does not dominate the group and the leadership shifts from time to time. A young man's individualised programme results from the deliberations of this group. He will be the main actor in the programme mapped out but he does not attend the conference because precipitate confrontation with his total circumstances could be harmful. Take the view of a child quoted from *Who Cares?*, 1977:[12] "For example, some children at their review know nothing at all about their parents. And they find out—all of a sudden—that their mother is a whore, they weren't wanted and their father didn't care."

However, the youngster is still involved in his conference because his views about his present circumstances and his own ideas about his future are relayed to conference by a staff member who by using his skill and relationship in a non-threatening setting has discovered the boy's ideas and has made clear to the youngster the reasons for needing to know his own views. The ideas and wishes of the boy's family are obtained in a similar way by the field social worker who attends the conference which takes place in the unit.

Because of the comparatively small number of boys and the number of staff (necessary because of the nature of the boys and the demands of security) it is possible to operate an individualised approach. This is superimposed on the institutional life to which the writer will return later. In the interdisciplinary method teachers will teach and use relationships, residential social workers will form and use relationships and teach, psychiatrists will provide psychiatric treatment to the small proportion who will respond and will act in a consultative and supportive role for staff members, field social workers will bring to the programme the wider view of the boy's total circumstances so that the individual is not treated in isolation from his main areas of life, and the medical staff will provide medical attention based on a much wider foundation than the physical factors alone.

The efforts of the interdisciplinary approach can be seen more clearly by considering the specific recommendations for Joseph, a disturbed, emotionally and socially deprived, delinquent 13-year-old boy. He had been subject to a Care Order since the age of 8 because he was beyond control. He was the seventh of 10 children. His father, a long-distance lorry driver, was a heavy drinker and had appeared in court for assaulting mother. Mother was in poor health and talked of divorcing father; the family were not on good terms with neighbours because of the unruliness of the children; father had handed over the responsibility of caring and controlling the children to mother who lacked confidence to do this without support. Mother spoiled the children and father favoured corporal punishment. There was continued family disharmony. Joseph had been rejected by the family for a considerable period of time—the typical scapegoat. One of his reactions to this rejection was antisocial behaviour. At the age of 8 years he was referred to Child Guidance for refusing to attend school and running away from home. Mother said he was beyond control and the family was referred to the social services department as mother was threatening suicide. Joseph continued his delinquent behaviour and the police were demanding that he be controlled. A Care Order was made and removal from home was agreed. Six different residential homes and schools failed to help Joseph because he kept running away and committing numerous offences of theft and burglary. His need for affection was such that he was vulnerable in the companies he sought when he was absent from care and was considered to be in moral danger. He was also a danger to himself because of suicidal attempts. Apparently the making of the Care Order had not resulted in better care. Admission to secure accommodation was agreed upon in the expectation that better care, education, treatment and control would result. This is not obtained merely by using a secure building but by the efforts of the professional staff who work there. It is the way in which security is provided that matters.

After a settling period, during which time Joseph had the opportunity to weigh up his new surroundings and then to test them out, the staff team was in a position to give careful consideration to Joseph's circumstances in the hope of preparing an individual programme designed to return to him in a gradual way responsibility for those areas of his life that he had not learned to manage in a way that was helpful to himself and acceptable to others.

The first recommendation in his programme was that he should continue his stay in secure accommodation. This was made in the belief that he could be better helped in secure accommodation than returning home or being transferred to another residential establishment. The special unit sets out to ensure that disturbed behaviour does not bring about rejection of the individual, and its purpose is to provide as much help as possible to those who have suffered a pattern of rejection.

It was agreed that Joseph should have a programme of weekend home leaves once a month. This was in agreement with his parents and it was judged that at that stage they could tolerate this amount of contact and Joseph needed to experience that he was not totally rejected at home. Joseph wanted to see his mother regularly and his responsibility in this arrangement was explained to him very clearly. Firmly placed on his shoulders was the responsibility of returning to the unit after his weekends at home and of keeping clear of delinquent behaviour.

Three members of staff—two men and a woman—were given, and they accepted, the responsibility for giving Joseph special attention in the hope of forming relationships that could be used to raise Joseph's self-esteem and give training in social skills. "Forming relationships" and "using relationships" are vague phrases in danger of losing significance because they mean different things to different people. Many would testify to the importance of the idea of forming a relationship but would hesitate when asked to say what something so personal and intuitive means. Others would say that with many of our children we are hampered by the problem that many of them have a limited ability to form appropriate relationships and adults and other children already have relation-ships with significant adults and do not need substitutes and are often so skilled at manipulating adults that they use relationships for undesirable ends. It is true that the job is difficult and demanding but those children who have difficulties in relationships with adults desperately need good experiences in this kind of interaction and those who can form relationships need the good example that can be provided by stable, caring adults. Without being exclusive it is useful to consider that the professional relationship should increase the child's communication with the adult, increase the child's respon-siveness to social reinforcement and increase the tendency of the child to copy the adult's behaviour.

A third recommendation was that Joseph should receive extra individual attention in the basic school subjects. Joseph had been deprived of formal schooling, but was of average intelligence and capable of learning given the circumstances to overcome his opposition to school and the time and attention of a skilled and sympathetic remedial teacher. It is not surprising that emotional development and development of cognition are so interdependent that development of the one frequently stimulates development in the other. Adolescents who have failed to learn to read, write and manipulate numbers at the time when most of their contemporaries have experienced success in these areas often carry on failing to learn because of emotional factors. The possibility of individual attention often brings surprising results and the experience of succeeding in learning to read usually brings increased self-esteem and social competence and acceptance.

One male residential social worker was given the task of counselling Joseph and agreed to give special attention concerning Joseph's feelings towards his father and also Joseph's attitude to delinquent behaviour. Joseph needed good-quality interaction with a man as compensatory experience because of his deprivation in this area. It was possible that Joseph was capable of insight learning given reasonable development of cognition and experience of a sound professional relationship.

It was also decided that Joseph needed psychiatric oversight so that his capacity to relate could be monitored and his emotional state observed because of his attempts to do himself physical injury. Joseph was not suffering from mental illness and his attempts at self-injury were regarded as ways of securing attention. Nevertheless this aspect of Joseph's behaviour needed careful observation without his experiencing the desired results of raising anxiety and securing special attention.

The field social worker on the unit's staff and the local authority's social worker accepted the task of co-operating in the necessary social work so that arrangements would be based on a full knowledge of the family's circumstances and of Joseph's needs.

It was anticipated that if Joseph's programme were successful then he would be in a position to move from the secure part of the special unit to the open part where he would be able to exercise more responsibility for his behaviour with the support of the same members of staff with whom he had appropriate relationships.

The obvious objective of the experience of this form of residential care is to bring youngsters like Joseph to a position when they can return to life in the community with-out being a danger to themselves or others. Delinquency is not cured as though it were a disease that would respond to treatment, but hopefully the youngster has been helped by all-round development and the minimising of problems and unhappiness.

A great deal has been written about the negative aspects of institutional life and it must be recognised that individual programmes must be carried out against a background of institutional life. Goffman[13] defined his total institution as: "a place of residence and work where a large number of like-situated individuals, cut off from the wider society for an appreciable period of time, together lead an enclosed, formally administered round of life".

It is important for secure establishments for children to cater for relatively small numbers so that each child can receive individual consideration. This means that such establishments would be in a position to minimise many of the negative aspects of institutional care and maximise the positive. One of the characteristics of total institutions is described by Goffman as follows: "each phase of the member's daily activity is carried on in the immediate company of a large batch of others, all of whom are treated alike and required to do the same thing".

In units for children this need not be so and in secure units the staff/child ratio should enable the institution to be flexible and permit different experiences to be given to different children according to individual need. There should be no large group of "managed people" and a small supervisory staff so that the "basic split" between the "managed group" and the staff is obvious. Staff should be in a position to form close professional relationships and to break down psychological distance so that the child is not given over to the influence and example of the most delinquent in his peer group.

Goffman commented on a block to the passage of information about staffs' plans for inmates: "Characteristically the inmate is excluded from knowledge of the decisions taken regarding his fate."

This is not necessary in a secure unit for children. In a sensitive way it is possible to involve the child and his family in plans for his future and to ensure that he is clear about his own commitment and responsibility.

It is necessary to be alert to what Goffman has termed "disculturation", by which he means an untraining which renders the individual incapable of managing certain features of daily life outside the institution. This disculturation can certainly be minimised by determining clearly those life-areas in which the individual needs help and making sure that responsibility for those areas in which he is capable is not taken away from him.

Efforts should also be made in secure accommodation for children to avoid what Goffman terms "mortification". When a child enters an establishment he should never be subjected to experiences which are "abasements, degradations, humiliations and profanations of self". The secure institution obviously places a barrier between the inmate and the wider world but the harmful effects of this can be minimised by field social workers keeping the child in touch with his real life and problems and devising a programme which carefully preserves contact with significant people and places. The child is a person and has a name, and what prevents this name from being used and what prevents the child from bringing to his institutional life some of those possessions that preserve his individuality? The institution need not indelibly stamp its label on the individual. In secure accommodation for boys an individual's bedroom can be regarded as a cell but it can also be regarded as safe personal space where he can be himself without molestation and where his private property can be around him without being stolen or broken by bullies.

Experience has shown that a great deal of acting-out behaviour by boys can be experienced and used to enable the young person to realise that although certain behaviour is not condoned he himself is not rejected. There should be no need to produce what has been described as "the routinely compliant inmate". Corporal punishment is not used. This kind of humiliating experience is not necessary. There is also no need to demand humiliating verbal responses. Sensible, purposeful activities render unnecessary the use of "patently useless makework".

Self-determination and freedom of action are certainly to a large degree taken away from young people who enter secure accommodation but these can gradually be restored as the young person develops greater responsibility for his actions.

Nevertheless, great care must be taken before the drastic step of depriving a young person of his freedom is taken. This care must be in the hands of skilled and experienced multi-disciplined assessment teams capable of considering the total circumstances of a young person's life and of determining the steps that need to be taken to provide for him better-quality life.

References

1. C. HIBBERT, *The Roots of Evil*, Penguin, 1963.
2. B. BEHAN, *Borstal Boy*, Hutchinson, 1958.
3. A. SILLITOE, *The Loneliness of the Long Distance Runner*, W. H. Allen, 1958.
4. D. CLEMMER, '*Prisonisation*'. *The Sociology of Punishment and Correction*, edited by JOHNSON, SAVITY and WOLFGANG. Wiley, 1962, pp. 148–51.
5. R. H. THOULESS, General and Social Psychology, University Tutorial Press, 1958.
6. M. A. SPIELMAN, *The Romance of Child Reclamation*, Butler & Tanner, Frome and London, Undated (c. 1920).
7. M. CARPENTER, *Reformatory Schools for the Children of the Perishing and Dangerous Classes and for Juvenile Offenders*, 1851, New Impression, The Woburn Press, 1968.
8. V. DURAND, *Disturbances at the Carlton Approved School on 29th and 30th August, 1959*, HMSO, 1960.
9. HMSO, *Report of the Committee on Children and Young Persons*, 1960.
10. D. WEST, *The Young Offender*, Penguin, 1967.
11. D. McGREGOR, *The Human Side of Enterprise*, McGraw-Hill, New York, 1960.
12. NCB, *Who Cares?* National Children's Bureau, 1977.
13. E. GOFFMAN, *Asylums*, Penguin, 1961.

CHAPTER 23

SEX AND THE RESIDENTIAL SETTING

LEONARD F. DAVIS

We are moving beyond the sexual liberation of the 1960s and 1970s into a post-permissive age where the Western world is ordered by a new set of values: sex education for 13- and 14-year-olds is explicit and detailed; contraceptives and contraceptive advice are more easily available to under-16s; short-lived sexual relationships no longer leave a natural burden of guilt; homosexual relationships become more acceptable; living together is an alternative to marriage; and elderly people expect to remain sexually active until later in life.

In the climate of relaxed relationships and frank exchanges encouraged by new approaches to group living, staff in institutions will have to show greater awareness of the needs of sexually active and potentially active residents, setting aside taboo, suspicion and ridicule, and lessening the need for victims and offenders. I do not underestimate the difficulties of accommodating a wide range of values but suggest that we cannot continue to measure sexual conduct with the yardsticks of another era, yardsticks already discarded by emerging generations. Residential social workers must educate, and challenge as necessary, those who, sometimes for political ends, set themselves up as the last bastions of moral concern. Within other sexual codes there are equally valid concepts of right and wrong.

As in many aspects of daily living in groups, residents now have sexual rights instead of privileges. Such rights extend to both heterosexual and homosexual relationships. It becomes the duty of their care givers to uphold these rights, regardless of the care givers' own beliefs and practices (which, in their turn, at an individual level, must be equally protected). The opportunity for sexual expression should not be reduced merely because a person lives in an institution and younger members of staff, the decision-makers of the 1980s and 1990s, are giving a lead in the understanding and interpretation of new sexual values as they apply to work in residential settings.

There are signs of progress. Physically handicapped people in residential care are beginning to demand equal opportunities for sexual freedom, reminding us that the environments we create for them may act as barriers to a sexual life and reinforce widely held assumptions that they are asexual. Action on behalf of physically handicapped people is especially needed at this time concerning their right to privacy; their right to live with a partner (male or female) with or without the marriage tie; and their right to the choice of a sexual life.[1]

Slowly, also, an appreciation grows of the need for intimate relationships, and sometimes sexual experiences, in the lives of those with mental handicap and, in the long term, only prisoners are faced with the prospect of a denial of their sexual needs as they live through the period of their sentences. I have some confidence that over time, although perhaps a considerable time, the sexual needs and aspirations of adults in residential care will be acknowledged and provided for.

Since publication of my earlier paper on touch, sexuality and power[2] there has been a steady response from members of staff wishing to share present and past concerns about the impact of their sexuality on others, and about their own reactions to the sexuality of residents. The latter, too, have made their feelings known. Most frequently, from both groups, the focus has been on some incident involving an adolescent.

The continuing debate about sex in residential establishments will undoubtedly be most heated in respect of living and working with young people, but as case law is built with one client group its effect will be felt by those working in other residential settings. This chapter dwells particularly on children and adolescents; on the sexual needs and rights of adolescents; and on sexual exchanges and relationships between adults and young people. The next two decades will witness shifts in attitude and practice calling for skill, sensitivity and compassion of the highest order.

Two distinguishing features of community homes working towards completion of the transition from approved schools (or from the more formal children's home of an earlier period) are: firstly, the quality of communication which exists between the adults and the young people, and between the adults themselves; and, secondly, the opportunities available through staff meetings, small group discussions and individual supervision for the exploration of incidents arising from the intimacies of daily living. Incidents of a sexual nature are appropriately brought to such meetings. Where there is no vehicle for discussion the individual is left to manage his feelings in the best way he can.

The following experiences of three female students and a newly appointed, unqualified member of staff, all in their mid-20's illustrate typical exchanges. Joy was initially taken aback by the behaviour of Alan, a slightly retarded but affectionate 13-year-old. Each night, when Joy was putting him to bed, he would fondle her breasts. She decided not to prevent him and used the occasion to give Alan a cuddle. This diverted him, did not make him feel rejected and was, in Joy's opinion, the way to return his affection. But the contact worried her. She found Alan an attractive young boy and warmed to his embrace. After a week or so the security of the unit staff meeting allowed Joy to express her anxiety. She found that two other young females were having similar experiences and they evolved a joint plan which allowed Alan to continue while they talked to him about more conventional ways for a young person to show his affection. Gradually Alan responded.

Tina's concern was also at bedtime, in a room shared by four young adolescents. She was usually the only female on duty on her shift. Each boy would have an erection, either in the bathroom or in the bedroom, subtly ensuring that Tina was near at hand. One evening the oldest boy started to masturbate in her presence. Tina needed to share her reaction to this demonstration of adolescent sexuality but staff meetings at the assessment centre were devoted to administrative matters and supervision was infrequent and superficial. Tina knew from her observations that reporting the boys to senior staff would lead to swift and severe punishment, probably corporal punishment, with no consideration given to a discussion of the underlying reasons for the boys' behaviour. She could not identify any staff member having the interest or ability to talk about masturbation with the boys. Tina could only contain her feelings and discuss them in the safety of the college setting.

Ann, also a CQSW student, was being shown around a CHE by a 15-year-old boy, Mark, on a pre-placement visit. They were walking along an upstairs corridor when Mark suddenly asked Ann to "wait a moment" as he hurried into one of the bedrooms. Within seconds he called her to the bedroom where, on entering, she found him standing naked. Calmly she ignored his tentative advances and suggested that, when he had dressed, they would resume the tour. This he did and they walked around the rest of the school as if nothing had happened. Ann added an amusing touch. As she left Mark to return to the principal's office, she remarked: "Thank you, Mark. That was an interesting visit. I think that you have shown me everything." The boy grinned.

This was only an observation placement; Ann felt unsure of staff reaction, did not want the boy to be punished and only shared the incident with the consultant to the school a few days before she left. Mark maintained an easy relationship with Ann during the period of her short stay but she felt unable to broach the subject with him. I am sure that, having talked about Mark's action with the consultant, this would have been her next step had she been remaining longer in the school.

Sue was "needled" by Eric, a physically well-developed boy of 15 years, during the whole of the first month of her new job in a boys' hostel. He often set others against her. At the time Sue did not know that she was the first female member of staff, other than the warden's wife, ever to be employed there. One evening Eric wandered into the office where Sue was alone and engaged her in conversation for a few minutes. Suddenly he said: "You want me to screw you, don't you? If you let me, I'll see that you get a quiet life." Sue acknowledged the proposal and the comment (the "want" and the "let" conveyed a double message) and, as far as an excited Eric would allow, talked the matter through with him. Later, in the quiet of her room, she began to shake and cried anxiously.

In a calmer frame of mind the next day, Sue was able to use her period of supervision to talk about the conversation with Eric, and with her supervisor rehearsed the points that had to be raised first in staff discussion and then in the community meeting. In the latter, there was no direct reference to the previous evening although most of the boys had some ideas about what had taken place. Other matters allowed the questions of aggression, bullying and intimidation to be aired and Eric responded to the signals emitted by the staff and boys.

After a further month in the hostel, Sue was able to spend time with Eric on his own in what amounted to sexual counselling, enabling him without embarrassment to share his ignorance of basic sexual facts, eventually helping him to find his first girlfriend and to engage in a sexual relationship without threats and aggression.

Male members of staff are also quickly caught up in intimate exchanges. John was 21 years of age when he went into a residential special school for younger boys. He worked well, was efficient and popular. Being touched affectionately by 9- and 10-year-old boys was a new experience for him but John became rather worried when three of the boys sought him out on their own or in pairs and wanted to kiss him, and in fact did so frequently. He was both excited and distressed by the feelings that welled up inside him but there was nobody with whom these could be shared. His responsive close physical contact with the boys, for example, in the bath—interfering in legal terms?—never became known and subsequently John moved on for training before taking up an appointment in fieldwork. Only later did he realise how his relationships with the boys would have been viewed had they ever come to light. Retrospectively, he saw himself at the age of 21 as in full adolescence, naïve, and effectively seduced by the physical exchanges initiated by the boys.

These accounts demonstrate a range of responses to the sexuality of young people in residential care. Joy, Ann and Sue were strengthened in their understanding; Tina left her placement disconcerted and dissatisfied; and John was lucky. Individually, Alan and Eric received help in growing up; Mark encountered someone able to set limits without punishing him; and the other boys were left with adults who, through no fault of their own, failed to draw boundaries or to use the experiences of daily living as points for discussion. The above illustrations show the value of individual and group supervision but, regrettably, also offer examples of children's centres where denial is still the first refuge, punishment the second, and a forum for the regular examination of resident–staff exchanges, including those of a sexual nature, is not available.

The age at which young people become sexually active is falling and in many day schools efforts are made within the sex education programme of the social education course to acknowledge this. Young people in mixed classes talk freely about reproduction, contraception, masturbation and venereal diseases, although some local education authorities still suggest that homosexuality should not be discussed unless the subject has first been raised by the pupils.[3] For those living away from home such curriculum developments have two implications: firstly, if young people attend day schools, the work of the school must be extended to take account of the additional intimacies of group living; and, secondly, in institutions with education on the premises, we must ensure that a comparable programme of sex education is available together with discussion and sexual counselling suited to the needs of those already wrestling with emotional and social problems. Much of the sexual excitement, anguish and confusion in adolescence feeds directly into other areas of behaviour and it is surprising that even young people who have come into care for reasons of a sexual origin—either as victims or offenders—are rarely given the opportunity to "talk sex" in a way which will allow them to explore in a safe environment their past experiences.

Turning to the sexual relationships of young people, and especially of young people living in institutions, I take as my base line the report of a working party of the World Health Organisation on young people aged 14 to 18 years:

> While induced abortion may be better than an unwanted child, contraception is better than an unwanted pregnancy and the best path to improved contraception is education for responsible sexual behaviour. Increasing sexual activity among teenagers is a fact and, rather than ignoring its existence or trying to stamp it out, it would seem more expedient to educate young people so that such activity becomes a positive and constructive experience in the developmental process leading to responsible adulthood.[4]

A major survey of 14-year-old Danish pupils carried out in 1976 showed that, of those questioned, 16% of boys and 13% of girls had had sexual intercourse.[5] In the United Kingdom, nearly a quarter of 15-year-olds regularly engage in genital apposition and about 10% have sexual intercourse.[6] Some would suggest that figures for young people living in community homes are higher. Certainly, many adolescents in care are sexually active. Some young people of 14 or 15 years are able to find in a sexual relationship a comfort which, in its level of satisfaction, outshines the interventive techniques so carefully (or otherwise) designed by the institution. Because of the nature and extent of their deprivation, the sexual needs of adolescents in care not infrequently go beyond the age-related exchanges associated with the normal development of young people living in their own homes. These needs relate to three basic factors of physiological and psychological origins.

Firstly, there is the need for close human contact which involves touching and stroking. Berne suggests that: "Of all the forms of sensation the one preferred by most human beings is contact with another human skin. This provides not only touch, but also warmth or heat of a special kind."[7] Such contact, it is said, may make the difference between physical and mental health or breakdown. The taboo on touch remains strong in many institutions while the need for close physical contact is compounded by the isolation (either occasional or permanent) experienced by many adolescents in group living. As plants turn towards the light, young people respond to a nervous system hungry for physical sensation. In *The Prodigy* Hesse describes the growing relationship between Hans Giebenrath and Hermann Heilner, two boys under stress in a boarding school:

> They looked at each other. It was probably the first time they had ever studied each other's face and felt that behind each other's smooth features lived an individual person, a kindred spirit, with his own peculiarities.
> Slowly Hermann Heilner stretched out his arm, gripped Hans by the shoulder and drew him towards himself until their cheeks were quite close. Then Hans in a sudden exquisite panic felt his friend's lips touch his own.[8]

Secondly: "For the majority of the human race, self-esteem is chiefly rooted in sexuality . . . the object of physical passion is thus not only a means whereby the drive of sexuality can be expressed and assuaged, but also a vital source of self-esteem."[9] Adolescents in care are especially low in self-esteem. In matters of bodily attraction and sexual performance they feel, at least temporarily, able to regain some of the self-esteem lost in other areas of their lives, for example, in social and educational performance.

Thirdly, with young people in residential establishments, there seems a particularly fine interplay between sexuality and aggression. As Storr remarks, we know little about the biochemical states underlying tension but:

> One interesting fact is that the state of the body in sexual arousal and in aggressive arousal is extremely similar. Kinsey lists fourteen physiological changes which are common to both sexual arousal and anger, and in fact can only discover four physiological changes which are different in the two states of emotion.[10]

The high levels of aggression (not necessarily "fighting") in many institutions are only marginally lowered by the traditional efforts directed towards diversion and sublimation. Downes maintains that the fall in the age of marriage has done more to keep delinquency rates down than all the intervention we so relentlessly employ.[11]

The body mechanism does not respond to an arbitrary "age of consent" of 16 years in its need for sexual activity. As I have pointed out, this need may be increased by the deprivation suffered by many adolescents in residential care. In view of the evidence that young people under 16 do enjoy sexual relationships, some adults find difficulty in equating the current age of consent and certain sections of the Sexual Offences Act 1956 with the falling age of puberty. A healthy sexual relationship in adolescence may, in the long term, be better for mental health than an adolescence spent furtively exploring pornographic magazines and bearing the guilt imposed by the taboos of adults caught up in the tentacles of an outwardly prudish Victorian era. Institutions have borne longer than anywhere else the repressive climate of that period.

Of course we have to protect the young against exploitation but, as in other fields, we must be prepared to think and act laterally when the inevitable event occurs. If a sexual relationship does arise in the life of a 15-year-old the task of the residential social worker does not lie in making the young person feel guilty and of low esteem (yet again), thereby increasing the need for secrecy. It seems preferable to help her (or him) to understand it, to control it and (dare we ever suggest?) to enjoy it. The adult look of disapproval and the imposition of obstacles and unreasonable restrictions leading to scenes of confrontation, alienation and despair are rarely constructive, especially in the face of the agonising searches made by many young people in residential care as they strive to "belong". Helping the adolescent to manage the relationship within the boundaries he or she desires would appear to be a better approach. Adult fears of promiscuity are usually ill founded.

I am aware that "the development of an individual's sexuality is a long and complicated process involving the interaction among biological, psychological and social factors"[12] and that there is often a gap between psychological and biological development. In filling this gap, however, the residential social worker has to ensure that he does not give the negative messages likely to widen it, but, more fruitfully, provides understanding as sexual relationships emerge. The earlier example of Sue and Eric is helpful in this respect.

Under the Family Law Reform Act 1969 16-year-olds have the right to consent to their own medical treatment without parental knowledge, and this includes advice and practical assistance in matters of contraception. Hopefully, this right is given active support by those working with older adolescents. For those under 16 a preventive service is also available and it is the adults who are irresponsible if they block access to such measures, particularly in view of the DHSS circular dated May 1974:

> It is for a doctor to decide whether to provide contraceptive advice and treatment, and the Department is advised that if he does so for a girl under the age of 16 he is not acting unlawfully, providing he acts in good faith in protecting the girl from the potentially harmful effects of intercourse.
>
> The Department is also advised that other professional workers who refer, advise or persuade a girl under 16 years of age to go to a doctor in his surgery or at a clinic for the purpose of obtaining contraceptives or treatment would not by such an act alone be acting unlawfully.
>
> The Medical Defence Union have advised that the parents of the child, of whatever age, should not be contacted by any staff without his or her permission even though as a matter of clinical judgement the refusal of permission to involve the parents may affect the nature of the advice given to the child.[13]

Residential care is often experienced as restrictive by many adolescents. It is not difficult to increase these feelings if the advice and practical help about contraception available to their peers of 14 or 15 living in their own homes is not made available to young people in care. That a girl of 15 years in a children's home is taking the "pill" will be known by several people, a fact which in itself takes away a right to privacy enjoyed by her peers. Some members of social services committees and managers of voluntary bodies find it necessary to oppose contraception for girls under 16. Such an attitude needs to be taken up in discussion by senior officers of departments and voluntary organisations in a way which indicates support for those working closely with teenagers in residential homes.

Oral contraceptives (the pill) do present special problems for adolescents as: "The biological maturation process is probably not complete until 2 or 3 years after menarche. Since there is a lack of knowledge about the effects of hormonal contraception during maturation, it is recommended that young women at risk of sexual exposure and unwanted pregnancy during the early adolescent period use non-steroidal contraceptives."[14]

For many adults the "pill" is the easiest method of contraception to discuss and the most "distanced" from the act of sexual intercourse. In view of these warnings, however, it is important to consider other available methods and, further, to work with boys in discussing their responsibilities. I suspect that this is rarely done with adolescent boys in care and that too many engage in sexual activity without adequate information about contraception, later regretting the pregnancies of their girlfriends. A young member of staff told me recently that she is purchasing condoms for two of the 15-year-old boys in the voluntary children's home where she works as a group leader, "because they are too embarrassed to buy them themselves". She has not been able to share this yet with the officer-in-charge or any other members of staff and fears their reaction. The girl is extremely concerned about developing sexually responsible attitudes in the boys in her care but is aware of her delicate position if the managers of the home learn of her actions.

The most difficult statements from adolescents to senior members of staff in institutions must surely be: "Last night when I was ill Mr A. came into my room to take my temperature and put his hand on my breast" or "When we were at camp on Saturday Mr Z. came into my tent and played with me". There are even greater complications when such a remark is made about the officer-in-charge to a comparatively junior member of staff. We are all on trial from that moment. Sitting down with the young person and asking for an elaboration of the statement means that the story is told without a witness. Often it is impossible to strike a balance between belief and disbelief as, at that time, the whole of the named adult's reputation and "residential contribution" over the past years or months flash in front of the member of staff engaged in the interview. The absence of a witness may mean that the story has to be told on yet another occasion, each account reinforcing the previous one and making it more difficult for the young person to retract or to modify his original statement if he so chooses.

On the other hand, if it is decided to call in the person concerned to hear the accusation first-hand, the risk is run of embarrassing or inhibiting the adolescent so that he is fearful of telling his story.

Questions of suspension, whether to inform the police and what to tell the staff and other adolescents arise immediately. I use the word "immediately" because quick thought and instant decision making are necessary, even if the decision is to do nothing. The choice between inaction or communication to others is in itself significant and can have later repercussions for the member of staff to whom the story is told, the "accused" and the adolescent. At worst, this decision may be the first step leading towards criminal charges and possible imprisonment.

Of one thing we can be certain: details of the alleged conduct will not be hidden from others in the building. Suspension more often than not carries with it some assumption of guilt but, from another standpoint, if an individual remains on duty, does this indicate to the adolescent: "I don't really believe you"?

There is no complete answer. In my experience this is one of the incidents most clumsily dealt with by external managers of residential establishments, their widespread fears quickly changing to aggression and unspoken reprobation. Elsewhere I described a role-play of such an event, one in which the officer-in-charge was himself under suspicion:

> The members of the group played out the incident as administrators, homes advisers and "duty" fieldworkers from firm desk positions placed around the edge of the room (with much telephoning, uneasy laughter and character smearing) whilst the main subjects remained stunned and unattended on the open floor space. He who five minutes earlier had been a friend and colleague had suddenly become a different kind of being.[15]

Local authorities and voluntary organisations should have available (and frequently discussed and updated) a broad code of conduct for such emergencies, and the rights of each person involved should be widely known. But, of equal importance, there should be guidance on how to lessen the trauma for all concerned. Under ideal conditions, I favour an immediate meeting between the adolescent, the adult and the staff member to whom the incident is reported. But such an approach can only be made in an open climate which supports the similar discussion of all other problems. Too few establishments operate at such a level, and the risks in dealing with "accusations" in this way are great. More frequently, it seems better to see each party separately in the presence of a witness acceptable to those being interviewed. It is difficult for a junior member of staff if he is spoken to first by a young person. In climates such as those created where Tina and John worked it may be necessary to seek outside advice before proceeding.

In general, the avoidance of suspension appears preferable, unless the person wishes to go off duty. Sometimes he does. The seriousness of the accusation will enable the individual to decide for himself which course to adopt. From the adolescent's point of view, it seems important to indicate to him that nobody is "telling" anybody to go off duty. It must be remembered that frequently adults and young people who become linked in this way have previously had—and still have—an established relationship, and its destruction by formal (and sometimes legal) action can leave the young person with unbearable guilt about the part he has played. Caring for someone and then knowing that you have perhaps lost him his job, blighted his career, forced him out of his accommodation and broken up his family are heavy burdens for the "victim" to bear, and often they have to be carried for a long time.

The sexual games and the sexual rivalries of children and young people are no less powerful than those enacted by adults. They may indeed be more powerful, lacking sophistication and thereby more readily ending in accusation or blackmail. There are many young people in care who are well aware of their power over the adult through the use of their sexuality. Both boys and girls will employ it as the ultimate weapon in response to feelings of jealousy, frustration or deprivation. "I can get you into trouble" is far reaching in its implications.

Resignation, the "gentleman's way out", is like pleading guilty without a fair hearing, but occasionally a person feels that this is the procedure for him. Sometimes, of course, for an officer-in-charge or homes manager not to involve the police means treading on

mined ground but I have a feeling that more incidents are being bravely and professionally examined internally, putting into perspective the intensity of sexually based interactions which are bound to happen within the intimacies of group living as the most
complicated dyadic and triadic relationships are being worked out. Cases of exploitation
and serious assault, although rare, will remain but the brutal and all-condemning nature
of their proceedings need not necessarily be extended to all other incidents. The essence
of residential social work demands that, whenever possible, we should seek to heal and
not to destroy, using each complexity of daily living as a learning experience. The way
in which an incident is approached can leave a greater scar than the incident itself. I
cannot believe that it would have been right to punish John or that, under the circumstances, he was to blame for his actions in the residential special school. Undeniably, with
advice and counselling on the job he would have been in a far better position to set
boundaries and to understand what was happening.

I spoke to Angela recently. She had left a children's home to move into a shared flat.
When she was 15 she was found in bed with Tony, a temporary member of staff who was
filling in the period between leaving school and going to university. He was dismissed,
charged and received a custodial sentence. Angela's distress was considerable and no
adult had yet been able to convince her that any man should be punished thus—or
indeed at all—for having had sexual intercourse with her as a result of the fondness that
had grown between them. Press reports glibly referred to "scandal" and "assault" and
justice was seen to have been done. Are we able to speak of "justice" when two lives have
been so strongly affected by the aftermath rather than the act and as an outcome of
overwhelming forces that would have operated regardless of the law or fear of its consequences? Adults saw fit to punish and destroy when neither person involved in the
event which brought about legal proceedings could identify the crime allegedly committed. Righton reinforces this point:

> It remains true . . . that staff are much more likely to be forgiven seven times for
> vicious cruelty to a resident than *once* for a sexual liaison with him—even when the
> relationships is fully desired and enjoyed by both. . . . Provided there is no question
> of exploitation, sexual relationships freely entered into by residents—including
> adolescents—should not be a matter for automatic enquiry; nor should a sexual
> relationship between a resident and a worker be grounds for automatic dismissal.[16]

Female staff, too, carry the past with them. Mary, 32 years of age and now working
with her husband in a CHE, recalls how 12 years ago she frequently had sexual intercourse with a 15-year-old boy, Clive, in the large children's home where she worked.
The relationship continued for nearly a year after both had left the home. Clive and Mary
parted amicably, the former to live with his married sister, the latter to a job in a
different part of the country. Mary still thinks about that time, wondering what would
have happened had they been "caught" and even questioning the security of her present
appointment "should the department get to know". Clive, she feels, found concern and
comfort at a painful period of his life. Mary herself would not now encourage such a
relationship—at the time it just "happened"—but she remembers with affection the one
senior member of staff in whom she confided before leaving the children's home. He
chose to use counselling skill with both Mary and Clive rather than his power to destroy.

Sexual fears, sexual attractions and sexual taboos are stronger forces in the dynamics of group living than we care to admit. Often we fail to provide the meeting places where their complexities can be unravelled. The support systems we do offer rarely touch the edge of the dilemmas facing staff and residents. Each year the intensity of sexual feelings and experiences in residential settings results in a number of bruised and disillusioned people, those for whom everything has gone wrong. We cannot change the norms of society but we can display levels of understanding and tolerance unknown elsewhere. We can clear our minds of much suspicion, of the need to punish, and of the desire for excessive control. I am not celebrating the post-permissive society, lauding unbridled sexual activity and suggesting licence for free sexual exchanges in residential care. I am advocating a hard look at institutional frameworks with a view to lessening the embarrassment, guilt and harshness which surround all aspects of sexuality in residents and staff. But I go further than that, placing a responsibility on staff, as part of their caring task, to facilitate sexual expression among those who may be unnaturally prevented from doing so, and calling for a far greater degree of kindness in our responses to events which, on first examination, may rouse in us the need for retribution.

References

1. L. F. Davis, The ancient monuments to chains of residential care, *Health and Social Service Journal*, **LXXXVI** (4514), p. 1932, 1976.
2. L. F. Davis, Touch, sexuality and power in residential settings, *The British Journal of Social Work*, **5** (4), 397–411, 1975.
3. See, for example: *Health Education in Schools*, HMSO, 1977, p. 118; and a news item in *The Times Educational Supplement*, 24 Jan. 1975, p. 5.
4. *Problems of Children of School Age (14–18 Years)*, Report of a Working Group, Regional Office for Europe, World Health Organization, Copenhagen, 1978, p. 31.
5. Report in *The Times Educational Supplement*, 4 Mar. 1977, p. 15.
6. *Problems of Children of School Age (14–18 Years)*, op. cit., p. 10.
7. E. Berne, *Sex in Human Loving*, Penguin, Harmondsworth, 1973, p. 190.
8. H. Hesse, *The Prodigy*, Penguin, Harmondsworth, 1973, p. 67.
9. A. Storr, *Human Aggression*, Penguin, Harmondsworth, 1968, p. 97.
10. *Ibid.*, pp. 33 and 34, referring to A. C. Kinsey *et al.*, *Sexual Behavior in the Human Female*, Saunders, Philadelphia, 1973, p. 704.
11. D. M. Downes, *The Delinquent Solution*, Routledge & Kegan Paul, London, 1966, pp. 251–3 and noted in the chapter by S. Millham, Who Becomes Delinquent? in *Working Together for Children and their Families*, HMSO, 1977, p. 62.
12. *Problems of Children of School Age (14–18 Years)*, op. cit., p. 9.
13. *Family Planning Service: Memorandum of Guidance*, HSC(1S) 32, DHSS, May 1974.
14. *Problems of Children of School Age (14–18 Years)*, op. cit., p. 11.
15. L. F. Davis, Feelings and emotions in residential settings: the individual experience, *The British Journal of Social Work*, **7** (1), 26, 1977.
16. P. Righton, Sex and the residential social worker, *Social Work Today*, **8** (19), 12, 1977.

PART III: QUESTIONS AND EXERCISES

1. How much choice do residents in your home have in the following aspects of their life: time of getting up and going to bed; meal times and diet; going out into the community?
2. How far are residents involved in important decisions affecting their lives? Discuss this in relation to establishing a plan of care and treatment, case conferences and reviews.
3. What opportunities exist for residents to express their feelings, wishes and problems? Who would they turn to discuss: (a) their wish to return home; (b) difficulties in a relationship with someone of the opposite sex; (c) annoyance at the way a member of staff had behaved to them?
4. How would you set about establishing a management group for your establishment. Who would be represented and what would its function be?
5. Examine an incident in which you or another member of staff has disciplined a resident. Why was this action taken and were there any other ways of handling the situation?
6. Are there any rules or conventions about relationships between the sexes in your establishment (whether between residents or staff and residents)? What are the reasons for them and how are they justified?
7. Set up the following role-play situation; one member of staff plays a staff role and a second plays the role of a 15-year-old girl who asks to be put on the pill. Let the interview continue for 5–10 minutes, taping it if possible, and then discuss the content of the interview.
8. The residents in an Old People's Home wish to have a staggered breakfast time. How is this request dealt with? Stage a management committee meeting in which staff take the role of staff, members of the community and residents to decide the matter, followed by a discussion by participants and observers.
9. What arguments are used to justify the deprivation of liberty in some establishments? How far does the practice of residential care in a secure setting violate social work values?

PART IV

Education and Training for
Residential Work

INTRODUCTION

The existence of a body of theory and practice relevant to residential living is no guarantee that it is disseminated broadly and actually incorporated in practice. This part addresses itself to the process of transmitting concepts and skills throughout residential services through a variety of training programmes and staff supervision. The extent of residential services and the lack of training opportunities for residential staff present a vast training gap which will not be easily filled. There are three kinds of problem which any education and training strategy has to face. Firstly, given a shortage of training resources, how might they be increased and where should limited resources be concentrated? What should be the balance between CQSW, CSS, in-service training and staff supervision? Secondly, how should the training opportunities be structured so that existing staff and new recruits have full access to the opportunities? Thirdly, what kinds of content should be included and how should it be taught?

At present there are no definitive answers to the questions, but the contributions included here give an indication of present thinking and possible future developments. Yet certain assumptions are implicit in whatever pattern emerges over the next decade. The nature of the tasks in residential care necessitate an emphasis on broad educational aims as well as detailed practice knowledge and skills. Residential care, as part of a network of service, and needing staff of maturity who are able to cope with the dilemmas of residential life, requires that staff have a broad as well as a narrow vision. If staff are to be effective they must have an understanding of society and of the variety of human need and personal service.

A further assumption is that the nature of residential tasks requires training broadly comparable with training for other social workers and as far as possible integrated with training for other social service staff. Unless these assumptions firmly underpin future training patterns, residential workers will themselves continue to be segregated from the mainstream of social work and this will contribute to a continued segregation of residential care as a second-best, poor-quality form of social service.

CHAPTER 24

THE TRAINING OF GROUP CARE PERSONNEL IN THE PERSONAL SOCIAL SERVICES*

FRANK AINSWORTH

This paper undertakes a review of the present situation in regard to training for group care (residential and day care) personnel. Although an array of disparate influences on this training are identified, a cohesive picture does not emerge from this review, simply because these influences have yet to be effectively ordered. An attempt is then made to clarify the different levels of training needed by group care personnel. This is done in a manner that requires the readers themselves to relate the material to practice illustrations. Training for direct care personnel is cited as the major area of unmet need and a new initiative in response to this is proposed. Finally, trends in service development are referenced and linked to potential changes in training. The material in this paper, because of its level of abstraction, has value as a tool for thinking about issues in group care training. It is not intended to offer a prescriptive device for constructing training courses. The more detailed material required for such an exercise represents another stage of development for this under-explored area of training.

The Present Situation

Some evidence now exists[1] which shows that in spite of intensive efforts in Britain over the last decade by central education and training bodies, service organisations, and educational institutions, growth in the number of trained group care personnel has remained small. This is surprising in view of the public commitment by all parties, expressed in their respective publications and press statements,[2] to increased training for this area of the personal social services. There has also been publicity urging that special attention be given to the training needs of group care personnel and that further resources be allocated to this end from the professional and occupational organisations concerned with this field of practice. Yet all this activity, whilst raising consciousness of the need for training of group care personnel, has apparently had little other impact.

Explanations for this lack of success in increasing the output of trained personnel who are willing to work in group care practice vary enormously. Little common agreement exists as to the reasons for this persistent problem. Consequently, a review of the many factors influencing the situation seems worthwhile.

---

* The views expressed in this article are the author's own and should not be taken to represent CCETSW views or policy.

Currently, the most favoured single explanation used in the personal social services stems from the part that employment conditions and patterns of remuneration play in maintaining this position. When contrasted with other areas of practice, the conditions and remuneration offered to trained personnel in group care practice appear to be inequitable. It is then suggested that this situation is responsible for the continuing loss of able individuals, from group care practice to other personal social service occupations both prior to and following acquisition of training. Whilst these two issues are undoubtedly influential and have a noticeable impact on the status awarded to group care practice, other matters can be seen to be of similar importance. Indeed, the history of group care services has been marred by an inability to recruit, train and hold on to high-calibre personnel. Even in an earlier era, when conditions and remuneration for group care personnel were less disadvantageous by contrast with other areas of practice than is the case today, this phenomenon was still conspicuously present.

Another important issue is the extent to which the group care practice is not confined within the boundaries of the personal social services. The major administrative systems concerned with health care, education and penal provision[3] are also committed to the provision of some forms of group care services. Group care when provided within these systems reflects the value preferences, organisational characteristics and occupational competences of the specialist field concerned. Certain qualifications acquired within one of the specialised systems may not, therefore, be assessed favourably when transposed into another system, especially in the personal social services arena.

In basic training for group care practice in the personal social services the primary concentration has to be on teaching material which equips personnel to provide the type of sensitive social care which is essential for human existence. This focus is different from that initially utilised for personnel who are trained to work in health care, education or penal provision. Clients in group care services in the personal social services, like every other member of the community, may need assistance from time to time from workers with knowledge and skills derived from training in specialist systems. But this will be supplementary to their basic social care needs and daily living requirements. Viewed in this way, the unwillingness of the personal social services to legitimise other patterns of training which have placed less emphasis on teaching about social care aspects is understandable. The development in the use of group care provision by the personal social services and the limited availability of trained personnel has, of course, led to the recruitment of many workers without training or with qualifications from one of the specialist supplementary areas. Regrettably, it has also led to confusion about the desired construction and content of training courses for group care personnel in the personal social services.

It is also important to recognise the wide range of practice contexts within which group care personnel may find employment. These range from small residential units to major institutions, all of which provide 24 hours, 7 days a week, care and treatment. All these programmes may be acceptable areas of practice for group care personnel, together with community-based enterprises which offer more time-limited and narrowly focussed living and learning opportunities. In addition to size and purpose, group care programmes are influenced by their environmental location. This occurs whether taking the form of geographic isolation from centres of population or being located within city or urban areas. All of these factors—size, purpose and location—are tempered by community expectations. Consequently, it is difficult to formulate and teach a comprehensive theoretical framework and practice skills applicable to group care situations. The fact that individual group care programmes are designed to respond to the needs of a specific population group—be it for children, adolescents, handicapped adults or the elderly— also adds complexity to the training issue. In particular it means that group care practitioners must be able to tailor daily events in these practice contexts in a manner which reflects substantive appreciation of the needs of a particular population group.

Yet another matter which has added to the training problem for group care personnel over the last two decades or more and which is still in process has been the advent of major research studies and theoretical writings about institutional care and treatment. Many of these writings have emphasised the negative aspects of life within institutional contexts. The studies[4] which have received extensive attention have largely emanated from the health care and penal practice fields, where they have mainly been undertaken by academic sociologists, psychologists and criminologists rather than by group care practitioners. They have, however, reinforced what Wolins[5] has described as the "anti-institutional movement" and have given us a literature which Jones[6] earlier referred to as "the literature of dysfunction". The over-generous use and sometimes uncritical acceptance of these materials and the tendency to characterise all 24-hour group living contexts—regardless of size, purpose and location—as harmful environments has had, and still continues to have, a negative impact on group care training and the recruitment of personnel. Even now, when some of these writings are being reviewed and more positive studies by practitioners are emerging, group care remains suspect. Indeed, some personnel employed in the personal social services can be shown to be ideologically opposed to its use.

These theoretical works also appeared for a time in the sixties to be in danger of unintentionally reinforcing the natural tendency of 24-hour group care programmes to be outside the mainstream of service development. This isolation from the continuum of community-based services and the creation of a false dichotomy between institutional and community care was, however, avoided. This was largely due to the personal social services reorganisation which welded these interests together under legislation enacted in the late sixties and early seventies.[7] Whether the same coalescence of interests has occurred in training courses for social work and social services personnel within which group care personnel find themselves is less certain. The limited presence amongst social work and social service educators of a group who in their own post-training or employment were engaged in group care practice or are now involved in research into group care raises this uncertainty. The lack of educators present at gatherings of those professional and occupational organisations concerned with practice in group care services also adds emphasis to this concern. When it is realised that in the personal social services growth of training for group care personnel is dependent on this body of educators, further alarm is liable to be felt.

The construction of a continuum of co-ordinated personal social services for all age groups which the legislation of the sixties and seventies sought to achieve requires at some point the type of 24-hour care and treatment provision which only the residential component of the group care field can provide. Indeed, it is the availability of more hours of care per day than can be made available by other forms or combinations of service that justifies the continued maintenance and development of 24-hour group care programmes. There is, however, ready agreement that such provision should only be used on a highly selective and, wherever possible, short-term basis. This is in order to limit possible negative influences which might occur in such protected environments. The author has indicated elsewhere[8] the limitations of a concentration solely on the residential 24-hour care context and the creation of an educational response around this. Such a concentration does not support integration of group care provision into a co-ordinated service continuum or provide a resolution to the problem of recruitment and retention of trained personnel. A shift in emphasis in training patterns towards considera-tion of the group care field as it spans a range of living and learning environments and time sequences valid for day care and residential practice is more productive. An educational development which teaches basic materials necessary for effective practice within group care and treatment services offers a viable alternative strand in social work and social services education to the well-established field practice sequences.

Post-Training Provision and Current Prospects

Historically there has been a sharper division between training for group care practice and field practice in the systems that now constitute the personal social services than has been the case for the comparable areas of health, education and penal provision. Within health care and education the initial qualifying training patterns have until very recently been considered suitable for personnel regardless of whether they intend to function within a group care context or in other types of community-based services. This is also true even in fields closely allied to the personal social services, namely the probation and penal services. With the movement of the probation and after-care service into some less traditional forms of group care, and penal services personnel into newer forms of community provision, there has, however, been growing support for the view that some new forms of training may be needed.

It is therefore interesting that training available in the personal social services for group care personnel should until recently have led to different qualifications and have been for a shorter duration than that for field practice. The explanation lies in the way in which the present pattern of social work training grew out of, and was mainly identi-fied with, field practice, whilst group care training emerged separately out of the residential child care service. When, in 1973, a policy commitment by the Central Council for Education and Training in Social Work was made, to ensure that "training for residential work shall be of equal length and standard with that of fieldwork within a single but flexible pattern of training and that a common qualification shall be awarded",[9] a major initiative was heralded, the potential of which has still to be realised. This policy can be shown to have influenced the amount of attention now given to teaching about group care practice in social work and social service courses. It can also be shown to have influenced recruitment patterns to these courses with many more participants now having pre-course experience in group care work.

Another influence of importance for field personnel has been the service reorganisa-tion brought about by the legislation referred to earlier, and the adoption of generalist practice perspectives.[10] Whilst these developments have assisted in altering perceptions of social work and social service and encouraged the growth of a common identity between field and group care personnel, some of the consequences have been less certain. Field personnel have undoubtedly been assisted in working with a variety of client populations, in broadening the range of interventive techniques and in recognising group care as a positive resource. Group care personnel, on the other hand, still provide services to single client populations. As a consequence personnel coming from and intending to return to group care positions require in-training courses teaching about specific client populations in a manner that may be less intense for those employed in the more generalist field services.

This comment is not intended to support an argument for the re-emergence or return to specialist residential qualifications, a proposition which finds favour with some commentators on the group care field. Indeed, a move in that direction would merely fragment the social work and social services training arena in a most unhelpful manner. Such a fragmentation between field and group care practice personnel when some coalescence of interests is just beginning to emerge would be entirely negative. Rather, it argues for a comprehensive training pattern for social work and social services in which preferences in studies are organised around the ultimate destination of course participants, be this either field or group care practice. A model for this type of approach has been offered by the author in an earlier paper.[11]

Most commentators on training for the personal social services have until recently assumed that staff recruited solely on the basis of personal merit would diminish and that positions in both field and group care practice would eventually be filled by qualified personnel. Whilst this may be desirable, the evidence[12] quoted earlier suggests that this aim as it affects group care practice will not be achieved in the forseeable future. Other statistics[13] also indicate that almost all qualified personnel who become involved in group care services occupy programme-planning, supervisory, service-monitoring or managerial positions. This suggests that the educational materials which to date have formed the curriculum for qualifying courses intended for group care practitioners might have to be reviewed, because some of these courses have been built around an assumption that they were training personnel for direct care positions.

The implications of accepting this analysis are many. One of the consequences is that in-service training courses are forced into assuming major responsibility for teaching the basic knowledge and skills required by direct care personnel. It also means that both the Certificate of Qualification in Social Work courses and Certificate in Social Service schemes have to consider building on this basic training and casting their contribution to take firm account of future work patterns of course participants. Courses and schemes have to illuminate further already acquired knowledge and skills, develop abilities in programme planning, supervision and service monitoring, as well as lay the foundation for future managerial studies.

The view that practice at a direct care level in group care services is likely to remain the preserve of unqualified or partially trained personnel, except in a few highly specialised programmes, may be unpopular. If accepted, it does, however, open up opportunities for thinking about new ways of responding to the training needs of the vast number of personnel employed in these posts. At a later stage in this paper a proposal for a new nationally validated group care qualification for direct care personnel will be made as a contribution to this new thinking.

Work Strata and Levels of Training

Using the different types of positions and levels of work referred to in this paper it is possible to construct a more precise yet still rudimentary model of three different levels of training for group care personnel. This model is derived from the work of Rowbottom and Billis[14] in personal social serivce organisations and refers to the work categorised by them as "prescribed output", "situational response" and "systematic service provision". This represents the first three levels of a five-stage conceptualisation of work stratification in an organisation. The work of direct care personnel is seen as level one; programme planning, service monitoring and supervisory work as level two; and the managerial function is equated with level-three activity. No attempt should, of course, be made to apply this model rigidly to a particular group care programme. Rowbottom and Billis make this point themselves in introducing the concepts of "zooming" and "transitional phase" which are designed to take account of both overlap in work levels and differential capacity amongst personnel in each work stratum. Used intelligently the model does, however, allow for greater clarity to emerge in regard to the training needs of group care personnel than might otherwise be the case. A general appreciation of the knowledge base required by group care personnel at each level and the associated practice skills can, in fact, be extrapolated from the model, provided some imaginative thinking takes place. The remainder of this section of this paper is an attempt to undertake the beginning steps necessary in linking work levels in group care services to patterns of training.

Clearly, all who work in group care situations at all levels require a general appreciation of this service context and its place in an overall spectrum of personal social services provision. This has to include:

—knowledge of the range of group care provision, including the historical development and current legislative position as it affects usage, and how this provision is placed within the overall spectrum of personal social services;
—understanding of the functioning of group care programmes including various models/patterns of provision and how these relate to achievement of unit objectives;
—appreciation of the processes associated with the cycle of events which is experienced by clients who enter, live, learn in, and leave group care programmes.

It is necessary for direct care personnel occupying the positions of care assistants, house parents, child care workers and those with similar titles to have at least some understanding of the following matters as they affect the client population of a programme:

—awareness of the continuum of human development and possible explanations for behavioral difficulties as manifested at each life-stage;
—familiarity with the range of approaches used by group care practitioners, especially the utilisation of daily living events, in work with both individuals and groups;

and for them to possess:

—a basic technical competence in providing individual and group interventions which aim to ensure that within a group care context essential nurturing and socialisation functions are achieved.

Obviously the significance of all this material has to be reinforced by personal experience. Great importance in any training course has therefore to be placed on linkage mechanisms whereby theoretical teaching and actual practice are married into a cohesive entity. Only when this has been achieved are further studies called for. These further studies need to reflect career prospects and the change in level of work which is entailed in moving from a direct care position to a programme-planning, supervisory or service-monitoring position. Those personnel who progress in this way then require more sophisticated teaching about the material already listed, but that is not the first or only need. A change in work focus from that of a direct care giver to that of planner, supervisor or monitor is substantial and calls for additional knowledge and skills. These posts generally titled team leader, senior, deputy or assistant officer-in-charge demand that the occupant has:

—an understanding of the various theoretical perspectives which can be used to under-pin group care programmes and the relative effectiveness of different approaches with differing client populations;

—knowledge of the principles of staff supervision and service monitoring, especially those which can be shown to be of use in group care situations;

—an appreciation of studies from a variety of disciplines outside the personal social services field which may contribute to group care programme design, planning and implementation.

This knowledge has then to be translated into practical skills which result in:

—an ability to devise and implement individual client care and treatment plans which take account of overall group needs within a total programme context;

—competence in monitoring, supervising and directing the work of direct care personnel, including appropriate methods of staff selection, training and assessment of job performance;

—a capacity to contribute to policy formulation for a total group care programme and devise procedures for internal use that accurately reflect overall policy and programme objectives.

Once this stage has been achieved, further steps in any career progression are likely to result in staff moving into third-level service management positions. Heads, principals, wardens, officer-in-charge posts are all third-tier positions and those who are promoted to this level deserve further training. This training has to be designed to fit onto the knowledge base that has been established by earlier studies. An essential characteristic of all these posts is that whilst they embody overall responsibility for programme development and the direction of a specific group care service, they also commit the holders to a great deal of work outside the actual programme in the larger personal social services structure and with even broader community interests. It is again possible to identify new areas of knowledge and skills which occupants of these management positions need. These include:

—a refined knowledge of the legislative framework which surrounds the client population serviced by the group care programme. This also includes legislation which relates to employment practices, health and safety regulations, trade union rights, malpractice law and similar complex issues;

—understanding of funding mechanisms and budgetry and financial control systems;

—appreciation of the structure and function of the allied care and treatment systems of health, education and penal provision with which the personal social services are actively engaged;

—awareness of new theoretical formulations and potential service innovations which reflect contemporary thinking and the possible direction of service developments.

This knowledge has then to be translated into skills in:

—working and negotiating with other organisations and allied systems outside the boundaries of the personal social services, services which are, however, used by clients from group care programmes;

—supervising the development of programme budgets and service costing techniques as a basis for acquiring financial resources, with submission writing and the assembly of supporting data and argument being an integral part of this process;

—promoting a positive programme image, especially with the local community, and activating media support when necessary;

—ensuring that staff recruitment and training at all levels are maintained and that matters of personnel management are undertaken in such a manner as to ensure that the group care programme maintains credibility.

It has, of course, to be said that training for management personnel from group care programmes might also be appropriate for a wide range of individuals occupying comparable positions outside this particular field. This may extend to other positions within the personal social services as well as beyond that system to the broad area of human services.

Personnel in level-three posts generally have limited contact with the actual client population in a programme. This is simply because their responsibilities take them away from the interaction between client snd direct care worker. Many of the achievements of management personnel have therefore to be gained by way of work through intermediaries. Characteristically, managers in all fields are concerned with ensuring the relevance of programme design in the light of contemporary thinking, acquisition of resources both of money and manpower, and the balancing of client and community interests. This is a highly skilled area of work and is vulnerable to gross distortion if earlier stages in training have not received adequate attention. The danger then is of abstract management techniques being applied without any real appreciation of their implication for clients in group care programmes. Management techniques invariably require careful blending and adaptation for use in that practice arena.

Direct Care Workers—a New Initiative

From the limited evidence presented earlier, which shows that the growth in the number of qualified group care personnel remains small, it can be concluded that for the foreseeable future the pattern of recruitment by which most direct care posts are filled with unqualified or partially trained personnel is likely to continue. If this is the case then an argument exists for considering a new approach to the training of direct care workers. This would be by way of courses specifically aimed at those who are engaged in tasks at this level. The material identified as required by level-one personnel both in terms of knowledge and skills would provide a framework for a training effort of this kind.

Even though some authorities within the personal social services are making major use of in-service courses, these efforts at present have substantial limitations. This is because attendance at in-service courses does not lead to the award of any recognised qualification. In consequence, attendance at these courses offers few career benefits to participants. Nor do internally promoted in-service courses have any standing with the external community and so they fail to enhance the image of group care services. This worthy effort also fails to add to the reservoir of nationally available qualified group care personnel. It can only be viewed as unfortunate that this should be the case at a time when the numbers of personnel who are qualifying as group care practitioners and acquiring nationally recognised qualifications presents such a gloomy picture.

The time to rethink radically the whole training strategy for the group care services may therefore have arrived. A new approach might be to accept that the existing qualifications in the personal social services (namely the Certificate in Social Service, and Certificate of Qualification in Social Work) are the relevant studies for those persons who intend to progress to second- and third-tier, planning, monitoring, supervision and management positions. This acceptance would then allow these courses to concentrate their efforts on developing teaching of the materials associated with level-two work with added provision for complementary skill development. The training requirements at the third level, namely those for senior management could be responded to by the creation of post-qualification study opportunities. These might be similar to those already available, possibly on too limited a basis, in the approved programmes of the Central Council for Education and Training in Social Work. In effect this would simply acknowledge what must surely be apparent to many observers of the group care field: namely that many direct care personnel now employed in group care programmes will not proceed to qualifying training for a variety of reasons such as educational attainment, age, geographic immobility and personal preference. It would also acknowledge that those direct care personnel who do undertake qualifying training are almost certain to be employed at an early stage in positions of a programme-planning, supervisory, service-monitoring kind, with this occurring almost immediately following qualification or in some instances because of personal potential prior to such a period of study.

By removing the assumption that most direct care personnel will progress to existing qualifying programmes, this approach opens up new potentials for untrained group care personnel. In fact it is arguable that the assumption that many of the untrained group would proceed to qualifying training might have limited in-service training commitments to them by some employing authorities. It is worth considering an alternative to the present simple forms of in-service training provided by authorities in an uncoordinated manner, and which also draws heavily on their resources. This might entail training departments in social services mounting upgraded studies jointly with a central validating body. Attendance and completion of studies in such a course of in-service training might then lead to a nationally accepted and transferable award. Within other human services organisations examples of this type of approach can be found. An illustration is to be found in nurse training within the health care sector where schools of nursing form the basis for producing a regulated supply of nursing personnel. These schools are integral parts of area hospital organisations whilst promoting nationally validated nurse training. This training has to conform to a centrally agreed curriculum with students being prepared for nationally promoted examinations. The result of this pattern of training is that nurse training is undertaken within a single service organisation and is in the hands of an employing body, although the existence of a central curriculum and national examining boards ensures maintenance of standards and wide acceptance of certification when achieved.

It is not difficult to imagine ways in which the present training sections of social services departments might constitute themselves in a similar manner, as schools of social service. It is equally possible to envisage ways in which a national body concerned with the personal social services might devise with employers an agreed curriculum for studies relevant to the group care field. Such a body might also constitute an examining board and guarantee the maintenance of national standards for any award.

This type of development might, of course, be seen by some as regressive, thought to diminish the importance of the group care field and encourage the re-emergence of specialist qualifications. This does not have to be the case, especially if such a development were not focussed on a single area of service. It is, for example, easy to see how a new group care award might provide a training for a large number of direct care workers. It might have appeal to residential, day care and some neighbourhood-based community work personnel. Such an award, available to all who are selected to work in group care services, might also be the first step towards the emergence of a more fully qualified group care service. The acceptance of a new low level point of entry training might lead in the end to the diminished employment in direct care positions of personnel with no training at all. Certainly, existing training provision is unlikely ever to achieve that end. The suggested new approach might therefore be developmental in impact. As always it would be used by some individuals as the first step in the incremented progression to full qualifying studies, and career advancement.

Service Trends and the Training Challenge

The newly established trend towards the greater allocation of personal social service resources away from 24-hour group care programmes and in favour of community-based services is, as far as can be seen, likely to continue. The emergence, however, of a balanced distribution of resources to all service areas, which emphasises their interdependence and linked importance, shows as yet few signs of being achieved. Any attempt to reduce the number of 24-hour group care programmes and replace these with community alternatives is, of course, to be encouraged. Paradoxically, this will not reduce the demand for trained group care personnel. This is because a reduction in the number of 24-hour care programmes will mean that the complexity of work in those that remain will increase. Other group care programmes designed as community alternatives but providing more limited daily time periods of care and treatment are also likely to be seen as suitable practice venues for group care personnel. These new programmes will in turn both draw off personnel from 24-hour programmes and create an additional demand for trained practitioners.

For example, the growth in the child care field of work on teaching parenting skills suggests an additional area of involvement for group care personnel. This emphasises, coincidentally, the nature of 24-hour group care programmes not as substitute care venues for children but as family support services. Group care practitioners involved with both retarded children and adults are also likely to be called on to offer advice and technical assistance to families who care for the retarded in family-life contexts. For the elderly a similar trend is likely to become visible with group care personnel being used to assist families and elderly individuals themselves to appreciate changing patterns of human functioning. Group care personnel can advise on the comfort and constraints of life in multi-generational family situations, with this understanding being derived from their own practice.

Finally, any diminished use of 24-hour group care services means that those programmes which remain would emerge as ideal locations for advanced research and experiments in practice. Much like teaching hospitals within the health care system, 24-hour group care programmes within the personal social services have the potential to become centres of teaching and advanced practice. Developed in this manner as special resource centres staffed by the most highly competent of practitioners, 24-hour group care programmes would become places in which new knowledge could be developed.

For the social work and social service training courses such developments in group care services would offer a major challenge. This challenge arises from many factors including the wide range of materials in the specialist fields of health care, education, penal provision and social work which have to be drawn on in assembling a valid training experience for group care personnel. Current forms of social work training which reflect the needs of field practitioners certainly seem unlikely unless modified substantially to meet this challenge. By contrast, the less well-established training provision which now leads to a social service qualification, because of the way it is jointly organised and managed may more easily respond to the training needs of group care personnel. In either case, the content of social work and social service courses, the emphasis given to teaching materials, the distribution of time to academic subjects and actual practice, the style of work supervision and the mode of examination all have to be re-examined when the training needs of group care personnel are considered.

For the social work and social services training system which responds to the needs of group care personnel the challenge is therefore enormous. It parallels and exceeds all previous challenges. This challenge has grown from the concern felt about the poor quality of much group care practice, and the consequence of this concern is that the training which is aimed at group care personnel needs to show how it will enhance the quality of practice. Social work and social service training as it refers to group care therefore warrants critical examination. The hope is that through this examination changes will occur and the challenge will be met.

References

1. See CCETSW, *Abstracts*, 1977; DHSS, *Personal Social Service Statistics*, 1976; D. ELLIOTT and R. WALTON, Attitudes to residential training, *Social Work Today*, 13 Feb. 1978.
2. For example, CCETSW Paper No. 3, *Social Work: Residential Work is Part of Social Work*, 1973. Back numbers of *Social Work Today*, or *Community Care* also provide evidence of RCA, BASW and ADSS views.
3. The Warnock Committee report (*Report of the Committee of Enquiry into the Education of Handicapped Children and Young People*, HMSO, 1978), provides evidence of this in regard to the educational services, whilst the activities of the National Association for the Care and Rehabilitation of Offenders illustrates the point in regard to penal provision. The Jay Committee report (*Report of the Committee of Inquiry into Mental Handicap Nursing and Care*, HMSO, 1979) offers a similar comparison for health care in respect of group care services for the mentally handicapped.
4. A summary of these studies is to be found in MAYER, RICHMAN and BALCERAK, *Group Care of Children*, Child Welfare League of America, 1978.
5. M. WOLINS, *Successful Group Care*, Aldine, 1974.
6. K. JONES, *New Thinking about Institutional Care*, Association of Social Workers, 1967.
7. Social Work (Scotland) Act 1968, Local Authorities Social Services Act, 1970.
8. F. AINSWORTH, *Teaching about Residential Services and Residential Practice on CQSW Courses*, CCETSW Discussion Paper, July, 1978.
9. *Social Work: Residential Work is Part of Social Work*, op. cit.
10. See, for example, the works of PINCUS and MINAHAN, *Social Work Practice, Model and Methods*, Peacock, 1974; GOLDSTEIN, *A Unitary Approach to Social Work Practice*, University of South Carolina Press, 1974.

11. AINSWORTH, *op. cit.*
12. ELLIOTT and WALTON, *op. cit.*
13. *D.H.S.S. Personal Social Service Statistics for England, 1976.* Similar statistics are available for Wales and Scotland.
14. ROWBOTTOM and BILLIS, Stratification of work and organisational design, *Human Relations,* **30** (1), 1977.

CHAPTER 25

IN-SERVICE TRAINING FOR RESIDENTIAL WORK

JOHN PHILLIPS and YVONNE DAVIES

Much is said and written about the value of training in social service agencies, but Training Officers attempting to carry out their role frequently find that their function is seen as peripheral to the main task of the organisation. Training is all too frequently viewed as little more than a pleasant interlude for staff where they can be given a break from the day-to-day pressures of work in a Social Services Department. This is often reflected in the way that training is separated organisationally from the rest of the structure of the agency. One wonders how it would be viewed if social service agencies were commercial organisations whose standard of service was to be more directly reflected in customer demand. Instead, our customers or clients have little choice in coming to our departments as each holds virtually a monopoly position in its local area. As training can show no immediate return to the organisation in the form of improved commercial prospects, its place on the priority list of activities is lowered. Indeed, social service agencies sometimes consider whether they need to train at all.

In this situation historically, residential staff have come off very badly. They have had notably less professional training, less in-service training, less opportunities to go on short external courses, and less planned induction than field staff, yet their day-to-day working situation is vulnerable and exposed. Their clients are totally dependent upon them for the whole quality and, indeed, the very existence of their lives. The quality of our services depends upon the quality of the staff who provide them, and the quality of the staff depends on three things—recruitment, motivation and training. These three things are themselves inextricably linked and the main variable open to agencies concerned about standards of service is training. Training might not offer a social service agency a quick economic return, but without it the whole *"raison d'être"* of an agency comes into question. If we are not concerned about providing a good service, is there any point in providing a service at all?

The reality of the situation, however, forces us to consider training by asking basic questions. We propose to consider why, who does it, and to whom, how, where, and when should training be carried out. We shall attempt to broaden the way in which the activity "training" is viewed so that it may be seen as not a peripheral activity, but rather a process which is central to management itself. We do not consider that training is something which only happens to residential staff on professional or ISS courses, or when the Training Officer is called in to provide some expertise, but rather it should be seen as part of the social-dynamic processes of the agency, an essential part of our provision of service.

First, why should we train residential staff? The task of the residential social worker today is increasingly complex and demanding. Residential social workers themselves frequently undervalue their role, but the responsibilities that are implicit in a task which directly affects the quality of life of individuals have to be acknowledged and staff themselves need to be made aware of their contribution. The basic purpose of training for residential staff is the same as the purpose of training for any group of staff—the acquisition of knowledge, skills and attitudes appropriate to the job to be done. However, for residential workers who frequently encounter situations which exhaust them physically and emotionally, the provision of in-service training programmes can further be seen as an important way in which the employers show that they recognise the demands made on staff. There is a need for residential staff to be encouraged by being given opportunities for learning and to explore with colleagues some of the dilemmas and problem situations which they encounter. Training situations can often provide a fairly detached neutral vehicle for such sessions where both evaluation of practice and confirmation of good care can occur. The physical care given in our establishments is frequently discounted as routine until staff have the opportunity to step back and examine closely the significance of what is being done.

Training, therefore, must first give staff the basic personal equipment for their job and will later refresh and update knowledge and practical skills. It provides staff with opportunities for improving job satisfaction because of greater understanding and it opens up new possibilities of career enhancement. For the agency it provides opportunities to communicate expected standards of good practice and an understanding of agency function. By the recognition of each staff member's potential, it is possible to improve motivation and to lay foundations for further professional training and development. Through this process the standard of care to the residents can be supported and improved. More fundamentally, the very process of demonstrating to staff that they themselves are cared about creates a caring environment in which they, in turn, are better able to provide the care that their residents need, which is the very purpose of residential care.

Who is this training for? The ultimate answer must be—for the residents, both present and potential. All training and, indeed, all activity in a residential establishment can be seen and perhaps measured in terms of how much it does for those that the establishment is intended to serve—the residents, their families and the community. It would be unrealistic, however, to suppose that all training is undertaken with effective service to residents in mind. Departments are concerned to impose their systems, standards and authority on establishments, and training provides them with an important vehicle for doing this. Staff are concerned about their income potential, job satisfaction and career prospects, and seek training as a means of improving these. Furthermore, "training" is part of the transaction between employers and their staff. It is often used as a reward, as a means of expressing concern about an individual or a situation, and can sometimes even be used as a means of temporarily removing an individual from a particular work situation. It is most importantly a point of common interest between management and staff within which both can express the positive aspect of the service they are providing. It can, therefore, be used as a means of healing when relationships between management and staff become fraught. All of these other motivations ultimately have an effect on service, but they are often more directly the reasons why training is engaged in, and as such they have a validity of their own.

Who, then, of all the people who make up a particular residential establishment is training directed at? There are the management and care staff, catering and domestic staff, the inevitable handyman, possibly administrative staff, the advisers, the other agency staff and people from other departments who have contact with the home, the volunteers, the relatives and the residents themselves. In one way or another all those can be seen as being helped by training. There is, however, some danger in extending the use of the word "training" to the point where it ceases to have meaning in relation to a specific kind of activity. Nevertheless, there will be elements of training needed for all these groups, though the training may be carried out in the context of liaison work, public relations, casework, groupwork or simple management.

What needs to be understood is that training is not something which is exclusive to care and management staff, but is instead something which can be relevant to all who are part of the establishment. Failure to understand this can result in training aims not being met because not all the individual needs have been perceived. The method, setting and timing of providing training may, indeed, vary amongst the different groups, but any group which is neglected in the process may exercise its power within the establishment to frustrate the objectives. This can easily be understood by an individual, even a Head of a Home, who has returned from a course full of good new ideas and has tried to introduce them into an establishment. What is perhaps less easy to accept is how the failure to involve one group, say the domestics or the residents themselves, can lead to the situation where training is frustrated. The social processes which go on in a home, however, involve them as much as any other people, and new staff and residents will often learn the attitudes and expectations from just these people. If by training in any establishment, therefore, we are seeking to improve working practices, change attitudes or functions, or simply improve the health and safety record, all can be undermined if we are not aware of the total establishment. The answer to the question, "who is training for?" must be that it is for all.

The other question is who does the training? Again, the answer is more complex than it might at first appear. Training is often seen as something which is organised by Training Officers as separate to the day-to-day life of a home. Training is understood as going on when people are taken away from their work and sat down in a classroom situation to be talked at by "experts". Much training does, indeed, have to go on away from the work situation, though a good Training Officer will recognise that it is the staff who are themselves the experts, and will plan his programme around the use of this expertise, developing knowledge or skill by the interchange of ideas of people working in a common field, and providing the opportunities for self-reflection which can in themselves often be the most valuable of all learning opportunities. Training in this situation may be organised by the Training Officer in consultation with other management staff, but the teaching and learning will be a process which involves all—the outside speakers, the training and management staff, and the course members.

However, this type of training, valuable though it is, is but a small part of the total training process. Training is part of the process of management by which anyone who delegates a task to someone else tries to ensure that that person has the knowledge, skills and attitudes necessary to carry out the task. Most training is, in fact, carried out in the work situation by the Manager himself or by someone to whom he gives the task. A new member of staff will learn from all the people with whom he comes into contact and the

Manager will be aware of those he wants to strongly influence and those whose influence he wishes to minimise. In a residential setting, a new member of staff will arrive with some knowledge already gained as a member of the community and to some extent developed at interview. She will need to be told the task, shown the physical environment and the working relationships and introduced to the people who make up the home. She is likely to be allocated to an experienced member of staff so that she can be given further knowledge, including an introduction to the informal expectation and channels of communication that exist in all working situations. She will meet residents who, in their turn, will be anxious to meet her to express their own wishes and needs, and she will talk to other staff members, to union representatives and to anyone else who happens to be heavily involved. This is partly the process of integrating a new member into the group, but it is also the most permanent training—for good or ill—that the new staff member is likely to receive. It will quickly be seen that any of the people involved in the home will participate in this "training" and, indeed, some will be very conscious that this is what they are about when they are doing it.

Responsibility for training after this remains with the management, both of the home and of the agency at large. For staff who regard themselves as "professional", however, there is also a responsibility resting on the individual to develop skills and knowledge appropriate to the task. The question of who does it at this stage, therefore, becomes complex. The individual will play an increasing role in developing his own knowledge. The Line Manager or Officer-in-Charge will probably play a diminishing role, though planned work allocation can be a most important developmental tool. The advisers who visit the home have a formal developmental role which links in with the Training Officer's role. A continuing development can often be seen, however, through the informal links that other agency staff bring to the home. Visiting social workers or the local General Practitioners, for instance, can be expected to be developing the profes- sional knowledge of staff in a home. The process of training is ongoing in a dynamic situation and the individual will learn sometimes in a planned way that has been thought out in advance, and sometimes in an unplanned informal manner, usually described as experience. What needs to be better understood is that training is a vital part of the ongoing work situation and not a detached activity which only takes place somewhere else. The "who is involved", therefore, comes down to everybody in the residential situation, including the individual himself.

The "where" and "when" questions have already been, in part, answered. The new staff member will learn most in his early days and weeks in his new work situation. It is the training task of the Manager to be aware of this situation and planning for it. At present, in residential care, the process of induction and orientation to work is carried out in a largely unplanned fashion. This does not mean that it does not happen, but rather that important learning opportunities which occur at this time are not necessarily being used to their best advantage. Typically, new care and domestic staff are taken on on a casual basis to begin with and this reduces the motivation of management to provide them with a systemised induction process. Yet very many of these casual staff will become permanent members of staff when the opportunity arises, and, even if they do not, their memories of how they were treated when they worked in what is usually their local home will have a considerable influence on community attitudes towards it in the future. It is important, therefore, to be aware of the training needs of all incoming staff and, by planning the process, to ensure that the vital influences which are brought to bear at this time are appropriate to the needs of the home and the agency.

After the induction period, which all staff need, the when and the where of their training becomes more diverse. There are training needs which apply to the whole establishment such as might arise if the home were changing its role or, more simply, the needs of health and safety training. These clearly need to be met as close to the work situation as possible. Alternatively, there are the specialised needs of the Officer-in-Charge, the Deputy, or perhaps the administrative staff, which might involve the creation of a situation where staff from a number of homes meet. There are situations between these where it may be appropriate to send a small group of staff together on a visit of observation, or where particular staff may be sent on developmental courses away from the establishment.

There is a problem, however. The closer training is organised to the work situation, the greater is its relevance likely to be to that situation. This is not an absolute theoretical law, and there can be on-the-job training which is a waste of time or even has negative results and, alternatively, staff can benefit greatly from courses which are external to the agency itself. Nevertheless, it remains a common observation that staff are most likely to absorb the contents of a training programme if they see it as having an immediate relevance to their work, and they are more likely to do this if they closely identify it with their work situation.

However, the need to provide residential staff with support through the opportunity for reflection can best be met away from the working situation. Indeed, training designed to achieve this must often involve different kinds of staff meeting together with the important secondary aim of helping them improve their understanding of one another and thereby improving their working communications. To achieve this, staff need to have had reasonable time and training to develop their understanding of their own role and often to be provided with a situation where there is an opportunity not only to discuss work but to relax and socialise as well.

Staff who go away from this work situation are much more likely to feed back to Training Officers about how much they have enjoyed the experience. Training Officers need, however, to remember when assessing the evaluation that this is a seductive answer if the purpose of training was more directly linked to developing practical knowledge and skills. The "where" of training thus needs a very clear understanding of the purpose it is intended to serve.

The "when", after the early period, depends on the development of the individual, the relevance to him of particular training courses, the developing role of the establishment he works in and the needs manifested there. Perhaps, above all, it depends on management and training staff being sufficiently aware to use opportunities which are relevant to the individual staff member, to groups or the whole staff, as they arise. In particular, when we consider the "when" of training, the relevance of thoughtful work allocation as a training tool becomes apparent. Learning opportunities very frequently occur in residential situations, but to take advantage of them management staff must be aware of the training needs and stage of development of individual staff members. Indeed, one would argue that the most important obstacle to more effective staff development in residential work is a lack of awareness amongst many of the management staff of our homes that they have both the basic responsibility for training their staff and the greatest opportunity for meeting it in the ongoing work situation. The "when" is largely a matter of planning work so that it includes the process of meeting training needs.

"How do we train?" The authors would suggest the following methods:

Information-giving sessions

These tend by definition to be mainly factual, and they need to be relevant and accompanied by handouts and/or guided reading for the most enthusiastic. This kind of session is difficult to accomplish effectively as residential care staff are often unused to the passive sitting and listening role which is required. The trainer, therefore, needs to have a stimulating style or the message will be lost in an indigestible mass of detail.

Practical sessions

Practical demonstration sessions are essential to most in-service training programmes —particularly when covering such areas as first aid, lifting techniques, health and safety and fire regulations. Maximum group and individual participation is necessary— observation is not sufficient for real learning to take place in these sessions.

Sitting by Nellie

"*Sitting by Nellie*"—asking an experienced staff member to take responsibility for showing a new member of staff the job she is supposed to do. The success of this method is dependent on the quality of "Nellie", her personality and ability to teach, and the way in which this type of training is monitored, guided and supported from above.

Topic or case-centred discussion groups

These groups can function with or without a leader and can often be a very productive method of training. Through the vehicle of the group, staff can examine their own practice in relation to theories and exchange ideas; these sessions can be both challenging and stimulating.

Trainers should be aware that such groups may need some focussing and monitoring if the time spent in them is to be effectively used. The leader will require a clear brief, and in his role as facilitator and enabler can make the sessions a valuable experience, particularly for those staff whose views have not been sought before and who find through the group that their contributions are valid. The spontaneous discussions which occur over coffee and lunch breaks can often be productive learning experiences for the staff involved if Officers-in-Charge and other senior management staff are able to use these informal discussions productively.

Films

Films are frequently found on in-service training programmes and are sometimes used as a gap-filler. The useful film material that is available requires careful selection and timing. Suggesting that staff focus their observations on the film on particular areas can be productive for the discussion that follows.

Visits of observation

Careful selection and timing of visits are required if the experience is to be useful. Visits can provide staff with a broader knowledge of the total agency and where their own establishment fits within the services that are provided. Staff given the opportunity to compare and contrast establishments similar to their own can be stimulated to question and evaluate their own work situation.

Group exercises

This method comprises discussion groups with a set task or problem-solving exercise of some kind. Here there is a clear purpose to the discussion with usually some expectation that the group will provide a feedback of their findings. This method can often provide the group with a useful experience of teamwork—its benefits and disadvantages.

Experiential exercises

This method can include role play, structured experiences and games, and can involve groups of varying sizes with a heavy emphasis on individual participation. This is an excellent method for making training come "alive". It can effect a considerable impact on those taking part. Careful selection and timing is essential when experiential exercises are used. Skilled leadership of such sessions is imperative and the trainer should clearly spell out the objectives to all concerned. Experiential exercises can be very threatening and uncomfortable for some staff, and the trainer should be aware of his responsibility towards staff when running these sessions and, wherever possible, provide the opportunity for a de-briefing period afterwards when feelings can be discussed and learning points clarified.

Personal learning projects

The use of projects can provide staff with a valuable opportunity for examining in depth a particular area of practice which interests or concerns them. Careful briefing is required and some time should be set aside during the course programme for monitoring progress. The involvement and co-operation of Officers-in-Charge when projects are being undertaken can be very fruitful. Projects can be seen as a threatening task for some staff, but the final sharing of their findings can be a most stimulating and supportive method of examining the task, and a vehicle through which the valuable contribution made by individual staff can be clearly seen.

Finally, when reflecting on the "how" of in-service training, one is left with the feeling that perhaps one of the most important things for trainers is that they constantly assess and re-evaluate their methods so that the training provided "moves" and keeps pace with the demands of the service concerned.

To reiterate, we see training as a fundamental part of the process of work. For various reasons it has not been given sufficient attention in the setting of residential care. However, if the services provided through residential care are to be better adapted to meet the needs of the residents, we must increase the attention paid to the training needs of our staff. Considerable attention is paid to the planning of the building which forms the shell within which a home is built, but relatively little attention is so often given to the human resources of the staff who will convert that shell into a living organisation, how and where they will be recruited, how their tasks will relate to each other and to the needs of the residents, and how the people that we employ will be equipped to carry out these tasks and to go on living in this environment. We have asked the questions why, who, where, when and how should we train. The real question is still, all too often, why not train?

Further Reading

ABERCROMBIE, M. L. J., *Aims and Techniques of Group Teaching*, Society for Research into Higher Education, 1970.

BLIGH, D., *What's the Use of Lectures?* Penguin, 1971.

CCETSW, *A New Form of Training: the Certificate in Social Service*, 1973, Paper 9.

COPPEN, H., *Aids To Learning and Teaching*, Pergamon, 1974.

PFEIFFER, J. and JONES, J. (eds.), *A Handbook of Structured Experiences for Human Relations Training*, Vols. 1–6, University Associates, 1974.

SHARAN and SHARAN, *Small Group Teaching*, Educational Technology Publications, Englewood Cliffs, N. J., 1976.

TAYLOR, J. and WALFORD, R., *Simulation In The Classroom*, Penguin, 1972 (reprinted 1978 as *Learning and the Simulation Game*).

WITTLICH, W. A. and SCHULLER, C. F., *Instructional Technology, its Nature and Use*, Harper & Row, 1973.

CHAPTER 26

A STUDENT UNIT FOR
RESIDENTIAL PLACEMENTS

SHEILA J. LAMBDEN

Beginnings

Student Units have been in operation for 49 years and have increased greatly in number in response to the expansion of qualifying courses. The early Units were based in teaching hospitals where learning through practice is normal procedure. Since those early days Units have been formed in Local Authority Children's Departments, the Probation Service, Voluntary Agencies and the new Social Services.

A current issue of debate in social work training centres around the value of practice placements. Many difficulties are encountered in attempting to provide an effective learning experience in the practice setting which will complement that which is taught in college. The Student Unit model—well tried in a variety of settings—has proved a worthwhile venture in this field. The idea of developing a residential model in Coventry Social Services was based upon this premiss. It offered the advantage of full-time tutorial support for students plus the added advantage of providing an ongoing developing programme for the permanent staff.

In her special Social Work Research Study on Student Units in Social Education, Kathleen Curnock quotes Brown and Gloyne's description, which is as follows:

(1) The appointment to the agency of a person with special responsibility for student training, and a particular responsibility to ensure that supervision and teaching be provided for groups of students on practical placements in that agency.

(2) Most of the students should be on professional social work courses (or at least there should be sufficient numbers from these courses to form a group, that is three or more).

(3) There should normally be agreement between the Unit and agency and a course that placements for students will be available for required periods of practical training.

This general description still holds good. At a later point in her study Kathleen Curnock adds: "Not surprisingly, Student Units have seemed, to both courses and agencies, a means of making best use of the scarce supply of fieldwork teachers and of minimising demands on other staff who might otherwise be asked to take some responsibility for students over and above their other duties."

The particular advantages envisaged for a residential unit were felt to be:

(1) Students could have a full-time supervisor to monitor their work and progress and relate practice to theory.

(2) The provision of a student group to test out sundry "on-the-spot" ideas and theories.

(3) The provision of some relief from the immediate pressures of residential life.

All these opportunities seem valid for students requiring a specialised residential placement. It was immaterial whether the duration was of 6 weeks experience, or a lengthier assessable period of time, representing one of the chief practical experiences required at the college.

The need for more supervision in residential practice has been paramount for a long time. Several residential practitioners had been urged to take courses in supervising students. Ideas flowed freely on what one taught and how one planned the teaching within a residential home. But there were insufficient supervisors available. Thus, when one of the existing Student Units in an area team lost its supervisor, the chance was taken to rethink the use of this Unit.

Training and management staff turned their attention to residential work. A prescribed method was needed to highlight the need to use residential daily life with all its entails to the full. Students needed to be far more aware of what happens to all parties involved. Such a wealth of experience could be partially missed or not wholly understood. Many valuable facets of residential life are there before a students' eyes to be witnessed, reflected on, tested out and used.

Unlike the majority of Student Units, where all the students are together, Coventry's Unit for Residential Placements is only near two residential establishments and thus the students are well scattered across the city. The base office forming the Student Unit's accommodation is a conference room large enough for a student group to gather. It is within a purpose-built four-unit bungalow for physically handicapped adults. These residents have been involved in the plan to establish a Unit from the beginning, as have the staff of the home. In their own way they all appreciate the need for students to learn on the spot, as do nurses and doctors, and can quite understand the practicalities of the idea. The office has literature and many duplicated handouts available and can be a quiet retreat for students in which to work and read if it is not in use.

Aims of the Unit

(1) To give a clear focus on good practice.

(2) To supervise growth of skill development.

(3) To explore social work subjects, methods and feelings.

We therefore hope to establish a structure:

(1) To help the student to learn and practise identified differing skills.

(2) To develop understanding of the philosophies of residential social work.

(3) To have individual tutorials linked to individual programmes.

(4) To participate in group seminars of students who are working with different client groups in residential care.

The Student Unit base radiates out to eight or nine different residential establishments at a time. Its supervisor has many roles.

(1) A bridge between college and the residential establishment. This role is that of link with the Tutor who requested the placement itself.

(2) A broker concerned with facilitating a required plan for the placement.

(3) An interpreter of the needs and opinions of everyone concerned.

(4) A mediator between all parties should the need arise.

(5) A teacher of theory or practical application requiring further exploration and explanation.

(6) A seminar leader when students gather together.

(7) An overall objective viewer of each planned arrangement.

(8) An assessor.

The Residential Setting

The Head of Home where the students are placed may be a Warden of a hostel; a Principal of a Community Home School with Education on the premises; or an Officer-in-Charge of a Children's Home or a Home for the Elderly or for the Handicapped. It is his decision to take a student and allocate one of the staff to supervise on a daily basis and possibly another staff member to work alongside the student. He may be the daily supervisor himself, depending on other staff to help hour by hour. Each home has a Residential Adviser who is responsible for all homes in a set geographical area. He or she has the final say in student placement according to the state of play within each home and whether it is timely for a student to arrive and work therein.

Good communication and understanding all round is essential for the Unit approach to work. It is all too easy for differences of opinion to mar the work of the student and negate the effectiveness of the practical experience. Some homes have students from so many courses that confusion can arise on what particular work and supervision needs have to be offered. All students need to capitalise on the material provided in placement, for example: human resources, staff, residents, activities, etc. The detail of how, when and where can vary with the objective of the placement and the focus of the student. The range of groups is wide.

Coventry has provision for physical and mental handicaps; children in distress or trouble; frail, elderly and physical handicap of all ages. There are many differing styles of organising establishments according to the building structure but also mainly subject to the individual style. Methods of care, values and imaginative ideas vary tremendously. The student has to face many sad groups of people and wonder how to communicate, how to help.

The impact of a home is tremendous and it is possible for a student's theory, so seemingly relevant in college, to fly out of the window and leave him feeling questioning, critical and yet inadequate. Any two homes can be totally different, but good, sensitive and positive care is needed in both. Confusion can reign and the student can feel sandwiched between college demands to understand the latest teaching and produce essays which demonstrate his understanding, and the home's demands for its occupants.

Let us now look at the setting up of an individual placement. Data is collected from each student in order to work out a satisfactory programme and contract for the duration of any placement. The course may have set a piece of written work. The student may be endeavouring to fill one of his knowledge and experience gaps. The two factors together colour the request from the Tutor to the Student Unit Supervisor. When such a request comes, the Student Unit Supervisor contacts the Residential Adviser who authorises the use of any specific home or centre. The Unit Supervisor contacts a promising home and

CONTRACT

Name =

C.Q.S.W. course =

Tutor =

Special focus = Assessment

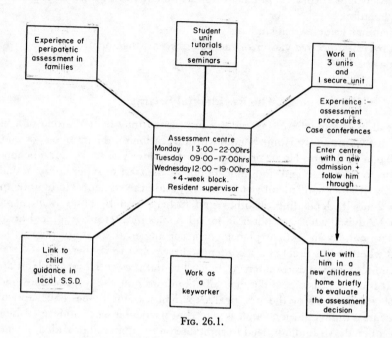

Fig. 26.1.

arranges to liaise with the Officer-in-Charge and any other staff likely to be involved in supervision and work arrangement. A plan is drawn up using the home as a base and looking out to other provisions of the agency which could be used as relevant experience. A plan could look diagrammatically like Fig. 26.1.

Thus we could have a structure as follows.

(1) A planned programme for each student in consultation with—Heads of Home; Daily Supervisor in the Home; Tutor; Student and Student Unit Supervisor. The programme should take into consideration:
    (a) The home's philosophy, aims and objectives.
    (b) Student's need and special focus.
    (c) CQSW course requirements, general and specific.
(2) Such a programme could become a package for the student with the Unit co-ordinating many aspects of the package. Each student would have a residential home and a base and from there radiate out to include visits of observation, and work with the local area office, local hospital or school, as appropriate.
(3) Planned tutorials with the Head of Home or nominated Supervisor or with the Student Unit Leader.
(4) Link with the college Tutor.
(5) Regular seminars to act as a forum for the residential social work teaching and a chance to air and share problems, skills, learning, distress, etc. There is obviously

here a great need for good liaison and understanding all round; a great need for good assessment; co-ordination and regular supervision formally and on an *ad hoc* basis.

Assessment usually follows each course's own special state of requirements. This could be followed by a Head of Home, either with the student and Tutor alone, or with the Student Unit Supervisor also, if requested. Supervision can be based from the start on these requirements stated by the college and supervisory sessions given as frequently as possible. Notes made at supervision sessions may be helpful in leading to the writing of the formal end-of-placement assessments. The Unit Supervisor need only be involved as a detached observer or a mediator if required, when disagreement occur. Increasingly, student self-assessment and participation in assessment is the order of the day now and such a joint exercise gained through the placement can be a joint advantage. The Student Unit Supervisor may be required to add her objective view of the placement with the additional comments on the student's performance in the seminar group.

The Seminar

There is value for people to gather where there is a common aim, interest or purpose. Students working within a practical experience enjoy such clustering to compare notes and share experiences. It is solace for the ones undergoing difficulties, and a stimulus for any who are anxious to learn more and test out ideas as they appear—bidden or un-bidden!

Operating from a detached academic background, students see many happenings which can puzzle, excite, pain and render them feeling sometimes effective and sometimes helpless. There is a wealth of material to air and share, and regular seminar gatherings give the opportunity to do this. Students come with a wide range of age and experience from varying universities and polytechnics. All participants are in specified residential settings and on a planned programme unique to each person. The hackneyed expression "theory to practice" here comes into its own. Yet there is more than a superficial look at such a concept because one has to have a base line of "What theory?". Which aspect are we all talking about? Has this said theory been covered yet on anyone's course or in anyone's reading or experience to date? Was it fully understood and can it be applied? What skills may be needed to apply this and who will guide, encourage and help as appropriate?

Logically there must follow "What is practice"? Each home will have its own philosophy and each individual works within the home according to this philosophy and his own integrity and professionalism.

Where staff communication is lively there should be a positive "climate" and way of working where students can "tune in" and use themselves as the tools of their trade. They may be able to test out ideas learned or evolved to benefit "clients" in group living. Given that there are a multiplicity of reasons for being in residential care and a multiplicity of homes as carers, then the topics for seminar discussion are endless. There is a tendency to see residents' needs as much "unmet" as "met" and the former given more talking time. Much that is basically good about people wishing to care for others in a loving, compassionate and sensitive way can easily be overlooked as we all wonder if our newly digested theories (mixed with our life-experience) can be put into operation!

The topics discussed will vary according to the needs of the students at the time. Obvious choices for those working with children range round "control", "discipline", "confrontation", "recognising the individual within the group". Concern for the childrens' checkered lives may lead to our discussing the tracing of their lives and piecing them together in a Life Story Book. A "Contract" made with a child, particularly a teenager, can be a helpful concept of caring but how does one do this? One can discern his needs to face the future from an unhappy, often deviant, past, but how can one help him modify his behaviour? Maybe the word "Contract" has thus far been used in the lecture room or on previous social work placements in connection with clients in a family. It can be helpful to discuss such use of an idea in a residential setting.

Words used in social work training can be explored as one faces "jargon" which is new and may not be the usual dictionary definition. General topics covering children, handicapped or elderly caring can use such words as "professionalism in residential social work"; "team work in homes"; "quality of life"—for those whose life-pattern has been broken and a new way substituted.

Some topics may be very practical others more academic. Some seminar groups alter their nature by the inclusion of residents or practitioners. Who better to tell us about physical handicap than two young ladies in wheel chairs who are willing to chat to the students and enjoy such a group "get-together"?

Who better to help with "theory to practice" than the practitioners themselves who can eloquently help us slot ideas into a home environment, and provide a realistic down-to-earth picture.

Ideas are never ending here. Different participants can help us by their willingness to join in a "forum" distanced from placement and the lecture room. Students can feel "safe" to explore ideas, ask questions and maybe try out role play to help understand the feeling elements in our work. Feelings are difficult to teach and to express. A quiet group, a good film, a sense of trust will all help.

So the seminar will alter each week both in topic and discussion and in "who is here". Its range can be tremendous and, hopefully, valuable. It should give strength to the student to return to look more closely at what is happening on placement. It could give confidence to try out, and inspiration to understand. It may help the feeling of isolation which residential work can and does convey.

Thoughts on this Venture

What are the implications from this experience for training in the residential sector? The Student Unit is less than a year old and the residential practitioners and the students themselves have helped enormously in thinking about its formation. I came to the Unit with a lengthy experience in residential work plus a college and polytechnic teaching of social work experience. These two much-enjoyed experiences are helping me to develop the Unit with the aforementioned help of those working within it.

I feel very strongly that students on courses need careful preparation for residential experience, both intellectually and emotionally. Some courses do not include much residential social work theory and thought. This negates any idea of the importance of such a provision of care and it can spin off onto the residents and residential staff in the placement. A positive informative approach towards the placement can only help all involved. The impact of the placement demonstrating an unusual way of life; a group often greatly handicapped all under one roof; a broken life-line; a questionable quality of life, etc. calls for much adjustment by the student and can daunt most of them. This situation calls for help and understanding and such thinking needs to be in-built into the course planning. A dual thoughtful approach to a placement by the college and the agency can enhance the experience offered by residential practitioners and not forgetting the residents themselves.

A mature student, leaving recently, gave me her views on the use of a Student Unit for residential placement. These were presented as facts felt by herself and echoed by others.

(1) The seminar was not just "nice to go to" but it gave an understanding of work outside the placement.

(2) It gave an understanding of the broadest scope of residential work; for example, children, mental handicap, physical handicap, the elderly. It afforded a chance to attend two or three in-service courses for Coventry staff run by the Unit Supervisor.

(3) It looked at issues away from a placement and gave the students a chance to feel they were away but also in touch.

(4) The contact with other students was more than helpful and gave a sense of "non-aloneness".

(5) The student role is a difficult one; a student is not a staff member despite the friendliness of the staff so can feel very alone. The Unit gave a chance for the student to test out with her "I think this was right" in a safe setting. It gave students a chance to clarify their own feelings and thoughts.

(6) The seminar was a forum to which one could bring feelings, hesitations and any thoughts or behaviour which could not be displayed in college through nervousness.

The seminar gave students strength to perform on their placement and a back-up to any situations occurring on the placement causing concern. Student Units for residential placements can help the student with any feelings which residential workers have on the insularity of their life.

We are still asking questions, such as can the Unit bridge the gap between college and placement, can it field the student when he feels overwhelmed and support him through his placement? He is, after all, the tool of his trade. Can it help him to recognise residential social work as a difficult job and residential life as a possible superb resource? Can it help him to link the variety of views shared in this job? Can the Unit support the student testing out his ideas, in looking at his skills, identifying them and using them? Residents in the home where the Unit is have been extremely intrigued by the students trooping in and out, talking to them and acting out in role-play many a scene which could happen in a residential setting. Some of these residents have joined in our seminars and made heart-rending contributions to our deliberations. The Unit will soon be a year old, and one must ask, is this a good method for social work practice? Can it be backed by polytechnics and universities and will it engender interest in residential social work practitioners? The more ideas which are injected and discussed the more the Unit will expand to meet the needs of students who welcome this particular way of appreciating the residential task placement.

The majority of students are primarily social workers and beyond this immediacy lies the need to identify the common ground on which all social work is based. In the final analysis the Unit justification must lie in the degree to which we are able to help our students link their experience positively to their college work. This facilitates the step yet to be taken of relating training to social work practice.

Further Reading

BROWNE and GLOYNE, *Field Training Of Social Workers*, Allen & Unwin.

CCETSW, Paper 3, *Residential Work is a Part of Social Work*, 1973.

CCETSW, Paper 10, Education and Training For Social Work, 1975.

CURNOCK, K., *Student Units in Social Work Education*, CCETSW, 1975.

DEACON, R. and BARTLEY, M., Becoming a Social Worker, in JONES, H. (ed.), *Towards a New Social Work*, Routledge & Kegan Paul, 1975, Chapter 5.

PEARSON, G., Making Social Workers: Bad Promises and Good Omens, in BAILEY and BRAKE (eds.), *Radical Social Work*, Arnold, 1975.

PETTES, D., *Supervision in Social Work*, Allen & Unwin.

Student Supervision in Residential Work with Children, Barnardo Social Work Papers, No. 1, 1977.

YOUNG, P., *The Student and Supervision in Social Work*, Routledge & Kegan Paul.

YOUNGHUSBAND, E., *Education for Social Work*, Allen & Unwin, NISW Series, 1968.

CHAPTER 27

A STUDENT PLACEMENT IN A
RESIDENTIAL SETTING

MARTIN PRICE

Like the courses that they attend, no two social work students' experiences are the same. Each student brings to a course his or her own perceived needs and attitudes to training. Social work courses are combinations of content, knowledge, personalities and also moral and political stances. What a student achieves on a course will depend, to a large extent, on the compatibility of his or her own expectations with the unique experience that the course has to offer, and also the ability and willingness of each party to change to meet each other's needs. Inevitably there is a lot of misunderstanding and disappointment. Working through problems of this nature can be a valuable educational experience. During the course the student is able to challenge ideas and structures, and in turn be challenged. Hopefully, by the end of the course he or she will have at least laid the foundations of a view of social work which is both consistent and integrated with his or her own personal feelings and outlook.

One vital area in social work courses are the placements. A poor placement, or one ill suited to a student's needs, will be of little value to the student and may induce strong negative feelings in the agency where the placement has taken place. Further, the time spent on placements is precious and it is vital that it is not wasted. Negative experiences can be valuable, though they are not always and are often detrimental.

Practical placements have two basic purposes. Firstly to introduce students to areas of work with which they will come into contact, though not necessarily be directly involved in. The hope is that in this way their understanding of these areas will be increased and the result will be an improved level of co-ordination and co-operation. In addition, there are skills common to all areas of social work, although different areas make greater use of some than others. For example, dealing with groups of children in a daily living situation is an essential and integral part of child care. The potential field social worker can develop such skills in a residential placement which would later be invaluable in an intermediate treatment or youth club setting.

The second function is to place students in the type of setting in which they are likely to work on leaving the course. This provides scope for teaching and assessment. Unless the student is on a residential care course, has a particular interest in entering residential work, or has an interest in a particular client group, for the majority of social work students the residential placement will be of the former type. The aim of this chapter is to discuss the problems in creating a professional placement in a residential setting.

The Residential Setting

The difficulties of setting up a residential placement do not only lie with meeting the students' needs. The establishment itself also has to make allowances and adjustments.

Any residential unit is in a constant state of flux. Residents and staff are continually maturing or regressing, each change altering the delicate balance of interaction within the group. New residents being admitted and others leaving will disrupt the life of the group. No establishment can expect a constant staff in the long term. The task of a unit may change, either due to internal re-assessment of needs or through change in policy which is imposed from outside. Maintaining continuity and a feeling of order and security is one of the basic tasks for any residential establishment. It is also one of the most difficult because the forces working against such a goal are often beyond the control of those involved. So why add a student to such a situation? Surely his or her presence can only disrupt the group life even further. Firstly, the student has to integrate with the group. Whether as an observer, participant, or in a professional role the student will inevitably cause a degree of disruption. When the placement has come to its end the same student must make an unnatural break. Staff and residents may come and go; hopefully, these separations will be meaningful and make sense to the rest of the group. The student's quitting of the establishment will not be decided by personal needs or the needs of the group, and thus related to his or her position in the group, but by a time-table. Separation is a very important area in residential care. It can be mishandled with disastrous consequences, but, if properly dealt with, it becomes a vital and meaningful learning experience. The student, unfortunately, has little time to establish relationships and even less time to make separation meaningful.

Residential social work is based on the relationships formed between workers and clients. These relationships tend to be complex and strong because they are formed over long periods of time and involve almost constant daily contact. In this area the student has two options. Either, providing the resident is capable of understanding, he or she can make relationships on the basis of the temporary nature of the placements. Both the student and the residents involved will have to be continually mindful of this situation, a difficult task when living together daily. Alternatively, the student can form relationships regardless of the firmness of the separation date. This might allow for greater depth in relationships but makes separation far more painful and less meaningful. Particularly in the case of young children in care this must be undesirable. There are usually enough broken and ill-informed relationships in these children's lives without imposing another avoidable one. "Another face for a child who may be new to a unit and very much troubled by home problems can in itself be overpowering. Too many adults can be overwhelming for a small child in any circumstances."*

Those unfortunate enough to be in residential establishments already feel different and alienated from the rest of the community. The introduction of a student into their midst can only increase this feeling. Any attempts to reduce alienation and to induce a feeling of the "normality" of their situation cannot be enhanced by the presence of students. The rest of the community do not have students imposed on their daily lives. Where the residents accept that they are in need of specialised help, then perhaps the notion of the student worker does not produce negative feelings. Where the residents feel

---

* See *Student Supervision in Residential Work with Children*, Barnardo Social Work Papers, No. 1, 1977, p.15.

that they are ordinary people in unfortunate circumstances, a student placed in their establishment might imply that they are more extraordinary; that they are in need of specialised treatment.

So far this discussion has implied that the placement of a student in a residential establishment will make no positive contribution to its being and will probably have a negative and disruptive effect. This need not be true, and as such underestimates the residents', staff's and student's capacity for coping with new and different situations. Further it does not take into account the positive work that a student can do. This can only be achieved if the first three safeguards set out in *Student Supervision in Residential Work with Children* are adhered to. Basically these safeguards are:

(1) Children should be made aware of the name and status of the student on the length of placement.
(2) Staff and student may need to keep their responsibilities separated, or at least differentiated.
(3) The student may be encouraged to undertake some type of activity or project that can be completed during the time of the placement and which can be left behind as a student contribution to the unit.

Regarding their residential placements, students commonly complain that, due to establishments being short- or under-staffed, they just become additions to the staff rota. No doubt students are sometimes mistakenly seen in the role of an extra member of staff by the other staff. This is understandable in situations where coping with the physical needs of the residents is about all the staff have time to achieve during any one day. In these circumstances the student releases staff to do extra work which would otherwise be left undone. Of course, this is not the function of a student placement but it is often a reality. It is essential that the student is involved in some of the daily practical routine of the unit, but also he or she could be responsible for some extra input that the staff do not have time for. If a balance can be achieved in this it is of benefit to both student and establishment and to the staff and residents.

Hopefully, the student will also bring new ideas into the work. Unfortunately, lack of tact and misunderstanding on the part of the staff often mean that they fall on stony ground or are firmly rejected. Being an outsider the student is able to view the establishment with a greater degree of objectivity than those working within. The viewpoint is fresh and the eyes less jaded. Again if the student is to make a positive contribution there must be careful consideration given to the feelings of the staff. They might not all want to know what an "immature, inexperienced and temporary interloper might have to say". If the barriers of mistrust can be broken down then the student can be a valuable contributor to any dialogue about the establishment.

One very important facet of a student's placement in a residential establishment is that it brings the staff into direct contact with the idea of training. They can discuss all the training possibilities with someone on the receiving end of the process, and hopefully see that training could be for them. The percentage of residential workers who are trained, are in training, or who are considering training is much lower than in the area of fieldwork. It is difficult to understand the complex reasons for this situation, but increased familiarity with training can only lead to some improvement in this area.

The Placements

The various forms of student placements can be divided into three basic categories, although each tends to overlap with the others, dependent on the individual student and the nature of the placement.

The first, and ostensibly the simplest, form is the observation placement. There the contact is limited to one or more day visits, and the student is merely introduced to the setting and the basic task. Personal involvement is limited and the role of the student is mainly that of an observer. The second type of placement is one in which the emphasis is on experiential learning. The student is involved with the task of the work place and directly with the clients, though it is unlikely that the student would take any responsibility except for personal actions. Here the role of the student will be that of participant observer, with more emphasis on participation than in the previous case. The third type of placement will involve supervised teaching, and naturally takes in all aspects of the first two placement types—observation and experiential learning. The student is placed in a professional role, hopefully with all its attendant responsibilities, frustrations and tensions. The work input will be related as far as is possible, to that normally carried out in the particular work place. Further, there will be regular supervision by trained staff who will aim to support, criticise and assess the work of the student. Ideally, in each of the three types of placement there should be a tutorial role linking with the college and theoretical input. In practice this tends to happen only in the second and third type mentioned.

The type of setting provides few problems in the case of the observation placement, and a residential unit can easily cope. Though when a group of students troop around an establishment the residents often complain, with justification, of being specimens under observation. The second type of placement, experiential learning through participation and observation, is also well suited to residential care. Its form has been developed through the need to give students experience of residential and community work. There are the problems mentioned earlier, but these have to be accepted and worked with. The professional placement in a residential setting provides further difficulties. These are related to responsibility and self-direction, supervision, and the role of the student as a professional worker.

1. *Responsibility and self-direction*

The ultimate responsibility for a residential unit lies with the senior worker. However much the responsibility is distributed amongst the other workers it is the senior who has the most influence over the direction and policy of the unit. Each member of staff has a shared responsibility, a commitment to teamwork which is essential to the well-being of both clients and all staff concerned. By comparison, the fieldworker has far greater personal self-direction over his cases than the residential worker in a similar position. The student in the role of a fieldworker will take on more personal responsibility than the student as a residential worker. This supervised and controlled responsibility is an important part of training in social work. The student whose interest lies in residential work needs to feel and to learn to cope with a similar level of responsibility. Though this is not to deny the importance of learning to work as a member of a team and the responsibility which this entails. To do this he or she would have to take over as senior in a residential establishment. This is possible but will obviously meet with reluctance on the part of the agency and the existing senior. It is also fraught with many simple but basically intractable problems. Not only is there the question of accountability but also that of power—it is a difficult thing to relinquish and easy to misuse. For the student to work alongside the senior is not the answer. With the best intentions on both sides it would have to be an unequal partnership in favour of the latter. Even if it were equal, shared responsibility would bear little relation to the reality of individual responsibility. If the student were able to take over in full he would most certainly be bound by existing unit policy and accepted patterns of staff and client behaviour. To change this the student would need time, which would not be available, and the approval of the senior and the staff. Unless they are in full agreement with the changes, and keen to carry them on, the clients and the unit would be bound to suffer. So, if the student cannot change the direction of the unit and is not free to take on a full measure of responsibility, is there any real value to be gained from a residential placement above being a participant observer?

2. *Supervision*

Although it is accepted as a valuable tool and used extensively in fieldwork, the personal supervision of staff is found only in a small minority of residential establishments. Supervision is an essential and integral part of a student's professional placement. Unfortunately, it follows that if the concept of staff supervision is alien to most residential staff there will be few residential establishments suitable to take the student in need of a professional placement. The elements of staff supervision in a residential setting are as yet unclear, most of the experience being in the area of fieldwork. Even if the staff of an establishment are familiar with supervision, the techniques in use may be unsuited to residential work and the student's development. A further problem is the requirement that the student supervisor be experienced and preferably qualified in social work or residential care.

To find a suitable professional placement in a residential setting is difficult where the possibilities are so restricted due to inadequacies in the area of supervision. One solution to this problem is the residential student unit as described by Sheila Lambden.* Another is the supervision of students in residential units by staff not directly involved, for example, agency training officers and also student supervisors who might usually specialise in fieldwork.

3. *The student's role*

This will vary from establishment to establishment—and will also depend on the needs of the student. There will always have to be some compromise between what an establishment has to offer and the student's requirements. The contract between the parties involved must be realistic, functional and conducive to their mutual growth. It is vitally important that the student role be defined previous to the commencement of the placement. However, there is no reason why mutually agreed adjustments cannot be made in the light of experience. Further, the definition of the role must be sufficiently specific to combat the vagaries of role definition in residential care. It is easy to lose sight of

---

* See Chapter 26 of this reader: A Student Unit for Residential Placement, Sheila Lambden.

individual roles and establishment tasks because of the pressures of the client staff groups and the demands of the daily living situation. Conversely, to require that the student should only be involved in tasks which arise out of a specified role would be unrealistic. Only working within the roles defined for individuals is not always expedient, and unfortunately expediency is very much a part of residential care. Under-staffing and under-training means that until the situation alters dramatically there will always be gaps to be filled.

Placement at a Hostel

The first half of this chapter has discussed some general points relating to the student's professional placement in a residential setting. This second section will describe my own professional placement in an adolescent hostel.

The hostel

Run by a voluntary agency the hostel caters for up to 15 boys and girls of working age, it concentrates on young people who have a history of extended periods in care. It takes adolescents whom it is felt can be helped and can benefit from the particular environment of the hostel. The environment is not static in structure, the establishment's task being continually re-assessed. Factors which influence the hostel's change in task include the needs of the individual residents, the character of the resident group, the state of staff development and the considered staff strengths and weaknesses. For example, it may be considered appropriate to admit an adolescent at a particular time where 6 months earlier a similar admission might have been felt to be inappropriate. The management of the hostel—that is the entire staff group—have complete control over selection of adolescents for admission and its running. The basic task of the hostel is to nurture the personal growth and maturity of the individual adolescents. To meet this need the hostel has to continually assess its own collective well-being. The emphasis is always on the individual resident and his needs, though not in isolation from the needs of the group or the demands of the community outside the hostel. A great emphasis is placed on the internal code of ethics, not rules, which relate well to the world outside the establishment.

Although a staff hierarchy exists there is maximum delegation of responsibility throughout the staff structure. The superintendent has overall administrative responsibility for the hostel, and in his absence the deputy would assume his role. This being so, most decisions are democratic and where possible the adolescents are consulted and their opinions given serious consideration. The most important role of the seniors appears to be the formal support of staff. There are weekly individual staff supervision periods where the member of staff is supervised by a senior. Staff development meetings are also held weekly.

The aims of the placement

The basic aim of the placement was to provide structured working and learning in a relatively unstructured environment. My previous work experience had included a working boys' hostel and an assessment centre. In the former situation the environment was unstructured and, as this was my first experience of social work, so my work was lacking in direction. As in the case of the assessment centre my aim was to survive from day to day. The regime at the assessment centre, an ex-remand home, had been extremely authoritarian and regimented. A placement was needed that enabled me to develop my own framework for working. Consequently the informality of the hostel was seen as a suitable environment where this development might occur.

The placement was to include a period of 2 weeks when I would take over as superintendent. This would provide an opportunity for the pressure of being in charge to be felt and also give a role to work towards. During my period in the superintendent role I was to be responsible for all administrative co-ordination and supervision of staff, chairing internal meetings wherever this was appropriate, and attending meetings outside the hostel. Further, I would work continually for the 2-week period and do sleeping-in duty when appropriate.

The period in the role of superintendent was to take up the eighth and ninth week of a 12-week placement. The first 7 weeks were seen as a period of familiarisation and skill development and extension. Staff and adolescents were hopefully to come to some understanding about me and my projected role. I was to learn about them, the hostel and the organisation it was a part of. The 3 final weeks of the placement were seen as reflective, both for myself, when I would write a comprehensive report of the placement, and for the staff and residents, who would supply the feedback. It was also seen as a period when I would make preparation for separation.

With the exception of the weeks in the role of the senior my role was to be that of a student—observing interacting and carefully being involved, without impinging too dramatically on the relationships which existed and hopefully would continue to exist after my leaving. I was to be supervised regularly by the superintendent, and to join him and his deputy in their supervision session with the senior social worker attached to the hostel.

Entry into the hostel

Before the above contract could be agreed, although its bare bones had been already worked out, the staff and adolescents had to be consulted at their weekly community meeting. Did they want a student in their midst and could they accept him as a temporary superintendent? Although it was impossible for anyone to foresee what this would involve in reality, a general agreement had to be reached. I was not present at this meeting and as yet known only by the superintendent, whom I had known as a visitor to a previous hostel in which he had worked. The basic agreement having been accepted I made my first visit to the hostel and after consulting the group I was allowed to sit in on the next community meeting. Except to take a few meals there and to fill out the contract, my next involvement with the hostel was when my placement commenced there a month later.

The procedure outlined here is important. It was unlikely that the adolescents would object to the placement since they had been consulted and consequently were part of the commitment. They were party to the decision whether in retrospect it turned out to be right or wrong. It was probably advantageous that the superintendent knew something of me before the basic idea of the placement had been suggested. Firstly, because he was able to project, to some degree at least, my effect on the hostel. Secondly, he was able to present a more accurate impression to his staff and residents. Further, he might not have had the courage to commit himself to hand over the hostel for 2 weeks, albeit under his supervision, to someone of whom he knew nothing.

The first 7 weeks

On admission to the hostel each adolescent is allotted one of the staff as his or her residential social worker (RSW). This should become one of the primary relationships for the adolescent whilst at the hostel and in some cases for a period after leaving. Consequently it was impossible for me to take on such a role as this was never intended and it did not fit in with hostel policy or good practice. I was able to take on the role of secondary RSW for a few adolescents, committing myself to certain tasks worked out in conjunction with existing arrangements.

In this case of one particular boy, Stephen, I feel that the result of my secondary role and intervention was detrimental, though at the time the results appeared positive. One area in which Stephen's RSW was having difficulty with him was that of finding work. She could not find the time that she felt was needed to help him over this matter. My timetable was more flexible and it was agreed that I should work with the boy. Together we were successful in finding him employment in a job that he liked and kept for a very long period in comparison with his previous efforts. What we failed to take into account was the effect that my relationship with Stephen might have on his relationship with his RSW. His family background was overshadowed by an authoritarian and physically oppressive father. The mother took no responsibility for discipline and tended to collude with Stephen against the father. As a result the mother–son relationship was very one-sided—the mother gave and the son took. When Stephen arrived at the hostel his mother had recently died and his dislike and fear of his father meant that the family connection had completely broken down. One of his basic needs was to form a relationship with an adult, particularly a female as his RSW was, that was based on equality. Unfortunately he was increasingly beginning to take on his father's attitudes which made this difficult. As Stephen and his RSW were beginning to hit difficult times I came upon the scene. He was now able to attach himself to me and to avoid the difficulties involved in reaching an equal relationship with his RSW. Although his behaviour improved and he kept his job I feel that false progress was made. His relationship with the hostel broke down soon after my leaving. This is not to imply that I have any special qualities which the staff at the hostel did not have. But I provided Stephen with an escape-route from the painful process of maturing. As a student I was not quite a member of staff, consequently Stephen saw me as less of a threat. I had wanted to show success and as a result was blind to the other tasks in which I was not involved.

During this first 7-week period I worked a typical, though not prescribed, staff rota, working with all the possible combinations of staff teams. I attended all meetings, staff development meetings and supervision sessions except those between the seniors and the individual staff. Also two members of staff and myself with most of the adolescents spent a long weekend camping on the coast.

Just before taking over as superintendent I arranged a supervision session with each member of staff, with me in the role of supervisor. This was by way of an introduction to myself and my projected methods. There were also the administrative duties of the senior staff which I had to spend some time becoming familiar with.

Working as the superintendent

The role of a student in a residential setting is not one that I enjoy. Primarily, there is the problem of working within the constraints of the temporary nature of the placement. Secondly, I have a tendency to get over-involved in the emotional, physical, business and political aspects of the residential situation. By the time I was to take over as super- intendent I saw myself as a temporary member of staff and not as a student. It appears that the staff and adolescents tended to see me in this role also. One of the aims of the hostel is that the lines of demarcation between staff and residents should be at a mini- mum, and that all should be seen as individuals living and working within the com- munity. Perhaps, then, I became another person with a particular role within that community.

Although I had been at the hostel for 7 weeks before taking charge there was still a great deal of the body of knowledge surrounding the hostel that I had not acquired. Especially that relating to the outgroup—that is, those adolescents who had left the hostel but were still relying on it for varying degrees of support. Also occasional adminis- trative matters arose, over which I was ignorant of the precedent involved, or which needed a precdent to be created. The routine matters proved to be no problem. These factors combined with the natural difficulty that the staff found in investing in the superintendent role, and the need to make long-term decision which would affect the hostel after I had left. Further, although the staff and adolescents recognised me as superintendent it was not easy for them to be continually aware of this. One of the reasons being that the present superintendent has delegated responsibility throughout the staff and adolescents, making his role less clear cut than it otherwise might have been. Also, the superintendent tends to take unilateral responsibility for the hostel with the deputy superintendent, with the effect that, whilst I was in charge, there were three seniors plus the Senior Social Worker attached to the hostel. Because of the lengthy period spent at the hostel prior to my taking over, the transition proved to be smooth, perhaps too smooth in that it was hardly noticed. This is possibly also a demonstration of the hostel's structure—that it continued to function without a strongly overt leader. At first there was an underlying feeling that the superintendent was still, in fact, in charge. It did not appear to be a conscious desire to maintain control on his part but a function of the reality of the situation. I found myself answering the telephone every time it rang, to maintain or achieve a monopoly over the information moving in and out of the hostel. I also involved myself in tasks which could be delegated. Probably because the delegation was natural and would occur without directive, and therefore did not appear to be coming from me. Thus, by being directly involved I increased my apparent level of usefulness and control. The task of taking over the role completely was impos- sible, however much all parties co-operated, and it was difficult to fully assess those areas in which this was not happening.

It is certainly true that my role as superintendent was confused by my previous role as a student, which made it very difficult for the adolescents to relate to me in this new role. There was also the requirement that I become more authoritarian where necessary and consequently upset the student/friend relationship which I previously had with most of the adolescents. I could see that it was most important for me that I did this in order that I was able to feel comfortable in the job. Had the situation been longer term it would have enabled me to create my own superintendent/adolescent relationship and not attempt to copy that of the present senior staff. As the hostel was already well established before I took over for the 2-week period the manner in which it functioned very much reflected the personalities of the superintendent and his deputy. Consequently it was impossible for me to step outside the existing functioning structure and to create my own as this would have been disruptive and impractical. It was only during the personal supervision of individual members of staff that I was able to work more closely to the manner which I would have had my position been more permanent.

During the first week I had a supervision session with one of the RSWs. It proved to be very task oriented and set the pattern for the others. As I was not very familiar with the members of staff it was difficult for me to give them the personal support they would normally receive from their seniors who had known them for much longer. However, I did find that using a task-orientated approach in supervision sessions seemed to help staff relate to me as their senior. One member of staff and myself managed to disagree over most matters, possibly a clash of personalities. Through circumstances beyond our control and a degree of reciprocated wariness of each other, a personal supervision session was never arranged. My feelings now are that over this matter I had abdicated my responsibilities. This might have been a part of the 2 weeks which would have stretched me much more than the rest.

Also during the first week I led the staff development meeting. There were no problems in taking over the role of leader of the group in this situation as it was well defined. It was always easier to do so as the normal leader was absent. As the 2 weeks progressed I found that both staff and adolescents were relating much better to me in my role, using me in a similar way as they would normally do with the existing senior. In fact this tended to carry over into the period after finishing the 2 weeks.

It must be stressed that without the co-operation of both staff and adolescents it would have been impossible to take on the role, and it might be too easy to underestimate the amount of co-operation and help I received from all areas. Conversely, however much the superintendent might try, he had real difficulty in relinquishing his position, although I do not feel that this was consciously done on his part, or that he was unaware after the fact. Further, the superintendent has long-term responsibility for the establishment. The experiment of placing a student in a senior role would probably meet very different problems if it took place in a far more hierarchical structure. It is doubtful whether such a change would be possible where the roles were more formal and the structure more rigid.

It was probably more difficult for those who were responsible for but external to the hostel to accept the role-change which occurred. Possibly due to the fact that firstly they were not so closely in touch with the situation as it unfolded, and their greater distance from it meant that although fully supporting the idea, they felt a loss of control; and that secondly, should anything go drastically amiss, then the ultimate responsibility rested upon them. This is not intended as a criticism of those who were in higher authority, especially in this case, as I feel that a sincere attempt was made to accept me in the role. Unfortunately there were many times I got the feeling that although the position was accepted it was never given full credence. It appeared that it was either convenient or genuinely easy to forget that the role had been changed. Consequently, although taking on the role of superintendent meant fitting into its normal occupier's shoes, there were areas in which this would not and could not occur. This was one very difficult area. The hostel could not be viewed in isolation but as part of a wider agency, its character and policies.

The hostel also continually works with outside agencies, in particular local authority social service departments. Social workers from these agencies were used to dealing with the superintendent and were not party to the planning of the placement. Even on the understanding that they must comply with any internal changes made within the hostel it was difficult for them to accept and relate to a student in the role of the hostel's senior. Unless a social worker was completely willing to accept the role then I felt that it was unjustifiable to force the issue. There were many areas related to this problem of which I had no knowledge. Social workers could not formulate long-term planning in conjunction with me in the role—to do so would have been unrealistic. It was therefore essential that any matters arising out of these areas should be dealt with by other members of staff or the senior where appropriate. However long the placement before taking on the role, it is unlikely that I would have become familiar with all these areas. The essential lesson here was to learn to delegate and re-assign whenever appropriate.

By general agreement the placement was relatively successful. It had shown that to place a student in a senior role was possible. The major problem area was where the work of the hostel met with that of outside agencies. Resolving this matter would have taken more time than was available. The complete absence of the superintendent would have helped to define the temporary role for others, but this was neither professionally, structurally nor educationally realistic.

Feedback from the hostel staff suggested that they had gained from the experience. A change of senior had shown there were alternative strategies possible. Although a little reticent over the more directive approach of leadership, they felt that the change had helped them place the various roles within the hostel in perspective. The presence of a student had also released time in which they could concentrate on areas of work where it would not have otherwise been possible. Further, there were small projects—for example, a weekend camping on the coast—which would probably not have been contemplated without the extra time and support which a student has available to offer. The important point there is that I, as a student, was not expected to conform to the ethos or the timetable of the establishment. Consequently my input was personal and I was able to structure my own working. This being true I was always aware of the expected ways of working and continually adjusted my responses to situations accordingly. This, I feel, was essential in order to maintain continuity within the establishment. Without this adjustment the disruption to the establishment ethos would have been detrimental to both staff and adolescents.

At this establishment the residents were able to fully understand the role and temporary nature of a student placement. It appeared that as far as they were concerned I came, stayed and eventually left. Some were unsure why anyone needed to be a student of residential care. A few began to look for relationships which would need to go beyond the time-limits of any placement. If the placement had continued for any longer the problem of disengagement would have become acute. It became necessary in the final few weeks to take on an academic role, slowly becoming separate from the hostel community and concentrating on recording my experience. On the day of my leaving I felt almost the stranger I was when I first entered the hostel.

Further Reading

ADVISORY COUNCIL ON CHILD CARE, *Fieldwork Training for Social Work*, DHSS, 1971.

AINSWORTH, F., Are today's CQSW courses right for residential work? *Residential Social Work*, **16** (11), 1976.

AINSWORTH, F. and BRIDGFORD N., Student supervision in residential work, *British Journal of Social Work*, **1** (4), 1971.

ELLIOTT, D., Residential placements: an undervalued resource in social work education and training, *Community Home Schools Gazette*, Sept. 1978.

MATTINSON, J., Supervising a residential student, *Case Conference*, **14** (12), 1968.

RIGBY, A., Residential placements, *Social Work Today*, 7 Sept. 1972.

WRIGHT, G., A model of supervision for residential staff, *Social Work Today*, **9** (45), 1978.

CHAPTER 28

STAFF AND STUDENT SUPERVISION
IN THE RESIDENTIAL SETTING

SUE EVANS and DAVID GALLOWAY

In this chapter our aim is to describe the staff and student support systems evolved in a particular unit for adolescents. We are assuming that the need for supervision is established, and are attempting to explain precisely what we do, and how and why we do it.

We also hope to draw out key areas of practice which could be transferred to work in other settings.

The chapter content will be described in subsections:

I   The contribution of theory to supervision practice.
II   Organisational setting.
III   Organisational structure.
IV   Staff group consultancy—(a) case-focussed,
                               (b) development-focussed.
V   Staff and student individual supervision.
VI   Senior social worker: superintendent support.
VII   Applications and conclusion.

The work we describe has evolved over a 3-year period of collaboration. Space demands that the presentation is fairly concentrated and requires the reader to work at expanding some ideas.

This work exists as a long-term process but is described as a whole: we do not do everything, at once, all the time! Nor do we dwell on our inadequacies as much as our competence. Nevertheless, hopefully it will be as useful to readers as the exercise of writing has been to us.

I. The Contribution of Theory to Supervision Practice

It would be quite impossible to give a detailed breakdown here of all the writers whose influence and ideas have been integrated into our own thinking and practice over the years. All we can attempt to do is to mention some significant contributions which have been important in developing our approach to our work. Published theory and descriptions of practice communicate other people's thoughts about their work and world, and the use which the reader makes of these is highly individual. Everyone builds up from theory and practice a set of unconscious assumptions about their understanding of their work; here we have tried to look at the derivation of some of our assumptions and models for practice.

The derivation of these ideas extends well beyond, but includes, social work literature. There seemed to be four main areas of input which directly affect supervision practice in this residential setting and we shall consider:

(1) Basic philosophical orientation.
(2) Assumptions surrounding management style and theories of learning.
(3) Child care theorists.
(4) Residential social workers staff support needs.

1. *Basic philosophy*

Everyone finds some model or models by which they understand and make sense for themselves of the world they inhabit. The need to consider these "roots" of our perceptions in relation to child care practice and in particular in relation to supervision came through miscommunication early on in supervision, where a lot of misunderstanding derived from lack of awareness of how the other person interpreted events to themselves. To find a basis of communication we had to establish common concepts and aims. The superintendent relates primarily to Freud[1] as a basic framework for understanding normal growth and development, whereas the senior social worker uses Maslow's[2] concept to achieve this understanding. The common base we found, to which we both relate, where these diverse interpretations can be unified is a shared enthusiasm for Carl Rogers'[3] work, in particular his ways of mobilising individuals' strengths and his belief in the capacity for health in each individual. This established the basis of how we would attempt to work together with the staff and the unit.

2. *Management and learning*

Although the disciplines are formally separate we need to consider management style and the understanding of learning process as a whole. This is partly because some aspects of management require a teaching input, but is primarily because what we learn in one area, if properly applied, affects other related areas of work. Thus the understanding of how people learn, rather than how they are taught, which has been profoundly affected by our reading of John Holt[4] and Ivan Illich's[5] works, has also influenced our evaluation of our relationship to our colleagues, which in turn influences the way in which we undertake management tasks. Holt and Illich both show that learning is a spontaneous inherent growth activity which can be inhibited by inept teaching. Their thoughts reinforce Carl Rogers'[6] comments on people-oriented management and lead us to trust responsible learning and participation to emerge from democratic involvement in management issues. Heal and Cawson[7] confirm the importance of involvement, autonomy and management style, emerging from their studies of different residential regimes. In a different setting Elizabeth Richardson[8] draws similar conclusions from her longitudinal study of change in a comprehensive school.

Relating these principles to a staff consultancy role, Westheimer[9] makes a useful contribution in offering operational guidelines to enable learning, seeing the consultant as at the service of the staff. Banner[10] clarifies the functional importance of a co-operative team approach to consultancy; whilst at a wider level Joyce Wareham[11] sets these understandings in the context of agency role and its relationship to social policy.

3. *Child care theory*

It seems crucial for work with any client group that the workers have a well-established understanding of normal development through childhood and adolescence. Its use in this setting lies not only in understanding our clients, but also in understanding staff and ourselves. If there is a recognition of normal needs and stages of growth one can deduce from adolescent or adult regression the level of need to which they are reverting and gain clues to satisfy that need. We make frequent use of Erikson's[12] concepts in this way, and have also found the work of the Newsom's[13] invaluable in increasing our understanding of the "normal". This has to be defined before one can identify any patterns as being "abnormal".

Barbara Dockar-Drysdale[14] and Bruno Bettelheim[15] are also of constant value in working with disturbed adolescents. Their sensitivity and warmth in communicating their understanding of children's needs and ways of showing these opens up our own awareness and stimulates new thinking and understanding whilst engaging our whole attention.

Similarly, articles in the Browndale Publications[16] series offer new food for thought and challenge existing ideas and assumptions.

4. *Residential social worker staff support needs*

The importance of staff care in enabling client care in residential work has been increasingly recognised, researched and documented, in the last decade. Juliet Berry[17] has written comprehensively and with real understanding about staff needs in such a way that she actually inspires enthusiasm for the task of meeting them. Less directly, the need for staff support and training is easily deduced from the research described by Tizard[18] *et al.* and such support is implicit in Doctor Drysdale's writing. Beedell[19] highlights the worker's tasks in residential settings in such a way as to point up the support systems; and Peter Righton[20] draws attention to the need to acquire specialist skills appropriate to the individual work setting. Finally, the "In Residence" page of *Social Work Today* offers frequent relevant articles focussed on particular areas of staff needs which constantly force us to re-assess the effectiveness of our own practice—we owe a particular debt to Chris Payne[21] in this area.

II. Organisational Setting

The unit in which these supervision experiences took place is a mixed-sex hostel catering for 12 adolescents, all of whom have experienced emotional disruption or deprivation to some degree. The aim of the unit is to equip the adolescents emotionally and practically for survival outside. We attempt this through a combination of close remedial relationships and a gradual thrusting of responsibility and independence onto the adolescent. Maintaining such relationships and handling disturbed behaviour in a relatively structured setting places residential social work staff under mild but continuous stress.

Staff support has therefore been of major importance throughout the units' evolution.

With the exception of the superintendent the residential staff are not professionally qualified although each brings relevant skills and experience to their work. These experiences and individual learning resulting from them are very diverse. Another major focus has been to share and expand the staff group's understanding, to develop professional awareness and conscious control of their skills.

III. Organisational Structure

To clarify the roles of superintendent and senior social worker in the unit a brief description of the wider organisational structure is necessary. This national voluntary organisation has headquarters in London and eight divisions throughout the United Kingdom. Major policy and resource allocation decisions are based upon recommendations submitted by the Central Child Care Committee, consisting of divisional and headquarters staff to the Barnardo Council. Divisional directors are responsible for internal policies, resources and development of divisional work. The organisational hierarchy has been moving gradually towards a more democratic participation in decision-making processes; in this division superintendents and senior social workers have a collateral relationship and are both directly responsible to an assistant divisional director. Superintendents have prime responsibility for child care, staff care and management of their units; senior social workers attached to units have prime responsibility for field social workers attached, and offer consultation and support to residential social workers and superintendents. These roles and responsibilities overlap to a large extent; the inherent conflict forces clear and explicit definition of tasks which derive from the roles.

Within this unit, responsibility for the individual supervision of residential social workers and students is delegated to the superintendent; individual supervision of the superintendent and deputy, and of the field social worker is delegated to the senior social worker, who also offers group consultation to the staff as a whole.

IV. Staff Group Consultation

The need for someone to fill the role of consultant to the unit, to bring an objective and informed viewpoint to bear upon the close working of the staff group, has always been recognised by staff and management. The use of the senior social worker in that role represents a compromise between needs and use of available resources, in that consultation forms only a part of the senior social worker's role to the unit. Other aspects of the role are involvement with staff appointments, client selection, monitoring of staff development and linking the work of the unit to that of the wider organisation.

These roles inevitably contaminate each other; objectivity is reduced by direct involvement in staff selection, for instance. However, the main problem in making the consultant role operational depended upon structuring input in such a way that staff perceived it as useful; role conflict has only occasionally presented difficulties.

The mode of service delivery has utilised the very diverse skills which all members of the staff team bring to the group. It has happened that no two members have brought parallel but greater or lesser expertise; the senior social worker had considerable case and fieldwork experience but little residential experience; the superintendent reverses this pattern. The residential social work staff have divergent life and work experience and have included teachers, an anthropologist, cooks, and those with extended involvement in community groups. To use these skills and integrate them so that staff could share in maximising each individual contribution necessarily involved co-operative group learning. To make this real and operational involved making it practice based.

There are two regular weekly meetings for the staff team to focus on their practice; a client-centred meeting and a staff development meeting.

(a) *Client-centred consultation*

This 2-hour meeting provides a running assessment of each of the adolescents in the unit. This serves also as a hand-over sharing for staff coming on duty; it co-ordinates forward planning for work with each child; it tries to ensure that tasks are delegated properly and that each staff member understands their role with each adolescent.

From the sharing of people's different perceptions which occurs, an awareness of individual style and capacities emerges which can then be used by the group in planning work with the adolescents. Also different personal value systems can be examined and some consensus established which still enables individual variation.

The field social worker shares her practice co-equally in these meetings, which over time has led to better understanding of the different roles and more flexible and appropriate use of the different skills present. Local authority social workers attend the meetings periodically but the quality of their involvement depends more on their relationship with the particular residential social worker responsible for the child; time does not permit a closer involvement in the group process.

The senior social worker role is dual in this meeting, as both chairman and consultant. She must structure the meeting and utilise staff learning opportunities; she must also maintain detachment and perspective where necessary; and must clarify relevant policy guidelines.

The regularity of the meeting, and consequent familiarity with staff and clients, is crucial. Expertise in itself is insufficient unless it can be communicated; consultant contributions must therefore be pitched to match the readiness of staff to hear and use the input. Sharing practice in this way leaves workers very vulnerable. There must be security within the group before consultation can be useful. The core of the staff team has been relatively stable but each new worker needs time to adjust and the group as a whole are supportive of this.

(b) *Staff development meeting*

This second meeting originally had a specific training input where staff in turn brought aspects of their own expertise to share with the group. Its scope has widened in response to a need for more pragmatic learning and for a regular venue for other of the senior social worker roles to the hostel to be filled. Currently this meeting services both unit management and in-service training needs and these areas frequently overlap.

Table 28.1 shows the relationship between the meeting content and the learning which derives from it.

TABLE 28.1. *Content of staff development meeting*

Areas of learning	Extending functional skills	Understanding management issues	Extending theoretical knowledge
1. Administration	×		
2. Internal management	×	×	
3. Unit planning/problem solving	×	×	×
4. Policy—internal		×	×
5. Policy—organisational		×	
6. Feedback—organisational issues		×	×
7. Developmental needs defined	×		
8. Training input planned	×		×
9. Sharing projects within team	×		×
10. Pure theoretical input	×		×

Some examples to illustrate the issues involved may be useful:

2. *Internal management*

Content may range from planning staff cover, to re-allocation of rooms, to how to use the community meeting.

Learning is about coming to grips with the complexity of tasks and issues involved in running the unit. The team learns to evaluate and balance the priorities involved.

3. *Unit planning/problem solving*

Content can include occupancy; admission criteria; aftercare and residential social worker roles in this; public and professional relations. Recently we have worked on a longitudinal evaluation of the aims and functioning of the unit and its relationship to local need.

Learning. This area produces learning across the board since it involves implementing theory, relating it to the organisational setting and defining the task areas which result.

5. *Policy—organisational*

Content. Establishing and contributing to the formulation of policy as it affects the work of the unit.

Learning. Staff need to understand how the organisation expresses its aims through its policies. Particularly where there may be conflict between overall organisation's needs and the felt needs of the unit, communication must be established to get the best "fit" possible for both.

6. *Feedback—organisational issues*

Content. Passing on information about the wider work of the organisation.

Learning. Increase staff identification with other work. Make real the other priorities of the organisation; and increase staff involvement in sharing their work more widely.

8. *Training input planned*

Content. Acting to fill needs defined by the group (see table, heading 7) by inviting speakers; applying for short courses; or planning visits to other establishments.

Learning. Firstly extends knowledge of where to seek expertise and secondly increases competence in serving their own growth needs.

This seems to cover a great deal. In fact the content is variable and spread over long periods, and learning is often imperceptible. The importance lies in practice and learning being inextricably linked and therefore learning is relevant and usable. The slow growth which can result can be consolidated naturally into the staff group practice.

The importance placed on sharing management decisions with staff should perhaps be explained. There is a tendency in any residential setting to feel isolated from the parent organisation. This can lead to the development of devious practices to "get round" organisational constraints and to a unit identification which actively prevents staff using such support as is offered by their organisation.

To avoid this staff need firstly to develop an awareness of the wider pressures on the organisation, then to involve themselves in considering these and finally either to reach agreement with the organisational priorities or formally take issue with them. At this stage staff became able to evaluate their own contribution to the organisation's work.

Similarly, involvement in the internal management of the unit creates felt responsibility for this area, engaging staff's attention and effort, and stimulating growth in these skills. The responsibility for enabling this involvement falls upon the senior social worker as the person who links the unit with the organisation's middle management. Responsibility for formal development input derives from the senior's wider contacts with local training and professional resources. However, it is important that the staff group control this "resource" so that they also take responsibility for filling their own needs for growth and development.

V. Staff and Student Individual Supervision

To make use of the staff's collective experiences, sharing consciously had to take place at two levels; i.e. group consultation and individual supervision. Here we will look at individual supervision.

Language and communication

For supervision to be made meaningful within any establishment there must be, on the part of each party involved, a reaching out for communication. In doing so the building of a working relationship, which considers the personal part but sees the need for structure, can take place. This really is about sorting out the language that is going to be spoken, and listened to, as it is fairly well understood that each group of people—whoever they may be—has its own way of talking (e.g. jokes, slang, the way information is handled and passed on).

Being able to come to some understanding about the nature of communication and the way in which it should take place, a wider look at the surrounding environment is then required as unit culture plays a big part in deciding the direction supervision takes. Looking at what has taken place gives some idea of the direction needed for the future, and on this base supervision can grow. When enough time, effort and energy are given to constructing a base, trust and confidence between supervisor and supervised is often experienced. Very little can take place that is meaningful if there is no trust or confidence within the team.

The growth of supervision within the team

The team, in this case the residential social worker team, numbers six and is divided into two teams of three—the superintendent and deputy each leading a team. The only time that this group meets as a complete staff team is for one full day per week; therefore it is important that at this time communication is clear and informative. It was from this need to communicate clearly and to give opportunities to each individual to explore what was being said, that a crude form of supervision began.

Early supervision was a team affair whereby each team leader supervised his own staff. This was not successful as it tended to polarise the teams, since there was no consensus of values existing and so confusion over each other's values arose, causing teams to withdraw within themselves. Therefore security within the teams was bought at the expense of hostility towards the opposite team, creating competitiveness instead of collectiveness, which could have destroyed most of what constructive work there was.

In order to counteract the polarisation, cross-team supervision began with team leaders being responsible for the supervision of the opposite team members. One big problem arising from this form of supervision was the organisation and use made of time owing to the shift system in operation. When supervision was a team affair it was easy to organise time, but much harder to put it to use due to team familiarity. Cross-team supervision made it harder to organise time, but much more use of this time was made.

From such experiences of supervision it became very clear that more importance should be given to the environment in which supervision was taking place, i.e. if in the office, interruption can keep offering escapes from intensity. If supervision took place in some private room, one was committed to much deeper forms of intensity through the security from interruption, so supervision went from being a cosy experience to a more focussed approach, that at times could be painful. In the course of this process the need for professional support along with personal support took over from tea and chat.

It is easy to make out a check-list and run through this each time supervision takes place. This method has its uses when routine tasks are in question, e.g. which forms go where and why; why is it important to fill in reports and for whom? But supervision by residential social workers for residential social workers is not an easy thing to set up. Offering an environment where supervisor and supervised can get in touch with each other often extends outside the supervision sessions in a way that neither can control.

Because supervisor and supervised will work alongside each other as colleagues some of the time, the actual supervision process must create a space for withdrawing from this direct action and make reflection on work possible. It also requires a re-adjustment of roles, in that the supervisor is influential in affecting the work he is supervising. This leads us to consider whether and when it could be appropriate for supervision to be offered by an "outsider". We have been experimenting with this on a time-limited basis (the field social worker is offering supervision to two residential social workers for a period of 3 months). Two points emerge. Firstly, supervision then becomes closer to a field social work model where observations all derive from reported and recorded practices so what you gain in objectivity you lose in direct observation of work in progress. Secondly, in field social work supervision, to actually share practice you have to set up joint visits; conversely, in residential social work supervision, a similar effort has to be made to create settings which enable detachment from joint involvement.

To clarify the contents of supervision, Tables 28.2 and 28.3 look at some of the things that may take place. With time this could be altered, refined and geared to individual staff or student.

TABLE 28.2. *Supervision within the residential establishment*

Residential social worker[a]	Student[a]
Time involvement	
Long and continuing	Short—beginning and ending
Orientation	
Practical → theoretical How → why	Theoretical → practical Why → how
Primary focus	
Client— Direct service delivery	Academic— Skill acquisition

[a] Both RSW and student need to know the history of the unit/organisation.

TABLE 28.3. *Achievements*

Residential social worker	Student
Long-term Client-focussed	*Long-term* Personal growth and skill-focussed
Mid-term Reviews to be undertaken plus looking at the prospects of work to be gone into. Mostly the goals are still client-focussed, but through this there can be an assessment of the residential social worker's work, progress and development.	*Mid-term* Assessments of work and reports.
Short-term Working out small tasks that can be undertaken which will instil some worth to those with whom the residential social worker's work.	*Short-term* Accumulation of experiences and making some of these.

General aims and purpose of supervision

1. Developing awareness of what is really happening: (a) between the supervisor and the worker, (b) between worker and clients, (c) between client group and staff group.

2. Being able to understand the effects the above interaction has, and to thus identify the areas needing to be worked on. For the supervisor this may be: identifying problem areas; sorting out strengths and weaknesses; and working on them while offering advice, direction and support, and interpreting need. For the worker it is often a case of accepting what is being offered and being able to work with someone else's interpretation of what it is that they are trying to do.

3. There are some differences to be noted between the supervision of staff and that of students:

Unlike the residential social worker, the time in which the student has to be assessed is directed from the beginning in the pre-placement planning. At the end of placement some written evidence is gathered together to be assessed. Written into a student's contract should be time for writing, objectivity and reflections, etc. On the other hand, at no time is the residential social worker required to hand in any evidence of knowledge gained. Neither is there time given to writing, objectivity or reflection—often this is achieved at the expense of the residential social worker's own private time, which in most residential establishments is very valuable.

For supervision to be successful, regular time must be set aside so that exploration for personal and professional growth may take place. Time structuring is important but there can be no blueprint to this timing. An hour may be long enough for one person one time, half an hour the next, while on other occasions 2 hours may be insufficient.

Content, like time, should also be balanced, as an overfull agenda can be an escape for avoiding in-depth consideration of a piece of work that concerns both the supervisor and the supervised. Likewise, nothing to talk about or not having anything set up can also be made an escape.

The balance of content, style and time are the most important aspects of supervision and must be fitted to all individuals taking part in the experience.

VI. Senior Social Worker: Superintendent Support

Although the regular weekly meetings between senior and superintendent are called "supervision", they more closely resemble the relationship described by Dorothy Pettes[22] when she talks about the supervision of experienced workers. This she describes as moving toward consultation, where two colleagues talk over case or administrative problems together.

Because in many ways the deputy superintendent role is intended to duplicate and back up that of the superintendent he is also included in this weekly supervisory session.

Much of the content of this supervision is covered in less depth in staff development meetings; but, whilst management and policy issues are important, personal support and conflict resolution are most usefully tackled here.

Problems of role and task definition, staff or client difficulties, unit difficulties and forward planning, and public relations are all foci for discussion.

All these areas are capable of generating considerable divergent opinion and conflict; and the issues of conflicting power and authority need to be worked through in these sessions as they arise. This is an important part of offering support, which must be honest and therefore exist within a relationship which withstands open mutual criticism from time to time. To take conflict through to a resolution the relationship must also be based on an underlying respect for each other's separate skills and expertise.

The reality of these supervisory sessions is that they only partially succeed in meeting the needs of the superintendent and deputy for supervision in its developmental sense.

In part, this derives from the different assumptions about the nature and purpose of supervision in fieldwork and in residential settings, which were brought to the relationship by the participants and which remained largely unconscious for many months. This led to different and conflicting expectations of the aims and purpose of the meetings, the senior social worker assuming a more "clinical" and detached evaluative purpose, the superintendent assuming a more personally supportive purpose. An attempt to merge these two prime foci has not been wholly successful to either side because the adaptation still only accommodates a part of the other's viewpoint without abandoning the original "set" of assumptions.

Another factor inhibiting satisfactory supervision is the collateral relationship which assumes equal power and authority; after 3 years' work together the conflicts arising from this are (hopefully) largely exhausted, but considerable testing out has taken part on both sides, and there remains a reluctance to exercise authority deriving from greater specialist expertise on both sides. This inhibits the senior social worker from offering supervision aimed at professional growth and development.

At another level, the focus which has been mutually agreed for these meetings excludes examination of the direct child care practice of superintendent and deputy. Recently the need for thoughtful supervision of this direct practice is becoming recognised by all three participants, and revision of the aims of the meetings is again due.

Finally, the human drawback in this supervision is related to the routine regularity of the meetings. These can all too easily become unfocussed and responsive only to immediate work stimuli. The shared responsibility for the content is often useful but in this instance can mean that overall responsibility for long-term planning of work in the meetings becomes diffuse.

Nevertheless, these meetings have proved successful in sharing common problems and exploring new ideas for developing work in the unit. If such a forum for discussion were not available the bulk of the work in which the participants engage in the unit would be less effective, and much of the excitement which fuels our input to the work would be diffused in the struggle to force the implementation of conflicting individual aims for future work.

VII. Applications and Conclusion

In describing the actual practice of supervision and consultancy in a particular unit we hope that some of the patterns of work we have evolved may be useful in other settings, modified to the needs of particular units and staff groups.

Workers employed by voluntary agencies are often perceived as being in a privileged situation in having more freedom and more time than employees of statutory agencies. This view (whether true or false!) should not be used to dismiss the possibility of modifying new ideas to fit one's own work situation.

Freedom or constraints do not come wholly from organisational policy; much derives from the quality of thought and of relationships within the agency, which can be questioned at whatever level one works. Many restrictive policies are not in fact "policy" at all—they exist as unquestioned assumptions which could be amenable to change if properly approached. (N.B. conflict entrenches attitudes.)

While voluntary organisations are better able to control external pressures on their work, similar internal pressures exist in both types of organisation. These are equally subject to the personal priorities which determine one's own work management.

The particular staff support input in this unit is time-intensive but some key factors can be abstracted which are applicable to any staff support role.

1. *Style*

The ways in which staff needs, unit management, and decision making are approached are all subject to the personal style of the responsible worker. This style can enable or disable staff from using services offered, it can determine the residential social worker's response to the worker but it has also to be modified by the residential social worker's needs. We have sought to operate democratic involvement of staff in a co-operative learning model but initially had to introduce this gently at the residential social worker's pace. The style of service delivery is not influenced by the time available to the unit but may be inappropriately modified by the expectations the organisation has of the role as expressed by the workers' peers or superiors.

2. *Regular and predictable input*

If the staff support service is actually to fill the perceived needs of residential social workers they need to know when and in what manner their needs will be serviced.

The importance of weekly meetings is not that they are long or that they are weekly, it is that they are predictable in their timing and content, and other patterns of consultancy could fill this role as well in other units.

3. *Communication—internal*

In any shared living and working situation with a common client group there exists the potential for interpersonal staff conflicts. If the internal communication system is poor the chance of such conflict increases, creating additional tension and stress which decreases the potential for personal and professional growth. Similarly, practical blunders occur, causing problems for clients as well as staff and creating more ill feeling. The handover meeting is useful in planning and sharing work and creating team identity; but we also use house diaries for future appointments and immediate communication of significant incidents. These mechanisms all aim to reinforce the shared caring which counteracts competitiveness between individuals.

4. *Communication—external*

Similarly a unit can become isolated from its wider organisation if communication is not deliberately nurtured. If this happens the staff come to feel unrecognised and undervalued; support which they are offered seems illusory, which increases their felt stress because they feel alone. This can grow to the point where a unit can actively distrust its employers and shelter its practice from their attention. For unit staff to be maximally effective, residential social workers must feel they belong to a wider organisation of professional people with common aims who value and support the work and methods they are using. Residential social work staff must also have ways of communicating to the organisation things which make their practice more difficult, and must know of the ways in which modifications to these problems can be attempted. The likely time-scale for change must also be understood; disabling frustration can be utilised positively if ways are found of working on an issue together with the organisation, even if this may take months or years.

The key factors in offering staff support, then, seem to us to be style, regular input and communication. These core issues could be applied in most situations and support delivery systems devised to suit the particular demands and resources available.

To reiterate: residential work carries more concentrated stress and fewer escapes than a fieldwork setting. It needs at least as much skill and at least as much support. Some skills already exist in all staff already doing this job (many residential social workers are unaware of the very considerable skills they use day to day). Support to be effective must address itself constructively and imaginatively to enhancing these skills, and it must use the positive qualities of the work setting to enable sufficient learning opportunities to be available to staff to advance their professional development.

References

1. S. FREUD, *The Ego and the Id*, Hogarth Press, 1927.
2. A. H. MASLOW, Towards a Psychology of Being, Van Nostrand, 1968.
3. C. R. ROGERS, *On Becoming a Person*, Constable, 1967.
4. J. HOLT, *How Children Learn*, Penguin, 1970.
5. I. D. ILLICH, *Celebration of Awareness*, Penguin, 1969.
6. C. R. ROGERS, *Personal Power*, Constable, 1978.
7. K. HEAL and P. CAWSON, in *Varieties of Residential Experience* (ed. I. TIZARD), RKP, 1975.
8. E. RICHARDSON, *The Teacher, the School and the Task of Management*, Heinemann, 1973.
9. I. J. WESTHEIMER, *The Practice of Supervision in Social Work*, Ward Lock, 1977.
10. G. A. BANNER, Cooperation in Residential Care, in KELLMER-PRINGLE, *Caring for Children*, Longman, 1969.
11. J. WAREHAM, *An Open Case*, RKP, 1977.
12. E. H. ERIKSON, *Childhood and Society*, Penguin, 1965.
13. J. and E. NEWSON, *Patterns of Infant Care*, 1965; *Four Years Old in an Urban Community*, Penguin, 1970.
14. B. DOCKAR-DRYSDALE, *Consultation in Child Care*, Longman, 1973.
15. B. BETTELHEIM, *Love is Not Enough*, The Free Press, 1950.
16. *Family Involvement Journal*, Canadian Educational Programmes, 1977/8.
17. J. BERRY, Daily Experience in Residential Life, RKP, 1975.
18. J. TIZARD (ed.), *Varieties of Residential Experience*, RKP, 1975.
19. C. BEEDELL, *Residential Life With Children*, Routledge & Keegan Paul, 1970.
20. P. RIGHTON, The Development of Special Skills in Residential Care, *Residential Care Annual Review*, Vol. 21, 1973.
21. C. PAYNE, in *Social Work Today*, **8** (15); **8** (38); **9** (8); **9** (18).
22. D. PETTES, *Supervision in Social Work*, 1969.

PART IV: QUESTIONS AND EXERCISES

1. Discuss the advantages and disadvantages of part-time and full-time training for residential workers.
2. Draw up a list of the areas of knowledge and skill required by:
   (a) a head of a Home for the Elderly;
   (b) a housemother in a large Children's Home;
   (c) a housefather in a Community Home with education.
3. What content and educational methods would be effective in a teaching module concerned with admission to residential care?
4. In relation to your own establishment which educational and development resources are accessible to you? Use the following checklist:
   (a) Books and journals—list these;
   (b) Supervision from a senior member of staff;
   (c) In-service study provided by your training section;
   (d) Certificate in Social Services;
   (e) Certificate of Qualification in Social Work.
   If any of these are not available or are severely curtailed how can you make your training needs known to your agency?
5. What problems might be encountered in staff and student supervision in a residential setting? How could these be overcome?
6. Discuss with colleagues the possibility of establishing a small study-group meeting, weekly or fortnightly. Select a list of topics and books which you think may be helpful in your practice, and work out a programme for six meetings with a different member of the group starting the discussion of a topic or book each week. Extend this idea to discussing aspects of your practice. Are there other people who might be interested— social workers attached to your home, training officers, advisers, colleagues from other homes? A group of three to six members is perfectly adequate for meetings of this kind. Review what you think are any effects on your thinking and practice at the end of a series of meetings.
7. (a) What kind of training can best be provided "on the job", and what kind of training can outside institutions—universities, polytechnics, colleges of higher and further education—best provide? (b) What are some of the problems involved in linking these two aspects of training in the present situation? (c) How do you think these could be overcome in future patterns of training?
8. Facilities for staff consultation and support are limited in many residential establishments: (a) What are the effects of this situation on the quality of care? (b) How might the situation be improved in the short term using existing contacts and resources. (c) What long-term plans and increased resources would be needed to effect a real improvement?

CONCLUSION

Residential care is in a phase of great change. It would be incorrect to call this phase "a crossroads", as this implies that the choices of direction are clear and that selection of one path forecloses other avenues completely. It is more the case that the whole residential field is in a period of self-appraisal, attempting to integrate and adapt to a wide range of influences out of which future directions will emerge with greater clarity. The list of influences is extensive—population trends, social conditions, a wide variety of social work and social science theory, accessibility of training, content of courses, financial considerations. It is not surprising that because of the variety of influences there is a diversity in practice, well illuminated by the use of behavioural and psychotherapeutic methods in different establishments and by different balances in emphasis according to client groups. Diversity in approach also stems from the particular combination of professionals in such establishments. Residential social workers, doctors, nurses, psychiatrists, teachers and psychologists are all to be found in different constellations according to variations in client group and need, creating multi-disciplinary teams in many establishments. Volunteers, too, are beginning to play an increasing variety of useful roles in many units.

The richness and innovatory thinking which stem from such diversity generates simultaneously attempts to provide unifying concepts and frameworks. Some of these—for example, integrated methods, the keyworker, resident rights and participation—are in their early stages of foundation and incorporation into practice. Others, such as assessment, are being questioned and reformulated. It is our belief that it is too soon for the imposition of grand theory over the whole field. Much of the practice described in this volume is increasingly being adopted as "normal", although the processes of dissemination are slow and tortuous. But it would be hazardous to represent present practice as static and the norm for the future. It would be more desirable to view the task over the next few years as requiring further diffusion of a repertoire of theories, concepts and skills, subjected to careful evaluation by practitioners and researchers. Out of this corporate effort should emerge a clearer signpost for the future development of effective residential care and a more creative partnership between different groups of professionals working in residential settings. If contributions to this Reader have given a clear enough picture of the practice possibilities and issues, they will be of great help to all those engaged in the task of improving the quality of life for residents, whether practitioners, administrators or trainers.

BIBLIOGRAPHY

ADVISORY COUNCIL ON CHILD CARE, *Community Homes Design Guide*, HMSO, 1971.
AINSWORTH, F., Are today's COSW courses right for residential work? *Residential Social Work*, **16** (11), 1976.
ALDGATE, J., Advantages of residential care, *Adoption and Fostering*, **92** (2), 1978.
ALLEN, D., The residential task—is there one? *Social Work Today*, **9** (7), 1977.
ALLERHAND, M. E., WEBER, R. E. and HAUG, M., *Adaptation and Adaptability*, Child Welfare League of America, 1966.
ANONYMOUS, *Go Ask Alice*, Corgi, 1974.
ARDEN, N., *Child of a System*, Quartet, 1977.
ASW, *New Thinking about Institutional Care*, 1967 Education Sub-Committee Association of Social Workers.

BALBERNIE, R., *Residential Work with Children*, Pergamon, 1966.
BALBERNIE, R., The Management of an Evolving Care System, in HEY, A. *et al.*, *Residential Establishments*, Hunter Ainsworth, 1973, pp. 11–37.
BARKER, P. (ed.), *The Residential Psychiatric Treatment of Children*, Crosby, Lockwood, Staples, 1974.
BARTON, R., *Institutional Neurosis* (3rd edn), Wright, 1976.
BASW, *The Social Work Task* (Working Party Report), BASW, 1977.
BEEDELL, C., *Residential Life with Children*, Routledge & Kegan Paul (Library of Social Work), 1970.
BEEDELL, C., Working with individuals in the residential context, *Social Work Today*, **8** (26), 1977.
BEHAN, B., *Borstal Boy*, Hutchinson, 1958.
BERNSTEIN, S. (ed.), *Explorations in Group Work*, Bookstall Publications, 1972.
BERNSTEIN, S. (ed.), *Further Explorations in Group Work*, Bookstall Publications, 1972.
BERRY, J., *Social Work With Children*, Routledge & Kegan Paul, 1972.
BERRY, J., *Daily Experience in Residential Life*, Routledge & Kegan Paul, 1975.
BETTELHEIM, B., *Truants from Life. The Rehabilitation of Emotionally Disturbed Children*, Free Press; Macmillan, 1964.
BETTELHEIM, B., *Love Is Not Enough*, Free Press, 1960; Collier Macmillan, 1965.
BILLIS, D., Entry into residential care, *British Journal of Social Work*, **3** (4), 1973.
BION, W. R., Experiences in Groups and Other Papers, Tavistock, 1961.
BIOSS (Brunel Institute of Organization and Social Studies), Social Services Organisation Research Unit. Principal contributors: ROWBOTTOM, R., HEY, A., BILLIS, D., *Social Services Departments Developing Patterns of Work and Organization*, Heinemann, 1974.
BOLMAN, W. M., The future of residential care for children, *Child Welfare*, **XLVIII**, May 1969.
BOOTH, B. and BOOTH, H., From residential to family care, *Adoption and Fostering*, **92** (2), 1979.
BOSWELL, D. M., WINGROVE, J. M. (eds), Open University, *The Handicapped Person in the Community. A Reader and Sourcebook*, Tavistock, 1974.
BOWLBY, J., *Attachment and Loss*, Vol. I, *Attachment*, Penguin, 1971.
BOWLBY, J., *Attachment and Loss*, Vol. II, *Separation: Anxiety and Anger*, Penguin, 1975.
BREARLEY, P., *Social Work, Ageing and Society*, Routledge & Kegan Paul, 1975.
BREARLEY, P., *Residential Work with the Elderly*, Routledge & Kegan Paul, 1977.
BRIDGELAND, N., *Pioneer Work with Maladjusted Children*, Granada, 1971.
BROADHURST, J., *Old People in Institutions—Their Rights*, Age Concern Manifesto Series, No. 10.
BROCKLEHURST, J. C. *et al.*, Medical screening of old people accepted for residential care, *Lancet*, 15 July 1978.
BROMLEY, G., Interaction between field and residential social workers, *British Journal of Social Work*, **7** (3), 1978.

CAMPAIGN FOR MENTALLY HANDICAPPED, *Homes for Mentally Handicapped People*, Discussion Paper No. 4.
CARLEBACH, J., *Caring For Children In Trouble*, Routledge & Kegan Paul, 1970.
CARTWRIGHT, D. and ZANDER, A. (eds), *Group Dynamics Research and Theory* (3rd edn), Tavistock, 1968.

CAWSON, P., *Community Homes. A Study of Residential Staff*, HMSO, DHSS, 1978.

CCETSW, *Day Services—An Action Plan For Training*, CCETSW Paper 12, 1975.

CCETSW, *Teaching About Residential Services and Residential Practice on CQSW Courses*, London, 1978.

CENTRAL COUNCIL FOR EDUCATION AND TRAINING IN SOCIAL WORK (CCETSW), *Social Work: Residential Work is a Part of Social Work*, CCETSW Paper 3, 1973.

CIGNO, K., Where do they all come from? *Community Care*, No. 247, 18 Jan. 1979.

CLARK, D. H., The therapeutic community, *British Journal of Psychiatry*, **131**, Dec. 1977.

CLARKE, R. V. G. and MARTIN, D. N., *Absconding from Approved Schools*, Home Office Research Studies, 12, HMSO, 1971.

CLOUGH, D., Residential care: positive alternative, *Adoption and Fostering*, **92** (2), 1978.

COOPER, J., Group Treatment in Residential Care, in PRINGLE K. (ed.), *Caring for Children*, Longman, 1969.

CORNEY, G., Counselling in the residential setting—a counsellor's view, *Social Work Service*, **19**, Mar. 1979.

CORNISH, D. B. and CLARKE, R. V. G., *Residential Treatment and its Effects on Delinquency*, Home Office Research Study No. 32, HMSO, 1975.

CYPHER, J. R., Training for Residential Work, in *Personal Social Services: Manpower and Training*, BASW, 1977, pp. 40–3.

DAVIES, B., *The Use of Groups in Social Work Practice*, Routledge & Kegan Paul (Library of Social Work), 1975.

DAVIES, L. F., A case for consultancy? In residence. *Social Work Today*, **10** (7), 1978.

DAVIES, L. F., Feelings and emotions in residential settings: the individual experience, *British Journal of Social Work*, **7** (1), 1977.

DAVIES, L. F., Touch, sexuality, and power in the residential setting, *British Journal of Social Work*, **5** (4), 1975.

DAVIES, M., *Support Systems in Social Work*, Routledge & Kegan Paul (Library of Social Work), 1977.

DAWSON-SHEPHERD, R., Counselling in the residential setting. A consumer's view, *Social Work Service*, **19**, Mar. 1979.

DES, *Educating Mentally Handicapped Children*, Education Pamphlet No. 60, HMSO, 1975.

DES, *Boarding Schools for Maladjusted Children*, HMSO, 1965.

DHARAMSI, F. et al., *Caring for Children. A Diary of a Local Authority Children's Home*, Owen Wells, 1978.

DHSS, *Social Work Service. Hostels for Young People*, HMSO, 1975.

DHSS, *Priorities for Health and Personal Social Services in England*, A Consultative Document, HMSO, 1976.

DHSS, *Annual Report 1975*, HMSO, 1976.

DHSS, *Sharing Resources for Health in England*, HMSO, 1976.

DHSS, *Youth Treatment Centres*, HMSO, 1971.

DHSS, *A Review of the Mental Health Act 1959*, HMSO, 1976.

DHSS, *A Life Style for the Elderly*, HMSO, 1976.

DHSS, *A Classification of Staff in Homes for the Elderly*, Statistical and Research Report No. 18, Government Statistical Office.

DHSS, *Mentally Handicapped Children in Residential Care*, HMSO, 1974.

DHSS, *Manpower and Training for the Social Services*, HMSO, 1976.

DHSS, *Residential Care for the Elderly in London*, A Study by DHSS Social Work Service, London Region, 1979.

DINNAGE, R. and PRINGLE, M. K., *Residential Care—Facts and Fallacies*, Longman, 1967.

DOCKAR-DRYSDALE, B. E., Staff Consultation in an Evaluating Care System, in HEY, A. et al., *Residential Establishments*, Hunter Ainsworth, 1973, pp. 39–61.

DOCKAR-DRYSDALE, B. E., *Therapy In Child Care*, Longman, 1969.

DOCKAR-DRYSDALE, B. E., *Consultation in Child Care* (Papers on Residential Work), Longman, 1973.

DOUGLAS, T., *A Decade of Small Group Therapy, 1960–70*, Bookstall Publications, 1970.

DOUGLAS, T., *Groupwork Practice*, Tavistock, 1976.

DOUGLAS, T., *Basic Groupwork*, Tavistock, 1978.

DR BARNARDO's, Scottish Division, *Student Supervision in Residential Work with Children. A Handbook*, Barnardo's Social Work Paper No. 1, 1977.

DUNHAM, J., Staff stress in residential work, *Social Work Today*, **9** (45), 1978.

DUNLOP, A., *The Approved School Experience*, Home Office Research Unit, HMSO, 1975.

ELLIOTT, D., Integrated methods and residential work, *Social Work Today*, 14 Feb. 1978.

ELLIOTT, D., Residential placements. An undervalued resource in social work education and training, *Community Home Schools Gazette*, **72** (6), 1978.

ELLIOTT, D. and WALTON, R., Recording in the residential setting, *Social Work Today*, **9** (32), 1978.

ELLIOTT, D. and WALTON, R., Agency attitudes to residential training, *Social Work Today*, **10** (24), 1979.

FERGUSON, T., *Children in Care*, Oxford University Press, 1966.

FLINT, B., *The Child And the Institution: A Study of Deprivation and Recovery*, University of London Press, 1967.

FRANKLIN, M. E. (ed.), *Q Camp. An Experiment in Group Living with Maladjusted and Anti-Social Young Men*, The Planned Environment Therapy Trust, 1966.

GANTER, G., YEAKEL, M. and POLANSKY, N. A., *Retrieval from Limbo. Intermediary Group Treatment of In-accessible Children*, Child Welfare League of America, 1967.

GIL, G. G., Institutions for Children, in SCHORR, A. L. (ed.), *Children and Decent People*, Allen & Unwin, 1975, pp. 53–87.

GILL, O., *Whitegate, An Approved School in Transition*, Liverpool University Press, 1974.

GODEK, S., *Leaving Care. A Case Study Approach to the Difficulties Children Face in Leaving Residental Care*, Dr Barnardo's Social Work Paper No. 2, 1977.

GOFFMAN, E. *Asylums. Essays on the Social Situation of Mental Patients and Other Inmates*, Anchor, Doubleday, 1961; Penguin, 1968.

GOFFMAN, E., *Stigma. Notes on the Management of Spoiled Identity*, Pelican, 1963.

GOFFMAN, E., *Relations in Public. Microstudies of the Public Order*, Penguin, 1972.

GOLDBERG, M., *Helping the Aged*, Allen & Unwin, 1970.

GOLDSTEIN, J., FREND, A. and SOLNIT, A. J., *Beyond the Best Interests of the Child*, Free Press, Macmillan, 1973.

GREEN, H., *I Never Promised You A Rose Garden*, Pan, 1964.

GREY, M. and HARVEY, C., Forcing old people to leave their homes: the use of Section 47 of The National Assistance Act. *Community Care*, No. 254, 8 Mar. 1979.

HANSON, J., *Residential Care Observed*, National Institute for Social Work Training and Age Concern, 1972.

HARRIS, A. I., *Social Welfare For The Elderly*, HMSO, 1968.

HART, T., *A Walk With Alan*, Quartet, 1973.

HAY, A. *et al.*, *Residential Establishments: The Evolving of Caring Systems*, University of Dundee, 1973.

HAY, A., Analysis and Definition of the Functions of Caring Establishments, in HAY, A. *et al.*, *Residential Establishments*, University of Dundee, 1973.

HAZEL, N., Children in care should be children in transit. *Community Care*, 5 July 1978.

HENSTEIN, N. and SIMON, N., A group model for residential treatment, *Child Welfare*, **56** (9), 1977.

HERAUD, B. J., *Sociology and Social Work Perspectives and Problems*, Pergamon, 1970.

HINSHELWOOD, R. D. and MANNING, N., *Therapeutic Communities*, Routledge & Kegan Paul, 1979.

HITCHMAN, J., *King of the Barbareens*, Penguin, 1960.

HOGHUGHI, M., *Troubled and Troublesome*, Burnett, 1978.

HOLT, K. S. and REYNELL, J. K., *Observation of Children*, National Association for Mental Health, 1970.

JENKS, M., A case study of two old people's homes, *Architects Journal*, **167** (21), 1978.

JENSEN, G., Reassuring reviews, *Community Care*, 11 Oct. 1978.

JONES, H., *The Residential Community: A Setting for Social Work*, Routledge & Kegan Paul (Library of Social Work), 1979.

JONES, H., The Approved School as Theoretical Model, in MAYS, J. B., *The Social Treatment of Young Offenders*, Longman, 1975.

JONES, K., *A History of The Mental Health Service*, Routledge & Kegan Paul, 1972.

JONES, M., *Social Psychiatry in Practice*, Penguin, 1968.

JONES, M., *Beyond The Therapeutic Community*, University of Yale Press, 1973.

KAHAN, B. (ed.), *Approved School to Community Home*, HMSO, 1976.

KAHAN, B. and BANNER, G., *The Residential Task in Child Care* (Castle Priory Report), Residential Care Association, 1972.

KAHAN, U. L., *Mental Illness in Childhood. A Study of Residential Treatment*, Tavistock, 1971.

KASTELL, J., *Casework in Child Care*, Routledge & Kegan Paul, 1962.

KESEY, K., *One Flew Over the Cuckoo's Nest*, Picador, 1976.

KING, R. D., RAYNES, N. V. and TIZARD, J., *Patterns of Residential Care. Sociological Studies in Institutions for Handicapped Children*, Routledge & Kegan Paul, 1971.

KNAPP, M., Economies of scale in residential care, *International Journal of Economics*, **5** (2), 1978.

KNAPP, M. and DAVIES, B., The costs of residential care, *Social Work Today*, **9** (33), 1978.

KONOPKA, G., *The Adolescent Girl in Conflict*, (a Spectrum book), Prentice-Hall, 1966.

KONOPKA, G., *Group Work in the Institution* (revised edn), Association Press, 1970.

KONOPKA, G., *Social Group Work. A Helping Process*, Prentice-Hall, 1972.

KUSHLICK, A., Residential care for the mentally subnormal, *Journal of Royal Society of Health*, **90** (5), 1970.

KUSHLICK, A., The Care of the Profoundly Retarded Person, in *Patient, Doctor and Society*, Oxford University Press, 1972.

KUSHLICK, A., Residential Care for the Mentally Handicapped, in *Positions, Movements, and Directions in Health Service Research*, Oxford University Press, 1974.

LAMBERT, R. and MILLHAM, S., *The Hothouse Society*, Weidenfeld & Nicholson, 1968.

LAMPEN, J., Drest in a little brief authority: controls in residential work with adolescents. *Journal of Adolescence*, **1** (2), 1978.

LAWTON, M. P., Institutions and alternatives for older people, *Health and Social Work*, **3** (2), 1978.

LIPMAN, A. and SLATER, R., Homes for old people, A positive environment, *The Gerontologist*, **17** (2), 1977.

LITTNER, N., *The Stresses and Strains on the Child Welfare Worker*, Child Welfare League of America, 1957.

McCULLOUGH, M. K. and ELY, P. J., *Social Work with Groups*, Routledge & Kegan Paul (Library of Social Work), 1971.

MACLENNAN, B. W. and GELSENFELD, N., *Group Counselling and Psychotherapy with Adolescents*, Columbia University Press, 1968.

MAIER, H. W., *Three Theories of Child Development. The Contributions of Erik H. Erikson, Jean Piaget and Robert R. Sears, and their Applications*, Harper & Row (Harper International Edition), 1969.

MANARD, B., WOEHLE, R. E. and HEILMAN, J. M., *Better Homes for the Old*, Lexington, 1977.

MANTON, J., *Mary Carpenter and the Children of the Streets*, Heinemann, 1976.

MARSHALL and BOADEN, Residential care. How can we make admission less haphazard? *Modern Geriatircs*, **8** (1), 1978.

MAYER, M. F., *Supervision of House-Parents*, Child Welfare League of America, 1962.

MEACHER, M., *Taken For a Ride*, Longman, 1972.

MILLHAM, S., BULLOCK, R. and CHERRET, P., *After Grace—Teeth*, Human Context Books, 1975.

MILLHAM, S., BULLOCK, R. and HOSIE, K., *Locking up Children. Secure Provision within the Child Care System*, Saxon House, 1978.

MILLER, E. J. and GWYNNE, G. V., *A Life Apart*, Tavistock, 1972.

MILLER, M., Residential care. Some thoughts and speculations on the literature, *Social Work Today*, **5** (9), 1974.

MIND, *Starting and Running a Group Home*, 1972.

MINISTRY OF HOUSING AND LOCAL GOVERNMENT, *Grouped Flatlets for Old People. A Sociological Study. Metric Edition* HMSO, 1968.

MONGER, M., The English Probation Hostel, Probation Papers, No. 6, NAPO, 1969.

MORRIS, P., *Put Away*, Routledge & Kegan Paul, 1969.

MURPHY, J., Alternatives to residential care: a review of developments in North America this decade, *Community Home Schools Gazette*, **72** (9), 1978.

MURPHY, L. B., *Problems in Recognising Emotional Disturbance in Children*, Child Welfare League of America, 1963.

NATIONAL COUNCIL FOR SOCIAL SERVICE, *Caring for People: Staffing Residential Homes* (Williams Committee Report), Allen & Unwin, 1967.

NEIL, A. S., *Summerhill*, Penguin, 1970.

NICHOLSON, J., *Mother and Baby Homes*, Allen & Unwin, 1968.

NOPWC, (Report of the Working Party), *Role of the Warden in Group Housing*, Age Concern, 1972.

OSWIN, M., *The Empty Hours*, Penguin, 1973.

OTTO, S. and ORFORD, J., *Not Quite like Home: Small Hostels for Alcoholics and Others*, Chichester, Wiley, 1978.

OXLEY, G. B., A modified form of residential treatment, *Social Work*, Nov. 1977.

PAIGE, R. and CLARKE, G. A. (eds), *Who Cares?* National Children's Bureau, 1977.

PARKER, R., *Residential Care in Context: Comments on Some Statistics*, Concern No. 26, 1977/8.

PARKER, R. A., *Planning for Deprived Children*, National Children's Home, 1971.

PAYNE, C., Residential Social Work, in SPECHT, H. and VICKERY, A., *Integrated Social Work Methods*, Allen & Unwin, 1977, pp. 195–218.

PEPPER, J., *The Diary of Two Groups. Groupwork with Mothers of Pre-School Children*, Council for Children's Welfare, 1972.

PERSONAL SOCIAL SERVICES COUNCIL Working Group, *Living and Working in Residential Homes*, 1975.

PERSONAL SOCIAL SERVICES COUNCIL, *Residential Care Reviewed*, 1977.

PERSONAL SOCIAL SERVICES COUNCIL, *Policy Issues in Residential Care*, 1978.

PIZZAT, F., *Behaviour Modification in Residential Treatment for Children*, Behaviour Publications, 1973.

PLANK, D., Old people's homes are not the last refuge, *Community Care*, 1 Apr. 1978.

POLSKY, H. W., *Cottage Six. The Social System of Delinquent Boys in Residential Treatment*, Russell Sage Foundation, 1962.

POLSKY, H. *et al.*, *The Dynamics of Residential Treatment*, University of North Carolina Press, 1968.

POPE, P., Admissions to residential homes for the elderly, *Social Work Today*, **9** (44), 1978.

PROSSER, H., *Perspectives on Residential Care*, NFER, 1976.

PUGH, E., *Social Work in Child Care*, Routledge & Kegan Paul, 1968.

RAPPOPORT, R. N., *Community as Doctor: New Perspective on a Therapeuiic Community*, Tavistock, 1960.

RCCA, *An A.B.C. of Behaviour Problems*, Printing Technical School, National Children's Home, Harpenden, 1962.

RCCA, (Annual Review), *The Anti-Social Child in Care*, RCCA, 1966.

RCCA, *Residential Staff in Child Care*, RCCA, 1968.

RCCA, (Study Group Report), *Residential Task in Child Care*, RCCA, 1969.

RCCA Groups, *Annual Review 1970–71*.

REDL, F. and WINEMAN, D., *Children Who Hate*, Free Press, Macmillan, 1965.

REDL, F. and WINEMAN, D., *Controls From Within*, Free Press, 1952.

REEVE, P., *Starting and Running a Group Home*, MIND/National Association for Mental Health, 1972.

REGENSBURG, J. and FRAIBERG, S., *Direct Casework with Children*, 4th Printing 66 Family Service Association of America, 1957.

REID, J. H. and HAGAN, H. R., *Residential Treatment of Emotionally Disturbed Children*, Child Welfare League of America, 1952.

RESIDENTIAL CARE ASSOCIATION, *Manpower Problems in Residential Social Work—The Dalmeny Papers*, RCA, 1976.

RESIDENTIAL CARE ASSOCIATION and BRITISH ASSOCIATION OF SOCIAL WORKERS, The Relationship between Field and Residential Work, Report of a Joint Study Group published simultaneously in *Residential Social Work* and *Social Work Today*, Sept. 1976.

RICE, A. K., *Learning for Leadership. Interpersonal and Intergroup Relations*, Tavistock, 1965.

RICKARD, H. C. (ed.), *Behaviour Interaction in Human Problems*, Pergamon, 1971.

RIGHTON, P., *A Continuum of Care. The Link Between Field and Residential Work*, 1973 Barnardo Lecture, Dr Barnardo's School of Printing.

ROBERTS, G., *Essential Law for Social Workers*, Oyez, 1978.

RODWAY, S., The concept of the keyworker—pie in the sky? An employer's viewpoint. *Social Work Service*, **19**, Mar. 1979.

ROSE, M., Residential treatment—a total therapy. The David Wills Lecture, *Journal of the Association of Workers for Maladjusted Children*, **6** (1), 1978.

RUDDOCK, R., *Roles and Relationships*, Routledge & Kegan Paul, 1969.

RUTTER, M., *Helping Troubled Children*, Penguin, 1975.

SACKVILLE, A., The concept of the keyworker—a challenge to traditional thinking, *Social Work Service*, **19**, Mar. 1979.

SCHORR, A., *Children and Decent People*, Allen & Unwin, 1975.

SEARGEANT, B., Sex and sexuality in the residential setting, *Social Work Today*, **9** (28), 1978.

SHAW, I. and WALTON, R., Transition to Residence: An Evaluation of Selection and Admission to Homes for the Elderly, in *Residential Care Association, Annual Review 1979*.

SHEARER, A., Provision for handicapped children, *Social Work Today*, **10** (31), 1979.

SINCLAIR, I., *Hostels for Probationers*, Home Office Research Study, 6 Nov., HMSO, 1971.

SINCLAIR, L., *The Bridgeburn Days*, Gollanz, 1956.

SMITH, G., *Social Work and the Sociology of Organisations*, Routledge & Kegan Paul, 1970.

SMITH, G., Institutional dependence is reversible, *Social Work Today*, **6** (14), 1975.

SPARKS, R. F. and HOOD, R. G. (eds), *The Residential Treatment of Disturbed and Delinquent Boys*, Institute of Criminology, Cambridge, 1968.

SPARROW, J., *Diary of A Delinquent Episode*, Routledge & Kegan Paul, 1976.

STAPLETON, B., Avoiding residential care for the old, *Community Care*, 10 May 1979.

STEPHEN, E. (ed.), *Residential Care for the Mentally Retarded*, Pergamon, 1970.

STEVENSON, O., *Strength and Weakness in Residential Care*, The first Quetta Rabley Memorial Lecture, Quetta Rabley Trust Fund, printed by Aldon & Mowbray, 1972.

TAYLOR, D. A. and ALPERT, S. W., *Continuity and Support Following Residential Treatment*, Child Welfare League of America, 1973.

THOMAS, L., *This Time Next Week*, Pan, 1967.

TILBURY, C., The element of control in residential care, *Social Work Today*, **10** (7), 1978.

TIMMS, N., *Rootless in the City*, National Council for Social Service, 1968.

TIMMS, N. (ed.), *The Receiving End*, Routledge & Kegan Paul, 1973.

TIZARD, J., SINCLAIR, I. and CLARKE, R. V. G. (eds), *Varieties of Residential Experience*, Routledge & Kegan Paul, 1975.

TIZARD, J. and TIZARD, B., The Institution as an Environment for Development, in RICHARDS, M. (ed.), *The Integration of the Child into a Social World*, Cambridge University Press, 1974.

TOBIN, S. S. and LIEBERMAN, M. A., *Last Home for the Aged*, Jossey-Bass, 1976.

TOD, R. J. N. (ed.), *Papers on Residential Work, Vol. 4*, Longman, 1973.

TOD, R. J. N., *Disturbed Children (Papers on Residential Work)*, Longman, 1968.

TOWNSEND, P., *The Last Refuge*, Routledge & Kegan Paul, 1964.

TOWNSEND, P., The Institution and The Individual, in *The Social Minority*, Penguin, 1973, Chapter 9.

TOWNSEND, P. and WEDDERBURN, D., *The Aged in The Welfare State*, Bell, 1965.

TRIESCHMANNS, A., WHITTAKER, J. K. and BRENTANO, K., *The Other 23 Hours*, Aldine, 1969.

TUTT, N., *Care or Custody. Community Homes and the Treatment of Delinquency*, Darton, Longman & Todd, 1974.

TUTT, N., The nature and scope of control, *Social Work Today*, **10** (30), 1979.

VINTER, R. D. (ed.), *Readings in Group Work Practice*, Campus, 1967.

WALTON, R., The development of the residential care of deprived children, *Child Care Quarterly*, July 1969.

WALTON, R., Important themes in the development of the residential care of deprived children, *Child Care Quarterly*, Jan. 1970.

WALTON, R., A new balance, "In Residence", *Social Work Today*, 29 Nov. 1977.

WALTON, R., Research for practice, "In Residence", *Social Work Today*, **9** (22), 1978.

WALTON, R., Continuity and support for children in homes, "In Residence", *Social Work Today*, **9** (40), 1978.

WALTON, R., The language of therapy, "In Residence", *Social Work Today*, **10** (10), 1978.

WALTON, R., Training for risk taking: applications in residential care, *Social Work Service*, **18**, Dec. 1978.

WALTON, R., A quiet revolution, *Social Work Today*, **10** (33), 1979.

WARD, L., Clarifying the residential social work task, "In Residence", *Social Work Today*, **9** (2), 1977.

WARD, L., The centre way to caring, *Community Care*, 5 Oct. 1977.

WARD, L., Learning from others' experience, "In Residence", *Social Work Today*, **9** (35), 1978.

WEBER, G. H. and HABEALEINE, B. J., *Residential Treatment of Emotionally Disturbed Children*, Behavioural Publications, 1972.

WEST, D. J., *The Young Offender*, 1967, Penguin.

WHIFFEN, C., Case conference—two models for analysis of its function in the assessment of children in a residential setting, *Social Work Today*, **9** (38), 1978.

WHITTAKER, J. K. and TRIESCHMAN, A. E., *Children Away From Home*, Aloine, Atherton, 1972.

WHITTAKER, J. K., The changing character of residential child care: an ecological perspective, *Social Service Review*, **52** (1), 1978.

WIJNBERG and SCHWARTZ, Models of student supervision. The apprentice, growth and role systems models, *Journal of Education for Social Work*, **13** (3), 1977.

WILLS, D., *A Place Like Home*, Allen & Unwin, 1970.

WILLS, D., *Spare The Child*, Penquin, 1971.

WINNICOT, C., *Child Care and the Social Worker*, Caldicot, 1964.

WINNICOTT, D. W., *Playing and Reality*, Tavistock, 1971.

WRIGHT, G., A model of supervision for residential staff, *Social Work Today*, **9** (45), 1978.

INDEX